USING THE GUIDE

THIS BOOK is a handy pocket-sized guide that will help in choosing plants for specific conditions or places in the garden.

PLANTS FOR PLACES

Once you have identified the areas on your property for which you need plants, turn to the relevant chapter where you will find a "shopping list" of suitable choices. Knowing which plants are most likely to succeed in a particular place will lessen the chances of disappointing results and allow you to make plans and designs with confidence. Your needs may be practical, such as plants for a damp, shady site (*see p.238*), or you may be looking for plants that will add structure (*see p.472*), or flowers to attract wildlife (*see p.494*).

Even the smallest garden area can offer several different planting options: perhaps a shaded area, which may be predominantly dry or damp, as well as a need for climbers with, say, containers for added interest. To arrive at a "wish list" of plants you will often need to refer to two or more chapters, and you will find that many plants are suitable for more than one place or function.

SYMBOLS USED

SOIL MOISTURE PREFERENCES/TOLERANCES

◊ Well-drained soil

◖ Moist soil

● Wet soil

SUN/SHADE PREFERENCES/TOLERANCES

☀ Full sun

☀ Full shade

☀ Partial shade; either dappled shade or shade for part of the day

NB Where two symbols appear from the same category, the plant is suitable for a range of conditions.
Min is the minimum temperature that a tender plant will survive.
f Fragrant flowers or aromatic leaves.

All the featured plants in this book are given a minimum hardiness zone number (see map) except for annuals, and tender plants that are commonly wintered indoors (which have their minimum temperature noted). Plants in the "also recommended" panels are also given a zone number if it varies from that of the featured plant, or if the species is different.

These zones are given only as a guide; microclimates within your garden may enable you to grow less hardy plants, (or conversely, in an exposed garden you may be a zone colder). The hardiness of perennials is problematic since this depends on the depth and persistence of snow cover.

KNOW YOUR SOIL

THE SOIL ON YOUR PROPERTY has a strong influence on the plants that are likely to thrive there, so it is important to identify its type before you make any decisions on what to grow. It is always better and easier to choose plants adapted to your soil than to try to alter the conditions to suit the plant. Plants put in unsuitable soils struggle to survive, are a waste of money, and will only be a disappointment.

WHICH SOIL IS THAT?

In most soils, the relative proportion of clay, sand, and silt particles influence its physical and chemical nature. The main exception is peaty soil, which is dark in color and rich in organic matter. Peaty soils are derived from sedges or mosses, which have decomposed in waterlogged conditions. They are acidic and moisture-retentive, providing ideal conditions for acid-loving plants like rhododendrons (*see p.92*).

There are laboratories that will analyze your soil for a fee, but you can get a good assessment of your soil type simply by looking at its color and feeling the texture. Begin by rubbing a small amount

of moist soil between your fingers. Clay soils easily form a cohesive ball that holds its shape when molded, developing a shiny surface when smoothed. They are fertile but are slow to warm in spring, sticky, and slow-draining after rain, baking hard in dry weather. Silty soils feel silky or soapy and are easily compacted. Sandy soils feel gritty and will not stick together to form a ball. They are light and free-draining and quick to warm in spring, but they will need frequent irrigation and fertilizing. Chalky soils are alkaline, usually pale in color and stony, with chunks of alkaline minerals visible on the surface. They are often shallow and sometimes sticky.

The ideal soil type is a loamy one, which has an approximately equal mixture of clay, silt, and sand. This much-envied combination gives the very best combination of good drainage and moisture- and nutrient-retention. Loamy soils are good for the widest possible range of plants. If you are not blessed with a loamy soil, a sure way to improve any soil is to introduce plenty of well-rotted organic matter.

ACIDIC AND ALKALINE SOILS

The soil's pH value is a measure of its acidity or alkalinity and also influences the range of plants that can be grown. pH is measured on a scale of 1–14, with the neutral point being pH 7. Below pH 7, soils become progressively more acidic, and above, increasingly limy or alkaline. The most accurate way to gauge soil pH is using a pH-testing kit or electronic meter; both are inexpensive, easy to use, and available from garden centers. You can get a rough idea of your soil pH by observing the type of plants

ACID TEST
Like all rhododendrons, deciduous, fragrant R. luteum *needs acidic soil.*

that succeed in your area. For example, if rhododendrons thrive in neighboring gardens, and mophead hydrangeas have clear blue flowers, it indicates that the local soil is acidic. If nearby hydrangeas are pink, the soil is probably neutral or slightly alkaline. The vast majority of plants thrive in soils that are neutral or nearly so, and a great number tolerate slightly alkaline or slightly acidic soils.

SUN AND SHADE

ALL PLANTS NEED light to manufacture the compounds they need for growth, although they vary considerably in their tolerance of shade. Choosing the best exposure for an individual plant is crucial if it is to produce healthy and sustained growth. Many plants, however, are flexible about the amount of light they need. A particular specimen may prefer full sun, but it may still grow reasonably well in light, dappled shade, perhaps flowering a little less profusely and producing slightly lankier stems. Conversely, a shade-loving plant may tolerate full sun, but only in a site where the soil remains moist during the growing season.

GARDEN OBSERVATIONS

Surveying areas of light and shade in a garden area is not a technical task – you could even do it on a

A PLACE IN THE SUN
Many plants such as daisy-flowered anthemis and Oriental poppies produce their finest displays if given a sunny site.

warm, sunny day from the vantage point of a patio chair. The aim is simply to observe which areas of your property are in sun or shade, and how this changes through the day as the sun moves across the sky. Take account of the fact that the sun is lower in winter and casts longer shadows, but bear in mind that trees may be leafless and cast far less shade through the winter.

LEVELS OF SUN AND SHADE

It is helpful to categorize sunny and shady areas so that you can choose plants to fit the site.

FULL SUN: This category includes areas that are open to the sun for most of the day and are not subject to shade from nearby trees or buildings. Generally, they are good for most plants that are grown for their flowers or fruits, since flower and consequent fruit production demands considerable energy. The sun and the warmth it gives also helps woody growth to mature, and only mature growth will be able to survive the winter.

PARTIAL SHADE: Areas shaded by buildings or vegetation may actually receive between two and six hours of sun during the day as the sun moves across the sky. In these conditions, only the most committed sun- or shade-loving plants will fail to thrive. In many cases, partially shaded sites may actually prove to be advantageous to the gardener, especially if it protects both flowers and foliage from the scorching heat of the midday sun in summer.

LIGHT, DAPPLED SHADE: This is the sort of shade cast by the open canopies of deciduous trees such as birches, locusts, and flowering cherries. They create a moving patchwork of light and shade, which alters with the sun's daily course. Seasonal variation is dramatic here; shade is relatively deep when the trees are in leaf, but it is almost nonexistent in winter, when the sun is low in the sky. These are admirable spots for woodland plants in the summer and for early spring bulbs that finish blooming before the leafy canopy finally closes over.

DEEP SHADE: This category defines areas where tall buildings or dense vegetation – most typically of evergreen plants – block the light for much or all of the day during the growing season. Little or no sunlight reaches the ground, but ther are some ferns and many woodland plants that thrive in these conditions.

WORKING WITH THE SITE

THERE ARE many suggestions in this book for plants that thrive in a variety of locations, some of which are quite taxing on plants, such as damp or dry places in shade, coastal gardens, exposed sites, and hot and sunny areas prone to drought. While there are plants for even the most stressful conditions, there is much that the gardener can do to make such conditions more hospitable. The optimistic gardener will always seek to turn apparent disadvantage into positive advantage.

TOUGH SITES

Exposed and coastal gardens can be among the most difficult for vegetation. Both sites experience strong winds and, by the ocean, the winds carry salt spray and scouring airborne sand. Here, conditions can be improved by planting windbreaks or wind-filtering hedges (see pp.118, 138, 166) to create a gentler microclimate within your property. In coastal areas, this makes an almost magical difference to the types of plant that will thrive there. Given shelter, coastal gardens can be milder than inland, enjoying balmy humidity and some degree of temperature moderation by virtue of their proximity to a large body of water, which cools down more slowly than land. Marginally hardy plants may often be grown without much winter protection. Inland exposed gardens do not benefit from the ameliorating effect of the water so, unless windbreaks are planted, few plants will survive.

Hot, dry sites can be hard on plants, too, since they need to tolerate an almost continual shortage of water during summer, unless the gardener takes steps to remedy this. Of course, choosing drought-tolerant plants is the first and best approach, but if the soil's capacity to retain moisture is improved, many plants will give their spectacular best in such sunny, warm conditions. Dig copious amounts of well-rotted organic matter into the soil, and mulch deeply around the plants. Try to make sure that you supply water by the most economical means, such as using trickle irrigation. Sun and warmth mature the growth of woody plants, and mature wood – replete with ample food reserves – not only flowers and fruits more freely but is also more resistant to winter cold.

FROST POCKETS AND SHADE

Frost pockets can be dealt with by choosing the hardiest plants and avoiding those that emerge very early in the year. Mulch deeply in autumn to insulate the plant roots from the worst of the cold, and even if the first shoots are bitten by frost, new shoots will follow.

Shade can really be considered a disadvantage only when it is really deep or accompanied by poor, dry soil. The more experienced a gardener becomes, the more shade is seen as an opportunity to grow some or the world's most beautiful woodland flora. These plants cannot tolerate unrelenting sunshine. While there may not be a wealth of highly colored flowers to choose from, there are many that deserve cultivation for their luscious foliage alone or for their characteristically pale flowers, which become positively luminous in the gloom.

IDEAL HOME

A pocket in a wall is the perfect place for Erigeron karvinskianus.

PLANTS FOR CLAY SOILS

THE NEW GARDENER often views a heavy clay soil with despair because it is slow to warm in spring, poorly drained, and backbreaking to dig. It is also prone to compaction when walked on, impossibly sticky when wet, and as hard as brick when dry. Such inhospitable conditions can test even the most durable of plants as well as the patience of most gardeners, but these drawbacks are far from insurmountable. Once improved by careful digging and the use of soil additives, clay can prove the most fertile of soils. Clay benefits from a remarkable ability to retain nutrients and water, so it is rich in the ingredients needed for good plant growth.

CHOOSING PLANTS

With time, a little work, and good management, an enormous range of plants will thrive in clay. They may be slow to get going, but once they are established they can attain their maximum dimensions.

Realistically, it takes several seasons to create the perfect growing medium, however, and the avid gardener may wish to delay planting until it is achieved. Choosing plants that either thrive in (or at least tolerate) heavy clay soil is a sensible starting point. This way, you will not waste money and be disappointed by failure, and the plant roots will do much to improve drainage and aeration as they penetrate the soil. The plants included in this chapter tolerate, or positively thrive in, soils that are heavy and slow-draining. Regard them as a starting point for creating a beautiful garden full of scent and color; they will form the backbone of a garden, which will become more diverse as the soil conditions improve.

Improving Clay Soils

A clay soil can be improved by a variety of techniques. First, it can be dug over in autumn, with the clods left exposed through winter. As soil water freezes and thaws it expands, breaking up the clods to create a more open structure. Avoid undoing the good work by walking on and compacting the soil. Delay planting until late spring to reduce the damaging effects of cold, wet soil, which cause fragile new roots to rot; they will establish better in summer. Digging in coarse sand will also open up the structure, especially if it is incorporated along with copious quantities of relatively low-nutrient organic matter – in the form of compost, composted bark, well-rotted manure, or leaf mold. Apply these materials as an autumn or spring mulch on cultivated soils, then let the worms do the work of gradually mixing it. Lime or gypsum can be applied to cause tiny clay particles to clump together into crumbs. This crumb structure improves aeration and water percolation and makes it easier for roots to penetrate. Lime will make soil more alkaline, however, and may damage roots if overdone, especially on already alkaline soils – in this case use gypsum, which causes clumping without affecting alkalinity.

AESCULUS HIPPOCASTANUM

The horse chestnut is a vigorous, spreading tree, valued for its dense, conical "candles" of creamy white flowers in early summer. Spiny fruits that enclose shiny brown seeds follow in autumn. The palmately divided, dark green leaves flush red, yellow, and rich brown before falling. An excellent specimen tree for larger gardens. Prune in winter, when fully dormant, if necessary. It tolerates alkaline soils (*see p.64*).

ALSO RECOMMENDED: *'Baumannii' has double flowers and does not bear fruit;* A. × carnea *'Briotii'* (see p.120).

☼ ◖ Z5   **Deciduous tree**
↕ 80ft (25m) ↔ 70ft (20m)

JUGLANS NIGRA

The black walnut has a wide-spreading crown of aromatic, dark green leaves, and it makes an excellent, long-lived specimen tree. Its edible nuts need long summers to ripen fully, so a hot, dry site is desirable (*see p.190*). Walnuts do not transplant well, so set in their final position when no more than 24in (60cm) tall. Pruning should be done in late summer to avoid bleeding of the sap.

ALSO RECOMMENDED: J. regia *is the English walnut with smaller leaves, which are purple-flushed when young.* Z6

☼ ◗◖ Z3   **Deciduous tree**
↕ 100ft (30m) ↔ 70ft (20m)

+ LABURNOCYTISUS *'Adamii'*

An unusual small tree with curiously beautiful flowers that hang from its branches in spring. It bears pealike flowers in separate clusters in three colors: purple, yellow, and pink-purple with a yellow flush. A fine specimen for small gardens, it looks especially effective when grown in groups. Keep pruning to a minimum, but remove any shoots that arise from below the graft union.

☼ ◊ Z7 **Deciduous tree**
↕ 25ft (8m) ↔ 20ft (6m)

MAGNOLIA × SOULANGEANA

It is the huge, goblet-shaped, pink, violet, or white flowers that are treasured on this shrubby tree, and they emerge just before the new leaves in late spring. Preserve them from frost damage by growing as a specimen in a sheltered niche or by training the plant against a warm wall (*see p.280*). It withstands urban pollution and tolerates acidic soils (*see p.92*).

ALSO RECOMMENDED: *'Lennei' has deep pink-purple, white-centered flowers; 'Rustica Rubra' has deep purplish red flowers.*

☼ ◊ Z5b **Deciduous tree**
↕ 20ft (6m) ↔ 20ft (6m)

MALUS *'John Downie'*

This vigorous tree has beautiful white flowers in late spring and bears orange-red crabapples in autumn. The bright green leaves darken as they mature. An ideal small garden tree that produces its best fruits and flowers when planted in full sun. It also grows in alkaline soils (*see p.64*).

ALSO RECOMMENDED: M. × zumi *'Golden Hornet' bears pink-flushed white flowers in late spring, followed by yellow crabapples that persist well into winter.* Z4b

☼☀ ◊◗ Z3   **Deciduous tree**

↕ 30ft (10m) ↔ 20ft (6m)

POPULUS TREMULA *'Pendula'*

The weeping aspen is a fine specimen tree for small gardens, with pendent branches clothed in leaves that tremble and rustle in the breeze; they are bronzed when young and butter yellow in autumn. It bears a profusion of elegant, purple-gray catkins in late winter. Also tolerant of sandy and acidic soils (*see pp.38, 92*), and coastal and exposed gardens (*see pp.118, 166*). Plant all poplars well away from drains or foundations. Needs minimal pruning.

ALSO RECOMMENDED: P. alba (*see p.169*); P. nigra *'Italica', the Lombardy poplar, is narrowly columnar to 100ft (30m) tall* Z4.

☼ ◗ Z2   **Deciduous tree**

↕ 20ft (6m) ↔ 25ft (8m)

QUERCUS ROBUR
F. FASTIGIATA

This narrow and upright form of the English oak is a rugged-looking tree with fissured, gray-brown bark. It is densely furnished with the characteristic dark green, round-lobed oak leaves. Acorns appear from the end of summer. It is best as a specimen tree in a large garden. Also suitable for acidic soils (*see p.92*), exposed and coastal gardens (*see pp.118, 166*), and hot, dry sites (*see p.190*).

ALSO RECOMMENDED: *'Concordia' is a smaller, rounded tree with bright yellow young foliage that turns to green.*

☼☀ ◊ Z5   **Deciduous tree**
‡ 50ft (15m) ↔ 40ft (12m)

TAXODIUM DISTICHUM

This shapely, conical conifer is an ideal specimen tree, especially for very wet sites (*see p.372*); at the edge of water, it produces kneelike, protuberant aerial growths. The narrow, pale green leaves are late to emerge in spring and turn brilliant shades of russet brown in autumn. Hanging, red male cones emerge in winter. It grows in most wet or moist ground, including acidic soils (*see p.92*). Little or no pruning is required.

ALSO RECOMMENDED: *The shoots of 'Nutans' become pendent when mature.*

☼☀ ◊◖ Z5   **Deciduous tree**
‡ 80ft (25m) ↔ 25ft (8m)

KALMIA LATIFOLIA

A dense bush valued for its long-lasting display of pale to deep pink, occasionally white flowers that open from crimped, dark pink or red buds from late spring to midsummer. Equally at home in a shrub border or woodland garden, it flowers best in sun in reliably moist soil, which must be acidic (*see p.92*). Deadhead regularly, and remove any dead wood and overly long shoots in spring.

ALSO RECOMMENDED: *'Ostbo Red' is similar but has pale pink flowers opening from bright red buds.*

☼☀ ◐ Z5b   **Evergreen shrub**
‡↔ 10ft (3m)

NEILLIA THIBETICA

The gracefully arching, zig-zagging branches of this shrub bear dense clusters of bell-shaped, rose-pink flowers at their tips in early summer. It is perfect for either mixed and shrub borders or a woodland garden. It forms thickets by suckering, so is useful for barrier plantings. Trim after flowering. Also tolerant of alkaline, acidic, and permanently moist soils (*see pp.64, 92, 372*).

ALSO RECOMMENDED: N. sinensis *has dense clusters of pale pink to white flowers in late spring and early summer.* Z7

☼☀ ◐◑ Z7   **Deciduous shrub**
‡↔ 10ft (2m)

OXYDENDRUM ARBOREUM

The sourwood is a large shrub, valued for its late summer flowers and colorful autumn foliage. The small, fragrant white flowers are produced in large clusters that droop from the branches, and the elliptical and finely toothed, glossy dark green leaves turn to brilliant shades of red, yellow, and purple before they drop. For the best overall growth and autumn color, grow on an acidic soil (*see p.92*). Suitable for wild areas (*see p.494*).

☀☀ ◊ *f* Z6　　　**Deciduous shrub**
↕ 30–50ft (10–15m) ↔ 25ft (8m)

PYRACANTHA *'Mohave'*

This firethorn makes a bushy plant, admired for its clusters of small white flowers in early summer and its bright red berries, which persist well into winter and are a food source for birds (*see p.494*). The leaves are glossy dark green. It is ideal in a shrub border or against a wall (*see pp.262, 280*); its spiny branches make for a good boundary hedge (*see p.138*). For best results, choose a site that is sheltered from wind.

ALSO RECOMMENDED: *'Golden Charmer'* (see p.159); *'Soleil d'Or'* (see p.269); *'Watereri'* (see p.505).

☀☀ ◊ Z6　　　**Evergreen shrub**
↕ 12ft (4m) ↔ 15ft (5m)

SAMBUCUS RACEMOSA
'Plumosa Aurea'

Delicately cut, golden leaves make this plant a fine focal point in a mixed or shrub border or as a specimen in a woodland garden. Cut the stems back hard in early spring for the best foliage effect. If unpruned, creamy white flowers appear in spring and give rise to red berries that attract birds (*see p.494*). Tolerant of alkaline and permanently moist soils (*see pp.64, 372*). May scorch in full sun.

ALSO RECOMMENDED: *'Sutherland Gold' is less liable to sun scorch; 'Tenuifolia' is shorter with finely cut green leaves.*

☼ ◐ ◊◗ Z3   **Deciduous shrub**
‡↔ 10ft (3m)

SPIRAEA JAPONICA
'Little Princess'

A low but wide-spreading shrub, forming a dense mound of small, dark green leaves that makes a good ground-cover (*see p.304*). In mid- to late summer, it bears a profusion of rose-pink flowers. Ideal for edging a sunny border or for a rock garden. Tolerant of alkaline soils (*see p.64*) and urban pollution. Cut back to a low, permanent framework in spring.

ALSO RECOMMENDED: *'Goldflame' is taller with bronze young leaves that turn bright yellow, then green with the arrival of the flowers; 'Nana' is more compact.*

☼ ◊ Z2b   **Deciduous shrub**
‡ 20in (50cm) ↔ 3ft (1m)

SYRINGA VULGARIS *'Congo'*

This densely flowered form of the common lilac bears conical clusters of fragrant, lilac-purple flowers in early summer above heart-shaped, dark green leaves. Like other lilacs, it also thrives on well-drained soils, including shallow and alkaline (*see p.64*), and it tolerates coastal sites (*see p.166*) and urban pollution. A fine backdrop for a shrub or mixed border. Little pruning is necessary.

ALSO RECOMMENDED: *'Andenken an Ludwig Späth' has dark purple-red flowers; those of 'Charles Joly' are double and deep purple.*

☼ ◊ *f* Z2   **Deciduous shrub**
↕↔ 22ft (7m)

THUJA OCCIDENTALIS *'Hetz Midget'*

This slow-growing, dwarf variant of white cedar has yellowish green, scale-like leaves that are fruit-scented when bruised. It forms a spherical bush and is good for a rock garden or for providing strong contrasts of form in a conifer collection. Tolerant of most well-drained soils including alkaline (*see p.64*). Provide shelter from cold, drying winds.

ALSO RECOMMENDED: *'Caespitosa' has bluish foliage, making a bun-shaped bush to 12in (30cm) tall; 'Golden Globe' makes a golden yellow sphere to 3ft (1m) tall.*

☼ ◊ Z2   **Evergreen shrub**
↕↔ 32in (80cm)

WEIGELA FLORIDA *'Foliis Purpureis'*

This compact bush has arching shoots bearing generous clusters of funnel-shaped, dark pink flowers with pale insides in late spring and early summer. The foliage is bronze-green. It is ideal for a shrub or mixed border in an urban garden. Prune out some older branches at ground level each year after flowering. Also suitable as a hedge plant (*see p.138*), and it tolerates alkaline soils (*see p.64*).

ALSO RECOMMENDED: W. *'Minuet' has two-toned light pink flowers with a yellow throat and purple-tinged foliage.* Z5

☼ ◊ Z4b   **Deciduous shrub**
↕ 3ft (1m) ↔ 5ft (1.5m)

HUMULUS LUPULUS *'Aureus'*

The golden hops is grown for its prettily lobed, bright golden yellow foliage, which will twine over a fence or trellis, or up into a small tree. Hanging clusters of papery, conelike, greenish yellow flowers appear in autumn, and they dry well for garlands and swags. It can be grown on a partially shaded wall (*see p.262*), but leaf color is best in full sun. Give the twining stems support, and cut back any dead growth to ground level in early spring.

ALSO RECOMMENDED: H. lupulus, *the traditional hops, is similar but with pale green leaves.*

☼◐ ◊◊ Z4   **Climber**
↕ 20ft (6m)

VITIS COIGNETIAE

This vigorous, woody-stemmed climber has large, heart-shaped leaves that turn bright red in autumn; the color is best in full sun. It climbs using its tendrils and is ideal for clothing a warm wall (*see p.280*), pergola, or large tree; if pegged down it also makes a good groundcover (*see p.304*). It tolerates sandy and slightly alkaline soils (*see pp.38, 64*). Prune in midwinter.

ALSO RECOMMENDED: V. vinifera *'Purpurea'* (see p.303).

☼ ◑ ◊ Z5   **Climber**

↕ 50ft (15m)

ACONITUM × CAMMARUM *'Bicolor'*

Arching branches of hooded, blue and white flowers appear on this upright plant from mid- to late summer, well above the deeply lobed, glossy dark green leaves. It needs staking. Good for late color in herbaceous or mixed borders, and it will tolerate full sun where soils are reliably moist. All parts are highly toxic if ingested.

ALSO RECOMMENDED: *A. 'Bressingham Spire' has deep violet flowers; 'Newry Blue' has dense spires of mid-blue flowers.*

☼ ◊ Z3b   **Perennial**

↕ 4ft (1.2m) ↔ 12in (30cm)

ARUNCUS DIOICUS

Goatsbeard forms clumps of rich green, fernlike foliage, from which loose and arching clusters of creamy or greenish white flowers emerge in the first half of summer. A graceful woodland plant that is also good for damp shade (*see p.238*) and permanently moist soils (*see p.372*), such as around the edge of a pond. Cut stems to the ground in autumn.

ALSO RECOMMENDED: *'Kneiffii' has very finely divided leaves and cream flowers; A. aethusifolius is more compact, with leaves that turn yellow in autumn Z4.*

☼☀ ◑◐ Z3b   **Perennial**

‡ 6ft (2m) ↔ 4ft (1.2m)

ASTER NOVI-BELGII *'Jenny'*

This New York aster is grown for its sprays of daisylike, red-purple and yellow flowers that appear from late summer to midautumn above stout clumps of midgreen leaves. This is a useful plant for a perennial border. Fertilize and water well in spring and summer. Mildew may be a problem if conditions become too dry. Also good for wildlife areas (*see p.494*).

ALSO RECOMMENDED: *'Alice Haslam' has rose-red flowers; those of 'Audrey' are lavender-blue; 'Fellowship' has large, double, deep pink flowers; 'Little Pink Beauty' has soft pink flowers.*

☼☀ ◑◐ Z3   **Perennial**

‡ 5ft (1.5m) ↔ 24in (60cm)

ASTILBE *'Deutschland'*

Branching, feathery spires of many tiny, creamy white flowers rise above the dense mass of finely divided, bright green leaves in late spring and early summer on this versatile, clump-forming perennial. It is ideal for damp borders (*see p.238*), woodland gardens, and waterside plantings (*see p.372*). Divide the clumps every few years to maintain vigorous growth.

ALSO RECOMMENDED: *A. × arendsii 'Fanal' has long-lived, deep crimson plumes Z3b; A. × crispa 'Perkeo' (see p.377).*

☀ ◊◓ Z3b   **Perennial**
‡ 20in (50cm) ↔ 12in (30cm)

ASTRANTIA MAJOR

Ground-level clumps of deeply lobed leaves give rise to tall stems in early and midsummer, topped by small, green or pink, sometimes deep purple-red flowers. They are good for dried flower arrangements (*see p.524*). In a suitable position, such as damp woodland (*see p.238*) or anywhere with moist soil (*see p.372*), the plant will self-seed and form clumps. The leaves die down in winter.

ALSO RECOMMENDED: *'Hadspen Blood' has dark red flowers; 'Sunningdale Variegated' has cream-margined leaves and pink flowers.*

☼☀ ◊◓ Z5   **Perennial**
‡ 12–36in (30–90cm) ↔ 18in (45cm)

CAMPANULA LATILOBA
'Hidcote Amethyst'

A clump-forming bellflower with cup-shaped, pale amethyst blooms that appear against midgreen foliage in the second half of summer. An ideal border perennial that can also be naturalized in a wildlife garden (*see p.494*) or in gaps in paving (*see p.348*); the delicate flowers are best preserved in partial shade. Cut back after flowering to encourage further blooms. Also good for alkaline soils and hot, dry sites (*see pp.64, 190*)

ALSO RECOMMENDED: *'Percy Piper' has rich violet-blue flowers; C. latifolia 'Brantwood' is upright with violet flowers.*

☼ ◑ ◊◊ Z3 **Perennial**

‡ 36in (90cm) ↔ 18in (45cm)

CAREX OSHIMENSIS
'Evergold'

This evergreen sedge forms a low tussock of narrow, dark green leaves, each with a broad, creamy yellow central stripe. Brown flower spikes appear in mid- and late spring above the foliage. Tolerant of more freely drained soils than many sedges and is suitable for a mixed border or a sunny container (*see p.412*).

ALSO RECOMMENDED: *C. morrowii 'Fisher's Form' is slightly less hardy and grows to 20in (50cm) tall with cream-striped, dark green leaves.* Z5

☼ ◑ ◊◊ Z6b **Perennial**

‡ 12in (30cm) ↔ 14in (35cm)

CENTAUREA MACROCEPHALA

This stout knapweed with robust stems bears rich yellow flowers in mid- and late summer. The bases of these thistle-like blooms are fringed with shiny brown bracts. The leaves are soft and mid-green. Bees and butterflies are drawn to the bright flowers, which makes this plant suitable for a wildlife garden (*see p. 494*) as well as a traditional border. Tolerant of coastal sites (*see p.166*).

ALSO RECOMMENDED: C. simplicicaulis *grows to 10in (25cm) tall, has rose-pink flowers in early summer, and needs full sun and well-drained soil.* Z3b

☼ ◐ ◊ ◖ Z3   **Perennial**

↕ 5ft (1.5m) ↔ 24in (60cm)

EUPATORIUM RUGOSUM

White snakeroot forms clumps of purple-tinged, stiffly upright stems that are topped by domed clusters of pink, pinkish purple, or creamy white flowers from midsummer to early autumn. Whorls of coarse, purplish green leaves decorate the stems. Suitable for a reliably moist border (*see p.372*) or woodland garden (*see p.238*). It tolerates alkaline soils (*see p.64*).

ALSO RECOMMENDED: E. album *'Braunlaub' bears brown-flushed young leaves and brown-tinged flowers.* Z4

☼ ◖ Z4b   **Perennial**

↕ 5–6ft (1.5–1.8m) ↔ 24in (60cm)

FILIPENDULA PURPUREA

An upright, clump-forming plant that looks nice when planted in groups to form drifts of elegant, dark green foliage. Feathery clusters of red-purple flowers are carried above the leaves on purple-tinged stems in summer. Suitable for a waterside planting or bog garden (*see p.372*), it can also be naturalized in damp woodland (*see p.238*).

ALSO RECOMMENDED: *f. albiflora has white flowers; 'Elegans' has greenish yellow leaves.*

☼ ◐ ◊◊ Z3b   **Perennial**
‡ 4ft (1.2m) ↔ 24in (60cm)

HELENIUM *'Moerheim Beauty'*

From early to late summer, this robust and upright, undemanding perennial bears a succession of rich, coppery red, daisylike blooms with dark brown centers; they are attractive to bees (*see p.494*) and good for cutting (*see p.524*). Deadhead regularly and divide the clumps every third year to maintain vigor. Also suitable for large containers in sun (*see p.412*).

ALSO RECOMMENDED: *'Butterpat' bears golden flowerheads from midsummer; 'Wyndley' (see p.85).*

☼ ◊◊ Z3b   **Perennial**
‡ 36in (90cm) ↔ 24in (60cm)

HELIOPSIS HELIANTHOIDES
'Sommersonne'

Also sold as 'Summer Sun', the bright, golden yellow daisylike flowers of this vigorous perennial are borne from midsummer to early autumn, making it invaluable in a sunny border. A little unobtrusive support and regular deadheading improves the display, and dividing the clumps every third year will maintain vigor.

ALSO RECOMMENDED: *'Goldgefieder' has double, bright yellow flowerheads with green centers.*

☼ ◊◖ Z4   **Perennial**
‡ 36in (90cm) ↔ 24in (60cm)

HEMEROCALLIS
'Stella de Oro'

With vigorous, dense clumps of bright green leaves, this daylily makes a good groundcover (*see p.304*), especially in permanently moist soil (*see p.372*). The bright gold-yellow flowers are borne repeatedly from early summer. Ideal at the front of a sunny border or in a sunny container (*see p.412*).

ALSO RECOMMENDED: *'Gentle Shepherd' is taller, spreads more widely, and bears ivory white flowers; 'Stafford' is also taller and has star-shaped scarlet flowers.*

☼ ◖ Z3b   **Perennial**
‡ 12in (30cm) ↔ 18in (45cm)

HOSTA VENTRICOSA

This plantain lily forms dense mounds of broad, shiny dark green, overlapping leaves with slightly wavy margins. Spires of bell-shaped, deep purple flowers arch above the luxuriant foliage in late summer. Good at the front of a mixed border, but also suitable for containers (*see p.448*), as a groundcover under deciduous trees (*see p.326*), or in permanently moist soils (*see p.372*). .

ALSO RECOMMENDED: *var.* aureomaculata *has yellow-splashed leaves; those of H. 'Aureo-marginata' are margined yellow.*

☼ ◑ ◊ Z4   **Perennial**

‡ 20in (50cm) ↔ 3ft (1m)

HOUTTUYNIA CORDATA

In damp shade, at the margins of streams or ponds, or in shady containers (*see pp.238, 372, 448*), the blue-green, heart-shaped leaves of this vigorous, spreading plant make an excellent groundcover (*see p.326*). Small white flowers appear in spring. Protect roots of plants grown in wet soils with a winter mulch in cold areas.

ALSO RECOMMENDED: *'Chameleon' (syn. 'Tricolor') spreads less vigorously and has variegated leaves in shades of pale yellow, green, and red.*

☼ ◊ ◑ Z5b   **Perennial**

‡ 6–12in (15–30cm) ↔ indefinite

HYACINTHOIDES NON-SCRIPTA

English bluebells are perfect for
naturalizing in grass, in a wildlife area
(*see p.494*), or in a damp woodland
garden (*see p.238*). Although they
prefer moist soils, they tolerate dry
shade (*see p.216*) and are good for
underplanting a shrub border. The
spires of scented, soft violet-blue
flowers are borne in spring and look
best in massed plantings. They will self-
seed where conditions are favorable.
Plants bulbs in autumn.

ALSO RECOMMENDED: H. hispanica *is
more robust with denser flower spikes.* Z3

☀ ☀ ◗ *f* Z6   **Perennial**
‡ 8–16in (20–40cm) ↔ 3in (8cm)

KIRENGESHOMA PALMATA

A handsome, upright perennial with
broad, lobed, pale green leaves. In late
summer and early autumn, these are
topped by loose clusters of nodding,
pale yellow flowers, which are
sometimes called nodding wax bells. It
brings a gentle elegance to a cool and
damp, shady border (*see p.238*), and it
thrives in acidic soils (*see p.92*). Shelter
from wind, and enrich the planting
site with leaf mold.

☀ ◗ Z4   **Perennial**
‡ 24–48in (60–120cm) ↔ 30in (75cm)

MONARDA *'Mahogany'*

This beebalm forms clumps of dark green, aromatic leaves on upright stems. From midsummer to early autumn, a profusion of rich red, shaggy flowerheads appear, making a colorful addition to any herbaceous or mixed border. Since the flowers are also very attractive to bees and hummingbirds, beebalms are excellent for wildlife gardens (*see p.494*).

ALSO RECOMMENDED: *'Beauty of Cobham' has pale pink flowers; those of 'Gardenview Scarlet' are scarlet-red; 'Croftway Pink' (see p.517).*

☼ ◑ ◊ ◊ *f* Z3b   **Perennial**
‡ 36in (90cm) ↔ 18in (45cm)

PERSICARIA CAMPANULATA

This knotweed is grown for its display of small, white or pink, fragrant flowers that appear on upright stems in loose clusters from midsummer to early autumn. The plant forms a clump of spreading, slender, and wiry stems with bright green leaves. An undemanding plant for a border, as a groundcover (*see pp.304, 326*), or in containers (*see pp.412, 448*). Also good in cracks between paving or in permanently moist soils (*see pp.348, 372*).

ALSO RECOMMENDED: *'Rosenrot' is more upright in habit with deep pink flowers; 'Southcombe White' has white flowers.*

☼ ◑ ◊ *f* Z6   **Perennial**
‡↔ 36in (90cm)

POLEMONIUM CARNEUM

An upright perennial with dense clumps of decorative, divided leaves that are topped in early summer by loose clusters of shallowly bell-shaped flowers in pale pink, yellow, or sometimes deep purple or lavender. Remove dead flowerheads for a second flush of flowers. Grow in a border or wildlife garden (*see p.494*).

ALSO RECOMMENDED: *P. caeruleum has violet-blue flowers and reaches 36in (90cm) tall; f. album has white flowers; P. pauciflorum has pale yellow, red-flushed flowers. All Z3b*

☼◑ ◊◊Z3b　　　　　　**Perennial**

↕ 4–16in (10–40cm) ↔ 8in (20cm)

POLYGONATUM HIRTUM

Solomon's seals are valued for their fresh green foliage and tubular flowers. From late spring to midsummer, this species carries a few hanging, green-tipped, greenish white flowers from the axil of each leaf. Spherical black fruits follow. A favorite plant for a shady border (*see p.216*). Cut dead stems back in winter when the plant is dormant.

ALSO RECOMMENDED: *P. × hybridum 'Striatum' is shorter with late spring flowers and cream-striped leaves. Z4*

☼● ◊◊Z4b　　　　　　**Perennial**

↕ 4ft (1.2m) ↔ 24in (60cm)

PULMONARIA 'Sissinghurst White'

Slowly spreading to form a carpet of dark green, white-spotted leaves, this plant is spangled in spring with a mass of pure white flowers that open from pale pink buds. Excellent as a ground-cover beneath shrubs or in a woodland garden (*see p.326*); it is best in shade but tolerates full sun. Also suitable for a wildlife garden (*see p.494*). Divide and replant clumps every few years.

ALSO RECOMMENDED: P. angustifolia *bears deep blue flowers;* P. longifolia *has deep blue-purple flowers from late winter.* Z4

☼ ☀ ◑ Z4 **Perennial**

‡ 12in (30cm) ↔ 18in (45cm)

RODGERSIA AESCULIFOLIA

The deeply crinkled, horse-chestnut-like leaves of this architectural plant (*see p.472*) form a foil for the plumes of tiny, pink or white, star-shaped flowers that appear in midsummer. It makes an excellent groundcover (*see pp.304, 326*), especially for permanently moist soil (*see p.372*) or in a damp, shady border (*see p.238*). Also good in for a container in shade (*see p.448*).

ALSO RECOMMENDED: R. pinnata *'Superba'* (see p.391); R. sambucifolia *has white or pink flowers in early to midsummer.* Z5.

☼ ☀ ◑◑ Z5 **Perennial**

‡ to 6ft (2m) ↔ 3ft (1m)

SANGUISORBA CANADENSIS

The Canadian burnet produces fluffy, long-stemmed spikes of tiny white flowers in midsummer and autumn above a clump of divided, dark green leaves. It is perfect for naturalizing in permanently moist soils (*see p.372*). The long-lived flowers, which open from the bottom of the spike upward, are excellent for cutting (*see p.524*).

ALSO RECOMMENDED: S. obtusa *is shorter, to 24in (60cm), and has nodding spikes of pink flowers.* Z4b

☼ ◐◗ Z3   **Perennial**
‡ 6ft (2m) ↔ 3ft (1m)

SCROPHULARIA AURICULATA '*Variegata*'

The variegated water figwort forms a mound of wrinkled green leaves that are boldly splashed with cream; the bright variegation is maintained even in deep shade. An ideal marginal plant, it thrives in permanently moist soils and shallow water (*see pp.372, 394*); it is also good in a damp wildlife area (*see p.494*) or woodland garden. Cut the flowerheads off as they form to keep clumps neat and to maintain variegation.

☼ ◐◗ Z6   **Perennial**
‡↔ 36in (90cm)

SILPHIUM PERFOLIATUM

The cup plant forms a clump of resinously aromatic, triangular leaves and bears branching heads of yellow daisylike flowers from midsummer to autumn. They attract a variety of pollinating insects, which makes this plant ideal for naturalizing in a wildlife garden (*see p.494*). It also tolerates alkaline and permanently moist soils (*see pp.64, 372*).

ALSO RECOMMENDED: S. laciniatum, *the compass plant, is taller with nodding heads of yellow flowers.* Z6

☀️◐ ◊ *f* Z6　　　　　**Perennial**
‡ 8ft (2.5m) ↔ 3ft (1m)

SOLIDAGO *'Golden Wings'*

With broad heads of golden yellow flowers borne from late summer to early autumn, this vigorous plant is ideal for late color at the back of a mixed or herbaceous border; it will also naturalize in a wildlife area (*see p.494*) or woodland garden. The flowers are excellent for cutting (*see p.524*). This plants also tolerates sandy soils and maritime conditions (*see pp.38, 166*).

ALSO RECOMMENDED: *'Goldenmosa' is more compact, with yellow flowerheads; 'Crown of Rays' is shorter still with radiating golden yellow flowerheads.*

☀️ ◊�◊ Z4　　　　　**Perennial**
‡ 6ft (2m) ↔ 36in (90cm)

THELYPTERIS PALUSTRIS

The marsh fern is a spreading plant that forms substantial clumps of arching, finely divided, pale green fronds with deeply lobed segments. It thrives in permanently moist soils (*see p.494*), where it is ideal as a groundcover (*see pp.304, 326*), such as at the edge of a pond. It grows well in full sun or shade but will produce spores only in good light. It may be invasive.

☼ ◑ ◊◊ Z4b   **Perennial fern**
↕ 24in (60cm) ↔ 3ft (1m)

THERMOPSIS RHOMBIFOLIA

An upright, unbranched plant with pretty, laburnum-like, midgreen leaves clothed in silky silver hair. The short spires of soft yellow flowers in early summer are attractive to bees. This spreading plant is worth naturalizing in a wildlife area (*see p.494*) or woodland garden, although it may be invasive.

ALSO RECOMMENDED: T. villosa *is taller with downy yellow flowers in late spring and early summer.* Z5b

☼ ◑ ◊◊ Z2   **Perennial**
↕ 36in (90cm) ↔ 24in (60cm) or more

PLANTS FOR SANDY SOILS

Sandy soils are a joy to work. They are well-aerated and very free-draining, and, unlike clay soils, they can be worked at almost any time of year without harming the structure. As a rule, if you can walk on the bare soil without it sticking to your boots, it is safe to dig. All a sandy soil will need is the lightest of cultivation before it is planted. Sandy soils also warm quickly in spring, giving plants a head start into growth.

There is a price to pay for such a plethora of advantages, however. Sandy soils are generally very hungry and thirsty, as a result of being open and free-draining. Water is lost rapidly both by evaporation from the surface and drainage, and as the water drains away, it takes dissolved plant nutrients with it. Organic matter also degrades rapidly, which compounds the loss of nutrients.

SPECIAL PLANTS

Plants that thrive on sandy soils include many annuals plus those that are either tolerant of, or

adapted to survival on, low-nutrient soils, and they are often accustomed to drought in their natural habitat. For example, the foxtail lily (*see p.55*) grows in the dry, stony hills of Afghanistan, and its thick, fleshy roots have evolved to conserve what little moisture they can find. Sun-loving helianthemums (*see pp.46, 72, 351*) naturally dwell in dry, rocky places and on sand dunes, and their small, tough, often white-hairy leaves conserve vital moisture while deflecting the sun's burning rays. Many such plants have a waxy, bluish bloom to their foliage, another method of conserving water. The beauty of their foliage is often one of their most enduring features and can be used to create exciting mixtures of colors and textures. In the race to set seed before conditions become too dry, many plants also flower freely and attract pollinating insects with exuberant colors and fragrances. Some plants may even flower themselves to death if they exhaust the soil nutrients in the process.

CULTIVATION TIPS

If you garden on sand, be prepared to apply well-rotted, nutrient-rich organic matter, such as well-rotted manure or compost, on an annual basis, and to give additional plant food in the form of a balanced, preferably slow-release, fertilizer. Organic matter will be most effective if applied as a mulch, 2–4in (5–10cm) thick, to previously weeded ground. There is little point in digging organic matter and nutrients deeply into sandy soil, because this will damage the structure you are trying to improve. The natural actions of rainfall and beneficial soil organisms will carry them down to the plant roots, where they are needed. A mulch also helps reduce evaporation of water from the soil surface and moderate fluctuations in temperature, which may harm the roots. A ground-covering carpet of evergreen foliage will also help (*see pp.304, 326*), particularly in wet seasons, when increased rainfall leads to a greater leaching of nutrients.

BETULA ERMANII

Erman's birch is a conical tree with rough, warty shoots and pinkish or creamy white bark. Long, yellow-brown catkins open as the foliage emerges in spring; the dark green leaves turn yellow in autumn before they fall. Like most birches, this tree is an excellent landscape tree planted alone or in clumps. Also tolerant of clay and acidic soils (*see pp.12, 92*).

ALSO RECOMMENDED: B. pendula *'Tristis'* (see p.474); B. utilis *'Jermyns'* (see p.121).

☼ ◊ Z5　　　　　　**Deciduous tree**
‡ 70ft (20m) ↔ 40ft (12m)

CASTANEA SATIVA *'Albomarginata'*

This vigorous, broadly columnar tree has toothed, glossy dark green leaves margined with cream. In summer, it produces creamy white, catkinlike flowers in large clusters; these are followed by edible fruits – chestnuts – in autumn. A good specimen for larger gardens. Little pruning is required. Best in slightly acidic soils (*see p.92*).

ALSO RECOMMENDED: *'Aspleniifolia' has deeply cut leaves; 'Marron de Lyon' is grown for its fruit.*

☼ ◔ ◊ Z5b　　　　　**Deciduous tree**
‡ 100ft (30m) ↔ 50ft (15m)

CERCIS SILIQUASTRUM

The Judas tree is a handsome small tree. It bears clusters of pealike, bright pink flowers on the previous year's wood, either before or with the heart-shaped leaves in mid-spring. The foliage is bronze when young, maturing to dark blue-green, then to yellow in autumn. Also good for alkaline soils (*see p.64*) and hot, dry sites (*see p.190*). Prune young trees to a balanced shape in early summer.

ALSO RECOMMENDED: C. canadensis *'Forest Pansy' has dark red-purple leaves.* Z5b

---

☼ ◑ ◊◐Z7   **Deciduous tree**

↕↔ 30ft (10m)

ROBINIA PSEUDOACACIA *'Frisia'*

This variety of black locust is a fast-growing, broadly columnar tree much admired for its gentle yellow-green foliage, which is golden yellow when young and orange-yellow in autumn. Hanging clusters of small white flowers appear sparsely in summer. The stems are spiny. When young, maintain a single trunk by removing competing stems as soon as possible. Also suitable for alkaline soils (*see p.64*).

ALSO RECOMMENDED: R. hispida (see p.296).

☼ ◊◐ Z4   **Deciduous tree**

↕ 50ft (15m) ↔ 25ft (8m)

BALLOTA PSEUDODICTAMNUS

A low subshrub that forms mounds of aromatic, yellow-gray-green foliage on upright, white-woolly stems. Whorls of small, white or pinkish white flowers, each enclosed by a pale green funnel, are borne in early summer. It is ideal for a sunny border. Cut back in early spring to keep plants compact. Protect from excessive winter moisture.

ALSO RECOMMENDED: *B. acetabulosa is slightly larger with purple-pink flowers in mid- and late summer.* Z8

☼ ◊ *f* Z8b   **Evergreen shrub**
‡ 18in (45cm) ↔ 24in (60cm)

CALLUNA VULGARIS
'Kinlochruel'

A distinctive heather with double white flowers in long clusters that are borne very freely from midsummer to late autumn. It forms a spreading mound of bright green foliage that turns to bronze during winter. Hundreds of different cultivars of heather exist, most of which make good ground cover on acidic soils (*see pp.92, 304*). Good for wildflower gardens (*see p.494*).

ALSO RECOMMENDED: *'Wickwar Flame' has gold leaves that turn red in winter.*

☼ ◊ Z5   **Evergreen shrub**
‡ 10in (25cm) ↔ 16in (40cm)

CERATOSTIGMA WILLMOTTIANUM

Chinese plumbago is valued for its long-lasting display of pale to mid-blue flowers from late summer; autumn flowers appear at the same time as the diamond-shaped, mid-green leaves turn to blazing red. It dies back in cold winters but usually regenerates in spring. Grow in a sheltered mixed border. It also tolerates urban pollution and alkaline soils *(see. p.64).*

ALSO RECOMMENDED: C. plumbaginoides *is a shorter perennial form with bright blue flowers and crimson leaves in autumn.* Z6

☼ ◊ Z7   **Deciduous shrub**
‡ 3ft (1m) ↔ 5ft (1.5m)

CISTUS × SKANBERGII

A beautiful and compact rock rose that bears small clusters of pale pink blooms in profusion throughout summer. They are saucer-shaped with crinkled petals and a central boss of gold stamens – similar to single rose flowers. The narrow, slightly wavy-margined leaves are gray-green. Good for sunny shrub borders or containers, against warm walls, or in hot, dry sites *(see pp.190, 280. 412).*

ALSO RECOMMENDED: C. × cyprius *has white flowers with crimson marks at the petal bases and is twice the size;* C. × purpureus *has dark pink flowers.* Z7b

☼ ◊ Z7b   **Evergreen shrub**
‡ 30in (75cm) ↔ 36in (90cm)

CONVOLVULUS CNEORUM

This small, rounded bush bears masses of funnel-shaped, sparkling white flowers with yellow centers from late spring and into summer. They stand out against the dark silvery green, narrow leaves. Excellent as a largish plant in a rock garden or on a sunny bank. In areas with cold, wet winters, grow in a container (*see p.412*) and move into a cool greenhouse in winter. Trim back after flowering, if necessary.

ALSO RECOMMENDED: C. sabatius (see p.432).

☀ ◊ Z8   **Evergreen shrub**

↕ 24in (60cm) ↔ 36in (90cm)

CYTISUS × PRAECOX 'Warminster'

Warminster broom has slender, arching green branches, wreathed in fragrant, pealike, creamy yellow flowers in spring. Good for a shrub border or large rock garden; hot, dry sites (*see p.190*); and warm walls (*see p.280*). Pinch out branch tips to promote bushy growth. Cut shoots back by up to two-thirds after flowering; do not cut into old wood. Also tolerant of clay and acidic soils (*see pp.12, 92*) and coastal conditions (*see p.166*).

ALSO RECOMMENDED: *'Allgold' has deep yellow flowers.*

☀ ◊ **f** Z5b   **Deciduous shrub**

↕ 4ft (1.2m) ↔ 5ft (1.5m)

ERICA AUSTRALIS

Unlike many heathers, the Spanish heath is a relatively tall and upright shrub. It bears masses of bell-shaped, purplish pink flowers from midspring to early summer against a backdrop of fine, needlelike, dark green foliage. Grow in a heather garden or among other shrubs. Prone to damage by wind or snow; cut back damaged growth after flowering. Also good for acidic soils (*see p.92*).

ALSO RECOMMENDED: *'Mr. Robert' produces white flowers; 'Riverslea' bears lilac-pink flowers.*

☼ ◊ Min 35°F (2°C) **Evergreen shrub**
↕ 6ft (2m) ↔ 3ft (1m)

✕ HALIMIOCISTUS WINTONENSIS *'Merrist Wood Cream'*

A spreading shrub that bears roselike, creamy yellow flowers with red bands and yellow centres against grayish foliage in late spring and early summer. Good for a raised bed or rock garden, or for the front of a mixed border. It is also good for warm walls, hot, dry sites, and containers (*see pp.190, 280, 412*). It may perish during cold winters if not sheltered from excessive rain. Pruning is rarely needed.

ALSO RECOMMENDED: ✕ *H. sahucii is more compact with pink flowers in summer.* Z8a

☼ ◊ Z8 **Evergreen shrub**
↕ 24in (60cm) ↔ 36in (90cm)

HEBE CUPRESSOIDES
'Boughton Dome'

This dwarf shrub is grown for its neat shape and dense, cypresslike foliage that forms a pale green dome. Flowers are infrequent. An excellent addition to a rock garden, giving a topiary effect without any clipping. It also thrives in coastal gardens (*see p.166*) and can be grown as a low hedge (*see p.138*).

ALSO RECOMMENDED: H. albicans *forms a compact mound of gray-green foliage to 24in (60cm) tall, and white flowers appear from early to midsummer.* Z8

☼ ☼ ◊◊ Z8b   **Evergreen shrub**
‡ 12in (30cm) ↔ 24in (60cm)

HELIANTHEMUM
'Raspberry Ripple'

This rock rose is a spreading shrub that bears grayish green leaves and a profusion of saucer-shaped white flowers with irregular, purple-pink centers. They open in succession from late spring to summer. Good in a rock garden and makes a good ground-cover, especially in hot, dry sites (*see pp.190, 304*). Grow in neutral to alkaline soil (*see p.64*).

ALSO RECOMMENDED: *'Rhodanthe Carneum' (see p.72); 'Wisley Primrose' has pale yellow flowers; those of 'Wisley White' are creamy white.*

☼ ◊ Z6   **Evergreen shrub**
‡ 8in (20cm) ↔ 12in (30cm)

HIBISCUS SYRIACUS
'Woodbridge'

This rose of Sharon is a fast-growing, upright shrub that bears large, deep rose-pink flowers from late summer to mid-autumn. They have maroon blotches around the centers and stand out against the dark green leaves. Valued for its late season of interest. Prune young plants to encourage branching; keep this to a minimum once established. Also good for alkaline soils and hot, dry sites (*see pp.64, 190*).

ALSO RECOMMENDED: *'Oiseau Bleu' (syn. 'Blue Bird')* has lilac-blue flowers.

☼ ◊◊ Z5b   **Deciduous shrub**
↕ 10ft (3m) ↔ 6ft (2m)

LAVANDULA STOECHAS
SUBSP. PEDUNCULATA

French lavender is a small, neat shrub that blooms from spring to summer. Dense spikes of tiny, fragrant, dark purple flowers, each spike topped by distinctive long bracts, are carried on upright stalks above the narrow, woolly, silver-gray leaves. Effective in sheltered shrub borders, hot and dry sites, rock gardens, and wild areas (*see pp.190, 494*). The flower stalks are good for cutting (*see p.524*). It can also be clipped as a hedge (*see p.138*).

ALSO RECOMMENDED: *'Kew Red'* has red flowers; *f.* leucantha has white flowers.

☼ ◊ ƒ Z8   **Evergreen shrub**
↕↔ 24in (60cm)

LAVATERA *'Kew Rose'*

This pink-flowered mallow is a small shrub with purplish shoots and gray-green leaves. Its bright sprays of large flowers appear over a long season throughout summer. A fine, fast-growing but short-lived plant for a shrub border or coastal garden (*see p.166*). Where marginally hardy, grow against a warm wall (*see p.280*).

ALSO RECOMMENDED: *'Barnsley' has red-eyed white flowers; 'Bredon Springs' has dusky pink flowers; those of 'Burgundy Wine' are rich deep pink; 'Rosea' also has deep pink flowers.*

☼ ◊ Z5   **Evergreen shrub**
↕↔ 6ft (2m)

LESPEDEZA THUNBERGII

The bush clover is a small shrub with arching shoots and divided, blue-green leaves. A profusion of purple-pink, pealike flowers are borne in pendent spikes in early autumn. Good for late color in a sunny mixed border. The top-growth will die back in winter, but it will regenerate in spring. Cut back to a low, permanent framework in spring.

ALSO RECOMMENDED: *L. bicolor has dark green leaves and purple-pink flowers in mid-to late summer. Z4*

☼ ◊ Z4   **Deciduous shrub**
↕ 6ft (2m) ↔ 10ft (3m)

PEROVSKIA *'Blue Spire'*

This easily grown, upright subshrub, valued for its foliage and flowers, is good in a mixed or herbaceous border. Its branching, airy spikes of tubular, violet-blue flowers are borne in profusion during late summer and early autumn above the aromatic, silvery gray, deeply cut leaves. Prune back hard each spring to a low framework for vigorous, bushy growth. Also tolerates coastal conditions (*see p.166*), alkaline soils (*see p.64*), and hot, dry sites (*see p.190*).

ALSO RECOMMENDED: *'Hybrida' has darker flowers.*

☼ ◊ *f* Z5   **Deciduous shrub**
‡ 4ft (1.2m) ↔ 3ft (1m)

PHLOMIS FRUTICOSA

Jerusalem sage is an aromatic, grayish leaved shrub that forms a fine foil for dark- or purple-leaved plants in a shrub or mixed border. From early to midsummer it bears whorls of deep golden yellow flowers; it blooms later if pruned hard in spring to achieve the best foliage effects. Tolerates hot, dry sites (*see p.190*), alkaline soils (*see p.64*), and coastal exposure (*see p.166*), but it will suffer in cold, wet winters.

ALSO RECOMMENDED: *P. chrysophylla has gray-green leaves (golden in late summer); P. italica is less cold tolerant with silver-gray leaves and pink flowers* Min 40°F (5°C).

☼ ◊ Z8   **Evergreen shrub**
‡ 3ft (1m) ↔ 5ft (1.5m)

SALIX EXIGUA

One of the most elegant willows, the coyote willow has slender stems bearing long, narrow, gray-green leaves that are densely covered in silky, silver hair when young. This thicket-forming shrub bears gray-yellow catkins in spring. It makes a fine specimen and a beautiful backdrop for purple- or dark-leaved plants in a shrub border. Needs little or no pruning. It tolerates coastal conditions (*see p.166*), and clay and permanently moist soils (*see pp.12, 372*).

ALSO RECOMMENDED: *S. gracilistyla is slightly smaller; 'Melanostachys' has unusual black catkins with red anthers.* Z4b

☼ ◊ Z3b   **Deciduous shrub**
‡ 12ft (4m) ↔ 15ft (5m)

SANTOLINA PINNATA 'Sulphurea'

A dense and rounded, small shrub that is grown chiefly for its finely cut, aromatic, bright green leaves, although attractive pale yellow flowers appear at the tips of slender stems from midsummer. Useful for filling gaps in a sunny border; its bushy habit can also be trimmed to form a low hedge (*see p.138*). Remove old flowers in autumn and cut back straggly plants in spring. Tolerant of alkaline soils (*see p.64*).

ALSO RECOMMENDED: *'Edward Bowles' has grayish foliage and cream flowers.*

☼ ◊ ƒ Min 35°F (2°C)   **Evergreen shrub**
‡ 24in (60cm) ↔ 3ft (1m)

ECCREMOCARPUS SCABER

The Chilean glory flower is a fast-growing, scrambling climber with clusters of brilliant orange-red, tubular flowers throughout summer. Grow as a short-lived perennial to decorate an arch, pergola, or large shrub. Choose a sheltered, sunny site, and cut the stems back to within 12–24in (30–60cm) of the base in spring. Where not hardy, grow as a trailing annual. Also good for hot, dry sites (*see p.190*).

ALSO RECOMMENDED: *f. aureus has gold flowers; f. carmineus has red flowers.*

☼ ◊�él Min 35°F (2°C)   **Climber**
‡ 10–15ft (3–5m), sometimes more

ROSA *'American Pillar'*

A rose that is easily trained onto a sunny wall (*see p.280*), pergola, or up into a tree. Its large clusters of carmine-red, single flowers with white eyes are quite sensational when seen to full effect in late spring and early summer. The midgreen foliage is leathery and glossy. The majority of roses do not thrive on sandy soils, preferring moister conditions. This one also tolerates partial shade.

ALSO RECOMMENDED: *'Chaplin's Pink Climber' has bright pink flowers; 'Zéphirine Drouhin' is thornless with very fragrant, deep pink flowers.*

☼ ☼ ◊◊ Z6   **Climber**
‡ 15ft (5m) ↔ 12ft (4m)

ACHILLEA FILIPENDULINA *'Gold Plate'*

This strong-growing yarrow forms clumps of luxuriant, grayish, fernlike foliage. Flat-headed clusters of bright golden yellow flowers are borne on tall stems from early summer to autumn. Good for cutting (*see p.524*), and tolerant of hot, dry sites (*see p.190*) and alkaline soils (*see p.64*). Grow in a mixed or herbaceous border or as a groundcover (*see p.304*). Contact with the foliage may aggravate skin allergies.

ALSO RECOMMENDED: *'Cloth of Gold' has light green leaves and deeper gold flowers.*

☼ ◊◖ Z3   **Perennial**

‡ 4ft (1.2m) ↔ 18in (45cm)

ARTEMISIA PONTICA

An evergreen, upright artemisia that is valued for its dense dome of aromatic and feathery, silver-green leaves. Grayish yellow flowerheads appear in early summer. An excellent ground-cover plant for poor soils in full sun (*see p.304*). Cut back to the ground in autumn. Its vigorous spread can be invasive. Tolerant of coastal conditions (*see p.166*) and hot, dry sites (*see p.190*).

ALSO RECOMMENDED: A. absinthium *'Lambrook Silver' has silver foliage and spreads less vigorously – good in a herbaceous border.* Z5

☼ ◊ *f* Z5b   **Perennial**

‡ 16–32in (40–80cm) ↔ indefinite

COREOPSIS VERTICILLATA

This pretty tickseed bears a mass of starry, daisylike yellow flowers throughout summer above finely divided, feathery, bright green foliage. The flowers are good for cutting (*see p.524*) and are attractive to bees (*see p.494*). It also tolerates alkaline soils (*see p.64*) and can be grown in a sunny container (*see p.412*), or mixed or herbaceous border.

ALSO RECOMMENDED: *C. 'Moonbeam' has lemon yellow flowerheads.*

☼ ◑ ◊ Z3b   **Perennial**

‡ 24–32in (60–80cm) ↔ 18in (45cm)

CRAMBE CORDIFOLIA

This imposing perennial forms a clump of large and puckered, bristly, dark green leaves and bears airy sprays of small, honey-scented, creamy white flowers that form a gauzy screen from late spring to midsummer. The whole plant dies back by late summer. An architectural plant for the back of a sunny border that tolerates coastal sites (*see pp.166, 472*). The flowers are attractive to bees (*see p.494*).

ALSO RECOMMENDED: C. maritima (see p.183).

☼ ◑ ◊ Z5   **Perennial**

‡ 8ft (2.5m) ↔ 5ft (1.5m)

DICTAMNUS ALBUS

Burning bush is an aromatic plant with
divided, leathery, lemon-scented leaves.
It bears spires of white, or palest pink
flowers with very long stamens and
darker veins in early summer. In hot,
still weather, as the seedheads ripen,
the aromatic oils vaporize and surround
the plant, and they can be ignited. It
tolerates alkaline soils (*see p.64*) and
hot, dry places (*see p.190*).

ALSO RECOMMENDED: *var.* purpureus *has
purple-mauve flowers with darker veins.*

☼ ◐ ◊ *f* Z3   **Perennial**

‡ 16–36in (40–90cm) ↔ 24in (60cm)

ECHINOPS SPHAEROCEPHALUS

This majestic globe thistle forms a
clump of spiny, divided, gray-green
leaves. From mid- to late summer it
produces branching spires of spherical,
silver-gray flowerheads on sturdy gray
stems. Excellent as a focal plant in
a mixed or herbaceous border. The
flowerheads are popular with bees and
birds and with flower arrangers (*see
pp.494, 524*). It tolerates alkaline soils
and hot, dry places (*see pp.64, 190*).

ALSO RECOMMENDED: E. ritro *'Veitch's
Blue'* (see p.207).

☼ ◐ ◊ Z3   **Perennial**

‡ 6ft (2m) ↔ 36in (90cm)

EREMURUS ROBUSTUS

This foxtail lily bears imposing spires of pale pink flowers that appear in early and midsummer. They make this fleshy rooted perennial an ideal focal plant in a sunny border. Its narrow, grasslike leaves wither by flowering time. Mulch with compost in autumn, avoiding the crown. Excellent for cutting (*see p.524*) and tolerant of alkaline soils (*see p.64*).

ALSO RECOMMENDED: E. himalaicus *is shorter, with white flowers in late spring.* Z5

☼ ◊ Z5   **Perennial**
‡ 10ft (3m) ↔ 4ft (1.2m)

ERIOPHYLLUM LANATUM

The woolly sunflower displays a profusion of bright yellow, daisylike flowers throughout summer above clumps of white-woolly, silver-gray leaves. It needs sharp drainage and is tolerant of poor soils and hot, dry sites (*see p.190*). Grow on a sunny bank, a dry border, or between paving crevices (*see p.348*). Position with care in a rock garden; it may overwhelm smaller plants.

☼ ◊ Z4   **Perennial**
‡↔ 8–24in (20–60cm) or more

ERYNGIUM × TRIPARTITUM

This plant forms a mound of lobed, few-spined, glossy dark green leaves. From midsummer to autumn it bears branched heads of small, almost spherical, violet-blue flowers, each with a ruff of narrow, gray-blue bracts beneath; they are good for cutting and drying (*see p.524*). Tolerant of alkaline soils (*see p.64*), and coastal and hot, dry and sites (*see pp.166, 190*).

ALSO RECOMMENDED: E. bourgatii (see p.208); E. variifolium *has white-marbled leaves and blue-violet flowers* Z5.

☼ ◊ Z4   **Perennial**

‡ 24–36in (60–90cm) ↔ 20in (50cm)

LIMONIUM PLATYPHYLLUM

Sea lavender attracts bees and butterflies (*see p.494*) with its airy clusters of tiny, papery, lavender-blue flowers in mid- to late summer. They are good for cutting and drying (*see p.524*) and are borne on wiry stems above rosettes of leathery, dark green leaves. Suitable for a mixed border or gravel plantings, especially in coastal or hot, dry sites (*see pp.166, 190*).

ALSO RECOMMENDED: 'Violetta' *has blue-violet flowers*; L. bellidifolium *is much shorter, suitable for border edging in sharply drained soil* Z5b.

☼ ◊ Z4   **Perennial**

‡ 24in (60cm) ↔ 18in (45cm)

LUPINUS *'The Chatelaine'*

The stately, pink-and-white-flowered spires of this lupine, which rise above a mound of palmate, midgreen leaves, are excellent for lending height and color to a mixed or herbaceous border from early to midsummer. Lupines are generally short-lived but last longest in slightly acidic to neutral soils (*see p.92*) with good drainage. Good for cutting (*see p.524*). Protect from slugs.

ALSO RECOMMENDED: *'Chandelier' has creamy yellow flowers; 'Lulu' is shorter with flowers in a mixture of pinks, reds, blues, purples, and whites; 'The Governor' has blue and white flowers.*

☼ ◊ Z3   **Perennial**
‡ 36in (90cm) ↔ 30in (75cm)

LYCHNIS × ARKWRIGHTII *'Vesuvius'*

This clump-forming perennial has lance-shaped, dark maroon leaves that form a perfect foil for the cross-shaped, brilliant orange-scarlet flowers that are borne from early to midsummer. Good for a sunny, mixed or herbaceous border, especially those with a hot-colored theme. Often short-lived.

ALSO RECOMMENDED: L. coronaria (see p.318).

☼ ☀ ◊ Z4   **Perennial**
‡ 18in (45cm) ↔ 12in (30cm)

NERINE BOWDENII

This is one of the best late-flowering bulbs. In autumn, it bears open sprays of trumpet-shaped, bright pink flowers with curled, wavy-edged petals. The straplike, fresh green leaves appear after the display at the base of the plant. Provide a deep, dry mulch in winter; where marginally hardy, grow at the base of a warm, sunny wall (*see p.280*), in a hot, dry site (*see p.190*), or as pot plant (*see p.412*). The scented flowers are good for cutting (*see p.524*).

ALSO RECOMMENDED: *'Alba' has white or very pale pink flowers; 'Mark Fenwick' has pink flowers on dark stalks.*

☼ ◊ *f* Z8   **Perennial bulb**
↕ 18in (45cm) ↔ 5–6in (12–15cm)

OENOTHERA MACROCARPA

Ozark sundrops produces a long succession of cup-shaped, golden yellow flowers from late spring to early autumn. They appear above a mat of trailing, red-tinted stems and green foliage. It makes a good groundcover (*see p.304*), especially in gravel or scree gardens and in coastal and hot, dry sites (*see pp.166, 190*). Tolerant of poor and stony soils.

ALSO RECOMMENDED: *O. fruticosa 'Fyrverkeri' is taller and more upright, with clusters of bright yellow flowers. Z3b*

☼ ◊ Z4   **Perennial**
↕ 6in (15cm) ↔ 20in (50cm)

ORNITHOGALUM UMBELLATUM

The star of Bethlehem produces clumps of grasslike leaves that wither as the starry white flowers open in early summer. Vigorous (it can become a serious weed) and suitable for naturalizing in short grass, it is especially effective in gravel plantings. It thrives in sunny or partially shaded sites (*see p.216*) and hot, dry places (*see p.190*). Plant bulbs in autumn.

ALSO RECOMMENDED: *O. nutans also has white flowers* Z5; *O. oligophyllum has white petals, green on the insides* Z6.

☼ ◐ ◊ Z4   **Perennial bulb**
‡ 4–12in (10–30cm) ↔ 4in (10cm)

PARAHEBE PERFOLIATA

Digger's speedwell has a spreading habit and bears short spikes of saucer-shaped blue flowers in late summer. The bluish or grayish, evergreen, overlapping leaves are oval and slightly leathery. Suitable for gaps in old walls or in a rock garden; it needs an open, sunny site.

ALSO RECOMMENDED: *P. hookeriana is a mat-forming species with white to lavender-blue flowers in summer.*

☼ ◊ Min 35°F (2°C)   **Perennial**
‡ 24–30in (60–75cm) ↔ 18in (45cm)

PETRORHAGIA SAXIFRAGA

The creeping, wiry stems of the tunic flower root to form mats of grasslike, rich green leaves that are spangled throughout summer with many tiny, white or pink flowers. It thrives in poor soils and makes a good groundcover for a sunny bank (*see p.304*), or at the top of a wall or raised bed. Good for a rock garden. Grow in any poor to moderately fertile, well-drained soil.

ALSO RECOMMENDED: *'Rosette' is more compact with double pink flowers.*

☼ ◊ Z4   **Perennial**

‡ 4in (10cm) ↔ 8in (20cm)

PHLOX BIFIDA

Sand phlox makes a good groundcover for rock gardens or sunny banks (*see p.304*). Mounds of grassy, dark green foliage are studded with a profusion of starry, fragrant, lavender-blue to white flowers from spring to early summer. Grow in gritty or poor, well-drained soil in sun, or in dappled shade in areas with low rainfall. Thrives in hot, dry sites (*see p.190*) and in paving crevices (*see p.348*).

ALSO RECOMMENDED: *'Colvin's White' has white flowers;* P. douglasii *is larger with white, lavender-blue, or pink flowers* Z5.

☼ ◊ *f* Z4   **Perennial**

‡ 8in (20cm) ↔ 6in (15cm)

POTENTILLA NEPALENSIS
'Miss Willmott'

A summer-flowering, clump-forming plant that carries its loose clusters of small pink blooms with cherry red centers on wiry, red-tinged stems. The leaves are divided and mid-green. A colorful perennial for a cottage-style planting or at the front of a hot and sunny, herbaceous border (*see p.190*). Tolerant of clay soils (*see p.12*).

ALSO RECOMMENDED: *'Roxana' has copper-pink flowers with red centers.*

☼ ◐ ◊ Z4   **Perennial**
↕ 12–18in (30–45cm) ↔ 24in (60cm)

SALVIA OFFICINALIS *'Tricolor'*

This variegated sage is a low, shrubby perennial suitable for a sunny border or wildlife garden (*see p.494*). Its woolly, gray-green leaves with cream and pink markings combine well with the short spikes of early to midsummer, lilac-blue flowers. The colorful foliage is aromatic and is used in cooking; it will add interest to a herb garden. Trim to shape each year after flowering. Tolerant of alkaline soils (*see p.64*) and hot, dry sites (*see p.190*).

ALSO RECOMMENDED: *'Icterina' has yellow and green leaves; 'Purpurascens' bears red-purple young leaves.*

☼ ◑ ◊◊ *f* Z5b   **Perennial**
↕ 32in (80cm) ↔ 3ft (1m)

STROBILANTHES ATROPURPUREA

This upright, branching plant forms a dense, basal clump of deeply veined, dark green leaves and produces spikes of hooded, 2-lipped, indigo or purple flowers along the length of the stems in summer. Excellent for a sunny, mixed or herbaceous border, but it must have good drainage. Protect the crowns with a dry winter mulch.

☼ ◊ Z7b   **Perennial**
↕ 4ft (1.2m) ↔ 3ft (1m)

TANACETUM PARTHENIUM

Once introduced to the garden, feverfew becomes a permanent fixture with its copious self-seeding. The aromatic, fresh green leaves form a bright foil for the white, daisylike flowers that are produced through summer. Suitable for edging in borders and herb gardens. It tolerates most well-drained soils, including alkaline ones (*see p.64*).

ALSO RECOMMENDED: *'Aureum' has golden leaves and single white flowerheads.*

☼ ◊ *f* Z3   **Perennial**
↕ 18–24in (45–60cm) ↔ 12in (30cm)

TULIPA HAGERI *'Splendens'*

A bulbous perennial that bears large, star-shaped flowers on upright stems from early spring. They are crimson-scarlet with brownish red insides and are carried singly or in clusters of up to four. The basal leaves are lance-shaped and light green. After flowering, remove spent blooms, but allow the foliage to die back naturally. Suitable for a rock garden, hot and dry site, or in a container (*see pp.190, 412*). Plant bulbs in autumn.

ALSO RECOMMENDED: T. pulchella *has pale red to purple flowers, often in threes.*

☼ ◊ Z4   **Perennial bulb**
‡ 14in (35cm)

VERBASCUM OLYMPICUM

The towering, white-woolly, yellow-flowered spires that arise like candelabra from the large, basal rosette of silver-white leaves make this verbascum one of the finest of architectural plants (*see p.472*). It thrives in hot, dry sites (*see p.190*) and is set off to brilliant effect in gravel plantings. It often dies after flowering, but it self-seeds freely. Tolerant of alkaline soils (*see p.64*).

ALSO RECOMMENDED: V. bombyciferum *is slightly shorter; 'Silver Lining', often grown as an annual, is densely silver-woolly.* Z4

☼ ◊ Z5   **Perennial**
‡ 6ft (2m) ↔ 24in (60cm)

PLANTS FOR ALKALINE SOILS

MANY OF THE world's favorite plants occur naturally on alkaline or limestone soils, so the choice of plants for the gardener who is presented with these conditions is huge. They include pinks (*see p.82*), clematis (*see p.76*), and many of the jewel-like alpine plants found growing on the limestone mountains of Europe and Asia.

Soils over limestone are almost invariably alkaline in nature, but they can also be very fertile if they are deep and rich in organic matter – a wealth of

plants thrive and give their ornamental best on such soils. Their growth is not entirely limited by the soil's alkalinity, but chiefly by its ability to hold moisture. Therefore, plants such as the Madonna lily (*see p.490*) will grow well on alkaline soils, as long as they are rich in well-rotted organic matter.

Alkalinity, however, does exclude a small proportion of plants. In particular, it will not be possible to grow committed acid-lovers like rhododendrons (*see pp.108, 160, 243, 454*).

SHALLOW, ALKALINE SOILS

If alkaline soil is very shallow over a layer of stone, the chief problem – even for lime-tolerant plants – is rapid drainage, which can lead to very hot and dry soil conditions in summer. For these sites, many of the plants listed for sandy soils, hot and dry sites, and coastal conditions will thrive, provided that they do not also demand an acidic soil (see pp.38, 190, 166). Plants such as *Crocus* 'E.A. Bowles' (see p.81) or *Pulsatilla vulgaris* (see p.89) are so well-adapted to free-draining, alkaline conditions that they may rot and die in deep and moist, fertile soils rich in organic matter. Deep or very sticky alkaline soils need to be treated as for clay soils (see p.12).

WORKING ALKALINE SOILS

Shallow alkaline soils are usually light and easy to work at almost any time of year, but, because they drain so quickly, they often lack organic matter and plant nutrients; both are leached or washed away by natural rainfall.

Apply a well-rotted organic matter, such as leaf mold, manure, or compost as a deep, annual mulch to help build their levels in the soil. Organic matter helps retain moisture and nutrients, and it keeps the plant roots cooler. It also helps counteract the effects of the soil's alkalinity. If this is done regularly and over many seasons, it will eventually build up a useful depth of soil. As a result, the range of plants that can be grown successfully will expand.

The addition of well-rotted organic matter can also help reduce the problem of yellowing leaves, which some plants experience in alkaline soils. Even some fairly lime-tolerant plants, such as *Chaenomeles speciosa* 'Moerloosei' (see p.264), begin to show these symptoms after several seasons of growth due to vital nutrients, including iron, being "locked up" by the soil's alkaline chemistry. A simple remedy is to apply sequestered (chelated) iron annually as new growth begins in spring.

ARBUTUS UNEDO

The strawberry tree has a spreading crown of glossy deep green foliage and attractive, rough and shredding, red-brown bark. Hanging clusters of small, urn-shaped, white or pink-tinged flowers open during autumn as the previous season's strawberry-like red fruits open; they are not palatable. Keep pruning to a minimum. Excellent for a large, sheltered shrub border. It is also good in acidic soils (*see p.92*).

ALSO RECOMMENDED: *'Elfin King' is compact and flowers and fruits freely when small; f.* rubra *has dark pink flowers.*

☼ ◐ Z7   **Evergreen tree**
‡↔ 25ft (8m)

CHAMAECYPARIS LAWSONIANA *'Intertexta'*

This cultivar of Lawson's cypress makes a distinctive specimen tree with a conical crown of drooping branchlets bearing flattened sprays of dark blue-gray, scalelike foliage. It forms a strong leading shoot naturally, seldom needing formative pruning. The strongest growth occurs on moist but well-drained, neutral to slightly acidic soils (*see p.92*).

ALSO RECOMMENDED: *'Kilmacurragh' has bright green foliage on upswept branchlets; 'Lanei Aurea' has golden yellow foliage.*

☼ ◐ Z6   **Evergreen tree**
‡ 80ft (25m) ↔ 15ft (5m)

FRAXINUS ORNUS

The manna ash forms a rounded crown of divided, dark green leaves that turn dark purple before falling in autumn. In spring and early summer it produces dense clusters of many tiny, fragrant, creamy white flowers. A shapely specimen tree that thrives in fertile, well-drained or even hot and dry, chalky or acidic soils (*see pp.64, 92, 190*). It needs little pruning; cut out any badly placed or crossing shoots in winter.

ALSO RECOMMENDED: F. americana *'Autumn Purple'* (Z4) *and* F. nigra *'Fallgold'* (Z2b) *both with good fall color.*

☼ ◊ ƒ Z7 **Deciduous tree**
↕↔ 50ft (15m)

MORUS NIGRA

Black mulberry makes a picturesque, gnarled tree with age, forming a broad crown of large, heart-shaped leaves. Tiny green flowers in spring give rise to edible, juicy, black fruits that attract birds (*see p.494*). It tolerates coastal sites (*see p.166*) and urban pollution. This long-lived tree needs minimal pruning, in late autumn or early winter if necessary; it bleeds sap if pruned at other times.

ALSO RECOMMENDED: M. alba *bears less palatable, white then red fruits;* 'Pendula' *is a small, weeping tree.* Z4

☼ ◊◊ Z6 **Deciduous tree**
↕↔ 30ft (10m)

PINUS NIGRA

The Austrian pine has dense, spreading branches and deeply fissured, grayish, dark brown, or black bark. It forms a dark green, domed canopy of paired, needlelike leaves. The cones are yellow-brown. This tree also grows in clay soils (*see p.12*) and is tolerant of coastal exposure (*see p.166*).

ALSO RECOMMENDED: *subsp.* laricio, *the Corsican pine, is narrower with gray-green needles.*

☼ ◊ Z4 **Evergreen tree**
‡ 100ft (30m) ↔ 20–25ft (6–8m)

PRUNUS *'Pink Perfection'*

One of the most reliably floriferous of flowering cherries, this spreading tree bears a profusion of double, rose-pink flowers in heavy, drooping clusters amid bronzy young leaves in late spring. Effective as a single specimen and fabulous in groves or avenues, it is relatively easy to grow. Keep pruning to a minimum; remove dead or diseased wood in summer.

ALSO RECOMMENDED: *'Accolade' has pale pink flowers in early spring.* Z7

☼ ◊ Z6 **Deciduous tree**
‡↔ 25ft (8m)

BUDDLEJA LINDLEYANA

A slightly arching, late-flowering shrub
with dark green foliage that is suitable
for a mixed or shrub border. Its
tapering spikes of dark violet flowers
nod from the branches in late summer.
Prune branches hard in early spring to
encourage a neat, denser shape. Where
marginally hardy, it will fare better
against a warm wall (*see p.280*).

ALSO RECOMMENDED: B. globosa *has
round clusters of orange-yellow flowers in
early summer* Z7b; B. salviifolia *has pale
blue, fragrant flowers in late autumn* Z8.

☼ ◊ Z8   **Deciduous shrub**
↕↔ 6ft (2m)

CEANOTHUS *'Autumnal Blue'*

A vigorous California lilac that bears its
brilliant and profuse display of dense,
rich sky blue flowerheads from late summer
to autumn. They are complemented by
the glossy dark green leaves. Good for
a sheltered border and will perform
better against a warm wall where
marginally hardy (*see p.280*). Trim to
shape after flowering.

ALSO RECOMMENDED: C. × delileanus
*'Gloire de Versailles' is deciduous and
hardier with pale blue flowers from
midsummer to autumn.* Z7b

☼ ◊ Z8a   **Evergreen shrub**
↕↔ 10ft (3m)

CORNUS MAS

The Cornelian cherry makes a fine specimen plant for late winter, when small clusters of yellow flowers appear in profusion on the bare branches. The fruits ripen to bright red in summer, and the oval, dark green leaves turn red-purple in autumn. Also suitable for a woodland garden. Keep pruning to a minimum.

ALSO RECOMMENDED: *'Aurea' has yellow young leaves; 'Variegata' is compact, with white leaf margins and abundant fruit.*

☼ ◑ ◊ Z4b   **Deciduous shrub**
↕↔ 15ft (5m)

COTINUS COGGYGRIA
Purpureus Group

This smoke tree has oval, light green leaves that turn to orange then red in autumn. Smokelike plumes of tiny, purplish pink flowers are produced on older wood. Good in a shrub border or as a specimen tree. Cut back hard to a framework each spring for the best foliage effect.

ALSO RECOMMENDED: *'Royal Purple' bears dark red-purple foliage, turning scarlet in autumn; C. 'Grace' has purple leaves, turning brilliant red in autumn.*

☼ ◑ ◊ Z5   **Deciduous shrub**
↕↔ 15ft (5m)

COTONEASTER STERNIANUS

A graceful shrub with arching branches that bear clusters of pink-tinged white flowers in summer. A profusion of large, orange-red berries follow in autumn, attracting birds (*see p.494*) and contrasting well with the glossy gray-green foliage. It is good grown as a hedge (*see p.138*). Trim lightly after flowering, if necessary.

ALSO RECOMMENDED: C. cashmiriensis (see p.306); C. frigidus (see p.218); C. horizontalis (see p.265); C. lacteus (see p.149).

☼ ◐ ◊ Z6   **Evergreen shrub**
↕↔ 10ft (3m)

DEUTZIA CRENATA *'Nikko'*

This spreading shrub is among the smallest of the deutzias. It has rich green leaves that turn red-purple in autumn and produces clusters of starry white flowers in late spring. Excellent for a rock garden or for the front of a shrub border.

ALSO RECOMMENDED: D. gracilis (see p.128); D. × rosea *has white flowers that are flushed with pink.* Z6

☼ ◊ Z5b   **Deciduous shrub**
↕ 24in (60cm) ↔ 4ft (1.2m)

HELIANTHEMUM
'Rhodanthe Carneum'

This long-flowering rock rose, also sold as 'Wisley Pink', is a low and spreading bush. Pale pink, saucer-shaped flowers with yellow centers appear from late spring to summer amid narrow, gray-green leaves. Good in a rock garden, raised bed, or mixed border. Trim after flowering. Also good for sandy soils (*see p.38*) and as a groundcover (*see p.304*).

ALSO RECOMMENDED: *'Fire Dragon'* (*syn. 'Mrs. Clay'*) *has vivid orange-red flowers;* *'Henfield Brilliant' has brick-red flowers;* *'Raspberry Ripple'* (see p.46).

☼ ◊ Z6   **Evergreen shrub**
↕ 12in (30cm) ↔ 18in (45cm) or more

INDIGOFERA HETERANTHA

A spreading plant with arching stems that is valued for its pretty, pealike flowers and gray-green foliage. It carries dense, more or less upright clusters of small, purple-pink flowers from early summer to autumn. Where marginally hardy, it is best trained against a warm wall (*see p.280*). Cut all stems to just above ground level in early spring. Also suitable for a sunny shrub border.

ALSO RECOMMENDED: I. amblyantha *bears spikes of pink flowers.* Z7

☼ ◊ Z7b   **Deciduous shrub**
↕↔ 6–10ft (2–3m)

KOLKWITZIA AMABILIS *'Pink Cloud'*

This beauty bush is well known for its abundant clusters of bell-shaped, bright yet deep pink flowers with yellow throats that appear during late spring and early summer. It grows vigorously and has arching stems clothed with dark green leaves. Excellent for a shrub border or as a specimen plant. Let young plants develop without pruning, then thin out some old stems each year after flowering.

☼ ◊ Z4b   **Deciduous shrub**
↕ 10ft (3m) ↔ 12ft (4m)

OSMANTHUS × BURKWOODII

A dense, rounded shrub with leathery, dark green leaves that bears profuse clusters of sweetly fragrant, tubular white flowers in spring. An ideal shrub as a backdrop in a mixed border or as a specimen in a woodland garden. It can be hard pruned and makes a very attractive flowering hedge (*see p.138*) that can be trimmed after flowering. It tolerates urban pollution.

ALSO RECOMMENDED: O. delavayi (see p.221); O. heterophyllus *has hollylike leaves and blooms in late summer* Z7b.

☼◑ ◊ ƒ Z7   **Evergreen shrub**
↕↔ 10ft (3m)

PHILADELPHUS MICROPHYLLUS

This compact mock orange is an upright shrub with peeling, chestnut-brown bark. It bears a profusion of single, highly scented white flowers in early and midsummer. Ideal for a mixed border in smaller gardens, it associates well with roses and is easy to grow on most well-drained soils. Its tolerance of pollution makes it well suited to city gardens. Good for cut flowers (*see p.524*). Cut a few of the oldest stems back to ground level after flowering.

ALSO RECOMMENDED: P. coronarius *'Variegatus'* (see p.156); P. *'Buckley's Quill' has double flowers.*

☼ ◊ *f* Z4   **Deciduous shrub**
↕↔ 3ft (1m)

POTENTILLA FRUTICOSA *'Red Ace'*

A compact and densely rounded shrub that has dark green foliage and rose-like, vermilion flowers from spring to autumn. It makes a good ground- cover (*see p.304*) or low hedging (*see p.138*), especially in coastal sites (*see p.166*). Also good for a mixed border. Trim after flowering. The flowers tend to fade in full sun.

ALSO RECOMMENDED: *'Abbotswood' has white flowers; those of 'Katherine Dykes' are canary yellow; 'Tangerine' has yellow flowers tinted orange-red.*

☼ ◐ ◊ Z3   **Deciduous shrub**
↕ 3ft (1m) ↔ 5ft (1.5m)

SYRINGA × PERSICA

The Persian lilac is a robust and stocky shrub that bears small but fragrant purple flowers in dense clusters in late spring. Tolerant of pollution, it is ideal for city gardens that are too confined for the common lilac (*S. vulgaris*). Its flowers are good for cutting (*see p.524*). It makes a fine informal hedge (*see p.138*), needing only a light trim after flowering.

ALSO RECOMMENDED: '*Alba*' *has white flowers;* S. pubescens '*Superba*' *(see p.165);* S. vulgaris '*Congo*' *(see p.21).*

☼ ◊ *f* Z2b   **Deciduous shrub**
↕↔ 6ft (2m)

CAMPSIS RADICANS

The common trumpet creeper is a vigorous climber with fine autumn color, bearing clusters of trumpetlike, orange to red flowers at the branch tips from late summer. They look striking against the dark green foliage. Grow against a wall, fence, or pillar, or up into a tree. Prune branches while they are bare in late winter.

ALSO RECOMMENDED: *f.* flava *(syn. '*Yellow Trumpet*') has yellow flowers;* C. × tagliabuana '*Madame Galen*' *has salmon-red flowers* Z6.

☼ ◊◊ Z5b   **Climber**
↕ 30ft (10m) or more

CLEMATIS *'The President'*

This early-flowering clematis is valued for its showy, early summer display of large, rich purple blooms with silvery undersides and red anthers. It is vigorous and flowers freely, making it ideal for covering a featureless or unattractive wall (*see pp.262, 280*). Allowed to grow through a deciduous shrub, it can make an attractive color combination with the shrub's flowers or bloom alone. Keep the roots shaded.

ALSO RECOMMENDED: *'Bill MacKenzie'* (see p.299); C. montana (see p.274); *'Nelly Moser'* (see p.273); C. rehderiana (see p.300); C. tangutica (see p.508).

☼ ◐ ◊◊ Z3b   **Climber**

‡ 10ft (3m)

JASMINUM NUDIFLORUM

This mound-forming winter jasmine displays its cheerful yellow flowers on bare green branches in late winter. It is grown to best effect if tied to a framework on a sunny wall (*see p.280*), but it tolerates most exposures except those facing due east. If allowed to sprawl unsupported, it makes a good ground- cover (*see p.304*). Cut back after flowering; the flowers are good for cutting (*see p.524*).

ALSO RECOMMENDED: *'Aureum' has gold-blotched leaves that are almost yellow.*

☼ ◐ ◊ Z7   **Climber**

‡↔ 10ft (3m)

PARTHENOCISSUS HENRYANA

Parthenocissus are prized for their colorful autumn foliage. The white-veined leaves of this one, however, are impressive from the moment they emerge in spring to the time they turn bright red and drop in autumn. The summer flowers are insignificant. Train over a wall or a strongly built fence (*see pp.262, 280*) and prune in autumn; young stems may need support. Leaf color is best in deep or partial shade. Good for wildlife gardens (*see p.494*).

ALSO RECOMMENDED: P. quinquefolia *has brilliant red autumn foliage* Z2b; P. tricuspidata (see p.277).

☼◐ ◊◑ Z7b   **Climber**
‡ 30ft (10m)

ROSA *'Albertine'*

This vigorous, very thorny rambler bears a mass of scented, fully double, soft salmon-pink blooms in midsummer. They are displayed to perfection on purple-flushed stems against glossy dark green leaves. An excellent specimen for a pergola; it also blooms well when trained on a trellis against a wall (*see p.280*). Prune after flowering.

ALSO RECOMMENDED: *'Albéric Barbier' has double white flowers and tolerates shaded walls; 'François Juranville' bears apple-scented, pale salmon-pink flowers over long periods.*

☼ ◊ *f* Z6   **Climber**
‡ 15ft (5m) ↔ 12ft (4m)

ALYSSUM WULFENIANUM

This evergreen plant forms mounds of gray- or white-hairy leaves and bears sweetly scented, pale yellow flowers in abundance in early summer. A fine rock-garden plant also for paving crevices and the tops of dry stone walls (*see p.348*). It tolerates hot, dry sites (*see p.190*) and most well-drained soils. Trim after flowering to keep compact.

ALSO RECOMMENDED: *A. montanum 'Berggold' forms mats of golden flowers* Z4; *A. spinosum 'Roseum' is mound-forming and shrubby with rose-pink flowers* Z4.

☼ ◊ *f* Z5   **Perennial**
‡ 4–6in (10–15cm) ↔ 20in (50cm)

ASPLENIUM TRICHOMANES

The maidenhair spleenwort is a short fern that occurs naturally on limestone outcrops, so it is perfectly suited to alkaline conditions. It bears tufts of narrow, dark green fronds that are divided into many rounded leaflets with glossy black or dark brown stalks. Very suitable for wall and paving crevices (*see p.348*) and rock gardens.

ALSO RECOMMENDED: *A. scolopendrium* (see p.225).

☼ ◊◊ Z4   **Perennial fern**
‡ 6in (15cm) ↔ 8in (20cm)

BERGENIA CILIATA

The large and rounded, paddle-shaped leaves of this fleshy plant form elegant, midgreen clumps at ground level. White or pinkish white flowers enliven the display from early spring. Mulch the plants in autumn; the foliage may die back in open winters. Suitable as a groundcover (*see pp.304, 326*) and tolerant of exposed sites (*see p.118*), permanently moist soils (*see p.372*), and damp or dry shade (*see pp.216, 238*).

ALSO RECOMMENDED: *f. ligulata has very pale pink flowers; B. 'Morgenröte' (syn. 'Morning Red')* (see p.333).

☼ ◐ ◊◊ Z6   **Perennial**
‡ 12in (30cm) ↔ 18in (45cm)

CAMPANULA PUNCTATA

This bellflower forms clumps of dark green leaves. It produces short clusters of hanging, bell-shaped, creamy white to dusky pink flowers on upright stems in early summer; they color better if the plant is grown in shade. Cut back after flowering to encourage further blooms. Suitable for a border.

ALSO RECOMMENDED: *C. 'Birch Hybrid'* (see p.358); *C. carpatica 'Bressingham White'* (see p.359); *C. glomerata 'Superba'* (see p.313); *C. isophylla* (see p.430); *C. lactiflora 'Prichard's Variety'* (see p.532); *C. latiloba 'Hidcote Amethyst'* (see p.26).

☼ ◐ ◊◊ Z4   **Perennial**
‡ 12in (30cm) ↔ 16in (40cm)

CHIONODOXA FORBESII

Glory of the snow produces a sheaf of narrow leaves topped by clusters of white-centered, starry, clear blue flowers in early spring. It is ideal for early color in a rock garden or for naturalizing beneath trees and shrubs. It self-seeds freely to form extensive colonies. Plant bulbs in autumn.

ALSO RECOMMENDED: *'Pink Giant' has white-eyed, pink flowers; C. sardensis has slightly pendent, deep clear blue flowers* Z3.

☼ ◊ Z3 **Perennial bulb**
↕ 4–8in (10–20cm) ↔ 1¼in (3cm)

COLCHICUM AUTUMNALE

The meadow saffron has weatherproof, goblet-shaped pink flowers that appear in autumn before the large, lance-shaped leaves emerge in winter or early spring. Grow at the front of a border, at the foot of rockwork in a rock garden, or naturalize in grass. All parts are highly toxic if ingested. Plant corms in summer.

ALSO RECOMMENDED: *'Album' has white flowers; 'Pleniflorum' has double, pinkish lilac flowers; C. agrippinum* (see p.360).

☼ ◊◊ Z4 **Perennial corm**
↕ 4–6in (10–15cm) ↔ 3in (8cm)

CROCUS CHRYSANTHUS *'E.A. Bowles'*

Spring-flowering crocuses are indispensable dwarf perennials, since they bring early color to the garden. This one, like other *C. chrysanthus* cultivars, is among the earliest to flower. The flowers are rich lemon yellow with purple feathering on the outer petals. Very effective in drifts at the front of a mixed or herbaceous border, naturalized in grass, or in a rock garden. Plant bulbs in autumn.

ALSO RECOMMENDED: *'Cream Beauty' has cream flowers; 'Ladykiller' has white flowers with purple marks; C. corsicus (see p.361).*

☼ ◊ Z3　　　　**Perennial bulb**

↕ 3in (8cm) ↔ 2in (5cm)

DELPHINIUM TATSIENENSE

A delicate variation on the more common theme of the showy, tall spires of hybrid delphiniums, this is a far more modest plant with clusters of elf-cap-shaped, bright cornflower blue flowers with hooded eyes and azure tips. They appear during the first half of summer against deeply divided, lobed leaves. Suitable for a rock garden or at the front of a border. It does not need to be staked. The flowers can be cut for indoor arrangements (*see p.524*).

ALSO RECOMMENDED: D. grandiflorum *'Blue Butterfly' (see p.534).*

☼ ◊◊ Z7　　　　**Perennial**

↕ 8–24in (20–60cm) ↔ 12in (30cm)

DIANTHUS *'Bovey Belle'*

The double, clove-scented, deep pink flowers of this modern pink are borne in profusion throughout summer above a mound of narrow, blue-gray leaves. The stiff-stemmed blooms are excellent as cut flowers (*see p.524*). Grow in a mixed or herbaceous border; they associate well with roses.

ALSO RECOMMENDED: *'Doris' has pale pink flowers with dark pink centers; 'Haytor White' has white flowers; 'Houndspool Ruby' has rose-pink blooms with currant red centers; 'La Bourboule' (see p.361); D. subacaulis (see p.314).*

☼ ◊ *f* Z4   **Perennial**
‡ 10–18in (25–45cm) ↔ 16in (40cm)

DICENTRA SPECTABILIS

Bleeding heart is an elegant, late-spring-flowering plant for a damp, shady border (*see p.238*) or woodland garden. The red-pink flowers are heart-shaped and hang in rows from long, arching stems; they contrast vividly against the hummock of bright green, deeply cut foliage. The plant usually dies back after flowering. Also suitable for acidic soils (*see p.92*).

ALSO RECOMMENDED: *'Alba' has white flowers; D. 'Stuart Boothman' has pink flowers and gray foliage Z4; D. 'Bacchanal' (see p.336); D. cucullaria (see p.229).*

☼ ◗ ◖ Z3   **Perennial**
‡ to 4ft (1.2m) ↔ 18in (45cm)

DORONICUM *'Miss Mason'*

A spreading plant with dense, basal clumps of heart-shaped leaves that are almost covered from spring to early summer by golden yellow daisylike flowers that are held well above the foliage. Good for a mixed or herbaceous border and can be naturalized in a woodland garden. It tolerates clay soils (*see p.12*), and the flowers are good for cutting (*see p.524*).

ALSO RECOMMENDED: D. × excelsum *'Harpur Crewe' has golden yellow flowers* Z5; D. pardalianches (see p.534).

☀ ◐ Z4   **Perennial**
↕↔ 24in (60cm)

ERODIUM MANESCAUI

Through summer and into autumn, this clump-forming perennial bears its geranium-like, bright magenta-purple flowers above basal clumps of softly hairy, divided leaves. Ideal for a rock garden, raised bed, or at the front of a mixed or herbaceous border. Grow in very well-drained, neutral to alkaline soil. It self-seeds freely.

ALSO RECOMMENDED: E. chrysanthum *has silver-green leaves and sulfur yellow flowers* Z5b; E. glandulosum *is smaller with lilac-pink flowers* Z5b.

☀ ◊ Z4   **Perennial**
↕ 8–18in (20–45cm) ↔ 8in (20cm)

ERYSIMUM *'Bredon'*

The bright, chrome yellow flowers of this shrubby evergreen appear from spring to early summer above a mound of gray-green foliage. Grow at the front of a mixed or herbaceous border in poor or not too fertile, well-drained soil. Trim after flowering to keep compact. Also suitable for hot, dry sites (*see p.190*) and sunny containers (*see p.412*).

ALSO RECOMMENDED: *'Butterscotch' has orange-yellow flowers; 'Constant Cheer' has dusky orange-red flowers that age to purple; 'John Codrington' has pale yellow flowers shaded brown and purple.*

☼ ◊ Z6   **Perennial**
‡ 12in (30cm) ↔ 18in (45cm)

FRANCOA SONCHIFOLIA

This plant is named bridal wreath for its tall spires of pink flowers that appear from midsummer. They are good for cutting (*see p.524*). The crinkled green leaves form rosettes at ground level. Suitable for border edging or in a woodland garden, so long as it is sheltered from winter moisture.

ALSO RECOMMENDED: F. ramosa *has white flowers with dark pink markings.* Z7b

☼ ◐ ◊◊ Z7b   **Perennial**
‡ 24–36in (60–90cm) ↔ 18in (45cm)

HELENIUM *'Wyndley'*

From early to late summer, this robust, upright, and undemanding perennial bears a succession of rich yellow blooms with orange-brown centers and irregular shades of dark orange; they are excellent for cutting (*see p.524*) and attract to bees (*see p.494*). Deadhead regularly and divide every third year to maintain vigor. It also tolerates clay soils (*see p.12*).

ALSO RECOMMENDED: *'Coppelia'* has copper-orange, brown-centered flowerheads; *'Moerheim Beauty'* (see p.28); *'Rotgold'* (syn. *'Red and Gold'*) has brown-centered flowerheads in shades of red and gold.

☼ ◐◑ Z3b   **Perennial**
↕ 32in (80cm) ↔ 24in (60cm)

HERMODACTYLUS TUBEROSUS

The widow iris is notable for the somber but nonetheless elegant combination of yellow-green and velvety dark brown in its irislike, fragrant spring blooms. Give it a prominent place in a mixed or herbaceous border or allow it to naturalize freely in grass. It also grows as an early-flowering container plant (*see p.412*). It must have sharp drainage and protection from excessive summer rain. It thrives and flowers most freely in hot, dry soils (*see p.190*). Plant tubers in autumn.

☼ ◊ *f* Z7b   **Perennial**
↕ 8–16in (20–40cm) ↔ 2in (5cm)

IRIS BUCHARICA

This fast-growing, spring-flowering iris bears up to six golden yellow and white flowers on each stem. The glossy, strap-shaped leaves die back after flowering. It must have good drainage and needs dry conditions when dormant after flowering. Plant bulbs in late summer or autumn.

ALSO RECOMMENDED: I. graeberiana *has blue flowers marked white and darker blue* Z6b; I. magnifica *has pale lilac flowers marked yellow and white* Z6b.

☼ ◊ Z5   **Perennial bulb**
↕ 8–16in (20–40cm) ↔ 5in (12cm)

KNAUTIA MACEDONICA

The deep purple-red, pincushion-like flowerheads of this clump-forming perennial are borne on slender, branching stems above grayish green leaves from mid- to late summer. Good for wildflower borders (*see p.494*) or meadow plantings. Also useful for late color in a cottage garden or herbaceous border. It self-seeds freely.

ALSO RECOMMENDED: K. arvensis, *the field scabious, is taller with pale bluish lilac flowers, and it may also be naturalized in meadow plantings.* Z5

☼ ◊ Z4   **Perennial**
↕ 24–32in (60–80cm) ↔ 18in (45cm)

LATHYRUS VERNUS
'Alboroseus'

This spring vetchling is a vigorous, clump-forming plant bearing very pretty, pink and white, pealike flowers on upright stems well above the mid-green foliage in spring. Suitable for a rock garden or herbaceous border, and it can be naturalized in a woodland garden or rough grassland. It tolerates poor soils but resents disturbance.

ALSO RECOMMENDED: *L. vernus has purplish blue flowers.*

☼ ☀ ◊ Z4b   **Perennial**
↕ 8–18in (20–45cm) ↔ 18in (45cm)

MALVA MOSCHATA

Musk mallow is a bushy, woody-based plant with faintly musk-scented foliage. A long succession of showy, pale pink flowers are borne throughout summer; they are long lasting and very pretty – ideal in a sunny, hot and dry, wildflower or herbaceous border (*see p.190*). It may be short-lived, but it self-seeds freely. Tolerant of poor soils and urban pollution.

ALSO RECOMMENDED: *f.* alba *has white flowers;* M. sylvestris *'Primley Blue'* (see p.539).

☼ ◊ Z4   **Perennial**
↕ to 36in (90cm) ↔ 12in (30cm)

NARCISSUS CANTABRICUS

This early spring-flowering hoop-petticoat daffodil bears delicate white flowers that are perfect in a rock garden and exquisite when naturalized in fine grass. This species needs very well-drained soil and warm, dry conditions during summer. Plant bulbs in autumn.

ALSO RECOMMENDED: *N. jonquilla has heads of up to five scented, golden yellow flowers with tiny cups and pointed perianth segments Z4; N. romieuxii has pale yellow, hoop-petticoat flowers Z7b.*

☼ ◊ Z7b   **Perennial bulb**
↕ 6–8in (15–20cm) ↔ 2in (5cm)

PAEONIA MLOKOSEWITSCHII

The Caucasian peony is an upright perennial with large, bowl-shaped, lemon yellow flowers in late spring and early summer amid bluish green foliage. Each leaf is divided into nine red-margined leaflets, and the flowers are followed by seed pods that split open when ripe. A fine addition to a herbaceous or shrub border.

ALSO RECOMMENDED: P. delavayi (see p.243); P. lactiflora 'Sarah Bernhardt' (see p.541).

☼ ☀ ◊◊ Z5   **Perennial**
↕↔ 26–36in (65–90cm)

PLATYCODON GRANDIFLORUS

The balloon flower forms clumps of purplish green foliage from which emerge clusters of large, purple to violet-blue flowers in late summer. They are borne on upright stems, which may need support, and the flowers open from balloon-shaped buds. Suitable for a rock garden or herbaceous border; do not allow the soil to dry out. Established plants resent disturbance. The flowers are good for cutting (*see p.524*).

ALSO RECOMMENDED: *'Apoyama' has deep violet flowers; 'Fuji Pink' has pink flowers; those of 'Mariesii' are violet-blue.*

☼ ☀ ◊ Z3b   **Perennial**
‡ to 24in (60cm) ↔ 12in (30cm)

PULSATILLA VULGARIS

The nodding, silky-hairy flowers of the pasque flower are deep to pale purple or occasionally white; they rise above the feathery foliage in spring and are followed by silky seedheads. Ideal for a rock garden, scree or gravel plantings, or for paving crevices (*see p.348*), and it can be naturalized in grass. The flowers are attractive to bees (*see p.494*). It resents disturbance.

ALSO RECOMMENDED: *'Alba' has white flowers; var.* rubra *has plum-red flowers.*

☼ ◊ Z3   **Perennial**
‡ 4–8in (10–20cm) ↔ 8in (20cm)

RUDBECKIA *'Herbstsonne'*

A robust, clump-forming plant for bold, back-border placement. It bears daisy-like, bright yellow flowerheads with protruding, cone-shaped green centers from midsummer to autumn. The plant is an imposing specimen when naturalized in a woodland garden. It tolerates clay soil (*see p.12*) and is a good source of cut flowers (*see p.524*). Also sold as 'Autumn Sun'.

ALSO RECOMMENDED: R. fulgida *var.* deamii *is shorter with orange-yellow and dark brown flowers* Z3b; R. *'Goldquelle'* (see p.543).

☼ ◑ ◊◑ Z3   **Perennial**
↕ 6ft (2m) ↔ 36in (90cm)

SAXIFRAGA *'Tumbling Waters'*

A slow-growing, white-flowered saxifrage that forms large and clustered rosettes of narrow, lime-encrusted, silvery green leaves at ground level. In spring, long and arching flowering stems arise from the centers of these leafy rosettes. Flowers will not appear for the first few years. Suitable for a rock garden or trough with shelter from excessive winter moisture.

ALSO RECOMMENDED: *'Southside Seedling'* has red-spotted white flowers.

☼ ◊ Z6b   **Perennial**
↕ 18in (45cm) ↔ 12in (30cm)

SIDALCEA *'Elsie Heugh'*

This prairie mallow bears its spires of satiny, purple-pink flowers with pretty, fringed petals over long periods in summer above a mound of lobed, glossy bright green leaves. Grow in a mixed or herbaceous border; the flowers are good for cutting (*see p.524*). Deadheading also encourages a second flush of bloom.

ALSO RECOMMENDED: *'Croftway Red' has rich red-pink blooms; 'Rose Queen' is taller with large, pink flowers; 'Sussex Beauty' has clear pink flowers; 'William Smith' has deep pink flowers.*

☼ ◑ ◊ Z4 **Perennial**
↕ 36in (90cm) ↔ 18in (45cm)

VERBASCUM *'Gainsborough'*

A short-lived plant that is much admired for its grand appearance and long flowering season. Throughout summer, it bears spires of saucer-shaped, soft yellow, purple-marked flowers above a rosette of gray-green leaves arranged around the base of the stem. A very beautiful plant for a hot and dry, sunny, herbaceous or mixed border (*see p.190*). Suitable for a wildlife garden (*see p.494*).

ALSO RECOMMENDED: *'Cotswold Beauty' has peach-pink flowers; 'Mont Blanc' has pure white flowers; 'Pink Domino' has rose-pink flowers.*

☼ ◊ Z5 **Perennial**
↕ 4ft (1.2m) ↔ 12in (30cm)

PLANTS FOR ACIDIC SOILS

THE MAJORITY OF acid-loving plants are originally from woodland areas, and they prefer a cool, more or less shady environment and a soil that is leafy, organic, and moist but well-drained. In nature, such soils are fairly fertile because nutrients are annually replenished by the recycling of fallen leaves. If you are one of the lucky ones to have such gardening conditions, all you really need to do is choose, plant, and admire your handiwork.

There are also many acid-loving plants that need or tolerate more open sites in sun, such as witch alder (*see p.103*), *Lithodora diffusa* 'Heavenly Blue' (*see p.104*), and most heathers (*see pp.42, 45, 102, 173, 306, 418*). Provided that the soil is not excessively acidic – perhaps on the acidic side of neutral – a huge range of plants are likely to thrive, excluding only those that positively demand alkaline conditions. Plan a display that lasts through the year, with woodland gems

that flower in spring or early summer, followed by plants that bloom later in the year. You can also enjoy creating blazing tapestries of autumn color using plants such as maples (*see pp.94, 95*), *Amelanchier lamarckii* (*see p.95*), or *Enkianthus cernuus* var. *rubens* (*see p.102*), since their foliage tints are best on acidic soils.

KEEP THE SOIL FERTILE

Relatively few acid-lovers thrive in poor, acidic soils. There are exceptions, however, such as bog rosemary (*see p.99*), brooms (*see pp.44, 198, 350*), heathers (*see pp.42, 45, 102, 173, 306, 418*), and vacciniums (*see pp.109, 376, 456*), which are found in the wild on wind-blasted moorlands and barrens. If you garden on peaty soil, the range of plants grown is usually limited by low fertility, so additional nutrients, preferably in the form of slow-release fertilizers, are needed to extend the range. If the soil is very acidic, it may fail to support even the most dedicated acid-lovers; in this case, careful liming can moderate the acidity. Adding organic matter to an already peaty soil may appear paradoxical, but it has value, as it adds a modicum of nutrients and improves drainage and moisture retention. Peaty soils are often poorly drained and can be difficult to wet again if allowed to dry out. Acidic clay or sandy soils also benefit from such treatment.

ACID-LOVERS IN CONTAINERS

Plants that thrive in acidic soils, like azaleas and rhododendrons (*see pp.108, 160, 243, 454*), often have such delicate glamour that gardeners yearn to grow them, even if they have totally unsuitable, alkaline soils. The best solution in this case is to choose small or dwarf cultivars of the plant in question and grow them in barrels or other containers filled with acidic (ericaceous) soil mix. Alternatively, create a raised bed on top of perforated plastic, which will allow drainage, and fill it with acidic soil. Be prepared to top-dress annually with more of the same.

ABIES LASIOCARPA
'Arizonica Compacta'

A compact and slow-growing form of the corkbark fir that develops into a small and densely foliaged, conical to oval tree with soft, corky bark. The blue-gray leaves give this tree a distinctive color. The upward-pointing fir cones are dark purple and ripen to brown. Grow in a shrub border or as a specimen tree.

ALSO RECOMMENDED: A. koreana (see p.496); A. nordmanniana *is columnar to 130ft (40m) tall with glossy foliage* Z6.

☼ ◊◊ Z3   **Evergreen tree**
↕ 10–15ft (3–5m) ↔ 6–10ft (2–3m)

ACER JAPONICUM
'Aconitifolium'

This Japanese maple forms a bushy tree and bears deeply lobed, mid-green leaves that turn brilliant dark red in autumn. It flowers very freely, producing upright clusters of conspicuous, reddish purple flowers in spring, followed by winged fruits. Where marginally hardy, provide a thick mulch near (but not up to) the trunk. Remove badly placed branches in summer or early autumn only.

ALSO RECOMMENDED: *'Vitifolium' has shallowly lobed leaves.*

☼ ◊ Z6   **Deciduous tree**
↕ 15ft (5m) ↔ 20ft (6m)

ACER PALMATUM
'Bloodgood'

The delicate, divided leaves of this small and graceful Japanese maple are dark red-purple and turn brilliant red in autumn. A fine specimen for a sheltered site in a small garden; it is also suitable for growing in containers (*see p.412*). Prune in summer only when young to remove any badly placed shoots.

ALSO RECOMMENDED: *f.* atropurpureum *has red-purple leaves that turn to bright red;* 'Burgundy Lace' *has deeply cut, dark red-purple leaves;* Dissectum Atropurpureum Group *has finely divided, dark red-purple leaves.*

☼◐ ◊ Z6   **Deciduous tree**

↕↔ 15ft (5m)

AMELANCHIER LAMARCKII

Juneberry is an upright, multistemmed shrubby tree that lends interest with its bronzed new leaves in spring and brilliant red and gold autumn color. The white flowers in hanging clusters appear in spring and are followed by purple-black fruits, which attract birds (*see p.494*). A fine specimen that forms its shape naturally, needing only minimal winter pruning, although it will also grow as a hedge (*see p.138*).

ALSO RECOMMENDED: *A.* canadensis *bears white flowers in upright clusters* Z3b; *A.* × grandiflora *'Ballerina' is more spreading, with arching flower clusters* Z4.

☼◐ ◊◊ Z4   **Deciduous tree**

↕ 30ft (10m) ↔ 40ft (12m)

EUCRYPHIA × INTERMEDIA 'Rostrevor'

Glistening white, cup-shaped flowers festoon this narrowly upright tree from late summer to autumn, and they are attractive to bees (*see p.494*). With its glossy dark green leaves, it makes an elegant specimen in any site that is sheltered from cold, drying winds. It grows best with its roots in shade and top-growth in sun. Overwinter indoors.

ALSO RECOMMENDED: *E. glutinosa is deciduous with orange-red fall color and is more tolerant of exposure (Tender); E. × nymansensis 'Nymansay' is taller (Tender).*

☼ ◯◑ Min 40°F (5°C) **Evergreen tree**
↕ 30ft (10m) ↔ 20ft (6m)

NOTHOFAGUS × ALPINA

This fast-growing, broadly conical southern beech, also known as *N. procera* of gardens, has beechlike leaves that are bronze when young, maturing to fresh green, and assuming glorious red, orange, and yellow tints before they drop in autumn. A fine specimen tree for larger gardens. It needs little pruning; cut out crossing or badly placed shoots in winter.

ALSO RECOMMENDED: *N. antarctica is smaller and often multistemmed Z7; N. obliqua is taller, with smaller leaves Z7b.*

☼ ◯◑ Z7b **Deciduous tree**
↕ 80ft (25m) ↔ 50ft (15m)

NYSSA SINENSIS

The Chinese tupelo is a conical tree valued for its colorful foliage. The leaves are bronze when young, maturing to dark green in summer, turning to brilliant shades of orange, red, and yellow in autumn before they drop. The flowers are inconspicuous. Ideal as a specimen tree near water, but choose a site that is sheltered from winds. Thin out crowded branches in late winter.

ALSO RECOMMENDED: *N. sylvatica is very similar but reaches 70ft (20m) in height* Z5b.

☼◐ ◊◊ Z7b   **Deciduous tree**
↕↔ 30ft (10m)

PSEUDOLARIX AMABILIS

The golden larch, although initially slow-growing, makes a beautiful specimen tree for larger gardens. The open, broadly conical crown of branches, which have purple-tipped shoots, bears soft, fresh green, needle-like leaves; they turn glorious shades of orange and old gold in autumn. In spring, it bears catkinlike male flowers, and the female cones are spiky and egg-shaped. It needs a warm, sunny site and deep, fertile soil; in cold areas, select a site with shelter from spring frosts. Areas with long, hot summers are the most suitable.

☼ ◊ Z6   **Deciduous tree**
↕ 50–70ft (15–20m) ↔ 40ft (12m)

STEWARTIA MONADELPHA

In midsummer, this elegant, slow-growing tree bears camellia-like, crystalline white flowers with a boss of violet anthers. The glossy dark green leaves turn deep orange and red in autumn and, at maturity, the bark is patterned gray and red-brown. A fine specimen for a woodland garden. Prune only to remove badly placed or damaged branches when dormant in winter.

ALSO RECOMMENDED: *S. ovata is a large shrub Z6; S. pseudocamellia has a tiered habit and is a smaller tree Z5b.*

☼ ◐ ◊ Z7   **Deciduous tree**
↕ 80ft (25m) ↔ 80ft (8m)

STYRAX JAPONICUS

The Japanese snowbell is a small and graceful tree with glossy leaves that turn red and yellow in autumn. In midsummer it is festooned with delicate, bell-shaped white flowers that hang beneath the branches. Suitable for a woodland garden or a shrub border in dappled shade. Choose a site with some shelter from winds. Prune only to remove badly placed branches in winter.

ALSO RECOMMENDED: *S. hemsleyanus is more columnar in habit Z7b; S. obassia is taller with more rounded leaves and fragrant flowers Z6.*

☼ ◐ ◊◗ Z5b   **Deciduous tree**
↕ 30ft (10m) ↔ 25ft (8m)

ANDROMEDA POLIFOLIA
'Compacta'

Bog rosemary forms a compact mound of wiry stems clothed in narrow and leathery, dark green leaves. In spring and early summer, it bears urn-shaped, light pink flowers. Excellent for a rock or woodland garden, or for a moist shady border (*see p.238*), it tolerates full sun where soils remain reliably moist. Good as a groundcover (*see pp.304, 326*). Trim after flowering.

ALSO RECOMMENDED: *A. polifolia is larger; 'Macrophylla' is also smaller, with larger flowers.*

☀◐ ◊ Z2   **Evergreen shrub**
‡ 16in (40cm) ↔ 24in (60cm)

CAMELLIA JAPONICA
'Lady Vansittart'

An upright shrub with dark green, leathery foliage. In early spring it is covered by masses of saucer-shaped, semidouble white flowers with rose-pink stripes or specks. Good for the back of a border or as a specimen shrub, sheltered from winds. Mulch around the base in winter, and prune young plants to shape after flowering. Also good for containers in shade (*see p.448*) and protected, north-facing walls (*see p.262*).

ALSO RECOMMENDED: *'Adolphe Audusson' (see p.450); 'Elegans' has pink flowers.*

☀ ◊◊ Z7   **Evergreen shrub**
‡ 28ft (9m) ↔ 25ft (8m)

CASSIOPE LYCOPODIOIDES

A heatherlike shrub with scalelike, dark green leaves that form a low and dense, ground-covering mat (*see pp.304, 326*). In late spring it is clothed by upright spikes of red-stemmed, narrowly bell-shaped white flowers. Good for a rock or woodland garden or a cool, shady border; it tolerates sun if the soil remains moist. It can also be grown in a wide, shallow pot (*see p.448*). Trim after flowering.

ALSO RECOMMENDED: *C. 'Edinburgh' is more upright with green-stemmed flowers; C. 'Randle Cooke' has taller-stemmed flowers in late spring.*

☼ ◑ ◊ Z7b   **Evergreen shrub**
‡ 3in (8cm) ↔ 18in (45cm)

CELMISIA WALKERI

The arching, spreading branches of this low-growing plant bear rosettes of narrow, leathery, dark green leaves at their tips; they are white and woolly beneath. In early summer it produces a mass of daisylike, yellow-centered white flowers. Good for a rock garden or a damp border; celmisias dislike hot sun and grow best in areas with cool, moist summers. Trim after flowering.

ALSO RECOMMENDED: *C. bellidioides is mat-forming with white flowerheads Z8; C. semicordata has rosettes of silky, hairy leaves and white flowers Z8.*

☼ ◑ ◊◊ Z8   **Evergreen shrub**
‡↔ 12in (30cm)

DESFONTAINIA SPINOSA

This dense bush has a hollylike appearance; unlike holly, showy hanging flowers are borne from mid-summer to late autumn. These tubular blooms are red with yellow tips and appear amid the spiny, glossy dark green leaves. Choose a shrub border in dappled shade with shelter from winds, such as against a north-facing wall (*see p.262*). It tolerates more open situations in areas of high rainfall. Trim in early spring, if necessary.

☀ ◊◊ Z8   **Evergreen shrub**
↕↔ 6ft (2m)

EMBOTHRIUM COCCINEUM

The Chilean firebush is a bushy and upright shrub with narrow, shiny dark green leaves. In early summer it bears clusters of showy, tubular, flaming scarlet flowers that stand out brilliantly if the shrub is grown as a specimen in the dappled shade of a woodland garden. Grow in the protection of a wall (*see pp.262, 280*), because it must have shelter from winds. Needs minimal pruning.

ALSO RECOMMENDED: *'Norquinco' is slightly hardier.*

☀☼ ◊ Min 35°F (2°C)   **Evergreen shrub**
↕ 30ft (10m) ↔ 15ft (5m)

ENKIANTHUS CERNUUS
F. RUBENS

A bushy plant with clusters of bright green leaves that assume dark red-purple tints before falling in autumn. The hanging clusters of bell-shaped, rich red flowers, which are delicately toothed at the mouth, are borne in late spring and early summer. Grow as a specimen in a woodland garden or in shrub border. If the soil is reliably moist, it thrives in sun and will produce its best autumn color there.

ALSO RECOMMENDED: *E. campanulatus is taller with pink-veined cream flowers and scarlet leaves in autumn.* Z5b

☼ ☀ ◑ Z6b   **Deciduous shrub**
↔ 8ft (2.5m)

ERICA CINEREA *'Romiley'*

This form of bell heather produces spires of magenta flowers from early summer to autumn above a dense clump of narrow, dark green leaves. It makes a good groundcover (*see p.304*) for a shrub border, rock garden, or when grown in a tapestry with other heathers. It associates well with dwarf conifers. Trim after flowering to keep compact. Tolerant of exposure (*see p.118*), and the flowers attract bees (*see p.494*).

ALSO RECOMMENDED: *'Eden Valley' has lavender-pink flowers; 'Pink Ice' has pink flowers and bronzed winter foliage.*

☼ ◑ Z6   **Evergreen shrub**
↕ 10in (25cm) ↔ 22in (55cm)

FOTHERGILLA GARDENII

Witch alder makes a dense bush with spikes of bottlebrush-like, fragrant white flowers on the bare branches in spring. It is also valued for its blaze of autumn foliage; the glossy dark green leaves turn orange, yellow, and red before they fall. An attractive addition to a shrub border or light woodland. Very little pruning is required.

ALSO RECOMMENDED: *'Blue Mist' has bluish foliage; F. major is very similar but larger and with later spring flowers* Z5b.

☼ ◐◊ ƒ Z6 **Deciduous shrub**
↕↔ 3ft (1m)

HAMAMELIS *'Brevipetala'*

Whether grown in woodland, in a shrub border, or as a specimen, this graceful witch hazel brings welcome scent and color in winter with its spidery yellow flowers that spangle the bare branches. In autumn, the leaves turn gold before falling. Pruning is best kept to a minimum, although the flowering branches are good for cutting (*see p.524*).

ALSO RECOMMENDED: *H. × intermedia 'Arnold Promise' has larger yellow flowers; 'Diane' has dark red flowers* Z6b; *H. mollis has yellow flowers* Z5.

☼◑ ◊ ƒ Z5 **Deciduous shrub**
↕↔ 12ft (4m)

KALMIA ANGUSTIFOLIA

The sheep laurel is a tough, rabbit-proof bush grown for its spectacular, rounded clusters of small, pink to deep red, sometimes white flowers. They appear in early summer amid the dark green leaves. Useful for a shrub border or rock garden, it naturally forms a mound; prune after flowering, if necessary. Mulch in spring with leaf mold or pine needles. It will tolerate full sun if the soil is kept moist, and it is suitable for a container (*see p.448*).

ALSO RECOMMENDED: *f.* rubra *has dark red flowers;* K. latifolia (see p.18).

☼ ◊ Z3   **Evergreen shrub**
‡ 24in (60cm) ↔ 5ft (1.5m)

LITHODORA DIFFUSA
'Heavenly Blue'

A spreading bush, sometimes sold as *Lithospermum* 'Heavenly Blue', that grows flat along the ground. Rich blue, funnel-shaped flowers are borne in profusion from late spring and on into summer. The leaves are dark green and hairy. Suitable for an open position in a rock garden or raised bed. Trim lightly after flowering.

ALSO RECOMMENDED: L. oleifolia *has sky blue flowers in early summer.* Z7

☼ ◊ Z6   **Evergreen shrub**
‡ 6in (15cm) ↔ 24in (60cm) or more

MAGNOLIA LILIIFLORA *'Nigra'*

A dense, summer-flowering shrub bearing goblet-shaped, deep wine red, fragrant flowers amid dark green leaves. Plant as a specimen or among other shrubs and trees. Unlike many magnolias, it begins to flower when quite young. Provide a mulch in early spring, and prune young plants in midsummer to encourage a good shape.

ALSO RECOMMENDED: M. campbellii (see p.478); M. grandiflora *'Goliath'* (see p.283); M. × soulangeana (see p.15).

☼ ◑ ◊◊ **ƒ** Z6   **Deciduous shrub**
↕ 10ft (3m) ↔ 8ft (2.5m)

MITRARIA COCCINEA

A weakly scrambling shrub with scarlet flowers over a long period from late spring to autumn. They contrast well with the glossy dark green foliage and are followed by fleshy berries. Keep the roots cool and shaded, and allow the top to grow into the sun. An easy plant to grow in a woodland garden or sheltered shrub border, where it will trail along the ground, spill over banks, or climb through a trellis. It will also cascade from a container or hanging basket in shade (*see p.448*). Trim in spring, if necessary.

☼ ◑ ◊◊ Min 40°F (5°C) **Evergreen shrub**
↕ 6ft (2m)

PHYLLODOCE × INTERMEDIA *'Drummondii'*

A bushy, low-spreading plant with stems that are densely clothed in narrow, glossy dark green leaves. In a rock garden, peaty soil, or shady border, it makes a goodground cover (*see p.326*). In spring, red stems bear clusters of nodding, narrowly bell-shaped, rich pink flowers. Trim after flowering to keep it dense and neat. It does not grow well where summers are hot and humid.

ALSO RECOMMENDED: *P. caerulea has purplish pink flowers Z2; P. empetriformis has purple-pink to rose-red flowers Z3.*

☼ ◑ Z2   **Evergreen shrub**
↕ 6–9in (15–23cm) ↔ 14in (35cm)

PICEA ABIES *'Ohlendorffii'*

This very slow-growing form of the Norway spruce makes a densely foliaged, rounded bush. It narrows to a more conical shape with age and has dark green, forward-pointing, needlelike leaves. Very little pruning is necessary.

ALSO RECOMMENDED: *P. abies grows to 130ft (40m) tall; 'Nidiformis' grows slowly to 5ft (1.5m) tall with a spreading habit; P. mariana 'Nana' (see p.423); P. omorika (see p.479).*

☼ ◐ Z2b   **Evergreen shrub**
↕ 10ft (3m) ↔ 10–12ft (3–4m)

PIERIS FORMOSA
'Wakehurst'

This upright shrub is valued for its brilliant red young foliage that fades to pink and matures to dark green. Also attractive are the large, slightly drooping clusters of small, fragrant white flowers in spring. Suitable for a woodland garden or shrub border. Trim lightly after flowering.

ALSO RECOMMENDED: *P. 'Forest Flame' is similar* Z5b*; P. japonica 'Little Heath' (see p.453)* Z5b.

☼ ◐ ◊◊ ƒ Z7   **Evergreen shrub**
↕ 24in (60cm) ↔ 12in (30cm)

PINUS SYLVESTRIS
'Gold Coin'

This dwarf and slow-growing cultivar of the Scots pine forms a rounded bush with bright golden yellow, needlelike foliage. It is suitable for small gardens and can be grown in a rock garden or as a specimen in a large container (*see p.412*). This shrub also tolerates exposed sites (*see p.118*) and sandy soils (*see p.38*).

ALSO RECOMMENDED: *Aurea Group is a selection of trees to 50ft (15m) tall with green foliage that turns to golden yellow in winter.*

☼ ◊ Z3   **Evergreen shrub**
↕↔ 6ft (2m)

RHODODENDRON LUTEUM

This azalea makes an open shrub with
midgreen, bristly, deciduous leaves.
In late spring and early summer,
clusters of up to a dozen funnel-
shaped, sticky and sweetly scented
yellow flowers cover the plant.
Unlike many rhododendrons, it grows
best in direct sun. Little or no pruning
is required.

ALSO RECOMMENDED: R. *Blue Diamond
Group* (see p.160); R. *'Homebush'* (see
p.454); R. *'Polar Bear'* (see p.243).

☼ △◑ *f* Z4   **Deciduous shrub**
↔ 12ft (4m)

SKIMMIA JAPONICA *'Rubella'*

A tough plant that bears dark red flower
buds in autumn and winter, which open
in spring as fragrant heads of white
flowers. The dome of oval leaves have
red rims. No berries are produced, but
it will pollinate female skimmias nearby.
It tolerates coastal areas (*see p.166*),
urban pollution, and dry shade (*see
p.216*), and it can be pot-grown (*see
p.448*). Requires little pruning, but cut
back any shoots that spoil the shape.

ALSO RECOMMENDED: *'Nymans' is female
with red berries; 'Robert Fortune' is a
hermaphrodite;* S. × confusa *'Kew Green'*
(see p.455); S. japonica (see p.223).

☼◐ ◑ *f* Z7   **Evergreen shrub**
↔ to 20ft (6m)

VACCINIUM VITIS-IDAEA
Koralle Group

This group of wide-spreading cowberries forms a mat of small and leathery, dark green leaves spangled with dense, nodding spikes of bell-shaped white flowers in spring and early summer. The shiny red fruits that follow are borne very freely. An excellent ground-cover for peaty soils in woodland or shrub borders (*see pp.304, 326*). Also suitable for sandy soils (*see p.38*). Trim to shape in spring, if necessary.

ALSO RECOMMENDED: *var.* minus *is smaller with pink flowers;* V. corymbosum (see p.376); V. glaucoalbum (see p.456).

☼ ◐ ◊ Z1　　　　　**Evergreen shrub**

↕ 10in (25cm) ↔ indefinite

ZENOBIA PULVERULENTA

The slender and spreading, arching shoots of this shrub are clothed in narrowly oval, bluish green leaves. In early to midsummer it produces upright clusters of fragrant, nodding, bell-shaped white flowers at the stem tips. An attractive specimen for a woodland garden or damp, shady border (*see p.238*). It tolerates sun where soils remain reliably moist and may be semi-evergreen in a sheltered site. To keep it compact, cut the stems back to strong buds after flowering.

☼ ◊ *f* Z6　　　　　**Deciduous shrub**

↕ 6ft (2m) ↔ 5ft (1.5m)

BULBINELLA HOOKERI

This sturdy perennial for a rock garden or peaty soil forms dense clumps of narrow and succulent, grasslike foliage. From spring to summer, spikes of golden yellow flowers appear on top of tall, upright stems above the foliage. Where marginally hardy, provide a thick mulch of leaf mold in winter.

☼ ◑ ◊◊ Z8   **Perennial**
‡ 24in (60cm) ↔ 12in (30cm)

DESCHAMPSIA FLEXUOSA 'Tatra Gold'

This evergreen grass forms a mound of arching threads of yellow-green leaves. In early to midsummer it bears airy heads of tiny bronze flowers on slender, wavy stalks. May be cut for fresh or dried flower arrangements (*see p.524*). Good for a mixed border or woodland garden. Remove old flowerheads as new growth appears in spring.

ALSO RECOMMENDED: D. flexuosa *is slightly taller with blue-green leaves and glistening, silver-tinted, purple or brown flowers;* D. cespitosa *'Goldtau' (syn. Golden Dew) (see p.228).*

☼ ◑ ◊ Z5   **Perennial**
‡ 20in (50cm) ↔ 12in (30cm)

DIANELLA TASMANICA

This plant forms clumps of long and arching, grasslike foliage from which rise branching sprays of star-shaped, lavender-blue to violet flowers with pale yellow anthers. These are borne on upright stems in early summer, then persistent, glossy deep blue berries follow. An enchanting plant for a woodland garden.

ALSO RECOMMENDED: *D. caerulea has blue, blue-green, or white flowers (Tender).*

☼ ◐ ◊ Min 35°F (2°C)   **Perennial**
‡ 4ft (1.2m) ↔ 18in (45cm)

GENTIANA SINO-ORNATA

This autumn-flowering gentian bears its trumpet-shaped, deep yet bright blue flowers, striped darker blue and palest green, above mats of trailing shoots carrying rosettes of narrow, dark green leaves. Ideal for a rock garden or the front of a damp, lightly shaded border (*see p.238*). It grows well in paving crevices (*see p.348*).

ALSO RECOMMENDED: *G. 'Inverleith' has pale blue flowers with dark blue stripes; G. × macaulayi 'Kingfisher' is more compact.*

☼ ◊ Z4   **Perennial**
‡ 2–3in (5–7cm) ↔ 12in (30cm)

IRIS INNOMINATA

This iris produces a clump of evergreen, very narrow, deep green leaves and bears cream, yellow, or purple to lavender-blue flowers in early summer. It is good for a herbaceous border, and its tendency to spread makes it good as a groundcover (*see p.304*). Mulch with compost in spring, and divide clumps every few years to maintain vigor.

ALSO RECOMMENDED: *I.* douglasiana *has flowers in shades of purple, blue, or white* Z7; *those of* I. tenax *come in lavender-blue, yellow, and cream* Z7.

☀ ◐ ◊ Z6   **Perennial**
↕ 6–10in (15–25cm) ↔ 6–10in (30cm)

LEIOPHYLLUM BUXIFOLIUM

Sand myrtle is an upright to mat-forming, shrubby evergreen grown for its glossy dark green foliage and its abundance of star-shaped, pinkish white flowers that appear in late spring and early summer. The leaves tint bronze in winter. A good, free-flowering underplanting perennial for a border or woodland garden. Protect from winds. Trim after flowering to contain its spread.

☀ ◐ ◊◊ Z6   **Perennial**
↕ 12–24in (30–60cm) ↔ 24in (60cm) or more

LILIUM SUPERBUM

The maroon-spotted orange flowers of the American turkscap lily, which rise on sturdy, purple-spotted stems in late summer and autumn, are spectacular if grouped in large clumps at the back of a border or in a woodland garden. Grow in deep, fertile, organic soil, siting the roots in shade and the tops in sun. Plant bulbs in autumn.

ALSO RECOMMENDED: L. martagon *has pink to purplish red flowers in early and midsummer* Z3; L. *Bellingham Group has yellow to orange and red, brown-spotted flowers in early and midsummer* Z3.

☀☀ ◊ Z4　　　　　**Perennial bulb**
↕ 5–10ft (1.5–3m) ↔ 12in (30cm)

MECONOPSIS NAPAULENSIS

This tall, evergreen poppy is worth growing for its overwintering, basal rosettes of large, tawny-hairy leaves alone. From spring to midsummer it bears branched stems of dusky pink, red, or purple poppy flowers. It dies after flowering. Best in leafy, organic soil in areas with cool, damp summers.

ALSO RECOMMENDED: M. betonicifolia *has sky blue flowers in early summer;* M. grandis *has deep rich blue to purplish red flowers in early summer.*

☀ ◊◊ Z4　　　　　**Perennial**
↕ 8ft (2.5m) ↔ 24–36in (60–90cm)

NOMOCHARIS PARDANTHINA

The nodding, white or pink flowers of this slender, elegant plant are borne in early summer above whorls of narrow stem leaves. An ideal companion for rhododendrons because it enjoys cool, damp conditions in partial shade, as found in woodland or shady borders (*see p.238*). It withstands sun in areas with cool summers where the soil remains moist. Plant bulbs in winter or spring. Protect from slugs.

ALSO RECOMMENDED: *N. aperta is shorter with pale pink, purple-spotted flowers.* Z7

☼ ◐ ◊ ♦ **Z7**   **Perennial**
↕ 36in (90cm) ↔ 4in (10cm)

PHLOX ADSURGENS
'Wagon Wheel'

This woodland phlox has trailing stems and forms a mound of light to mid-green foliage covered by salmon-pink flowers in late spring and early summer. The petals are very narrow, resembling the spokes of a wheel. Also useful as a groundcover in shade (*see p.326*).

ALSO RECOMMENDED: *'Red Buttes' has deep pink flowers.*

☼ ◐ ◊ ♦ **Z4**   **Perennial**
↕↔ 12in (30cm)

PODOPHYLLUM HEXANDRUM

The deeply lobed, purple-splashed leaves of this spreading perennial emerge fully after the cup-shaped, white or pale pink flowers bloom in spring. The plumlike red fruits that follow, though ornamental, are very toxic if ingested. Grow in damp, leafy soil in a woodland garden or shady border (*see p.238*). Tolerates permanently moist soils (*see p.372*).

ALSO RECOMMENDED: *P. peltatum* has *leaves that are well developed when it bears its fragrant, white or pink flowers. The fruits are yellow-green.* Z4

☼☀ ◐◖ Z4   **Perennial**
↕ 18in (45cm) ↔ 12in (30cm)

SEMIAQUILEGIA ECALCARATA

This delicate, usually short-lived plant carries clusters of diminutive, gracefully nodding, bell-shaped flowers in shades of dusky pink to purple-red in early summer; they are held above finely divided, fresh green leaves. A perfect plant for a sheltered niche in a rock garden. It grows well if it has some midday shade. Protect from slugs.

☼☀ ◖ Z5b   **Perennial**
↕ 12in (30cm) ↔ 8in (20cm)

SMILACINA RACEMOSA

False spikenard is a beautiful plant for a woodland garden or shady border, forming clumps of luxuriant, pale green leaves. Dense and upright, feathery spikes of creamy white, often green-tinged flowers arise from the clumps in late spring. These are occasionally followed by red berries. The foliage fades to yellow in autumn. Good as a groundcover in shade (*see p.326*).

ALSO RECOMMENDED: S. stellata *is shorter with smaller, less feathery flower spikes.* Z4

☀◐ ◑ Z4   **Perennial**
‡ 36in (90cm) ↔ 24in (60cm)

TRICYRTIS FORMOSANA

This toad lily is an upright plant with unusual flowers and is a fine choice for a shady border or open woodland garden. Its white, purple-spotted, star-shaped flowers appear in early autumn on zig-zagging, softly hairy stems above dark green, stem-clasping leaves. Where there is likely to be little or no snow cover, grow in a sheltered site and provide a deep winter mulch.

ALSO RECOMMENDED: T. hirta *is similar with flowers from late summer.* Z5

☀◐ ◑ Z4   **Perennial**
‡ 32in (80cm) ↔ 18in (45cm)

TRILLIUM ERECTUM

Purple trillium is a vigorous, upright perennial bearing whorls of broadly oval leaves atop sturdy stems. In spring, funnel-shaped, deep red-purple flowers appear just above them. Ideal for damp, shady borders (*see p.238*) or woodland gardens. Mulch annually with leaf mold to maintain optimum soil conditions. Protect from slugs.

ALSO RECOMMENDED: *f.* albiflorum *has white flowers;* T. grandiflorum *is shorter with more prominent white flowers.* Z4

☀️☀️ ◐ Z4 **Perennial**
‡ 20in (50cm) ↔ 12in (30cm)

UVULARIA GRANDIFLORA

Large merrybells forms slowly spreading clumps of slender, upright stems that bear bell-shaped yellow flowers in late spring. Like the midgreen leaves, they hang downward gracefully. An excellent plant for a shady border or woodland garden. Protect young plants from slugs and snails.

ALSO RECOMMENDED: *var.* pallida *has pale yellow flowers.*

☀️☀️ ◐◐ Z3 **Perennial**
‡ 30in (75cm) ↔ 12in (30cm)

PLANTS FOR EXPOSED SITES

ARDENS THAT SUFFER **extreme** exposure present some of the most difficult conditions for plants, the most detrimental feature being the force of the wind. Exposed gardens may be lashed by salt-laden coastal wind (*see p.166*), laid bare to the full brunt of the weather on a blasted hillside, or on flat, open land denuded of tree cover and hedges. High winds loosen plant roots, break fragile stems and shoots, and scorch foliage when the leaves lose water faster than they can replace it from the soil.

Some beautiful gardens, however, are sited in exposed locations, and the secret of their success is due largely to the creation of shelter belts or wind-filtering hedges around their margins (*see p.138*). Explore beyond the perimeter of such exposed gardens on a windy day, and compare the conditions outside and within; you will clearly feel just how effective a windbreak can be in creating a sheltered microclimate on the leeward side. With such shelter in place,

the range of plants that can be grown within the garden is so much wider – in fact, the choice is about the same as in a more naturally sheltered spot. If you have an exposed garden, therefore, your first priority is to lessen the full force of the wind's blast.

WINDBREAK PLANTS
The choice of windbreak or hedging material is more important in cold, exposed gardens than elsewhere, because the sheltering plants themselves must be very tough if they are to grow well enough to fulfill their function. Hawthorn (*see pp.123, 141*) makes some of the most resilient hedging, while Scots pines, maples (*see p.168*), poplars (*see pp.16, 169*), and willows (*see p.162*) are ideal windbreak material, not least because their flexible stems go with the flow, rather than crack in the teeth of the wind.

Even tough plants benefit from some protection in their early years in the form of temporary, artificial shelter, such as woven fencing, windbreak netting, or plastic tree shelters. Once the plants are established, the shelter can be removed.

THE REST OF THE GARDEN
In the lee of a windbreak, tough evergreen shrubs can be planted to further cut down the force of the wind and provide a background for the garden proper. This secondary defense should include leathery-leaved shrubs, such as *Prunus laurocerasus* 'Zabeliana' (*see p.131*) and *Viburnum rhytidophyllum* (*see p.134*). In more open areas, use lower-level plantings of small-leaved, ground-hugging plants, such as those that grow naturally on heathland or tundra. These include *Ledum groenlandicum* (*see p.129*), *Arctostaphylos* × *media* 'Wood's Red' (*see p.127*), or heather (*see p.102*). If you site the more robust plants carefully, they will begin to create sheltered niches within the garden as they grow. This creates more choice and will ultimately allow you to grow more delicate plants.

ACER PLATANOIDES *'Crimson King'*

This selection of Norway maple is a fast-growing tree with a crown of deep red-purple leaves divided into several pointed lobes. The leaves turn to red in autumn. Clusters of reddish yellow flowers clothe the bare branches in spring. Tolerant of most soils, including alkaline (*see p.64*), and urban pollution. Remove badly placed or unhealthy growth in late autumn to midwinter only.

ALSO RECOMMENDED: *'Drummondii' has attractive cream-margined green leaves;* A. campestre (*see p.496*).

☼ ☀ ◊◊ Z4b   **Deciduous tree**
‡ 80ft (25m) ↔ 50ft (15m)

AESCULUS × CARNEA *'Briotii'*

This cultivar of the red horse chestnut is a spreading tree, admired in early summer for its large, upright clusters of dark red flowers. They are followed by round, spiny fruits. The dark green leaves are divided into several leaflets. A tree for fairly large gardens only. Remove dead, damaged, or badly placed branches during winter.

ALSO RECOMMENDED: *'Plantierensis' has bigger flower clusters and shiny foliage.*

☼ ☀ ◊◊ Z6   **Deciduous tree**
‡ 70ft (20m) ↔ 50ft (15m)

ALNUS GLUTINOSA 'Imperialis'

This curious form of the black alder has deeply dissected, mid-green leaves. Groups of yellow-brown catkins are seen in late winter, followed by small, oval cones in summer. This beautiful foliage tree is not as tough as the species, but it is particularly good close to water, since it tolerates poor, wet soils (*see p.372*). If necessary, prune in autumn after the leaves have fallen.

ALSO RECOMMENDED: A. glutinosa *with oval leaves is a better choice for a cold, windy site;* A. incana (see p.140).

☼ ◊ Z4   **Deciduous tree**

↕ 80ft (25m) ↔ 15ft (5m)

BETULA UTILIS *'Jacquemontii'*

Himalayan birches should be grown where winter sun will illuminate the white, smooth, and peeling bark, which is particularly brilliant in this variety. Catkins are a feature in early spring, and the dark green leaves turn to rich golden yellow in autumn. Remove any damaged or dead wood in late autumn.

ALSO RECOMMENDED: B. ermanii (see p.40), B. nigra Z3, *and* B. papyrifera Z2, *are all good planted in clumps in exposed sites.*

☼ ◊ Z3   **Deciduous tree**

↕ 50ft (15m) ↔ 23ft (7.5m)

CHAMAECYPARIS PISIFERA *'Filifera Aurea'*

A broad conifer that develops into a conical tree with flattened sprays of golden green-yellow foliage. The fronds arch gracefully and are sometimes covered with small green cones, which ripen to brown. An excellent specimen tree that requires no regular pruning. The species is tougher and better as a windbreak; both are tolerant of permanently moist soils (*see p.372*).

ALSO RECOMMENDED: C. obtusa Z5 *and* C. pisifera *both make excellent windbreaks and can be trimmed as hedges.*

☼ ◐◐ Z4b   **Evergreen tree**
↕ 40ft (12m) ↔ 15ft (5m)

CORNUS FLORIDA *'Cherokee Chief'*

The flowering dogwood makes a beautiful tree with broad, midgreen leaves. These turn scarlet and purple in autumn before they fall. Dark pink flowers appear the following spring, succeeded by red berries that are attractive to wildlife. A good specimen tree that needs little pruning.

ALSO RECOMMENDED: C. alternifolia *'Argentea' (see p.476).*

☼ ◑ ◊ Z5b   **Deciduous tree**
↕ 20ft (6m) ↔ 25ft (8m)

CRATAEGUS LAEVIGATA
'Paul's Scarlet'

English hawthorn, or may, is a small
and thorny tree with a rounded crown.
This cultivar is valued for its abundant
clusters of double, dark pink flowers
that appear in late spring amid the
glossy green leaves. Red berries ripen
in autumn. Hawthorns tolerate urban
pollution and coastal sites (*see p.166*).
Prune after flowering; it is easily
trimmed as a hedge (*see p.138*).

ALSO RECOMMENDED: C. monogyna
(*see p.141*); C. × mordenensis *'Toba' is also
pink-flowered* Z3.

☼ ◐ ◊◊ Z6   **Deciduous tree**
↕↔ 25ft (8m)

CRYPTOMERIA JAPONICA
'Cristata'

This narrow and conical conifer is a
cultivated form of the Japanese cedar,
and it is also sold as 'Sekka-sugi'. It has
slender, feathery sprays of deep green
leaves and a neat growth habit that
needs little or no formal pruning.
All cryptomerias are tolerant of alkaline
soils (*see p.64*).

ALSO RECOMMENDED: C. japonica *is the
one to plant as a windbreak or hedge.*

☼ ◐ ◊ Z6   **Evergreen tree**
↕ 25ft (8m) ↔ 15ft (5m)

FRAXINUS EXCELSIOR *'Jaspidea'*

The yellowish foliage of this European ash make it a popular alternative to the species, which has dark green leaves. 'Jaspidea' is vigorous, and its broad crown of foliage is yellow in spring, darkening to pale green in summer, then fading to yellow again before dropping in autumn. An excellent specimen tree for coastal gardens (*see p.166*) and alkaline soils (*see p.64*). Prune in winter, if necessary.

ALSO RECOMMENDED: *F. excelsior makes a better windbreak; 'Pendula' has weeping branches.*

☼ ◊◊ Z4b　　　　**Deciduous tree**
‡ 100ft (30m) ↔ 70ft (20m)

LABURNUM × WATERERI *'Vossii'*

A tough tree suitable for small gardens, this golden chain tree bears long, hanging clusters of golden yellow, pealike flowers in late spring. The leaves are deep green. It can also be trained on an arch, pergola, or tunnel framework. All parts are toxic if eaten. Prune in winter or early spring, if necessary, and remove any growth that appears from the base of the trunk.

ALSO RECOMMENDED: *L. alpinum 'Pendulum' has weeping branches.* Z5b

☼ ◊ Z6　　　　**Deciduous tree**
‡↔ 25ft (8m)

PSEUDOTSUGA MENZIESII
VAR. GLAUCA

The blue Douglas fir is a conical tree with a bluish tinge to its dark green foliage. It makes an imposing specimen tree. The bark is scaly and dark gray, maturing to red-brown. The needlelike leaves are arranged in two ranks along the shoots. Protect from cold winds when young with a screen of plastic, row cover, or burlap. Little pruning is required.

ALSO RECOMMENDED: P. menziesii *has dark green foliage.*

☼ ◊ Z4   **Evergreen tree**

↕ 80–160ft (25–50m) ↔ 20–30ft (6–10m)

PYRUS SALICIFOLIA *'Pendula'*

The silvery gray leaves of the weeping pear are willowlike, and the spring display of small, creamy white flowers is followed by ornamental green pears in autumn. A fine tree that also tolerates pollution and is suitable for a small or urban garden.

ALSO RECOMMENDED: P. calleryana *'Chanticleer' has dark green foliage that reddens in autumn, and brown fruits.* Z5b

☼ ◊ Z5   **Deciduous tree**

↕ 25ft (8m) ↔ 20ft (6m)

SORBUS AUCUPARIA

This mountain ash is a good tree for cold exposed areas and to plant in clumps to make a windbreak. It has a crown of dark green leaves that color to red or yellow in autumn. Flat-headed clusters of white flowers appear in late spring, and these are followed later in the season by orange-red, inedible berries. It is also suitable for a small, urban garden or wildlife area (*see p.494*), and is tolerant of acidic soils (*see p.92*). Prune in winter, if necessary.

ALSO RECOMMENDED: S. aria, *whitebeam, is similar.* Z4

☼ ◑ ◊ Z3　　　　　　**Deciduous tree**

↕ 50ft (15m) ↔ 22ft (7m)

TILIA CORDATA

The littleleaf linden has a reasonably broad crown of rounded, dark green leaves that turn yellow in autumn. With age, the smooth, silvery gray bark becomes fissured and the tree becomes more conical. Grow in groups or as a specimen tree. Suitable for a wildlife garden: the small, fragrant, pale yellow summer flowers are attractive to bees (*see p.494*). Prune badly placed growth in winter.

ALSO RECOMMENDED: T. × euchlora *is rounded and is unaffected by aphids* Z3; T. platyphyllos *is taller with larger leaves.* Z4.

☼ ◑ ◊ *f* Z3　　　　　　**Deciduous tree**

↕ 50ft (15m) ↔ 25ft (8m)

ARCTOSTAPHYLOS × MEDIA
'Wood's Red'

This dwarf, pink-flowered form of the common bearberry is a very low and spreading shrub that may form a mat of small and leathery, dark green leaves. Its flowers appear in summer and are followed in autumn by large, shiny red berries. Suitable as a ground-cover in open windswept areas in sun or partial shade *(see pp.304, 326)*. Tolerant of acidic soils *(see p.92)*.

ALSO RECOMMENDED: *A. uva-ursi is similar but hardier.* Z3

☼ ◑ ◊◊ Z4   **Evergreen shrub**
↕ 4in (10cm) ↔ 20in (50cm)

BERBERIS × STENOPHYLLA
'Corallina Compacta'

While *Berberis stenophylla* is a large, arching shrub, ideal for exposed places as an informal hedge *(see p.138)*, this cultivar of it is tiny, making it suitable for a rock garden. It bears spine-tipped, deep green leaves on arching, spiny stems. Many small, orange-yellow flowers appear in spring, followed by inedible, blue-black berries. Cut back hard after flowering.

ALSO RECOMMENDED: B. thunbergii *is good as hedging* Z4b; B. × ottawensis *is very tough and intruder-proof* Z5.

☼ ◊ Z6b   **Deciduous shrub**
↕↔ 12in (30cm)

CORNUS ALBA *'Kesselringii'*

Red-barked dogwoods are usually grown for the winter effect of their colorful bare young stems, which are blackish purple in this variety. Small clusters of creamy white flowers appear from late spring amid the oval, dark green leaves that turn red and purple in autumn. Plant in clumps by water (*see p.372*), where the winter stems show up well. Cut back hard and fertilize every spring for the best stem color, although this will be at the cost of the flowers.

ALSO RECOMMENDED: *'Sibirica' has bright red shoots; 'Spaethii' has yellow-margined leaves.*

☀ ◊◊ Z2   **Deciduous shrub**
↔ 10ft (3m)

DEUTZIA GRACILIS

A graceful bush whose appearance belies its toughness. It has bright green foliage and bears its slender clusters of starlike, fragrant white flowers from spring to early summer. It has an upright, slightly spreading habit and is suitable for a mixed shrub border. Prune back after flowering.

ALSO RECOMMENDED: D. *'Mont Rose' has purple-pink flowers in early summer* Z6b; D. scabra (see p.150) *is tougher.*

☀ ◊ *f* Z5b   **Deciduous shrub**
↔ 3ft (1m)

LEDUM GROENLANDICUM

Labrador tea makes a rounded, white-flowering bush, a bit like a dwarf rhododendron. At the tips of the wiry, rusty stems in late spring, small flowers are borne in rounded clusters, which contrast with the dark green, aromatic leaves. This is a compact shrub for a cool position and combines well with heathers, since it is also tolerant of acidic soils (*see p.92*). Trim after flowering, if necessary.

☼ ◐ ◊ *f* Z2   **Evergreen shrub**
↕ 36in (90cm) ↔ 4ft (1.2m)

LONICERA TATARICA

This deep green, upright bush with white to pink or red flowers in late spring and early summer looks good in a mixed shrub barrier and can be grown as a hedge (*see p.138*). The tubular flowers absolutely cover the plant, and they are followed by red to deep yellow berries. Trim or prune after flowering.

ALSO RECOMMENDED: *'Hack's Red' has very deep purple-red flowers.*

☼ ◐ ◊ Z2   **Deciduous shrub**
↕ 12ft (4m) ↔ 8ft (2.5m)

MAHONIA AQUIFOLIUM 'Smaragd'

This popular variety of Oregon grape
is a low-growing shrub with stiff and
spiny, dark green leaves. These turn
brownish purple in winter. Large
clusters of bright yellow flowers open
in spring, followed by small, blue-black
berries. Tolerant of full sun only in
reliably moist soil. It can be grown as
a groundcover in shade (*see p.326*)
if sheared close to the ground every
two years.

ALSO RECOMMENDED: *'Apollo' has golden
yellow flowers; the young leaves of 'Orange
Flame' are rusty orange.*

☼ ◑ ◊◊ Z4b   **Evergreen shrub**
↕ 24in (60cm) ↔ 3ft (1m)

PINUS MUGO 'Mops'

This dwarf pine is a small, round bush
with scaly gray bark and thick, upright
branches. The shoots are covered
with long, dark to bright green needles
and the occasional dark brown pine
cone; these take a few years to ripen.
Effective in a large rock garden or,
where space allows, planted in groups.
Very little pruning is required.

ALSO RECOMMENDED: *Tall pines like
P. nigra are very wind tolerant and ideal
for windbreaks if you have the space.* Z4

☼ ◊ Z2b   **Evergreen shrub**
↕ 3ft (1m) ↔ 6ft (2m)

PRUNUS LAUROCERASUS *'Zabeliana'*

This short and spreading cherry laurel is an evergreen shrub with dense, glossy dark green foliage. Abundant spikes of white flowers are borne in spring and often again in autumn. Conical red fruits follow and ripen to black. Plant in groups as a low hedge (*see p.138*) or to cover bare ground (*see p.304*). Prune in late spring or early summer to restrict size. *P. laurocerasus* can be planted as a second line of defense in a windbreak.

ALSO RECOMMENDED: P. laurocerasus *and* P. lusitanica (Z7b) *make good infillers between windbreak trees* (see p.118).

☼ ◊◊ Z7 **Evergreen shrub**
↕ 3ft (1m) ↔ 8ft (2.5m)

ROSA PIMPINELLIFOLIA *'Plena'*

The Scots or burnet rose has a dense, spreading habit with very thorny and prickly stems. It has small, fernlike, dark green foliage, and this is covered with creamy white, double flowers in early summer; purplish black hips follow. The leaves turn to russet brown in autumn. Prune out some older stems after flowering, if necessary. Also good as a hedge or groundcover (*see pp.138, 304*), or in a wildlife garden (*see p.494*). The species is tougher.

ALSO RECOMMENDED: R. rugosa (see p.178).

☼ ◊◊ Z4 **Deciduous shrub**
↕ 3ft (1m) ↔ 4ft (1.2m)

SAMBUCUS NIGRA
'Guincho Purple'

This elder is an upright shrub with dark green leaves that turn black-purple then red in autumn. In early summer, musk-scented flowers are borne in flattened clusters, followed in late summer by small black berries. Elders are ideal to plant around the perimeter of a new garden, because they establish quite quickly. They also tolerate hard pruning in winter. *S. nigra* and *S. racemosa* are particularly good for providing food and shelter in wildlife gardens (*see p.494*).

ALSO RECOMMENDED: S. racemosa *also has some attractive foliage forms.* Z3

☀ ◑ ◊ Z4   **Deciduous shrub**
↕↔ 20ft (6m)

SPIRAEA NIPPONICA
'Snowmound'

This fast-growing and spreading, flowering shrub makes an invaluable contribution to any shrub border. It has arching, reddish green stems that bear neat clusters of densely packed, tiny white flowers in early summer. The foliage is bright green when young and darkens with age. Cut back flowered stems in autumn.

ALSO RECOMMENDED: S. japonica *is bushy with pink or white flowers in late summer.* Z5

☀ ◊ Z3   **Deciduous shrub**
↕↔ 4–8ft (1.2–2.5m)

THUJA OCCIDENTALIS
'*Rheingold*'

This bushy and spreading, slow-growing conifer is valued for its golden foliage, which has a pink tinge when young and turns bronze in winter. Small cones are carried amid the sprays of apple-scented, scalelike leaves. Trim in spring and late summer. Also suitable for hedging (*see p.138*) and for large containers in sun (*see p.412*). Protect from wind when young.

ALSO RECOMMENDED: *'Holmstrup'* makes a dense, cone-shaped shrub to 12ft (4m) tall; T. plicata 'Atrovirens' is the one to choose for a really tough hedge or screen Z5b.

☼ ◊◊ Z3   **Evergreen shrub**
↕ 3–6ft (1–2m) ↔ 10–15ft (3–5m)

ULEX EUROPAEUS

Gorse is a very spiny shrub with rigid, dark green shoots. It is impenetrable, with an upright to rounded shape. Yellow flowers appear sparsely through the year, but the main flush is seen in spring; brown-black seedpods follow. Suitable for a first defense against wind, especially in coastal areas, or as an intruder-proof hedge (*see p.138*). Tolerant of poor, sandy, and acidic soils (*see pp.38, 92*) and hot and dry, sunny sites (*see p.190*). Trim after flowering.

ALSO RECOMMENDED: *'Flore Pleno'* has double flowers and no seedpods, making it better for gardens.

☼ ◊ Z7   **Evergreen shrub**
↕ 8ft (2.5m) ↔ 6ft (2m)

VIBURNUM RHYTIDOPHYLLUM

The leatherleaf viburnum is named for its characteristic thick, dark green, and deeply veined foliage. It grows quickly and is decorated every spring with domed heads of creamy white flowers that form at the ends of the branches. Planted in groups, shiny red, inedible berries often follow, and they darken to black with age. Keep pruning to a minimum. It will tolerate alkaline soils (*see p.64*).

ALSO RECOMMENDED: *V.* lantana, *the wayfaring tree, is deciduous, with white flowers followed by red and black berries.* Z2b

☼ ◑ ◊◑ Z5b   **Evergreen shrub**
↕ 15ft (5m) ↔ 12ft (4m)

ASTER ALPINUS

This spreading, low-growing aster is good for the front of a border, a rock garden, or a wildlife area (*see p.494*). In the first half of summer it bears a mass of daisylike, purplish blue or pinkish purple flowerheads with deep yellow centers. These are borne on upright stems above the deep green leaves. Provide a mulch after cutting back in autumn. Also good for hot, dry sites (*see p.190*).

ALSO RECOMMENDED: *'Dunkle Schöne' (syn. 'Dark Beauty') has deep purple flowers; those of 'White Beauty' are white.*

☼ ◊ Z4   **Perennial**
↕ 10in (25cm) ↔ 18in (45cm)

CORNUS CANADENSIS

The creeping dogwood is a superb groundcover plant for a shady shrub border or woodland garden (*see p.326*) below wind-breaking shrubs and trees. In late spring and early summer, flower clusters with prominent, shining white bracts appear above the oval, bright green leaves, and these are followed by glossy red berries. Also tolerant of acidic soils (*see p.92*).

☀ ◊ Z2   **Perennial**
↕ 6in (15cm) ↔ indefinite

LATHYRUS LATIFOLIUS

The everlasting or perennial pea is a clambering plant that needs support. It bears pink-purple, pealike flowers and is ideal for growing through shrubs or over a bank. Its blooms appear in clusters from summer to early autumn amid the blue-green foliage; the seeds are inedible. Cut back to ground level in spring and pinch out the shoot tips of new spring growth to encourage bushiness. It resents disturbance. Also good for shady walls (*see p.262*).

ALSO RECOMMENDED: *'Rosa Perle'* has pink flowers; those of *'White Pearl'* are white.

☀◐ ◊ Z4   **Perennial**
↕ 6ft (2m) or more

LYSIMACHIA NUMMULARIA *'Aurea'*

Golden creeping Jenny is a rampant and sprawling plant that makes an excellent mat of golden yellow ground-cover (*see pp.304, 326*). The bright yellow summer flowers further enhance the foliage color. It tolerates light foot traffic and permanently moist soils (*see p.372*).

ALSO RECOMMENDED: L. nummularia *has green foliage.*

☼ ◐ ◊ Z4　　　　　　**Perennial**

↕ 2in (5cm) ↔ indefinite

MOLINIA CAERULEA *SUBSP.* ARUNDINACEA

Purple moor grass forms tall tussocks of dark green leaves from which gently arching spikes of purple flowers appear for a long season from spring to autumn on tall, light brown stems. *M. caerulea* is one of the toughest ornamental grasses and forms a fine architectural plant (*see p.472*) for a border or a woodland garden. Clay and acidic to neutral soils are tolerated (*see pp.12, 92*).

ALSO RECOMMENDED: *'Karl Foerster' is similar; 'Sky Racer' has golden foliage.*

☼ ◐ ◊ Z4　　　　　　**Perennial**

↕ 5ft (1.5m) ↔ 16in (40cm)

PHALARIS ARUNDINACEA *VAR*. PICTA

Gardeners' garters is a clump-forming grass with narrow, white-striped, evergreen leaves. Tall plumes of pale green flowers that fade as they mature are borne on upright stems during the first months of summer. It is good as a groundcover (*see p.304*) or in permanently moist soils (*see p.372*), but it can be invasive; lift and divide regularly to control spread. Cut back in early summer to encourage fresh growth.

ALSO RECOMMENDED: *'Feesey' is less invasive and has purple-flushed flowers.*

☼ ◑ ◊ Z3b **Perennial**

‡ 3ft (1m) ↔ indefinite

VERONICA SPICATA *'Rotfuchs'*

This red-flowered speedwell forms mats of hairy leaves. Its upright spikes of starlike flowers emerge from early to late summer. The bright flower display is ideal for a rock garden or a mixed border; choose a site that is sheltered from winter moisture. Most other speedwells have blue flowers. It is also good in coastal gardens (*see p.166*) and alkaline soils (*see p.64*). Sometimes sold as 'Red Fox'.

ALSO RECOMMENDED: *'Heidekind' is a silvery plant with dark pink flowers; subsp.* incana *is also silver with blue flowers.*

☼ ◊ Z3 **Perennial**

‡↔ 12in (30cm)

Plants for Hedges

The main reasons for planting a hedge are to define boundaries within and around the garden and to create a sense of security. By using evergreens, you can create privacy, too. There are also less obvious benefits. Perhaps the most important is wind protection. Unlike solid barriers, such as walls, which create turbulence on their leeward side, a hedge filters wind and slows it down over a distance of up to ten times the height of the hedge. When wind hits a solid barrier, it speeds up as it passes over, creating eddies on the far side.

Hedges are also used to keep children and pets safely inside an area. Planting against a chain-link fence sunk into the ground prevents pets from squeezing through any gaps at the base. Hedges can also be used to frame views or screen unwanted ones and – if prickly plants are chosen – to deter unwanted visitors. There are many types of plants to choose from, for both formal or informal styles, and all

will need to be kept attractive and constrained in height and spread by regular clipping.

CHOOSING A HEDGE

A boundary hedge is one of the garden's most permanent and prominent features. Dark hedges like yew (*see p.144*), for example, form a quiet backcloth to brilliantly colored borders, while flowering and fruiting hedges of mixed native species entice birds and other wildlife into the garden. Choose plants appropriate for your climate, site, and soil, and consider the desired height and spread. Fast-growing species achieve quick results, but they need frequent clipping to keep them in good shape once established. In the long term, slower-growing plants tend to make a denser, lower maintenance feature.

GROWING A HEDGE

Cultivate the site thoroughly before planting, to a width of 24–36in (60–90cm). Space plants 12–24in (30–60cm) apart, giving the more vigorous species the wider spacing.

Early training is vital to form a hedge that is dense at the base. Most evergreens and conifers need little initial pruning. Only remove the leading shoots to give a uniform height. For deciduous species, shorten weak shoots by two-thirds of their length, and strong shoots by up to one-third to encourage bushy growth. Continue to prune until the desired size and shape is established, then clip regularly at the recommended time to keep growth dense and healthy. The hedge should be wider at the base than at the top.

MAINTAINING FERTILITY

Every time you clip a hedge, you remove some of its food reserves. If plants are to maintain good growth, they should be fertilized every few years with a balanced fertilizer in spring or after clipping. Also remember to keep the base of the hedge free from weeds, which will compete for water and nutrients. After weeding, mulch with organic matter in spring to suppress weeds and reduce moisture loss from the soil.

ALNUS INCANA

Gray alder is a large, broad, conical tree with oval, dark green leaves and brown male catkins in winter and early spring. Female catkins, borne on the same plant, develop into small, woody fruits resembling pine cones; these persist for some months. It makes a good boundary hedge for moist sites and should be trimmed in autumn. Tolerant of a wide range of soil conditions including wet sites (*see p.372*). As a tree, it can be grown as a windbreak (*see p.118*).

ALSO RECOMMENDED: *Unclipped, 'Aurea', reaches 30ft (10m) tall and has pale green foliage;* A. glutinosa *is similar* Z4.

☀ ◐ Z4   **Deciduous tree**
‡ 70ft (20m) ↔ 30ft (10m)

CARPINUS BETULUS

Hornbeam makes an excellent medium to tall boundary hedge with a beech-like appearance, although the oval leaves are a duller green and sharply toothed. In autumn, the foliage turns to yellow then brown; if trimmed in late summer, a large proportion of the dead leaves are retained throughout winter and maintain privacy. It does especially well on alkaline soils (*see p.64*). Established hedges tolerate hard pruning if renovation is necessary.

ALSO RECOMMENDED: C. caroliniana, *the American hornbeam, is similar.* Z3b

☀ ◐ ○ Z5   **Deciduous tree**
‡ 80ft (25m) ↔ 70ft (20m)

CORYLUS MAXIMA *'Purpurea'*

This purple-leaved selection of the filbert has larger leaves than the common hazel (*C. avellana*) and also produces edible nuts. Purplish yellow male catkins hang from the branches in early spring. It makes a multistemmed shrub. It can be grown as a formal or informal hedge, which should be lightly trimmed late each summer.

ALSO RECOMMENDED: C. avellana *and* C. maxima *have green leaves that turn yellow in autumn.* Both Z5

☀️◐ ◊ Z5   **Deciduous tree**
‡ 20ft (6m) ↔ 15ft (5m)

CRATAEGUS MONOGYNA

The singleseed hawthorn makes a fine hedge plant that thrives under all but the wettest soil conditions. Its deterrent thorns make it good as a boundary, and it withstands severe and coastal winds (*see pp.118, 166*). The glossy leaves are attractively lobed, and spectacular white flowers appear in late spring to be followed by glossy dark red fruit. Trim hedges at any time but after flowering is best.

ALSO RECOMMENDED: C. × lavallei *is very similar.*

☀️ ◊◔ Z4b   **Deciduous tree**
‡ 30ft (10m) ↔ 25ft (8m)

× CUPRESSOCYPARIS LEYLANDII *'Castlewellan'*

A slower growing, yellow-foliaged form of the notoriously vigorous Leyland cypress, which will grow very quickly to a great height if left untrimmed. It makes an excellent, dense hedge or windbreak (*see p.118*) that tolerates a wide range of soils and situations, but it should not be planted unless it will be regularly trimmed. It will take a great deal of moisture from the soil. Unsuitable for small properties.

ALSO RECOMMENDED: × C. leylandii *is more vigorous with dark green foliage, and it should be planted with great caution.*

☼ ◑ ◊ Z7   **Evergreen tree**
‡ 80ft (25m) ↔ 15ft (5m)

CUPRESSUS MACROCARPA *'Goldcrest'*

This golden yellow-leaved form of the Monterey cypress is a popular conifer for trimming into a formal hedge. It grows quickly and is useful for coastal gardens (*see p.166*). The lemon-scented foliage is best trimmed in late summer. Protect very young plants from cold.

ALSO RECOMMENDED: C. macrocarpa *has bright green foliage;* C. sempervirens *has dark gray-green foliage* Z7b.

☼ ◊ Z7b   **Evergreen tree**
‡ 15ft (5m) ↔ 8ft (2.5m)

FAGUS SYLVATICA

The European beech makes a fine,
medium or tall hedge suitable for a
boundary and is relatively inexpensive.
The leaves are silky-haired and pale
green at first, becoming dark green and
glossy, then golden yellow in autumn.
Like hornbeam, beech hedges will
retain their attractive brown and dried-
out leaves through winter if trimmed in
late summer. Suitable for alkaline soils
(*see p.64*)

ALSO RECOMMENDED: *Atropurpurea
Group, the copper beech, has purple leaves.*

☼◐ ◊ Z6   **Deciduous tree**
↕ 80ft (25m) ↔ 50ft (15m)

LAURUS NOBILIS

The bay laurel has glossy dark green,
aromatic foliage. It is long-lived in
fertile, moist soil and is a fine choice
for hedging and topiary work. The
flowers are insignificant. Trim to shape
with pruners during summer, taking
care not to shred the large, oval
leaves. Specimen plants benefit from
wall protection in exposed areas. Also
useful for containers (*see pp.412, 448*).

ALSO RECOMMENDED: *'Aurea' has
glossy golden yellow leaves.*

☼◐ ◊◊ ƒ Z6   **Evergreen tree**
↕ 40ft (12m) ↔ 30ft (10m)

TAXUS BACCATA

Yew is a well-proven, coniferous hedge plant with small and linear, dark green leaves borne on green shoots. Small red fruits may appear at the end of summer, although these are orten clipped off. All parts of the plant are toxic except for the red, fleshy covering of the seeds. An excellent choice for topiary. It will grow in dry shade (*see p.216*) and tolerates alkaline soils (*see p.64*). It is one of the few conifers that can be cut back hard and recover. Trim in late summer or early autumn.

ALSO RECOMMENDED: T. cuspidata, *the Japanese yew, is hardier.* Z4

☼ ◐ ◊◊ Z6   **Evergreen tree**
↕ 20ft (6m) ↔ 12ft (4m)

THUJA PLICATA *'Stoneham Gold'*

This low-growing variety of western red cedar is amenable to trimming into a low, formal hedge. It has aromatic leaves borne in graceful, hanging sprays that are bright gold when young and become dark green as they age. Grow in any deep, well-drained soil and provide shelter from winds, especially when young. Trimming should be done in spring or preferably late summer.

ALSO RECOMMENDED: T. occidentalis Z3, T. plicata, *and its cultivar 'Atrovirens' are more vigorous and better for tall hedges.*

☼ ◊◊ *f* Z5b   **Evergreen tree**
↕↔ 6ft (2m)

TSUGA CANADENSIS

The Canada hemlock is a fast-growing conifer with glossy green, narrow, needlelike leaves arranged in two ranks along the branch tips. Like other hemlocks it is tolerant of shade, but it will not grow well in alkaline soils. As a hedge, it withstands formal trimming during summer. If allowed to grow, it forms a tall, conical tree.

ALSO RECOMMENDED: *'Jeddeloh' is very compact, to 5ft (1.5m) tall, with bright green foliage;* T. heterophylla, *the western hemlock, will make a tall hedge* Z7.

☼ ◐ ☀ ◊◊ Z4   **Evergreen tree**
‡ 80ft (25m) ↔ 30ft (10m)

ULMUS PARVIFOLIA

The Chinese elm has leathery, glossy green foliage that turns yellow or red in late autumn or early winter. It makes a reliable hedge plant, showing resistance to Dutch elm disease, and should be trimmed in autumn. Untrimmed specimens bear very small red flowers from late summer; green winged fruits follow in late autumn.

ALSO RECOMMENDED: U. pumila *also shows resistance to Dutch elm disease.* Z3

☼ ◐ ◊ Z5   **Deciduous tree**
‡ 60ft (18m) ↔ 25–40ft (8–12m)

AUCUBA JAPONICA

Spotted laurel is a rounded bush that, when planted closely, makes a natural hedge. The leaves are glossy deep green. If a male plant is grown among females, the latter bear bright red berries from late summer into winter. It tolerates most soils and is good in dry shade (*see p.216*) and in containers (*see pp.412, 448*). Trim shoots with pruners in spring to keep the hedge in shape.

ALSO RECOMMENDED: *'Crotonifolia' and 'Gold Dust' are both females with yellow-spotted leaves; 'Crassifolia' is a male with dark green foliage.*

☼ ☀ ◐ ◊ ◖ Z7   **Evergreen shrub**
↕↔ 10ft (3m)

BERBERIS JULIANAE

An evergreen barberry that can be grown as either a formal or informal hedge. The foliage is glossy deep green with strongly spined margins, and small yellow flowers decorate the bush in late spring; black berries follow. Its dense, very spiny growth makes it ideal as a perimeter hedge. Trim in summer; it can be pruned hard for containment.

ALSO RECOMMENDED: B. darwinii *has orange flowers* Z7; B. × stenophylla *has deep yellow flowers* Z6b; B. verruculosa *is similar but about half the size* Z4.

☼ ☀ ◐ ◊ Z6   **Evergreen shrub**
↕↔ 10ft (3m)

BERBERIS THUNBERGII
'Dart's Red Lady'

This dense and very spiny shrub makes an impenetrable boundary hedge with dramatic autumn color when the very dark red-purple foliage turns to bright red. Small, pale yellow flowers are borne in spring, followed by glossy red berries. It can be grown as a formal or informal hedge. Trim after flowering.

ALSO RECOMMENDED: *'Aurea' has bright yellow young foliage; 'Rose Glow' has red-purple, white-flecked leaves and is more tolerant of shade.*

☼ ☀ ◊ Z4b   **Deciduous shrub**
↕ 3ft (1m) or more ↔ 8ft (2.5m)

BRACHYGLOTTIS *'Sunshine'*

This low-growing shrub with white-hairy leaves makes a good low-maintenance screen. It produces an abundance of bright yellow daisy flowers from summer to autumn and is a suitable choice for hedging in seaside gardens (*see p.166*). It grows well as an informal hedge if trimmed in spring, but it can also be pruned back hard, preferably with pruners, at the same time of year for a more formal look. It tolerates hot and dry, sunny sites (*see p.190*).

☼ ◊ Min 35°F (2°C)   **Evergreen shrub**
↕ 5ft (1.5m) ↔ 6ft (2m) or more

BUXUS SEMPERVIRENS

Boxwood is very tolerant of clipping and well proven as hedging, edging, and topiary. The species has small, glossy green leaves. Trim hedges once a year in summer. Clip topiary twice a year from late spring to summer. Encourage new growth with a dressing of fertilizer and a surface mulch. Also good for alkaline soils (*see p.64*) and in shady containers (*see p.448*).

ALSO RECOMMENDED: *'Marginata' is similar; 'Suffruticosa' is slow-growing and ideal for edging; B. microphylla also grows slowly and is best in partial shade Z5.*

☼ ◗ ◊ Z6   **Evergreen shrub**

↕↔ 15ft (5m)

CHAMAECYPARIS PISIFERA 'Boulevard'

This blue-green form of the Sawara cypress is a large, coniferous shrub or tree with dense fans of aromatic, scale-like foliage. It is suitable for training into a formal hedge if trimmed closely from spring to autumn; do not cut into older wood, because it will not resprout. It grows well on acidic to neutral soils (*see p.92*) and tolerates alkaline ones (*see p.64*).

ALSO RECOMMENDED: *'Filifera Aurea' has yellow foliage; C. lawsoniana 'Green Hedger' and 'Pembury Blue' both make reliable hedges Z6.*

☼ ◗ *f* Z4b   **Evergreen shrub**

↕ 30ft (10m) ↔ 15ft (5m)

COTONEASTER LACTEUS

There are many cotoneasters suitable for hedging, and this one is an excellent choice. It has dense growth with tough, dark green leaves, white-felted on the undersides. White flowers are followed by large clusters of brick red berries that persist into winter. It benefits from light trimming in winter to maintain a formal shape.

ALSO RECOMMENDED: C. divaricatus *with pink flowers and good autumn leaf color* Z5; C. franchetii *is similar with pinkish flowers* Z7; C. frigidus (see p.218).

☼◑ ◊ Z7b　　　　**Evergreen shrub**
↕↔ 12ft (4m)

DEUTZIA LONGIFOLIA 'Veitchii'

This spreading shrub with grayish green foliage can be grown as an informal, summer-flowering screen. The deep lilac-pink, starry blooms are carried during the first half of summer at the ends of arching branches. Trim back after flowering. Most deutzias are also suitable for shrub borders.

ALSO RECOMMENDED: D. longifolia *has white flowers.*

☼◑ ◊◊ Z7b　　　　**Deciduous shrub**
↕ 6ft (2m) ↔ 10ft (3m)

DEUTZIA SCABRA

An easily grown and well-tried, upright, summer-flowering, informal hedge plant. Dense, upright clusters of white, sometimes pink-tinged, honey-scented flowers are borne in the first half of summer amid the dark green foliage. The mature shoots have attractively peeling bark. Prune to thin out the older stems immediately after flowering.

ALSO RECOMMENDED: *'Pride of Rochester' has double flowers;* D. gracilis *(see p.128) makes a dwarf hedge.*

☼ ◐◊ *f* Z6   **Deciduous shrub**
‡ 10ft (3m) ↔ 6ft (2m)

ESCALLONIA *'Langleyensis'*

This small-leaved shrub produces abundant clusters of small rose-pink flowers from early summer. It thrives in coastal sites (*see p.166*) as a formal or informal hedge, a windbreak, or in a shrub border. Clip annually for a formal shape in spring. It can rob the surrounding soil of moisture and nutrients.

ALSO RECOMMENDED: *'Donard Seedling'* (see p.173) E. rubra *and its cultivars are excellent hedging subjects* Z7b.

☼ ◊ Z7b   **Evergreen shrub**
‡ 6ft (2m) ↔ 10ft (3m)

EUONYMUS ALATUS

The burning bush makes a dense informal hedge with a spectacular display of foliage and fruits in autumn. At this time, the small, purple and red, poisonous fruits split to reveal orange seeds as the oval, deep green leaves turn to bright scarlet. The flowers are much less significant. Trim lightly after flowering. For the best autumn display, grow in full sun.

ALSO RECOMMENDED: *'Compactus' grows to 3ft (1m) tall; E. fortunei 'Silver Queen'* (see p.219) *and* E. japonicus (Z5b) *are both evergreen.*

☀ ◐ ◊ Z3   **Deciduous shrub**
↕ 6ft (2m) ↔ 10ft (3m)

FORSYTHIA OVATA *'Ottawa'*

This bushy and vigorous plant with finely toothed leaves makes a good flowering hedge of medium height. Its striking, bright yellow flowers bring the garden to life in early spring; they are good for cutting (*see p.524*) and emerge on the bare brown branches before the leaves. Prune or trim after flowering. A reliable shrub that looks good underplanted with spring bulbs. Flowering is less profuse in partial shade and growth is thinner.

ALSO RECOMMENDED: *'Northern Gold' has paler flowers* Z4; F. suspensa (see p.267).

☀ ◐ ◊ Z3   **Deciduous shrub**
↕↔ 10ft (3m)

FUCHSIA *'Riccartonii'*

This fuchsia hybrid is an upright shrub with bronze-tinged, dark green foliage. It carries its characteristic red and purple flowers throughout summer; they are small and delicate and hang like earrings from the graceful branches. A beautiful low to medium hedge that is at its best in mild-climate areas, especially by the ocean (*see p.166*). Prune back hard in spring.

ALSO RECOMMENDED: *'Genii* and *'Mrs. Popple'* are both shorter, about *3ft (1m)* tall; F. magellanica (see p.174).

☼ ◑ ◊◊ Z8   **Deciduous shrub**
‡ 6–10ft (2–3m) ↔ 3–6ft (1–2m)

GRISELINIA LITTORALIS *'Variegata'*

A dense and attractive shrub that carries glossy leaves variegated with irregular creamy white margins and gray-green streaks. It responds well to trimming with pruners in spring, and it thrives in coastal gardens (*see p.166*), where it is one of the quickest hedges to establish. If necessary, cut back hard from time to time to reduce spread.

ALSO RECOMMENDED: G. littoralis *has plain, apple green leaves and makes a more formal, medium to tall hedge.*

☼ ◊ Z8   **Evergreen shrub**
‡ 25ft (8m) ↔ 15ft (5m)

HEBE *'White Gem'*

A rounded, neat shrub that is suitable for low hedging. It has densely packed, deep green leaves and is covered by short spikes of white flowers from early summer. In mild regions, all hebes are worth considering as hedges, doing best on moist soil in full sun; they are good in coastal sites (*see p.166*). They regrow well from older wood – useful when renovating. Each year, prune lightly in spring or after flowering.

ALSO RECOMMENDED: H. albicans (*see p.46*), H. brachysiphon, *and* H. rakaiensis *are similar*; H. salicifolia *forms a taller hedge, to 6ft (2m), with pale blue summer flowers.*

☼ ◐ ◊◊ Min 35°F (2°C) **Evergreen shrub**
↕ 30–39in (75–100cm) ↔ 3ft (1m)

HIPPOPHAE RHAMNOIDES

Sea buckthorn is a spiny shrub with long and narrow, silvery green leaves. It produces tiny yellow-green flowers in spring, with male and female flowers on separate plants; if both are grown, female plants bear small, bright orange berries in autumn, which remain on the bush in winter. Very tolerant of salt-laden winds and also suitable as a windbreak for coastal gardens (*see p.166*). Trim shoots lightly in late summer to maintain a formal shape.

☼ ◊◊ Z2b **Deciduous shrub**
↕↔ 20ft (6m)

HYDRANGEA MACROPHYLLA
'Générale Vicomtesse de Vibraye'

A rounded shrub with large, oval leaves and big, spherical heads of flowers from midsummer. Like most hydrangeas, the flower color is influenced by soil acidity; on acidic soils (*see p.92*) the flowers are pale blue, ranging to pink on more alkaline soils (*see p.64*).
A good ornamental hedge of medium height that needs to be pruned in late autumn. Suitable for coastal sites.

ALSO RECOMMENDED: *'Mariesii Perfecta' (syn. 'Blue Wave') has flat flowerheads; 'Madame Emile Mouillère' has white flowers.*

☼ ◑ ◊ Z6   **Deciduous shrub**

↕ 6ft (2m) ↔ 8ft (2.5m)

ILEX AQUIFOLIUM
'Golden van Tol'

This female holly is fairly slow-growing, but it makes a very good, dense hedge. The yellow-margined leaves have few spines. In informal hedges, plant in an occasional male holly for the red berries, which attract birds (*see p.494*) and often persist into winter. Trim hedges regularly in summer. Also suitable for exposed and coastal sites (*see pp.118, 166*).

ALSO RECOMMENDED: *I. × altaclerensis (Z6) and I. aquifolium make excellent medium to tall formal hedges with plain green leaves; both have many cultivars also suitable for hedging.*

☼ ◑ ◊ Z7   **Evergreen shrub**

↕ 12ft (4m) ↔ 10ft (3m)

LAVANDULA ANGUSTIFOLIA
'Hidcote'

English lavender is compact with aromatic, grayish leaves. It is valued for its dense spikes of fragrant, dark purple midsummer flowers. Lavender does well on a wide range of soils and is ideal as a low hedge or edging. Trim below the flowering spikes in early spring, but do not cut into old wood. Replace hedges when they become woody and straggly. Good for hot and dry sites, as edging for paths and patios, and in wildlife gardens (*see pp.190, 348, 494*).

ALSO RECOMMENDED: *'Loddon Pink' has soft pink flowers;* L. dentata (*see p.200*).

☼ ◊ *f* Z6　　　　**Evergreen shrub**
‡ 24in (60cm) ↔ 30in (75cm)

LIGUSTRUM SINENSE

Privets are widely grown as medium to tall hedges. They are ideal for formal hedging and topiary if repeatedly clipped in summer. This one is tough, fast-growing, and good in well-drained soil. Cut it hard in spring to renovate or restore its shape and to keep the hedge within bounds. Clipping up to three or four times a year is necessary to keep a neat shape and to remove the white, musty-scented flowers. It may shed its leaves in harsh winters.

ALSO RECOMMENDED: *'Variegatum' is best in full sun;* L. lucidum (*see p.194*); L. ovalifolium *and* L. vulgare *are similar* Z5.

☼☀ ◊ Z7　　　　**Evergreen shrub**
‡↔ 12ft (4m)

LONICERA NITIDA
'Baggesen's Gold'

This form of shrubby honeysuckle is a foliage plant with tough shoots and small yellow-green leaves. *L. nitida* is green-leaved and also excellent for hedging. Both grow quickly and must be trimmed hard up to three or four times each summer to avoid a straggly appearance. This tolerance of clipping makes it good for simple topiary. If it becomes unkempt or bare at the base, cut it down to within 6in (15cm) of ground level.

ALSO RECOMMENDED: *'Silver Beauty' has cream-variegated leaves; 'Maigrün' (syn. 'Maygreen') has pale then dark green leaves.*

☼ ◐ ◊ Z7 **Evergreen shrub**
‡ 11ft (3.5m) ↔ 10ft (3m)

PHILADELPHUS CORONARIUS
'Variegatus'

This upright shrub makes a wonderful informal hedge on account of its small bunches of intensely fragrant, pure white, saucer-shaped flowers that are borne in early summer. The leaves are an added attraction with broad white margins. Remove one in four flowered shoots at ground level after flowering.

ALSO RECOMMENDED: *'Aureus' has lime-green to golden leaves that retain their color better in part shade; P. 'Snowbelle' and 'Manteau d'Hermine' (see p.74) are similar, but only half as tall.*

☼ ◐ ◊ *f* Z4 **Deciduous shrub**
‡ 8ft (2.5m) ↔ 6ft (2m)

PHYLLOSTACHYS BAMBUSOIDES *'Allgold'*

The giant timber bamboo has thick and shiny, rich golden yellow canes that can be used to good effect as a screening hedge. The leaves are glossy and dark green with the occasional yellow stripe. Suitable for a woodland garden in dappled shade. It has very vigorous roots, so plant it in a trench lined with concrete slabs (or equivalent) to prevent unwanted spread.

ALSO RECOMMENDED: *P. aurea has brownish yellow canes and golden green leaves Z7; P. nigra has dark green leaves and arching canes that age to black Z7.*

☀️ ◐ ◊◊ Z7   **Evergreen bamboo**
‡ 10–25ft (3–8m) ↔ indefinite

PITTOSPORUM TENUIFOLIUM

A fast-establishing, large shrub that is much valued for its tough, wavy-edged, glossy green leaves. Insignificant flowers appear from late spring. Trim hedges to shape in spring and again in autumn. It is especially good as a windbreak in coastal gardens (*see p.166*). The foliage is good for cutting (*see p.524*).

ALSO RECOMMENDED: *'Irene Paterson' has white-speckled leaves; 'Silver Queen' has grayish leaves with irregular white margins.*

☀️ ◐ ◊◊ Z8   **Evergreen shrub**
‡ 12–30ft (4–10m) ↔ 6–15ft (2–5m)

PONCIRUS TRIFOLIATA

The hardy orange is a formidable, thorny shrub with thick green stems armed with sharp spines. The leaves, made up of three leaflets, are dark green, turning yellow in autumn. Fragrant, cup-shaped white flowers are produced in spring with a second flush in autumn. Orangelike fruits follow. Cut young plants hard to help them establish bushy growth, trimming more established hedges twice in summer.

☼ ◊ *f* Z7   **Deciduous shrub**
↕↔ 15ft (5m)

PRUNUS LUSITANICA *'Variegata'*

This variegated form of Portugal laurel makes a relatively slow-growing but dense hedge with slender spikes of small, fragrant white flowers in early summer. The oval, glossy dark green leaves are narrowly margined with white. Purple berries appear later in the season. Prune to shape with pruners in spring.

ALSO RECOMMENDED: P. laurocerasus (Z7) *and* P. lusitanica *have plain dark green leaves, and both make excellent hedges and windbreaks.*

☼ ◊◊ Z7   **Evergreen shrub**
↕↔ to 70ft (20m)

PRUNUS SPINOSA *'Purpurea'*

Blackthorn is a dense and thorny shrub that makes a good protective barrier and tolerates hard trimming at any time. This red-leaved variety bears small pink flowers in early spring before the leaves appear, followed by very dark blue fruits (sloes). These persist until winter, during which time the foliage has turned purple and fallen.

ALSO RECOMMENDED: P. spinosa, *with green leaves and white flowers, makes a good stockproof hedge for a rural garden;* P. cerasifera *also has green leaves and white flowers, followed by plumlike, red or yellow fruits* Z4.

☼ ◑◔ Z6   **Deciduous shrub**
↕ 15ft (5m) ↔ 12ft (4m)

PYRACANTHA *'Golden Charmer'*

Spiny firethorns are excellent as a barrier hedge, and they attract hungry and nesting birds (*see p.494*). This one has golden yellow autumn berries. Profuse clusters of tiny white flowers appear in early summer against the glossy dark green leaves. Also suitable for clay soils (*see p.12*) and for covering sunny or shady walls (*see pp.262, 280*). Trim in early summer.

ALSO RECOMMENDED: *'Mohave'* (see p.20); *'Soleil d'Or'* (see p.270); *'Teton' has yellow-orange berries; 'Watereri'* (see p.500).

☼◐ ◔ Z7   **Evergreen shrub**
↕↔ 10ft (3m)

RHAPHIOLEPIS UMBELLATA

A dense and slow-growing shrub suitable for hedging. It has tough and toothed, large, deep green leaves. It bears tight clusters of white flowers, which are sometimes tinted pink, in early summer, and they are followed by bronze-black fruits. Trim to shape after flowering. Where marginally hardy, plant it as a specimen in an enclosed garden, protected border, or against a sunny wall (*see p.280*).

ALSO RECOMMENDED: *R. × delacourii grows to 6ft (2m) tall with pink flowers.* Z8

☼ ◊◊ Z8   **Evergreen shrub**
↕↔ 5ft (1.5m)

RHODODENDRON *Blue Diamond Group*

Many evergreen rhododendrons make spectacular hedges on moist but well-drained, acidic to neutral soils (*see p.92*). There is an immense range available, and it may be worth seeking the advice of a nearby nursery for a cultivar that grows well in your locality. The Blue Diamond Group has a compact habit and produce clusters of violet-blue flowers amid the relatively small leaves in late spring.

ALSO RECOMMENDED: *R. 'PJM' is a small evergreen with clusters of mauve flowers and foliage that turns purple in fall.* Z4

☼ ◊◊ Z7   **Evergreen shrub**
↕↔ 5ft (1.5m)

RIBES SANGUINEUM 'Brocklebankii'

This upright shrub is valued for its bright yellow-green, hairy leaves, and it makes an attractive informal hedge. A fine display of deep pink flowers in hanging clusters appears through spring. Flowering currants establish well on most soils; the majority do well in full sun, but this slow-growing form displays better foliage in partial shade, including dry shade (see p.216). Trim after flowering.

ALSO RECOMMENDED: *'King Edward VII' and 'Pulborough Scarlet' have dark red flowers; R. alpinum 'Aureum' (see p.222).*

☼ ◐ ◊ Z6b   **Deciduous shrub**
↕ 4ft (1.2m)

ROSA *Chinatown*

Many roses succeed as hedges, and this one is particularly vigorous, easy to grow, and resistant to disease. Clusters of large and rounded, double yellow flowers are borne from summer to autumn amid the glossy dark green leaves. They are suffused with pink and carry a heavy scent. Prune this shrub rose lightly when dormant, removing some of the oldest stems at the base each year.

ALSO RECOMMENDED: *R. 'Prairie Joy' has dense, upright branches and grows 3–4 ft (1–1.5 m) tall. Flowers are pale pink in early summer Z2; R. rugosa (see p.178).*

☼ ◊◊ ƒ Z6   **Deciduous shrub**
↕ 4ft (1.2m) ↔ 3ft (1m)

ROSMARINUS OFFICINALIS

The upright shoots of rosemary bear narrow and aromatic leaves, useful in cooking. Pale blue flowers appear along the stems in spring and autumn. Informal hedges require minimal pruning; it can be grown formally if clipped once or twice during summer. Otherwise, grow as an edging or in an herb garden. Also suitable for coastal and hot, dry sites (*see pp.166, 190*), and containers (*see p.412*).

ALSO RECOMMENDED: *'Miss Jessopp's Upright' is strong-growing and upright; the flowers of 'Tuscan Blue' are dark blue.*

☼ ◊ *f* Z7　　　　　**Evergreen shrub**
↕↔ 5ft (1.5m)

SALIX PURPUREA

The purple osier is notable for its arching, red-tinged shoots and dark bluish green leaves. Slender, silvery green catkins appear in early spring before the first leaves. Willows will succeed on wet sites (*see p.372*), but never plant them close to drains or building foundations. Cut back to the base each year when dormant for a temporary screen, or allow to grow up as a tall windbreak (*see p.118*).

ALSO RECOMMENDED: *S. alba and its colored-stem forms, such as subsp.* vitellina *and 'Britzensis' (see p.375), are tall and vigorous, good as an external shelter hedges.*

☼ ◊ Z4　　　　　**Deciduous shrub**
↕↔ 15ft (5m)

SANTOLINA CHAMAECYPARISSUS *'Lemon Queen'*

This compact lavender cotton makes a low hedging subject suitable for border edging, with slender, aromatic, grayish leaves. It bears small, button-ike, lemon-yellow flowers from midsummer. Trim after flowering to remove straggly shoots, or before flowering for the best foliage, and cut back hard every few years in spring to rejuvenate. Also good for coastal and hot, dry sites (*see pp.166, 190*).

ALSO RECOMMENDED: *S. chamaecyparissus is just as good; 'Pretty Carol' and 'Small-Ness' are even more compact; S. pinnata 'Sulphurea'* (see p.50).

☼ ◊ Z7   **Evergreen shrub**
↔ 24in (60cm)

SEMIARUNDINARIA FASTUOSA

Narihira bamboo is a very tall and upright bamboo, forming dense clumps of smooth green canes with plum-purple and brown stripes. The glossy foliage is borne mostly at the top of the canes. Where a tall screen is required, this bamboo makes an interesting option. Suitable for woodland gardens. It has vigorous roots, so plant it in a trench lined with concrete slabs (or equivalent) to limit its spread.

☼ ◐ ◊◗ Z7   **Evergreen bamboo**
↕ 22ft (7m) ↔ 6ft (2m) or more

SPIRAEA × VANHOUTTEI

This spirea, often call bridal wreath, makes a bushy, informal flowering hedge with dark green foliage. It bears masses of white flowers along the arching shoots during early summer. After flowering, prune the flowered shoots back to a strong bud, and cut a number of older shoots out at ground level. Good for clay soils and exposed sites (*see pp.12, 118*).

ALSO RECOMMENDED: S. *'Arguta'* is similar Z2b; S. japonica *'Little Princess'* (see p.20); S. nipponica *'Snowmound'* (see p.132).

☼ ◊◑ Z3　　　　　**Deciduous shrub**
‡ 6ft (2m) ↔ 5ft (1.5m)

SYMPHORICARPOS ALBUS *VAR.* LAEVIGATUS

Snowberry is a densely upright, robust shrub with rounded, dark green leaves. It carries tiny pink flowers in summer, followed by eye-catching, pure white berries in autumn. It grows on a wide range of sites but can be invasive, so it is best as a boundary, where it could be included in a mixed hedge. Prune selectively to the base in early spring. Tolerant of urban pollution, exposed sites, and dry shade (*see pp.118, 216*). Attractive to wildlife (*see p.494*).

ALSO RECOMMENDED: S. × doorenbosii *'White Hedge'* (see p.224).

☼◐ ◊ Z3　　　　　**Evergreen shrub**
‡↔ 6ft (2m)

SYRINGA PUBESCENS *'Superba'*

A bushy lilac with glossy dark green leaves that makes a fine informal flowering hedge. Its red-green young shoots ripen through summer to bear conical clusters of fragrant, purple-lilac flowers the following spring. Minimal pruning is required, after flowering if necessary; it tolerates the occasional hard prune to rejuvenate. Tolerant of clay and alkaline soils (*see pp.12, 64*).

ALSO RECOMMENDED: S. patula *'Miss Kim'* is much more compact, to 6ft (2m) tall Z2; S. × persica (see p.75).

☀ ◊◊ *f* Z3   **Deciduous shrub**
↔ 20ft (6m)

TEUCRIUM FRUTICANS

Tree germander is suitable as a low evergreen hedge. The grayish green, aromatic leaves are held on white woolly shoots, and if it is not trimmed in spring, light blue flowers emerge in summer. Prune in spring or trim to a formal shape in summer.

ALSO RECOMMENDED: T. × lucidrys *(syn. T. chamaedrys), wall germander, is hardier with dark green foliage and red, pink, purple, or white flowers, but better as border edging, since it grows to just 24in (60cm) tall Z4; T. polium (see p.352).*

☀ ◊ *f* Z7b   **Evergreen shrub**
↕ 24–39in (60–100cm) ↔ 12ft (4m)

PLANTS FOR COASTAL GARDENS

ON A SUNNY summer's day, with a balmy breeze blowing onshore, it is easy to view the prospect of gardening on the coast with rose-tinted glasses. In reality, many of the plants that grow there must be exceptionally tough to survive. Not only do they often need to contend with winter storms but also with the quantities of damaging salt spray that high winds bring with them (often several miles inland). Nevertheless, the proximity to the ocean moderates overall air temperatures to a degree, and light levels and humidity are often higher than inland. In coastal gardens, many slightly tender plants will thrive when they might otherwise fail in areas even a few miles from the protective effects of the water.

WINDBREAKS FOR SHELTER

The advantages of coastal gardens are magnified if the garden is surrounded by a windbreak to alleviate the worst effects of salt-laden winds (*see also Plants for Exposed*

Sites, p.118). On the coast, it is common to see even notably tough trees like hawthorn (*see pp.123, 141*) and many pines wind-trained into gnarled and stunted – though picturesque – versions of their inland counterparts. Planted as windbreaks, even a relatively low, wind-filtering barrier can provide shelter in its lee for five times its height. With such shelter in place, the range of plants that can be grown is greatly extended.

In a new garden, creating or planting a windbreak should be the first priority. A woven fence made of willow branches, for example, will give temporary shelter until a living windbreak grows tall enough to be useful. A driftwood fence can be effective, since it is attractive and perfectly appropriate to its setting. Although a wall is better than nothing, solid barriers should be avoided, because they create problems; instead of blocking the wind, the wind moves over them them and creates turbulence on the leeward side, which can cause damage.

MARITIME PLANTS

Many of the plants that succeed in coastal sites have special adaptations that enable them to shrug off the worst effects of wind and salt spray. Plants like *Eucalyptus gunnii* (*see p.168*), *Olearia nummularifolia* (*see p.176*), or *Phillyrea latifolia* (*see p.177*) have tough, leathery leaves, while others, like *Anaphalis margaritacea* (*see p.182*), have leaves with a protective covering of fine hair, which limits salt damage and helps conserve moisture. Some, like ground-hugging *Alchemilla conjuncta* (*see p.181*), survive simply by keeping their heads down. You can also be sure that any plant with "littoralis" (meaning "of the shore") or "maritima" in its name – *Griselinia littoralis* (*see p.152*) and *Crambe maritima* (*see p.183*), for example – will be in its element in a coastal garden. Listings of suitable plants often seem limited, but by observing native flora and the successes in other people's gardens, you will find many more, often surprising, survivors.

ACER PSEUDOPLATANUS *'Simon-Louis Frères'*

This compact sycamore maple is a slow-growing, round-headed tree with five-lobed leaves that are pink when young, later turning creamy green with white speckles. It tolerates a range of soils, including clay and alkaline (*see pp.12, 64*), urban pollution, and exposure (*see p.118*). Remove dead or badly placed growth from late autumn to midwinter only.

ALSO RECOMMENDED: *'Brilliantissimum' has bright pink young leaves that age to green; 'Leopoldii' has pink young leaves, later green with yellow and pink speckles.*

☼ ◑ ◊ Z5b   **Deciduous tree**
‡↔ 30ft (10m)

EUCALYPTUS GUNNII

The cider gum is a tall tree with peeling, pale green, gray, and pink bark, and narrow gray-green leaves. If hard-pruned, it produces attractive, rounded, blue-gray juvenile leaves, which are good for cutting (*see p.524*). Grow in neutral to acidic soil (*see p.92*) with shelter from wind. Cut all shoots back to the base or to a short trunk annually in early spring for the best foliage effect.

ALSO RECOMMENDED: E. coccifera, E. globulus, *and* E. pauciflora *subsp.* niphophila *all need pruning to maintain distinctive juvenile foliage (Tender).*

☼ ◊ Z7b   **Evergreen tree**
‡ 30–80ft (10–25m) ↔ 50ft (15m)

POPULUS ALBA

This tough tree makes an excellent windbreak in exposed, coastal gardens (*see p.118*). The silvery white under-sides of its lobed, dark green leaves are revealed as the branches move in the breeze. It tolerates urban pollution and any but waterlogged soils, including dry or alkaline ones (*see pp.64, 190*). It needs little pruning, in winter if necessary. Site at least 100ft (30m) away from drains or foundations.

ALSO RECOMMENDED: *f.* pyramidalis *is pyramidal in shape;* 'Raket' *is smaller and narrowly conical;* 'Richardii' *is smaller, with golden leaves.*

☼ ◊◊ Z2   **Deciduous tree**
↕ 70–130ft (20–40m) ↔ 50ft (15m)

ARGYRANTHEMUM FRUTESCENS

A close relative of the chrysanthemum, this small bush of divided, bright green leaves gives an abundant display of white and yellow, daisylike flowers. Cultivated varieties extend the color range to deep pink and yellow. Where not hardy, it can either be grown as temporary plant in a summer border or grown in a container (*see p.412*), which must be moved under cover in winter.

ALSO RECOMMENDED: A. 'Cornish Gold' *has yellow flowers;* 'Mary Wootton' *has pale pink flowers;* 'Vancouver' *(see p.416).*

☼ ◊ Min 35°F (2°C)   **Evergreen shrub**
↕↔ 28in (70cm)

ATRIPLEX HALIMUS

Tree purslane is a dense and bushy foliage plant with leathery gray leaves. It is very tolerant of coastal or dry and windy situations (*see p.118*), and it is a good choice for a hedge in such areas (*see p.138*). The flowers are of little ornamental value. Lightly trim damaged shoots in early spring. It can also be grown as part of a shrub border.

☼ ◊ Z7b   **Evergreen shrub**
↕ 6ft (2m) ↔ 8ft (2.5m)

BUPLEURUM FRUTICOSUM

This spreading, slender-stemmed shrub has leathery, deep sea green leaves and forms a dense mound that is clothed in rounded heads of tiny yellow flowers from midsummer to autumn. It is a good groundcover (*see p.304*) for a shrub or mixed border, and in cold areas it grows best against a warm, sunny wall (*see p.280*). It tolerates urban pollution. Prune to remove badly placed or damaged shoots in mid- to late spring.

☼ ◊ Z7b   **Evergreen shrub**
↕ 6ft (2m) ↔ 8ft (2.5m)

CASSINIA LEPTOPHYLLA
SUBSP. VAUVILLIERSII

This rounded bush has small, leathery, dark green leaves arranged on white, sticky-hairy shoots. The honey-scented white flowers of midsummer attract bees (*see p.494*). Grow in a shrub border; it associates well with heathers. Trim after flowering to keep the shape compact.

ALSO RECOMMENDED: *The stem and leaf undersides of var.* albida *are silvery white;* subsp. fulvida *has yellow stems and dark green leaves that are yellow beneath.*

☼ ◊ Min 35°F (2°C) **Evergreen shrub**
↕↔ 10ft (3m)

CHAMAEROPS HUMILIS

The dwarf fan palm is a bushy plant, producing several shaggy, fibrous stems from the base. They are topped by broad, blue- or gray-green, fanlike leaves with spiny stalks. Unspectacular flowers appear from spring. Where not hardy, it is best grown in a cool greenhouse or in a sunny container outdoors, which can be moved under cover in winter (*see p.412*).

☼ ◊ Min 45°F (7°C) **Evergreen palm**
↕ 6–10ft (2–3m) ↔ 3–6ft (1–2m)

COLUTEA ARBORESCENS

The bladder senna is a very tough specimen for a shrub or mixed border. It tolerates urban pollution, poor soils, and exposure (*see p.118*), and it thrives on dry, sunny banks (*see p.190*). During summer, above divided, bright green foliage, it bears clusters of yellow, pea-like flowers followed by translucent, bladderlike seedpods. It may be cut back hard in winter or early spring to renovate or keep compact.

ALSO RECOMMENDED: *C. × media has orange-brown flowers* Z5; *C. orientalis has copper-red flowers marked with yellow* Z6.

☼ ◊ Z5   **Deciduous shrub**
↕↔ 10ft (3m)

COROKIA × VIRGATA

This upright bush with glossy dark green foliage is treasured for its small and star-shaped, fragrant yellow flowers and colorful orange or yellow fruits. The blooms are displayed in late spring, and the berries color in autumn. Grow as a specimen plant in a sheltered shrub border or against a warm wall (*see p.280*). Trim after flowering.

ALSO RECOMMENDED: *'Bronze King' has bronze-tinted foliage; 'Yellow Wonder' is vigorous with golden fruit; C. cotoneaster is more tangled, like a cotoneaster* Z7.

☼ ◊ *f* Z7b   **Evergreen shrub**
↕↔ 10ft (3m)

ERICA ARBOREA *VAR.* ALPINA

The tree heath is much larger than other heathers, and this form is shorter than the species. Its upright branches are covered by small, honey-scented white flowers from late winter to spring, and the needlelike leaves are dark green. This specimen plant is good for sandy soils (*see p.38*) and, unlike most heathers, both alkaline and acidic soils (*see pp.64, 92*). Cut young plants back hard in early spring to promote bushiness.

ALSO RECOMMENDED: *'Albert's Gold' has golden foliage but rarely flowers; 'Estrella Gold' bears white flowers above lime green foliage, tipped bright yellow.*

☼ ◊ *f* Z7b   **Evergreen shrub**
‡ 6ft (2m) ↔ 34in (85cm)

ESCALLONIA *'Donard Seedling'*

A compact shrub that carries dense, glossy dark green foliage. During the first half of summer, a profusion of small, pink-flushed white flowers appear on the arching branches. Suitable for a shrub border, it can also be grown as a hedge (*see p.138*) or as a windbreak (*see p.118*). Trim after flowering.

ALSO RECOMMENDED: *'C.F. Ball' carries red flowers; 'Iveyi' bears fragrant, pure white flowers; 'Langleyensis' (see p.150).*

☼ ◊ Z7b   **Evergreen shrub**
‡↔ 8ft (2.5m)

EUPHORBIA MELLIFERA

Honey spurge is an attractive shrub with long and narrow, gentle green leaves. It is named for its rounded, honey-scented brown flowerheads that appear at the ends of the thick shoots in late spring. It forms a grand feature plant for sandy soils and hot, dry sites (*see p.38, 190*). Choose a sheltered position. Prune after flowering, if necessary, but wear gloves, becuase the sap irritates skin.

ALSO RECOMMENDED: *E. characias (see p.482); E. × martinii grows 3ft (1m) tall and wide with spikes of yellow-green, red-eyed flowers from spring to summer Z6.*

☼ ◊ Min 35°F (2°C) **Evergreen shrub**
‡ 6ft (2m) or more ↔ 8ft (2.5m)

FUCHSIA MAGELLANICA

Hardier than most fuchsias, this bears a profusion of hanging, red and purple flowers throughout summer. Useful in mixed borders or against a warm wall (*see p.280*). In colder areas of its hardiness range, the top-growth will die; cut back in spring, and it will regrow from the base. Provide a winter mulch. Good for informal hedging in warmer areas (*see p.138*).

ALSO RECOMMENDED: *var.* molinae *(syn. 'Alba') has very pale pink flowers;* F. 'Riccartonii' (see p.152).

☼ ◑ ◊◊ Z7b **Deciduous shrub**
‡↔ 10ft (3m)

HEBE *'Autumn Glory'*

A small bush that carries a long display of dark purple-blue flowers from midsummer to early winter. They are small and borne in short, dense spikes. The bronze shoots are covered with dark green, red-margined leaves. Useful as hedging and as a groundcover (*see p.138, 304*) if sheltered from winds. No regular pruning is necessary.

ALSO RECOMMENDED: *'Great Orme'* (see p.503); H. cupressoides *'Boughton Dome'* (see p.46).

☀◐ ◊◊ Min 40°F (5°C) **Evergreen shrub**
‡24in (60cm) ↔ 36in (90cm)

JUNIPERUS COMMUNIS *'Compressa'*

This slow-growing, dwarf form of the common juniper forms a dense shrub shaped like a tiny tree, with deep to blue-green, aromatic sprays of foliage. It is suitable for a rock garden. Small berries remain on the plant for three years, ripening from green through cloudy blue to black. Little or no pruning is needed.

ALSO RECOMMENDED: *'Sentinel'* is vigorous, to 1.5m (5ft).

☀◐ ◊ *f*Z4 **Evergreen shrub**
‡32in (80cm) ↔ 18in (45cm)

OLEARIA NUMMULARIIFOLIA

Daisy bush is suitable for shrub borders and informal hedging (*see p.138*). Its golden shoots are clothed in small, round, dark green leaves that are white- to yellow-woolly beneath. The fragrant, white and yellow, daisylike flowers of midsummer attract bees (*see p.494*). It thrives in most fertile, well-drained soils, including alkaline ones (*see p.64*). Shelter from winds and trim in spring; it tolerates hard pruning.

ALSO RECOMMENDED: *O. × haastii is similar,* O. macrodonta *is taller with spiny, hollylike leaves.* Both Min 35°F (2°C)

☼ ◊ *f* Z7b   **Evergreen shrub**
↕↔ 6ft (2m)

OZOTHAMNUS ROSMARINIFOLIUS

A compact shrub with rosemary-like, dark green foliage that is woolly beneath. Fragrant white flowerheads emerge from red buds in early summer, and they are carried in dense clusters at the ends of the upright stems. Suitable for a shrub border. Trim after flowering.

ALSO RECOMMENDED: *'Silver Jubilee' has silvery gray foliage;* O. ledifolius *has scented leaves and yellow-green shoots. (Tender)*

☼ ◊ *f* Min 35°F (2°C)   **Evergreen shrub**
↕ 6–10ft (2–3m) ↔ 5ft (1.5m)

PHILLYREA LATIFOLIA

A dense, rounded shrub or small tree with oval, glossy dark green leaves that make a fine backdrop in a shrub or mixed border. It is also useful for informal hedging (*see p.138*); trim after flowering. In late spring, inconspicuous but very fragrant, greenish white flowers appear, followed by spherical, blue-black fruits. Where marginally hardy, it flowers and fruits more freely against a warm, sunny wall (*see p.280*). Suitable for most well-drained soils. Also sold as *P. media*.

ALSO RECOMMENDED: *P. angustifolia grows to 10ft (3m), with narrower leaves.* Z7b

☼ ☀ ◊ *f* Z7b　　　　**Evergreen shrub**
↕↔ 28ft (9m)

ROMNEYA COULTERI 'White Cloud'

This vigorous tree poppy is actually a small shrub with gray-green foliage and showy white flowers through summer. They are large and sweetly fragrant with a prominent boss of golden yellow stamens. Choose a site sheltered from winds, and provide a deep, dry mulch in winter where marginally hardy. Grow in a border or against a sunny wall (*see p.280*). It spreads quickly once established.

ALSO RECOMMENDED: *The spread of* R. coulteri *is less vigorous.*

☼ ◊ *f* Z8　　　　**Deciduous shrub**
↕ 3–8ft (1–2.5m) ↔ indefinite

ROSA RUGOSA

The Japanese rose or sea tomato is a dense and very prickly shrub that can make a vigorous flowering hedge for cold, exposed areas (*see pp.118, 138*). It is decorative for most of the year, starting with the fragrant, deep pink, yellow-centered flowers from summer to autumn. Tomato-like, orange-red hips follow, and in autumn, the leathery, dark green leaves turn yellow and orange. Suitable for wild areas (*see p.494*). Trim after flowering.

ALSO RECOMMENDED: *'Alba' has white flowers; those of 'Rubra' are purple-red.*

☼ ◊◑ *f* Z2b   **Deciduous shrub**
↕↔ 3–8ft (1–2.5m)

SALIX RETICULATA

This diminutive willow has trailing branches bearing rounded, deeply veined, dark green leaves that are white-hairy beneath. In spring, it bears upright, pink-tipped catkins; these are a useful source of pollen for emerging bumblebees (*see p.494*). Excellent groundcover (*see p.304*) for the front of a border or rock garden. It tolerates poor soils.

ALSO RECOMMENDED: *S. retusa has glossy midgreen leaves and gray catkins Z3; S. serpyllifolia has small, dark green leaves and silky gray-green catkins Z3.*

☼ ◊ Z2   **Deciduous shrub**
↕ 3–4in (8–10cm) ↔ 12in (30cm)

SPARTIUM JUNCEUM

Spanish broom is an upright bush with dark blue-green shoots that are almost leafless. Masses of fragrant, pealike, rich yellow flowers appear at the stem tips from early summer to autumn, followed by brown seedpods. Particularly useful on poor, sandy soils, in hot, dry shrub borders, and against warm, sunny walls (*see pp.38, 190, 280*). Cut young plants back by half in spring to promote bushiness.

☼ ◊◗ *f* Z7b   **Evergreen shrub**
↕↔ 10ft (3m)

TAMARIX RAMOSISSIMA *'Pink Cascade'*

Tamarisks are versatile shrubs bearing billowing branches of feathery foliage. This one produces clouds of pink flowers in summer and autumn, adding to the general effect. It is also suitable as a windbreak hedge in coastal areas (*see pp.118, 138*) but requires shelter from winds if grown inland. It can become straggly if not hard pruned regularly to shape in early spring. Tolerant of sandy soils (*see p.38*).

ALSO RECOMMENDED: T. tetrandra *is shorter and flowers in spring.* Z6

☼ ◊ Z3   **Deciduous shrub**
↕ 24in (60cm) ↔ 3ft (1m)

BILLARDIERA LONGIFLORA

The climbing blueberry is a twining climber with narrow, deep green leaves grown for its pendulous, cream flowers in summer and big, deep purple-blue, edible berries that follow. It tolerates poor, neutral to acidic soils (*see p.92*). Choose a sheltered site, training its wiry stems against a wall (*see pp.262, 280*), over a structure, or into nearby shrubs. If the top growth is damaged, it may regenerate from its robust root system.

☼ ◐ ◊◊ Min 35°F (2°C)   **Climber**
↕ 6–10ft (2–3m)

TROPAEOLUM TUBEROSUM *'Ken Aslet'*

A colorful climber with bright orange-yellow flowers amid lobed, grayish green leaves from midsummer to autumn. It is ideal for growing over a fence, trellis, or nonflowering shrub, and it will trail over a bank or dry wall. Where not hardy, lift the tubers and store them in a frost-free place until the following spring; otherwise, cover them with a dry winter mulch.

ALSO RECOMMENDED: T. majus *'Alaska'* (see p.447).

☼ ◊◊ Min 35°F (2°C)   **Climber**
↕ 6–12ft (2–4m)

AGAPANTHUS *'Blue Giant'*

One of the hardiest of the African blue lilies, this is a useful plant in the late summer border. It is vigorous and forms clumps of strap-shaped leaves. From the center of these clumps emerge thick, upright stems that bear round heads of bell-shaped, bright violet-blue flowers in the second half of summer. Also good for large containers in sun (*see p.412*). Overwinter indoors where tender.

ALSO RECOMMENDED: *'Bressingham White' has pure white flowers.*

☼ ◐ Z7b   **Perennial**

↕ 4ft (1.2m) ↔ 24in (60cm)

ALCHEMILLA CONJUNCTA

This low, spreading plant is valued for its rounded, lobed leaves, which are finely silver-hairy beneath, and for the summer-long display of tiny, yellow-green flowers; deadhead these to prevent self-seeding and for cut flowers (*see p.524*). It makes a restrained groundcover (*see p.304*) in a rock garden or at the front of a border. It also tolerates clay and alkalne soils (*see pp.12, 64*).

ALSO RECOMMENDED: A. alpina (see p.354); A. mollis (see p.311).

☼◑ ◐◖ Z3   **Perennial**

↕ 16in (40cm) ↔ 12in (30cm)

ANAPHALIS MARGARITACEA

A clump-forming, spreading plant that is valued in herbaceous borders for its mounds of gray-green, white-woolly leaves; it makes a good groundcover (*see p.304*). White flowerheads appear in midsummer and autumn; they are excellent for cutting and drying (*see p.524*), and they are favored by bees and butterflies (*see p.494*).

ALSO RECOMMENDED: *A. triplinervis has narrower leaves; 'Sommerschnee' has brilliant white bracts.* Z3

☼ ◐ ◊ Z4   **Perennial**
↕↔ 24in (60cm)

ARMERIA MARITIMA 'Vindictive'

Sea thrift is a natural seaside plant, and it forms mounds of vary narrow, dark green leaves. This variety has hemispherical heads of dark crimson flowers borne on the tips of stiff stems from late spring to summer. It is ideal for a rock garden, trough, or border front. It tolerates sandy soils and hot, dry sites (*see p.38, 190*), and the flowers attract bees and butterflies (*see p.494*).

ALSO RECOMMENDED: *'Alba' has small white flowerheads; 'Bloodstone' has dark, blood red flowerheads.*

☼ ◊ Z4   **Perennial**
↕ 8in (20cm) ↔ 12in (30cm)

CICHORIUM INTYBUS

A familiar roadside plant in much of the
country, chicory is a clump-forming
plant with lance-shaped, basal leaves
and leafy stems bearing clear blue,
dandelion-like flowerheads in summer;
they are attractive to bees (see p.494).
Grow in a herbaceous border, in an
herb garden, or naturalize in grass.
It tolerates alkaline soils (see p.64).
Removed spent flowerheads to prevent
excessive self-seeding.

ALSO RECOMMENDED: *f. album has white
flowers; 'Roseum' has pink flowers.*

☼ ◊ Z4   **Perennial**

‡ 4ft (1.2m) ↔ 24in (60cm)

CRAMBE MARITIMA

Sea kale forms a sculptural mound of
twisted, irregularly cut, waxy blue-green
leaves. They die back after flowering,
so associate with other, more arching
plants to disguise any gaps. Thick
shoots arise in early summer, bearing
dense heads of small, honey-scented
white flowers that attract bees (see
p.494). It tolerates poor, gravelly or
sandy soils, and hot, dry sites (see pp.38,
190). Grow in a herbaceous border,
or as a specimen in a gravel garden.

ALSO RECOMMENDED: *C. cordifolia
is much taller (see p.53).*

☼ ◊ Z6   **Perennial**

‡ 30in (75cm) ↔ 24in (60cm)

CROCOSMIA *'Lucifer'*

This dazzling, deep red crocosmia makes a fabulous midsummer display when its spikes of upward-facing flowers arch over the fans of bright green leaves. It is particularly effective at the edge of a shrub border or by a pondl, and the flowers are good for cutting (*see p.524*). 'Lucifer' is a little hardier than other crocosmias. Plant corms in spring, and cover with a dry mulch in winter.

ALSO RECOMMENDED: C. × crocosmiiflora *'Emily McKenzie' has bright orange flowers; 'Lady Hamilton' has golden flowers Z6; 'Star of the East'* (see p.533).

☼ ◐ ◊◊ Z5   **Perennial corm**

↕ 3–4ft (1–1.2m) ↔ 3in (8cm)

DRABA MOLLISSIMA

This compact, rosette-forming evergreen forms a dense hummock of hairy and narrow, gray-green leaves. They are almost obscured in late spring by the tiny, cross-shaped, bright yellow flowers. It must have gritty, very sharply drained soil and will grow in gravel or on top of a dry stone wall (*see p.348*). Where winters are wet, it is best to confine it to an alpine house; outdoors, protect it with an open-ended cover.

ALSO RECOMMENDED: D. aizoides *forms slightly larger mounds of bristly, dark green leaves;* D. dedeana *has white flowers flushed pale violet at the base.* Z4

☼ ◊ Z4   **Perennial**

↕ 3in (8cm) ↔ 8in (20cm)

EPILOBIUM GLABELLUM

This semi-evergreen plant forms low mats of small and bronzed, dark green leaves. In summer, it bears branching spikes of creamy white or pink flowers. A good groundcover plant (*see pp.304, 326*) for a rock garden or damp, shady border (*see p.238*). It tolerates sun where soils are reliably moist, preferring some midday shade.

ALSO RECOMMENDED: '*Sulphureum*' *has pale yellow flowers;* E. crassum *has pink-veined white flowers.*

☀ ◐ ◊◊◊ Z5b   **Perennial**
↔ 8in (20cm)

ERIGERON '*Quakeress*'

This robust fleabane is popular for its lavish displays of daisylike flowers during the first part of summer. They are pinkish white with yellow centers and appear in clusters above the clumps of grayish green leaves. Good in a border, and the flowers are ideal for cutting if picked when fully open (*see p.524*).

ALSO RECOMMENDED: '*Dunkelste Aller*' (*syn.* '*Darkest of All*') *has dark violet, yellow-centered flowers.*

☀ ◊ Z4   **Perennial**
↕ 24in (60cm) ↔ 18in (45cm)

ERYNGIUM × OLIVERIANUM

This sea holly is a striking plant when naturalized in gravel or in a sunny, well-drained herbaceous border. In summer and autumn, branched flower stems rise above a mound of leathery, blue-green leaves armed with triangular teeth. The flower stems, which cut and dry well (*see p.524*), are topped by rounded flowerheads with ruffs of spiny, gray-blue bracts. It tolerates sandy and alkaline soils (*see pp.38, 64*) and hot, dry sites (*see p.190*).

ALSO RECOMMENDED: E. alpinum *has steely blue flowerheads* Z4; E. giganteum (see p.535); E. × tripartitum (see p.56).

☀ ◊ Z5 **Perennial**
‡ 36in (90cm) ↔ 18in (45cm)

GLAUCIUM FLAVUM

The yellow-flowered horned poppy produces a rosette of divided, blue-green leaves and branched stems of poppylike flowers in summer. The long, horned seedpods that follow are decorative if cut and dried (*see p.524*). Good for a sunny border or gravel garden; it tolerates hot, dry sites (*see p.190*). Often grown as a biennial that may self-seed once established.

ALSO RECOMMENDED: G. corniculatum *has red flowers with a black spot at the base* Z6; G. grandiflorum *has orange or crimson flowers* Z6.

☀ ◊ Z6 **Perennial**
‡ 12–36in (30–90cm) ↔ 18in (45cm)

KNIPHOFIA *'Percy's Pride'*

This red-hot poker bears tall, dense spikes of creamy yellow flowers in late summer and autumn above clumps of arching, grasslike leaves. The flowers attract bees (*see p.494*) and are good for cutting (*see p.524*). Grow in a herbaceous border, and mulch in the first winter (routinely where marginally hardy). Divide overcrowded clumps in late spring. It also tolerates sandy and alkaline soils (*see pp.38, 64*).

ALSO RECOMMENDED: *'Bees' Sunset' has orange flowers; 'Green Jade' has pale green flowers; 'Little Maid' is smaller with ivory flowers; 'Royal Standard' (see p.536).*

☼ ◐ ◊◊ Z6   **Perennial**
↕ 4ft (1.2m) ↔ 24in (60cm)

LYCHNIS FLOS-JOVIS

Flower of Jove forms a mat of gray-green leaves and a long display of pink, white, or scarlet flowers in summer. It is good as a groundcover on hot, dry sites (*see pp.304, 190*) and ideal for a gravel garden or the front of a mixed or herbaceous border. It thrives in most well-drained sites, including poor, sandy, alkaline, or acidic soils (*see pp.38, 64, 92*). The seeds may self-sow.

ALSO RECOMMENDED: *'Hort's Variety' is compact with clear pink flowers; 'Nana' is even more compact; L. coronaria is taller (see p.318).*

☼ ◊ Z4   **Perennial**
↕ 8–24in (20–60cm) ↔ 18in (45cm)

OSTEOSPERMUM JUCUNDUM

Also known as *O. barberae*, this perennial is famous for its striking, mauve-pink, daisylike flowers that give a long display from late spring until autumn. The grayish leaves form clumps at ground level. An excellent plant for wall crevices or at the front a border. Remove dead flowers to promote flowering.

ALSO RECOMMENDED: *'Blackthorn Seedling' has dark purple flowers.*

☼ ◊ Min 40°F (5°C)   **Perennial**
↕ 4–20in (10–50cm) ↔ 20–39in (50–100cm)

PHORMIUM *'Dazzler'*

New Zealand flax is a striking plant with its spiky clumps of tough, evergreen leaves. In this variety, they are bronze with pink, red, and orange stripes. Dusky red flowers appear in summer on thick, upright spikes that form seedheads for winter ornament. Where marginally hardy, choose a sheltered site and mulch deeply in autumn. It also makes a good architectural plant (*see p.472*).

ALSO RECOMMENDED: *'Yellow Wave' has yellow-green leaves;* P. tenax *Purpureum Group has deep copper-purple foliage* Z8.

☼ ◊◗ Z8   **Perennial**
↕ 3ft (1m) ↔ 4ft (1.2m)

PHYSOSTEGIA VIRGINIANA
'Variegata'

This variegated form of obedient plant
forms an erect clump of long, narrow
green leaves margined with white. The
hooded, magenta-pink flowers, which
appear from summer to autumn, are
good for cutting (*see p.524*); they
remain in a new position if moved on
the stalks, hence the common name.
Grow in a mixed or herbaceous border.

ALSO RECOMMENDED: *P. virginiana has
deep purple to bright lilac-pink flowers;
'Summer Snow' has white flowers;
'Vivid' has bright purple-pink flowers.*

☼ ◐ ◊ Z3b   **Perennial**
‡ 4ft (1.2m) ↔ 24in (60cm)

POTENTILLA
'Gibson's Scarlet'

An attractive flowering perennial that
should be used to add a bit of bold
color to a herbaceous border or
rock garden in summer. It forms dense
clumps of soft green, strawberry-like
foliage, covered by very bright scarlet
flowers in succession from early to late
summer. Tolerant of hot and dry, sunny
sites (*see p.190*).

ALSO RECOMMENDED: *'Monsieur
Rouillard' has deep red flowers with yellow
marks; 'William Rollison' has orange-red,
semidouble flowers.*

☼ ◊ Z3b   **Perennial**
‡ 18in (45cm) ↔ 24in (60cm)

PLANTS FOR HOT & DRY SITES

Y OU MAY FIND that there are several sites in your garden where conditions get very hot and dry during summer. For example, steeply sloping, sunny banks where drainage is rapid, the base of sunny walls that are in a rain shadow, and virtually any sunny site, protected from the worst effects of wind and rain by surrounding walls and fences, where the soil is very sandy, stony, or shallow and alkaline. All of these can prove difficult for any plant that is not adapted to cope. Hot, dry sites present a challenge to plant survival, not only because of the obvious lack of moisture needed for growth, but also because the leaves of many plants – even some committed sun-lovers – scorch in very hot sun, particularly where the water supply is short or unreliable.

PRACTICAL PLANTS

Many of the plants that will thrive in these conditions have characteristic features, which are as beautiful as they are practical. Gray- or silver-leaved

plants like *Senecio viravira* (*see p.202*), and blue-leaved ones like *Leymus arenarius* (*see p.211*), are clothed in fine hair or have a waxy surface bloom to deflect the burning rays of the sun. Plants with fragrant foliage, such as lavender (*see pp.47, 155, 200*), rosemary (*see p.162*), hyssop (*see p.504*), and *Phlomis purpurea* (*see p.201*), exude volatile oils that form a haze around the plant and act as an aromatic "sun-block." Then there are succulent species of low, neat habit, like sempervivums (*see pp.323, 370, 438*) and sedums (*see pp.323, 369, 370, 520*), whose thick, fleshy leaves store water to prevent dehydration. Many bulbs, such as *Amaryllis belladonna* (*see p.204*), demand a summer baking to enable their bulbs to mature so they can flower freely.

IMPROVING THE SITE

In exceptionally dry, free-draining soils, it is a good idea to incorporate some organic matter to aid water retention. Leaf mold is an excellent form of organic matter for such sites, because it does not add too many nutrients; compost is also good. However, many heat- and sun-loving plants perform best on soils that are not too fertile. High nutrient levels can produce soft, sappy growth that is more susceptible to damage by cold and moisture in winter, and it may induce plants to produce leafy growth at the expense of flowers.

A mulch of water-worn pebbles or gravel enhances this style of planting, forming beautiful tonal and textural contrasts, especially with gray-leaved plants. It also helps suppress weeds and conserve soil moisture. As the soil water evaporates, it condenses on the cooler undersides of the stones and is recycled back into the soil. At the same time, it keeps the roots cool and the vulnerable crown of the plants clear of accumulated moisture, which helps prevent rot. Crushed shells, a by-product of the shellfish industry, have a similar effect, and they are perfectly in keeping when used in coastal gardens.

CLADRASTIS KENTUKEA

Also sold as *C. lutea*, yellowwood has a spreading crown of large, divided, light green leaves that turn yellow in autumn. Hanging clusters of pealike, scented white flowers emerge in early summer. A fine specimen tree for larger gardens, needing shelter from strong winds because the wood is brittle. Prune after flowering or in winter when dormant to remove dead or badly placed growth only. It tolerates alkaline soils (*see p.64*).

☼ ◊ *f* Z4b   **Deciduous tree**
‡ 40ft (12m) ↔ 30ft (10m)

EUCALYPTUS DALRYMPLEANA

The columnar crown and creamy white bark of the mountain gum make it a fine specimen for larger gardens. It can be pruned hard each year to produce oval, blue-green juvenile leaves, which are valued by flower arrangers (*see p.524*); if unpruned, it bears narrow, bright green adult leaves. Choose a site sheltered from winds. It tolerates alkaline soils and coastal conditions (*see pp.64, 166*).

ALSO RECOMMENDED: *E. parvifolia has gray and white bark; E. perriniana has gray, yellow, green, and bronze bark. (Both tender)*

☼ ◊ Min 40°F (5°C)   **Evergreen tree**
‡ 70ft (20m) ↔ 25ft (8m)

FICUS CARICA

The common fig, with its spreading crown of large, lobed leaves, makes a very ornamental specimen. It is most productive of ripe, juicy figs if grown in a sheltered, sunny site with the roots confined in not-too-fertile soil or in large containers (*see p.412*). In areas with cool summers, train against a south-facing wall (*see p.280*). Remove wayward or crossing shoots in late winter.

ALSO RECOMMENDED: *'Brown Turkey', 'Brunswick', and 'White Marseilles' are the best cultivars for cooler climates.*

☼ ◊ Z6b   **Deciduous tree**
↕ 10ft (3m) ↔ 12ft (4m)

GLEDITSIA TRIACANTHOS 'Rubylace'

The divided leaves of this elegant, broadly conical tree are rich bronze-red on emergence, turning later to bronze-green, and borne on a canopy that is light enough to permit underplanting. Tolerant of urban pollution Prune from late summer to midwinter only to cut out diseased, damaged, or dead wood.

ALSO RECOMMENDED: *G. triacanthos has dark green leaves that yellow in autumn; 'Sunburst', to 40ft (12m), has gold foliage.*

☼ ◊ Z4   **Deciduous tree**
↕ 100ft (30m) ↔ 70ft (20m)

LIGUSTRUM LUCIDUM

Chinese privet is a small and conical, shrubby tree with lustrous, dark green leaves and open clusters of white flowers in late summer and autumn, followed by small, egg-shaped, blue-black fruits. A shapely specimen, good for a shrub border or for hedging (*see p.138*). Remove unwanted growth in winter; clip hedges twice in summer.

ALSO RECOMMENDED: *'Excelsum Superbum' has yellow-margined leaves; 'Tricolor' has green and grayish leaves with white margins, pink-flushed when young.*

☼ ◑ ◊ Z8　　　　**Evergreen tree**
↕↔ 30ft (10m)

MAACKIA AMURENSIS

An open, spreading tree with a crown of divided, dark green leaves. In late summer it produces upright clusters of white flowers, flushed palest slate-blue; it flowers even when young. An unusual specimen that is most easily grown as a multistemmed tree. Remove dead, diseased, or damaged growth between autumn and early spring. Grow in neutral to acidic soil (*see p.92*)

ALSO RECOMMENDED: *M. chinensis has bluish young shoots and leaves that have a dense, silver-silky down in spring.* Z6

☼ ◊ Z3　　　　**Deciduous tree**
↕ 50ft (15m) ↔ 30ft (10m)

PINUS ARISTATA

One of the most distinctive of small, slow-growing pines, the branches of the bristlecone pine are densely clothed in bright green, needlelike leaves, speckled with white resin. Egg-shaped brown cones have a bristlelike prickle on each scale, hence the common name. It tolerates exposed sites (*see p.118*) and grows best on neutral to acidic soils (*see p.92*). An attractive specimen that may be used as a low windbreak. It rarely needs pruning.

ALSO RECOMMENDED: P. mugo *is smaller, with dense, dark green leaves* Z2b; P. pumila *'Glauca' has gray-blue leaves* Z2.

☼ ◊ Z3   **Evergreen tree**
‡ 30ft (10m) ↔ 20ft (6m)

QUERCUS CANARIENSIS

Algerian oak is a vigorous, broadly columnar tree with rugged black bark; it makes a fine specimen for larger gardens. Lobed, glossy bright green leaves turn yellow before falling, often remaining on the tree until midwinter. In autumn, acorns are borne in scaly cups. It tolerates clay and alkaline soils (*see pp.12, 64*) and is best in deep, fertile soils. Little pruning is needed; cut out crossing or badly placed shoots in winter, if necessary.

ALSO RECOMMENDED: Q. ilex, *the holm oak, is evergreen* Z7b; Q. macranthera *has large, deeply lobed leaves* Z7.

☼ ◊ Z7b   **Deciduous tree**
‡ 100ft (30m) ↔ 50ft (15m)

SOPHORA JAPONICA

The Japanese pagoda tree forms a wide-spreading crown of finely divided, fresh green leaves that turn yellow in autumn. At maturity, it bears hanging clusters of pealike white flowers. Grow as a specimen tree and prune in winter only to remove dead, diseased, or damaged wood.

ALSO RECOMMENDED: *'Regent' starts to flower at a relatively young age.*

☼ ◊ Z6   **Deciduous tree**

↕ 100ft (30m) ↔ 70ft (20m)

UMBELLULARIA CALIFORNICA

California laurel is a low-branching and rounded tree with aromatic, glossy bright green leaves. It flowers most freely in a warm site with shelter from winds; the waxy, creamy green flowers appear in late winter and early spring, followed by egg-shaped purple berries. An attractive specimen for any well-drained soil. Keep pruning to a minimum, since the aromatic oils released when the branches are cut can cause severe headaches.

☼ ◊ Z8   **Evergreen tree**

↕ 60ft (18m) ↔ 40ft (12m)

CARAGANA ARBORESCENS *'Nana'*

This dwarf pea tree has a dense and curiously twisted habit with divided, bright green leaves in congested clusters on thorny stems. The pealike yellow flowers appear in late spring. Plant in a shrub border or as a low hedge (*see p.138*). It needs little or no pruning, but if necessary, prune in winter. It will grow in exposed positions (*see p.118*).

ALSO RECOMMENDED: *C. arborescens reaches 20ft (6m) tall; 'Lorbergii' is also tall, with narrower leaflets; 'Pendula' is a small and weeping form.*

☼ ◊ Z2   **Deciduous shrub**
‡ 5ft (1.5m) ↔ 3ft (1m)

CISTUS × ARGENTEUS *'Peggy Sammons'*

A rounded, bushy rock rose with gray-green leaves and profuse clusters of pale purplish pink flowers in summer. Good for sunny banks or borders, or large rock gardens, and it will also grow in a container (*see p.412*). Tolerant of alkaline soils and coastal gardens (*see pp.64, 166*). To keep it compact, trim lightly after flowering. Where marginally hardy, grow at the base of a warm, sunny wall (*see p.280*).

ALSO RECOMMENDED: *C. × purpureus has deep pink flowers Z7b; C. 'Silver Pink' has silvery pink flowers with paler centers Z7b.*

☼ ◊ Min 35°F (2°C)   **Evergreen shrub**
↔ 3ft (1m)

CYTISUS MULTIFLORUS

Portuguese broom is an upright shrub with narrow, simple or divided, dark green leaves. It bears clusters of pea-like white flowers along the length of the stems in spring and early summer. Grow in a shrub or mixed border in well-drained soil. Trim lightly after flowering; do not cut into old wood. Tolerates poor, acidic soils and coastal conditions (*see pp.92, 166*).

ALSO RECOMMENDED: *C. 'Hollandia' has cream and dark pink flowers; 'Zeelandia' has cream and lilac-pink flowers – both reach 5ft (1.5m) tall by as much across.* Z6

☼ ◊ Z7b　　　　　　**Deciduous shrub**
‡ 10ft (3m) ↔ 8ft (2.5m)

ERINACEA ANTHYLLIS

Hedgehog broom forms a slow-growing mound of hard, spine-tipped, intricately branched stems clothed in small, dark green, divided leaves. In late spring and early summer, the bush is covered in pealike, violet-blue flowers. This long-lived plant is ideal for a rock garden or scree bed or for clothing a dry, sunny bank; it needs gritty, very well-drained soil. It is especially effective when cascading over the edge of a raised bed.

☼ ◊ Z7b　　　　　　**Evergreen shrub**
‡ 12in (30cm) ↔ 3ft (1m)

EURYOPS PECTINATUS

This vigorous shrub with upright shoots bears daisylike, bright yellow flowers against the deeply divided, gray-hairy foliage from early summer and into autumn. Keep it above freezing and water sparingly in winter, and it may continue to flower. Trim lightly after flowering. In a container in sun (*see p.412*), it can be moved under cover during winter.

ALSO RECOMMENDED: E. acraeus *is hardier* (see p.350).

☀ ◊ Min 40°F (5°C) **Evergreen shrub**
↕↔ 3ft (1m)

GENISTA AETNENSIS

From midsummer, the weeping, rush-like branches of the Mount Etna broom are wreathed in fragrant, bright yellow pea flowers. A fine, large specimen shrub or tree for a sunny bank or lawn. It does best in poor, light and sandy, well-drained soils (*see p.38*). Too much pruning can spoil its weeping habit, and do not cut into old wood. A good architectural plant that will also grow in coastal gardens (*see pp.166, 472*).

ALSO RECOMMENDED: G. hispanica *is spiny* (see p.307); G. lydia *is short, to v24in (60cm) tall, with yellow early summer flowers* Z3b.

☀ ◊ *f* Z7 **Deciduous shrub**
↕↔ 25ft (8m)

Grevillea *'Canberra Gem'*

A spreading bush with narrow, spine-tipped, dark green leaves that are silky-hairy beneath. The waxy, pinkish red flowers appear between late winter and late summer in spidery clusters. Grow in well-drained, neutral to acidic soil (*see p.92*); it tolerates sandy sites (*see p.38*). Where marginally hardy, grow against a warm, sheltered wall (*see p.280*). Prune out dead or damaged wood in spring.

ALSO RECOMMENDED: G. rosmarinifolia *has cream, pink, or red flowers.* G. juniperina *f.* sulphurea *has yellow flowers. (Both tender)*

☼ ◊ Min 35°F (2°C)   **Evergreen shrub**
↕ 6–12ft (2–4m) ↔ 6–15ft (2–5m)

Lavandula dentata

This lavender is a fragrant shrub with dense spikes of mauve-blue, late summer flowers topped by purple bracts. It is suitable for most garden positions, and the soft, grayish foliage makes it particularly useful as an edging plant to lessen the harsh lines of paving (*see pp.138, 348*). Also good for cutting and drying (*see p.524*) or in sunny containers (*see p.412*). Grow against a warm wall where marginally hardy (*see p.280*).

ALSO RECOMMENDED: L. lanata *is shorter with dark purple flowers;* L. viridis *has white flowers and pale green leaves. (Both tender)*

☼ ◊ *f* Z8   **Evergreen shrub**
↕ 3ft (1m) ↔ 5ft (1.5m)

PHLOMIS PURPUREA

This compact and upright shrub with leathery leaves on white-woolly shoots bears showy whorls of hooded, purple to pink flowers in summer. It is very effective when massed in a sunny border; where marginally hardy, grow it against a warm, sunny wall (*see p.280*). Tolerant of poor, sandy, and alkaline soils (*see pp.38, 64*). Prune back any weak or leggy stems in spring.

ALSO RECOMMENDED: P. fruticosa (*see p.49*); P. cashmeriana *has yellowish, gray-green leaves and lilac-purple flowers* Z8.

☼ ◊ Min 35°F (2°C)   **Evergreen shrub**

↕↔ 24in (60cm)

RUTA GRAVEOLENS
'Jackman's Blue'

Common rue forms a rounded bush of aromatic and decorative, grayish blue-green, lacelike leaves. Clusters of cup-shaped, yellow-green flowers are borne in summer; they are good for cutting (*see p.524*), although contact in sunshine with the pungent oil in the foliage may produce a painful, weeping rash. Ideal for a herbaceous or mixed border. Prune in spring or after flowering.

ALSO RECOMMENDED: R. graveolens *is less compact and the foliage less blue.*

☼☼ ◊ Z5   **Evergreen shrub**

↕↔ 24in (60cm)

SENECIO VIRAVIRA

The finely divided leaves of this shrubby plant lend striking foliage contrasts in a sunny border; they are bright, velvety, and silver-white. Many gardeners prefer to remove the pale yellow flowerheads that appear from summer to autumn; trim lightly in early spring for the best foliage effects. It must have well-drained soil.

ALSO RECOMMENDED: S. cineraria *'Silver Dust'* (see p.425).

☀ ◊ Z8   **Evergreen shrub**
↕ 24in (60cm) ↔ 3ft (1m)

XANTHOCERAS SORBIFOLIUM

The thick shoots of yellowhorn bear finely divided, glossy dark green leaves that emerge in spring with the upright spikes of star-shaped white flowers. Good as a free-standing specimen or in a shrub border. Prune in winter only to remove damaged or badly placed shoots.

☀ ◊ Z4b   **Deciduous shrub**
↕ 12ft (4m) ↔ 10ft (3m)

ALLIUM CERNUUM

The nodding onion is one of many
alliums that thrive in hot, dry sites.
In summer, above a sheaf of narrow
leaves, stiff stems appear bearing
clusters of bell-shaped, mid- to deep
pink flowers. Grouped together in
a mixed or herbaceous border, they
look especially lovely alongside gray-
leaved plants. Plant bulbs in sandy
soil in autumn (*see p.38*). Tolerant of
coastal conditions (*see p.166*).

ALSO RECOMMENDED: A. caeruleum *has
round heads of bright blue, starry flowers*
Z2; A. carinatum *subsp.* pulchellum *has rich
purple, bell-shaped flowers* Z3.

☼ ◊ Z3   **Perennial bulb**
↕ 12–24in (30–60cm) ↔ 2in (5cm)

ALLIUM FLAVUM

This yellow-flowered onion, ideal
for the front of a border, produces
its loosely rounded flowerheads atop
upright stems in summer. As they open,
the flowers bend down toward the
narrow, grayish leaves below. Plant
bulbs in autumn, preferably in sandy
soil (*see p.38*). Tolerant of coastal
conditions (*see p.166*).

ALSO RECOMMENDED: A. karataviense
*has round heads of pale pink flowers in
summer* Z4; A. schoenoprasum (see p.510).

☼ ◊ Z4   **Perennial bulb**
↕ 4–14in (10–35cm) ↔ 2in (5cm)

AMARYLLIS BELLADONNA

The fragrant, funnel-shaped pink blooms of this autumn-flowering plant appear atop thick, purple-flushed stems before the strap-shaped leaves. It is suitable for herbaceous or mixed borders; where marginally hardy, grow at the base of a warm, sunny wall (*see p.280*). Provide some protection from cold and excessive rain in winter and when the plant is dormant. Plant bulbs just below the soil surface in late spring or summer in well-drained soil.

☀ ◊ *f* Z7   **Perennial bulb**
‡ 30in (75cm) ↔ 4in (10cm)

AMSONIA ORIENTALIS

The upright stems of this clump-forming plant carry willowlike, gray-green leaves. In early and midsummer, delicate clusters of many tiny, starry, violet-blue flowers appear. Grow at the front of a mixed or herbaceous border in well-drained soil; incorporating well-rotted organic matter to improve moisture retention will aid growth in very dry soils.

ALSO RECOMMENDED: A. tabernaemontana *is taller with pale blue flowers.* Z4

☀ ◊ Z4   **Perennial**
‡ 20in (50cm) ↔ 12in (30cm)

ANTHEMIS TINCTORIA
'E.C. Buxton'

Pretty, lemon yellow flowerheads are produced throughout summer above a mound of divided, grayish green leaves on this clumping perennial. The flowers are attractive to bees and good for cutting (*see pp.494, 524*). Grow in a mixed or herbaceous border; it also thrives in sandy and alkaline soils (*see pp.38, 64*), and coastal sites (*see p.166*). Cut back hard after flowering to increase longevity.

ALSO RECOMMENDED: *'Kelwayi' has clear yellow flowerheads; those of 'Sauce Hollandaise' are pale cream.*

☼ ◊ Z3   **Perennial**
‡ 18–28in (45–70cm) ↔ 24in (60cm)

ANTHERICUM LILIAGO

St. Bernard's lily produces elegant spires of delicate white flowers in late spring and early summer above a sheaf of grasslike leaves; these grow so densely as to be useful as a groundcover (*see p.304*). It lends emphasis to clump-forming plants in a herbaceous border and can be naturalized in grass. The flowers cut well (*see p.524*). It will grow in coastal gardens (*see p.166*).

ALSO RECOMMENDED: *var.* major *has larger, more open flowers;* A. ramosum *is shorter and flowers from early summer* Z4.

☼ ◊ Z7   **Perennial**
‡ 24–36in (60–90cm) ↔ 12in (30cm)

ASPHODELINE LUTEA

Yellow asphodel produces a clump of narrow, blue-green leaves that make an attractive feature before the dense, leafy spires of fragrant, starry yellow flowers appear in late spring. Grow in a border, where it is especially effective with gray- or silver-leaved plants, or on a dry, grassy bank. It must have a warm site and deep, well-drained soil; sandy ground is suitable (*see p.38*). Both flowers and seedheads are good for cutting (*see p.524*).

ALSO RECOMMENDED: *A. liburnica has pale yellow flowers in summer* Z6; *A. taurica has white flowers* Z6.

☼ ◊ *f* Z6   **Perennial**
↕ 5ft (1.5m) ↔ 12in (30cm)

BUPHTHALMUM SALICIFOLIUM

A good plant for attracting bees (*see p.494*), this robust perennial bears its daisylike, deep yellow flowers from early summer to autumn. When cut, they last well in water (*see p.524*). The stems, with willowlike, dark green leaves, are rather lax, so space plants closely or provide unobtrusive support early in the season. Grow in a border or naturalize on a sunny bank. It thrives on poor soils.

☼ ☀ ◊ Z3   **Perennial**
↕ 24in (60cm) ↔ 18in (45cm)

CATANANCHE CAERULEA
'Major'

A short-lived perennial that bears grassy leaves and cornflower-like, dark-centered, lilac-blue flowers. They have papery, silvery white bracts and appear from summer to autumn. It thrives in any well-drained site, including clay and alkaline soils (*see pp.12, 64*). Good for cutting and drying (*see p.524*); it flowers most freely in its second year.

ALSO RECOMMENDED: *C. caerulea has blue to lilac-blue flowerheads; 'Bicolor' has white flowerheads with purple centers.*

☀ ◊ Z4   s**Perennial**
‡ 20in (50cm) ↔ 12in (30cm)

ECHINOPS RITRO
'Veitch's Blue'

The deep blue flowerheads of this globe thistle, borne in succession from late summer, attract pollinating insects and are good for cutting and drying (*see pp.494, 524*). With a basal mound of spiny, divided, white-cobwebbed leaves, it is an excellent specimen for a border with a gray- or silver-leaved theme. Best in poor, well-drained sites, it also tolerates sandy soils and coastal sites (*see pp.38, 166*).

ALSO RECOMMENDED: *E. bannaticus has blue-gray flowerheads; 'Taplow Blue' has bright blue flowerheads. Z3b*

☀ ◊ Z3   **Perennial**
‡ 36in (90cm) ↔ 18in (45cm)

ERYNGIUM BOURGATII

The blue-gray flowerheads of this spiny plant, surrounded by silver bracts, appear from mid- to late summer above basal clumps of divided, dark green, silver-veined leaves. Grow in a herbaceous border or gravel garden; it tolerates sandy soils and coastal exposure (*see pp.38, 166*). The flowers are good for cutting and drying (*see p.524*) and attract bees (*see p.494*).

ALSO RECOMMENDED: *E. alpinum 'Amethyst' has violet-blue flowerheads* Z4; *those of* E. planum *'Blauer Zwerg' (syn. 'Blue Dwarf') are intense blue* Z4.

☼ ◊ Z4 **Perennial**
‡ 18in (45cm) ↔ 12in (30cm)

ERYSIMUM *'Bowles' Mauve'*

This bushy, evergreen wallflower forms a round mound of narrow, gray-green leaves. For most of the year it bears dense spikes of small, rich mauve flowers, most freely in spring and summer. It is ideal for growing on a sunny bank, at the front of a border, or on top of a dry stone wall (*see p.348*). Trim lightly after flowering to keep compact. It tolerates alkaline soils (*see p.64*) and is often short-lived.

ALSO RECOMMENDED: *E. linifolium has lilac- to lavender-blue flowers and plain, gray-green leaves.* Z6

☼ ◊ Z4 **Perennial**
‡ 30in (75cm) ↔ 24in (60cm)

FESTUCA GLAUCA
'Blaufuchs'

The narrow, bright blue leaves of this evergreen grass are its chief attraction. It is excellent in a border or rock garden as a foil to other plants. The flower spikes are less significant. Divide and replant clumps every two or three years for the best foliage color. Often sold as 'Blue Fox'. It tolerates sandy soils (*see p.38*) and can also be grown as a groundcover in sun (*see p.304*).

ALSO RECOMMENDED: *'Harz' has purple-tipped, dark olive-green leaves; 'Seeigel' (syn. Sea Urchin) has hair-fine, blue-green foliage in a tight bun.*

☀ ◊ Z3b   **Perennial**

↕ 12in (30cm) ↔ 10in (25cm)

FRITILLARIA IMPERIALIS

The sturdy stems of the crown imperial arise in spring to display hanging, bell-shaped, orange, red, or yellow flowers above whorls of narrow, fresh green leaves. It is ideal in a sunny border with fertile, well-drained soil; plant where they can be left undisturbed. The skunky scent can be unpleasant at close range. Plant bulbs in late summer. It tolerates shallow, alkaline soils (*see p.64*).

ALSO RECOMMENDED: *'Aurora' has golden orange flowers; those of 'Lutea' are yellow; 'Rubra' has red flowers.*

☀ ◊ Z5   **Perennial bulb**

↕ 3ft (1m) ↔ 12in (30cm)

GAILLARDIA *'Kobold'*

The brightly colored, daisylike flowerheads of this low-growing and bushy perennial bloom for a very long period, from early summer until the first frosts. It is good for a sunny border, especially one with a theme of hot colors, and is best on light, well-drained soils. It tolerates alkaline soil (*see p.64*). The flowers are good for cutting (*see p.524*).

ALSO RECOMMENDED: *'Burgunder' has wine-red flowerheads; those of 'Dazzler' are orange-red with yellow tips.*

☼ ◊ Z3   **Perennial**
‡ 12in (30cm) ↔ 18in (45cm)

GERANIUM CINEREUM *'Ballerina'*

This low-growing geranium is useful at the front of a border, in a rock garden, or as a groundcover (*see p.304*). From late spring into summer, a succession of light purple flowers with very dark veins open against the lobed, grayish foliage and face the sky. The soil must be sharply drained.

ALSO RECOMMENDED: *'Laurence Flatman' and subsp.* subcaulescens *are more vigorous;* G. dalmaticum (*see p.363*).

☼ ◊ Z4   **Perennial**
‡ 24in (60cm) ↔ 12in (30cm)

GERANIUM RENARDII

In early summer, this low-growing plant bears violet-veined, white to pale lavender flowers. Often shy-flowering, it is more highly valued for the dense clumps of rounded, velvety, grayish green leaves that make an excellent groundcover at border fronts or in gravel gardens (*see p.304*). Best in poor, light, well-drained soils; it may self-seed in ideal conditions.

ALSO RECOMMENDED: *'Whiteknights' has white, pale-blue-lilac-flushed flowers;* G. × riversleaianum *is more spreading, with light pink to deep magenta flowers* Z4.

☼ ◊ Z5   **Perennial**
↕↔ 12in (30cm)

LEYMUS ARENARIUS

One of the finest of the blue-leaved grasses, this spreading plant produces stiffly upright stems of tiny, blue-gray then buff-colored spikelets throughout summer; they are good for cutting and drying (*see p.524*). A fine architectural plant (*see p.472*) for specimen planting in gravel. It can be invasive, but it is suitable for a mixed or herbaceous border. Grow in sandy soil (*see p.38*). Cut down dead growth in autumn and, if necessary, divide mature plants when the soil has warmed up in spring.

☼ ◊ Z4   **Perennial**
↕ 5ft (1.5m) ↔ indefinite

LINARIA PURPUREA
'Canon Went'

This slender plant produces upright, wandlike stems clothed in grayish green leaves. They are topped by spikes of pale, dusky pink, two-lipped flowers throughout summer. An ideal choice for a cottage garden or herbaceous border. It self-seeds and comes true to type if isolated from the species. Grow in any light, well-drained soil; it tolerates sandy and alkaline soils (*see pp.38, 64*).

ALSO RECOMMENDED: L. purpurea *has violet-purple flowers;* 'Springside White' *has white flowers.*

☼ ◊ Z4 **Perennial**

↕ 36in (90cm) ↔ 12in (30cm)

OENOTHERA SPECIOSA 'Rosea'

A vigorous evening primrose that spreads by means of runners; it makes a good groundcover at the front of a border (*see p.304*). Scented, pink-flushed white flowers, veined with pink, remain open in daylight and appear in succession from summer to autumn above the rosettes of narrow leaves. Good in poor to moderately fertile, sandy soils (*see p.38*). It may be invasive.

ALSO RECOMMENDED: O. speciosa *has white flowers that may age to pink;* 'Pink Petticoats' *has pale pink, veined flowers.*

☼ ◊ ƒZ4 **Perennial**

↕↔ 12in (30cm)

PAPAVER ORIENTALE *'Allegro'*

This Oriental poppy forms a mound of bristly, divided leaves and, in late spring and early summer, produces bowl-shaped, satiny, vivid red-orange flowers, each with a black basal blotch. They are followed by characteristic poppy seedpods. Grow in any moderately fertile, well-drained site, including alkaline soils (*see p.64*). Oriental poppies make spectacular plants for herbaceous borders.

ALSO RECOMMENDED: *'Black and White' has black-blotched white flowers; 'Mrs. Perry' has pale salmon-pink flowers with blotches.*

☼ ◊ Z3   **Perennial**
‡ 12in (45–90cm) ↔ 24–36in (60–90cm)

PHORMIUM COOKIANUM *'Tricolor'*

This striking perennial, very useful as a focal point in a border, forms arching clumps of straplike, light green leaves to 5ft (1.5m) long; they are boldly margined with cream and red stripes. Tall spikes of tubular, pale green flowers emerge from the center of the plant in summer. Mulch deeply for winter where marginally hardy. A fine architectural plant that will grow in a large container (*see pp.412, 472*); it also tolerates coastal sites (*see p.166*).

ALSO RECOMMENDED: *'Cream Delight' is similar; P. 'Dazzler' (see p.188).*

☼ ◊◊ Z8   **Perennial**
‡ 2–6ft (0.6–2m) ↔ 1–10ft (0.3–3m)

TRITELEIA LAXA

This delicate plant with grassy leaves produces loose, showy clusters of pale to deep blue-purple flowers in early summer; the leaves usually wither by flowering time. It grows best in light, sandy soils (*see p.38*) and is very effective if grown *en masse* in a sunny, mixed or herbaceous border. It thrives in containers in sun (*see p.412*). Plant corms in autumn.

ALSO RECOMMENDED: T. hyacinthina *has white or pale blue flowers* Z7b; T. laxa *'Koningin Fabiola' (syn. Queen Fabiola) has purple-blue flowers.*

☼ ◊ Z7   **Perennial corm**

‡ 28in (70cm) ↔ 2in (5cm)

TULIPA PRAESTANS *'Unicum'*

Suitable for a raised bed or rock garden, this easy tulip produces several bright red flowers in spring. An appealing feature of this tulip is its large, cream-edged leaves. It makes a superior display when planted in clusters. Tolerant of sandy soils (*see p.38*), and it can be grown in a sunny container (*see p.412*). Plant bulbs in autumn.

ALSO RECOMMENDED: *'Fusilier' has bright orange-scarlet flowers;* T. *'Keizerskroon'* (see p.439); T. hageri *'Splendens'* (see p.63); T. *'Purissima'* (see p.545). All Z4

☼ ◊ Z4   **Perennial bulb**

‡ 12in (30cm)

VERBENA *'Peaches and Cream'*

A spreading plant with clusters of tiny summer to autumn flowers in pastel shades. They open pinkish orange and fade through apricot to cream. It is usually grown as an annual in a sunny border or container (*see p.412*), but it can be overwintered in a greenhouse.

ALSO RECOMMENDED: *'Homestead Purple' has red-purple flowers; 'Silver Anne' has pink flowers; 'Sissinghurst' (see p.439); V. bonariensis is hardier with purple flowers on stems to 6ft (2m) tall Z7b; V. rigida has fragrant purple flowers Z8.*

☼ ◊ Min 40°F (5°C)   **Perennial**

↕ 18in (45cm) ↔ 12–20in (30–50cm)

YUCCA WHIPPLEI

This almost stemless yucca forms a dense rosette of rigid, narrow, gray-green leaves at ground level; they are sharply spine-tipped, so site with care. It is an impressive architectural plant for well-drained borders or gravel gardens (*see p.472*). When mature, it produces spectacular spires of fragrant, creamy white flowers in summer, after which the flowered clump will die. Grow in sandy soil (*see p.38*).

ALSO RECOMMENDED: *Y. filamentosa 'Bright Edge' (see p.483); Y. gloriosa is larger and has blue-green leaves Z7b.*

☼ ◊ ƒ Z7b   **Perennial**

↕ 3ft (1m) ↔ 4ft (1.2m)

PLANTS FOR DRY SITES IN SHADE

There can be no denying that the combination of shade and drought presents a challenge to plants, and even experienced gardeners may despair when faced with such a difficult site. Many plants thrive in damp shade, but few are able to tolerate the combined lack of light and moisture.

Dry shade often occurs in urban gardens at the base of a wall or side of a building that faces away from the direction of prevailing wind and is therefore sheltered from rain.

It is also evident beneath large, shallow-rooting trees, which create a rain shadow beneath their leaf canopies, further parched by the moisture-depleting effects of their questing roots. If the soil is also free-draining, as in sandy and shallow, alkaline soils, the problems are worsened.

IMPROVE THE SOIL
As always, the first line of attack is to choose plants that are known to tolerate such sites, such as *Geranium phaeum*

(*see p.232*) or *Liriope muscari* (*see p.233*), although much can be done to improve soil conditions so the range of survivors is extended. The most important action is to improve the moisture retention of the soil by incorporating plenty of well-rotted organic matter, like farmyard manure, compost, composted bark, or leaf mold. The same materials can also be applied as a mulch in autumn or spring, but it is vital to do this when the soil is already damp. If applied to dry soil, it prevents rainfall from penetrating to the soil beneath, thus making the problem worse. In the absence of natural rainfall, give the soil a thorough soaking before mulching.

Another trick is to excavate a wide planting hole and lining it with perforated plastic, which is especially effective under shallow-rooting trees such as maple (*see p.120*). Mix the excavated soil with copious quantities of soil-based potting mix or well-rotted organic matter, then backfill with the improved soil.

PREPARE THE SITE

Establishing a carpet of drought-resistant groundcovers, made up of plants such as *Pachysandra terminalis* (*see p.235*) or *Tellima grandiflora* (*see p.236*), also helps retain soil moisture by reducing surface evaporation. Planting through permeable, woven landscaping fabric (often sold as geotextile membrane), especially if used in combination with a mulch, gives them the best possible chance of establishing good cover. Bear in mind that in such testing conditions, even the toughest plants may not achieve their expected height and spread, so you may need to plant more closely than is usually recommended. It is also vital that new plantings are kept well watered during the most vulnerable period before they develop a well-established root system. With shrubby plants, such as *Elaeagnus × ebbingei* 'Gilt Edge' (*see p.218*), take the reduced vigor into account, so there should be little need to prune.

COTONEASTER FRIGIDUS

A spreading shrub with matte green leaves that turn yellow before falling. In summer, it is covered by clusters of cream flowers, followed in late summer and autumn by a profusion of bright red berries that attract birds (*see p.494*). An easily grown, versatile shrub that can be clipped as a hedge (*see p.138*) or trained as a single-trunked tree. Tolerant of clay and alkaline soils (*see pp.12, 64*).

ALSO RECOMMENDED: *'Cornubia' is similar*; C. horizontalis (see p.265); C. lacteus (see p.149); C. sternianus (see p.71).

☼ ◑ ◊ Z7   **Deciduous shrub**
↕↔ 30ft (10m)

ELAEAGNUS × EBBINGEI *'Gilt Edge'*

This dense, fast-growing shrub is valued for its gold-margined, glossy green leaves; the creamy white flowers of autumn are fragrant but inconspicuous. Use in a shrub border or to brighten a dark corner. It may also be grown as informal hedging (*see p.138*); trim in late spring. Tolerant of exposed and coastal sites (*see pp.118, 166*), and it provides cover for wildlife (*see p.494*).

ALSO RECOMMENDED: *'Coastal Gold' has golden yellow leaves with irregular green margins; 'Limelight' has silvery young leaves, maturing to yellow and pale green.*

☼ ◑ ◊ f Z7   **Evergreen shrub**
↕↔ 12ft (4m)

EUONYMUS FORTUNEI
'Silver Queen'

An upright or scrambling shrub with white-margined, dark green leaves that tinge pink in cold weather. The spring flowers are insignificant. It makes a good groundcover (see pp.304, 326), can be clipped as a hedge (see p.138), and will climb against a lightly shaded wall (see p.262), reaching 20ft (6m) tall. Grow in any but waterlogged soil; good for coastal conditions and containers (see pp.166, 412, 448). Trim in spring.

ALSO RECOMMENDED: 'Emerald 'n' Gold' has yellow-edged leaves; Golden Prince (syn. 'Gold Tip') is compact with gold-tipped leaves.

☼◑ ◊◊ Z5   **Evergreen shrub**
‡8ft (2.5m) ↔ 5ft (1.5m)

GARRYA ELLIPTICA

The silk-tassel bush is a dense shrub with dark sea green, wavy-margined leaves, glossy or matte. It is prized for the gray catkins (borne on male plants) that may be up to 8in (20cm) long and dangle in clusters through winter and into spring; they make interesting cut flowers (see p.524). It can be treated as a hedge (see p.138) but is also fine in a shrub border or against a wall (see pp.262, 280). It tolerates coastal sites (see p.166). Trim after flowering.

ALSO RECOMMENDED: 'James Roof' is noted for having the longest catkins.

☼◑ ◊ Z7b   **Evergreen shrub**
‡↔12ft (4m)

HEDERA HELIX *'Erecta'*

English ivy is typically a climbing plant, but this unusual form is used mostly as a shrub or as a groundcover (*see pp.304, 326*), because the stiff stems are upright and self-supporting. The round-lobed leaves are dark green with prominent, pale green veins. Site in a shrub border or rock garden, or grow in a container (*see pp.412, 448*) or against a shady wall (*see p.262*). It tolerates alkaline soils (*see p.64*).

ALSO RECOMMENDED: *'Congesta' is less vigorous and forms a neat bush.*

☼☀ ◊◑ Z5b   **Evergreen shrub**
↕ 3ft (1m)

HYPERICUM × INODORUM *'Elstead'*

This vigorous shrub produces dense clumps of upright stems bearing aromatic, dark green leaves. The bright yellow flowers are borne at the stem tips in summer and autumn, followed by glossy red berries. Shear in early spring to produce the densest ground-cover (*see pp.304, 326*). Grow in any but waterlogged soil.

ALSO RECOMMENDED: *H. androsaemum 'Albury Purple' has purplish leaves and black fruits* Z4; *H. calycinum (see p.328).*

☼☀ ◊◑ Z7   **Deciduous shrub**
↕↔ 4ft (1.2m)

KERRIA JAPONICA
'Golden Guinea'

A suckering shrub that has glossy green, canelike stems and neatly toothed, bright green leaves. It bears large and single, sunshine yellow flowers during spring, making a cheerful and reliable, early-flowering shrub for a border or woodland garden or against a partially shaded wall (*see p.262*). Cut flowered stems back to different levels to obtain blooms at varying heights. It tolerates clay soils (*see p.12*).

ALSO RECOMMENDED: *'Picta' has cream-margined, gray-green leaves; 'Pleniflora' is taller with double, pomponlike flowers.*

☼ ◐ ◊ Z5b   **Deciduous shrub**
↕ 6ft (2m) ↔ 8ft (2.5m)

OSMANTHUS DELAVAYI

The arching branches of this rounded shrub bear small, glossy dark green leaves. Sweetly scented, pure white flowers appear in mid- to late spring. It thrives in most, fertile, well-drained soils, including alkaline ones (*see p.64*). A fine specimen for a border or for training against a partially shaded wall (*see p.262*); it can also be grown as a hedge (*see p.138*). Prune to shape after flowering; trim hedges in summer.

ALSO RECOMMENDED: O. decorus *has larger leaves Z7;* O. × burkwoodii *(see p.73).*

☼ ◐ ◊ Z7   **Evergreen shrub**
↕ 6–20ft (2–6m) ↔ 12ft (4m)

RIBES ALPINUM *'Aureum'*

A neat and adaptable flowering currant with dense growth that is clothed by beautiful, bright yellow-green, lobed leaves that color better in light, dappled shade. The foliage is accompanied by flowers of a similar color in spring. Bunches of scarlet berries follow if a male form is growing nearby. Trim after flowering; it may be clipped as a hedge (*see p.138*).

ALSO RECOMMENDED: R. alpinum *has mid-green foliage and is better for heavy shade.*

☼ ☀ ◊ Z2   **Deciduous shrub**
↕↔5ft (1.5m)

RUSCUS HYPOGLOSSUM

The tough, glossy green leaves of this small shrub are actually modified stems, and – on female plants only – they bear ornamental red berries from autumn to winter. The flowers are insignificant, although plants of both sexes are needed if the females are to bear fruit. Cut out any dead stems in spring. It can be grown as a groundcover (*see p.326*).

ALSO RECOMMENDED: R. aculeatus, *butcher's broom, is taller.* Z7

☼ ☀ ◊◊ Z7   **Evergreen shrub**
↕ 18in (45cm) ↔ 3ft (1m)

SARCOCOCCA CONFUSA

Christmas box is a dense, rounded shrub with small, dark green leaves, making it a good ground cover (*see p.326*). It is noted for the intense winter fragrance of its honey-scented white flowers – best appreciated near a frequently used door or entrance. Small, glossy black fruits follow. It can be pruned hard in late spring and makes a fine low hedge (*see p.138*). Grow in any fertile, well-drained soil, including alkaline (*see p.64*). It tolerates urban pollution.

ALSO RECOMMENDED: *S. hookeriana var. digyna is similar but more compact; var. humilis* (see p.244).

☀️◐● ◊◊ *f* Z7b   **Evergreen shrub**
‡ 6ft (2m) ↔ 3ft (1m)

SKIMMIA JAPONICA

This tough, rounded shrub bears heads of dark red flower buds in autumn and winter, which open in spring as cream flowers Red berries follow on female plants, as long as males grow nearby. They contrast well with the glossy deep green, leathery, red-rimmed leaves. Tolerant of urban pollution, coastal sites, and damp, acidic soils (*see pp.92, 166, 238*). Little pruning is required. It will grow in a container (*see p.448*).

ALSO RECOMMENDED: *'Fragrans' is male; subsp.* reevesiana *has both male and female flowers on one plant; 'Rubella'* (see p.108); *'Veitchii' is female.*

☀️◐● ◊◊ Z7   **Evergreen shrub**
‡↔ to 20ft (6m)

SYMPHORICARPOS × DOORENBOSII *'White Hedge'*

This snowberry is a vigorous, suckering shrub with upright stems and oval, dark green leaves. In summer, it bears clusters of white flowers, followed by white berries that attract birds (*see p.494*). As informal hedging (*see p.138*), it can be trimmed in winter. Its spread may become invasive.

ALSO RECOMMENDED: *'Mother of Pearl' is arching with pink-flushed white fruit;* S. albus *var.* laevigatus (*see p.164*).

☼ ◐ ◊◊ Z5   **Deciduous shrub**
‡ 5ft (1.5m) ↔ indefinite

HOLBOELLIA CORIACEA

A twining climber with ornamental, evergreen leaves divided into three dark green leaflets. In a sheltered site it can be trained up into a small tree or onto a support or wall (*see pp.262, 280*). Two types of small, bell-shaped flowers emerge in spring: sprays of mauve male flowers at the tips of the previous year's growth and clusters of purple-flushed, greenish white female flowers at the base of new growth. Sausage-shaped purple fruits follow. It may be rampant in favorable conditions.

ALSO RECOMMENDED: *the leaves of* H. latifolia *are divided into leaflets. (Tender)*

☼ ◐ ◊ Min 40°F (5°C)   **Climber**
‡ 22ft (7m)

AJUGA REPTANS *'Multicolor'*

The dark bronze-green leaves of this evergreen perennial are attractively marked with deep pink and cream. It is a good choice for groundcover (*see pp.304, 326*), spreading freely by its rooting stems. Spikes of dark blue flowers to 6in (15cm) tall appear in early summer. Invaluable for border edging under shrubs and perennials, and in wall and paving crevices (*see p.348*). Tolerant of clay and damp soils (*see pp.12, 238*).

ALSO RECOMMENDED: *'Burgundy Glow' has silvery leaves with deep red tints; 'Catlin's Giant'* (see p.354); *'Pink Elf' has pink flowers on stems 2in (5cm) tall.*

☀ ◐ ◊◊ Z3   **Perennial**

‡ 6in (15cm) ↔ 3ft (1m)

ASPLENIUM SCOLOPENDRIUM

The hart's tongue fern forms a crown of tongue-shaped, leathery, bright green, undivided fronds to 16in (40cm) long. The margins are usually rippled. On the undersides of mature fronds, rust-colored spore cases are arranged in a herringbone pattern. The are no flowers. It prefers gritty, alkaline soils (*see p.64*) and tolerates damp shade (*see p.238*). A fine architectural plant for a container (*see pp.448, 472*).

ALSO RECOMMENDED: *fronds of* Crispum Group *have very ruffled margins; those of* Cristatum Group *have curious crested margins;* A. trichomanes (see p.78).

☀ ◊◊ Z7   **Perennial fern**

‡ 18–28in (45–70cm) ↔ 24in (60cm)

BERGENIA *'Sunningdale'*

An early-flowering perennial bearing clusters of rich pink flowers in spring. They are carried on upright stems above the clumps of broad, rounded, leathery, evergreen leaves; these turn coppery in winter. Good underplanting for shrubs, which give winter shelter from winds, and also as a groundcover or pot plant (*see pp.326, 448*). Mulch in autumn. It tolerates alkaline soils and damp sites (*see pp.64, 238*).

ALSO RECOMMENDED: *'Bressingham White'* has white flowers; *'Morgenröte'* (see p.333); *'Silberlicht'* has white flowers; B. ciliata (see p.79).

☀️ ◐ ◊◊ Z3b **Perennial**
‡ 12–18in (30–45cm) ↔ 18–24in (45–60cm)

BRUNNERA MACROPHYLLA *'Dawson's White'*

This clump-forming perennial with attractive foliage is ideal as a ground-cover in borders and among deciduous trees (*see p.326*). In mid- and late spring, open clusters of small, pale blue flowers appear above the heart-shaped leaves, which have irregular, creamy white margins. Choose a cool position in light, damp or dry shade (*see p.238*). It tolerates clay soils and exposed sites (*see p.12, 118*).

ALSO RECOMMENDED: B. macrophylla *has plain green leaves; those of* 'Hadspen Cream' *have irregular cream margins.*

☀️ ◊◊ Z3b **Perennial**
‡ 18in (45cm) ↔ 24in (60cm)

CONVALLARIA MAJALIS VAR. ROSEA

This pink-flowered lily-of-the-valley is a creeping perennial bearing small, very fragrant flowers that hang from arching stems in late spring above a pair of narrowly oval leaves; they are good for cutting (*see p.524*). It makes an excellent groundcover in damp or dry shade (*see pp.238, 326*), spreading rapidly under suitable conditions. Add a dressing of leaf mold in autumn. It tolerates sandy soils (*see p.38*).

ALSO RECOMMENDED: *C.* majalis *has white flowers; the leaves of 'Albostriata' are attractively cream-striped.*

☼ ◐ ● ◊◊ *f* Z2   **Perennial**
‡ 8in (20cm) ↔ 12in (30cm)

CORYDALIS LUTEA

This low perennial forms a mound of delicately lobed, bright green foliage, decorated over a long season from spring to early autumn by unusually spurred, bold yellow flowers. It self-seeds freely and is suitable for a rock garden or in crevices within dry stone walls or paving (*see p.348*).

☼ ◐ ◊ Z4   **Perennial**
‡ 16in (40cm) ↔ 12in (30cm)

CYCLAMEN COUM
F. ALBISSIMUM

The rounded, green or silver-marked leaves of *C. coum* will carpet the ground beneath shrubs or trees. They appear in winter and spring with the flowers, which have upswept petals. This form has white flowers with carmine-red mouths. Grow in gritty, well-drained soil that dries out in summer. In cold areas, apply a deep, dry mulch annually as the leaves wither. Plant tubers in autumn.

ALSO RECOMMENDED: *C. coum has white to pink flowers; the Pewter Group has silvered leaves.*

☀ ◊ Z5   **Perennial**
↕ 2–3in (5–8cm) ↔ 4in (10cm)

DESCHAMPSIA CESPITOSA
'Goldtau'

This evergreen grass forms tussocks of narrow, rigid leaves. Through summer, it bears clouds of glistening, red-brown flowers that age to golden yellow; they are good for cutting (*see p.524*). Grow in a border or woodland garden with neutral to acidic soil (*see p.92*). In dry soils, dig in compost before planting. Remove old flowerheads in early spring. Also sold as 'Golden Dew'.

ALSO RECOMMENDED: *'Bronzeschleier' (syn. Bronze Veil) has bronze flowerheads; 'Goldschleier' (syn. Golden Veil) is taller with bright, silvery yellow flowerheads.*

☼☀ ◊ Z4   **Perennial**
↕↔ 30in (75cm)

DICENTRA CUCULLARIA

The feathery, blue-green leaves
of Dutchman's breeches form low
hummocks beneath the upright stems
of small, trousers-shaped white flowers.
These appear in early spring, and the
entire plant dies back after flowering.
It needs gritty soil and should be kept
almost dry when dormant in summer;
dry spots beneath trees or shrubs make
an ideal site. It is also suitable for
shady niches in rock gardens and as
a groundcover (*see p.326*). Most other
dicentras prefer moist soils. It tolerates
alkaline soils (*see p.64*).

☀ ◊ Z4　　　　　　　　　　　　**Perennial**
‡ 30in (20cm) ↔ 10in (25cm)

DIGITALIS OBSCURA

Foxgloves are imposing plants when in
flower, producing tall spires of flowers
that are attractive to bees (*see p.494*).
This one has rusty, yellow or orange
flowers from late spring to midsummer.
It has a subshrubby appearance with
lance-shaped, grayish green leaves,
and it tolerates most soils, preferably
in partial shade. Suitable for a border
or woodland garden.

ALSO RECOMMENDED: *D. purpurea has*
purple flowers and is more tolerant of
dry conditions. Z4

◐☀ ◊◊ Z4　　　　　　　　　**Perennial**
‡ 12–48in (30–120cm) ↔ 18in (45cm)

EUPHORBIA AMYGDALOIDES VAR. ROBBIAE

Mrs. Robb's bonnet, also known simply as *E. robbiae*, is a spreading, evergreen perennial bearing open heads of yellowish green flowers in spring. The long, dark green leaves are arranged in rosettes at the lower ends of the stems. Dig up invasive roots to control spread. The milky sap can irritate skin. Also useful for hot, dry sites (*see p.190*) and as a groundcover (*see pp.304, 326*).

ALSO RECOMMENDED: *'Purpurea' has purple leaves and yellow flowers.*

☀️◐ ◊◊ Z6   **Perennial**
‡ 24in (60cm) ↔ 12in (30cm)

EUPHORBIA DULCIS 'Chameleon'

This spreading plant has upright stems carrying narrow, rich purple leaves and, at their tips, open heads of purplish, yellow-green flowers in early summer. The leaves assume orange, red, and gold tints in autumn. Good as a groundcover (*see pp.304, 326*) and for foliage contrasts in a shady border. It grows in any well-drained soil, including alkaline and those in hot, dry sites (*see pp.64, 190*). It self-seeds freely.

ALSO RECOMMENDED: *E. dulcis has dark or bronze-green leaves and yellow-green flowers.*

☀️◐ ◊ Z7b   **Perennial**
‡↔ 12in (30cm)

GALANTHUS NIVALIS
'Flore Pleno'

This double-flowered form of common snowdrop, *G. nivalis*, bears drooping, pear-shaped, pure white flowers from late winter to early spring. There are green markings on the tips of the inner petals, and the narrow leaves are gray-green. A reliable bulb for naturalizing in damp shade under deciduous trees or shrubs in a wild garden (*see pp.238, 494*). Plant bulbs in autumn, and divide clumps after flowering.

ALSO RECOMMENDED: *G. elwesii*, *G. 'Magnet'*, and *G. 'S. Arnott'* are twice as tall, with single flowers. All Z4

☀ ◐◑ Z3　　　　　**Perennial bulb**
↕↔ 4in (10cm)

GERANIUM NODOSUM

With a creeping habit and dense mounds of lobed, glossy leaves, this geranium makes a great groundcover (*see p.326*) in any dry, shady spot. The purplish pink flowers with darker veins are borne on red-tinted stems from spring to autumn. Very easy to grow, it tolerates any but waterlogged soil. Remove faded flowers and leaves to encourage new growth. It can be grown in a container (*see p.448*).

ALSO RECOMMENDED: *G. macrorrhizum 'Czakor'* (see p.339).

☀-◐ ◑ Z5b　　　　**Perennial**
↕ 12–20in (30–50cm) ↔ 20in (50cm)

GERANIUM PHAEUM

Dusky cranesbill is a densely clump-forming perennial with deeply lobed, soft green leaves. In spring and early summer, tall, slender stems carry a profusion of dusky violet-blue, black-purple, or maroon flowers. Excellent in containers (*see p.448*) or as a groundcover under shrubs or trees (*see p.326*); cutting back hard after flowering makes for denser cover and more flowers. Grow in any but waterlogged soil.

ALSO RECOMMENDED: *'Album' has white flowers;* G. endressii (see p.316).

☀️ ⛅ ◐ ◊◊ Z4   **Perennial**
‡ 20in (80cm) ↔ 18in (45cm)

HELLEBORUS FOETIDUS

The stinking hellebore is an upright, evergreen perennial forming clumps of dark green, deeply divided leaves that smell unpleasant when crushed. In winter and early spring, pale clusters of nodding, cup-shaped flowers appear above the foliage; their green petals are often edged with red. An intriguing specimen for a winter border or for cut flowers (*see p.524*). Best on dry or damp, neutral to alkaline soils (*see pp.64, 238*). Attractive planted among snowdrops.

ALSO RECOMMENDED: H. orientalis *subsp.* guttatus (see p.253).

☀️ ⛅ ◊◊ Z6   **Perennial**
‡ 32in (80cm) ↔ 18in (45cm)

IRIS FOETIDISSIMA
VAR. CITRINA

The stinking iris is not as unpleasant as it sounds, although the evergreen, silvery leaves do have a unpleasant scent if crushed. This vigorous plant bears pale yellow flowers in early summer, which cut well for indoor display (*see p.524*) and are followed by seed capsules that split in autumn to display decorative, scarlet, yellow, or more rarely, white seeds. Tolerates alkaline soils (*see p.64*).

ALSO RECOMMENDED: I. foetidissima *has purple flowers.*

☼ ◐ ◌ Z7   **Perennial**
↕ 12–36in (30–90cm) ↔ indefinite

LIRIOPE MUSCARI

The narrow, arching, dark green leaves of this tuberous perennial spread slowly to produce dense, ground-covering carpets (*see p.326*). In autumn, purple-green stems appear bearing crowded spikes of long-lasting, beadlike, violet-mauve flowers. Excellent in a woodland garden or beneath shrubs in a border. It also tolerates acidic soils and hot, dry sites (*see pp.92, 190*).

ALSO RECOMMENDED: *'Monroe White' has white flowers; 'Variegata' has white-striped leaves;* L. exiliflora *(syn.* L. muscari *'Majestic') has tall spikes of rich lavender-blue flowers.*

☼ ◐ ◌ Z6   **Perennial**
↕ 12in (30cm) ↔ 18in (45cm)

LUNARIA REDIVIVA

This perennial honesty forms dense clumps of triangular, dark green leaves and bears heads of very fragrant, pale lilac flowers during spring and early summer; these attract butterflies and bees (*see p.494*). The silvery seedpods that follow are good for cutting and drying (*see p.524*). Excellent for a border or for naturalizing in woodland. Grow in any well-drained soil; it tolerates alkaline conditions (*see p.64*).

ALSO RECOMMENDED: *L. annua is a biennial with purplish flowers. Z3*

☼ ◑ ◊ *f* Z6   **Perennial**

↕ 24–36in (60–90cm) ↔ 12in (30cm)

MECONOPSIS CAMBRICA

The Welsh poppy forms loose, basal tufts of divided, pale to bluish green leaves. From spring to autumn, on slender, leafy stems, it bears cup-shaped, lemon- to orange-yellow, delicate poppy flowers. A noted self-seeder, it is ideal for naturalizing in a wild or woodland gardens in sun or shade, tolerating alkaline soils (*see p.64*). Remove dead flowers to prevent nuisance self-seeding.

ALSO RECOMMENDED: *var.* aurantiaca *has orange flowers;* 'Flore-Pleno' *has double yellow flowers.*

☼ ◑ ◊◊ Z4   **Perennial**

↕ 18in (45cm) ↔ 18in (25cm)

PACHYSANDRA TERMINALIS

This freely spreading plant is valued
mainly for its glossy, dark green foliage.
It is an excellent groundcover plant for
a dry or damp woodland garden or
under trees and shrubs (see pp.238,
326). Small spikes of fragrant white
flowers appear in early summer at the
stem tips among a cluster of leaves.
In very dry soils, dig in compost before
planting. It tolerates acidic soils
(see p.92).

ALSO RECOMMENDED: *'Green Carpet'*
is more compact; 'Variegata' is less
vigorous, with white-margined leaves.

☼ ◑ ● ◊ ƒ Z3　　　　**Perennial**
↕ 8in (20cm) ↔ indefinite

SYMPHYTUM TUBEROSUM

The tuberous comfrey is named for
its creeping, rhizomatous roots, which
may spread rapidly. They give rise to
upright, hairy stems with long, dark
green leaves. These are topped in
early summer by heads of pale yellow,
tubular flowers. Like other comfreys,
it makes an excellent groundcover plant
(see pp.304, 326).

ALSO RECOMMENDED: S. *'Goldsmith'* (see
p.346); S. × uplandicum *'Variegatum'* has
blue flowers and variegated leaves Z3.

☼ ◑ ● ◊ ◑ Z6　　　　**Perennial**
↕ 16–24in (40–60cm) ↔ 3ft (1m)

TELLIMA GRANDIFLORA

Fringe cups forms a ground-smothering mound of lobed, fresh green leaves. From late spring to midsummer, it produces slender spires of small, greenish white flowers with fringed petals. It makes an excellent ground-cover beneath trees or shrubs (*see p.326*) and good edging at the front of a border. Grow in any moderately fertile soil, including clay (*see p.12*). It self-seeds freely.

ALSO RECOMMENDED: *'Purpurteppich' has purplish, red-tinted leaves and green-fringed red flowers; Rubra Group has purplish red leaves.*

☀ ◐ ◑ ◊◊ Z4   **Perennial**

↕ 32in (80cm) ↔ 12in (30cm)

TOLMIEA MENZIESII *'Taff's Gold'*

A spreading plant grown for its clumps of semievergreen, ivylike, pale lime green leaves mottled with cream and pale yellow. An abundance of tiny, nodding, green and chocolate-brown flowers appear in slender, upright spikes during early summer. Plant in groups to cover the ground in a woodland garden or in a container (*see pp.326, 448*). Direct sun will scorch the leaves. It tolerates acidic soils (*see p.92*).

ALSO RECOMMENDED: *T. menziesii, piggyback plant, has plain green leaves.*

☀ ◐ ◑ ◊◊ Z7   **Perennial**

↕ 12–24in (30–60cm) ↔ 3ft (1m)

VINCA MINOR

The lesser periwinkle is a trailing subshrub with long, slender shoots. It gives a long season of violet-blue flowers from spring to autumn amid the oval, dark green leaves. A useful plant for groundcover (*see pp.304, 326*), but it can be invasive if not cut back.

ALSO RECOMMENDED: *'Argenteovariegata' has cream-margined leaves*; V. major (*greater periwinkle*), *is very vigorous, 'Variegata' has cream-edged leaves* Z7.

☼ ◐ ◑ ◊◊ Z4   **Perennial**

‡ 4–8in (10–20cm) ↔ indefinite

WALDSTENIA TERNATA

A vigorous woodland plant that spreads quickly to form a thick mat of strawberry-like, palmately lobed leaves. Loose clusters of golden yellow flowers illuminate the plant in late spring and early summer; they resemble small, single rose flowers. Good as a groundcover for dry, shady banks or at the front of border (*see pp.304, 326*), but it may be invasive.

☼ ◐ ◊◊ Z4   **Perennial**

‡ 4in (10cm) ↔ 24in (60cm)

PLANTS FOR DAMP SITES IN SHADE

AN OLD GARDENING adage states that if shade did not exist in a garden, it would be necessary to create some, for some of the most beautiful and desirable plants need at least a modicum of shade to show their best. The world's forests provide an abundance of bulbs, perennials, ferns, and shrubs that thrive in damp shade. They illustrate the opportunities of color and beauty through the seasons, from spring-flowering gems like *Anemonella thalictroides* (*see p.245*) to the luscious berries of *Gaultheria × wisleyensis* 'Pink Pixie' (*see p.241*) in autumn. In the cool, humid environment that characterizes damp shade, foliage plants, such as most ferns and the many forms of hosta (*see pp.254, 318*), grow lush and remain in better condition for longer than in more open sites. As a result, sophisticated tapestries of textured foliage can be created to clothe the ground. Flowering perennials such as *Digitalis × mertonensis* (*see p.250*) often

perform for longer periods in shade and retain their color better when not exposed to the bleaching effects of the sun, while those with pastel-colored flowers, like *Aquilegia fragrans* (see p.246), appear at their most luminous in shade.

IDEAL SHADY PLACES

Many properties are not large enough to accommodate a patch of woodland, which would be the natural choice of site for shade-loving plants. Instead, many have areas that are shaded by high walls, specimen trees, or borders of shrubs, and the most desirable form of shade is dappled or partial shade, since relatively few shade-lovers thrive in deep, permanently sunless shade. If the shade cast by trees is too dense, prune the lower branches from the trunk, and thin the canopy to allow more light through. On large, mature trees, however, where the branches are large and heavy, this is most safely done by a professional arborist. In shady courtyards, or where heavy shade is cast by tall walls,

you can increase ambient light levels by painting the walls in pale colors and by using pale-colored gravel and paving at ground level. In a shrub border, especially if it is an otherwise open site, the shade beneath the shrubs is likely to be a patchwork of varying intensities that changes through the days and seasons as the sun moves across the sky. Plants that need partial shade are likely to do best here, but they should be positioned so that they receive at least midday shade; otherwise, their foliage is likely to scorch. Such a site is also ideal for shade-loving bulbs like snowdrops (see p.231) and anemones (see pp.332, 528), which perform before the deciduous canopy closes over by late spring.

Since most of these plants are from woodland, they grow best in soils that are moist but well-drained and rich in leafy organic matter. Unless your soil is like this naturally, add well-rotted organic matter to the soil when planting, and apply a mulch of the same annually in spring.

CAMELLIA JAPONICA *'Janet Waterhouse'*

This elegant shrub for a shrub border or wooded area can also be grown as a free-standing specimen in the open ground, in a container, or against a shady wall (*see pp.262, 448*). The glossy dark, oval leaves heighten the brilliance of the semidouble white flowers in spring. These can be cut for indoor decoration (*see p.524*). Prune young plants to shape after flowering. Tolerant of acidic soils (*see p.92*).

ALSO RECOMMENDED: *'Adolphe Audusson' (see p.450); 'Lady Vansittart' (see p.99); 'Tricolor' has flowers striped red and white.*

☀◐ ◊◊ Z7   **Evergreen shrub**
↕ 28ft (9m) ↔ 25ft (8m)

DAPHNE LAUREOLA

Although the spurge laurel is less showy than other daphnes, it does well in deep, damp or dry shade (*see p.216*). It is bushy, with glossy dark green, leathery foliage. Clusters of small, night-scented, pale yellow-green flowers emerge from the leaf axils in late winter; black berries follow. Grow in woodland or in a shrub border. It resents transplanting. All parts are toxic, and contact with the sap may irritate skin. Keep pruning to a minimum.

ALSO RECOMMENDED: *subsp.* philippi *is a spreading dwarf form, about 16in (40cm) tall, suitable for groundcover.*

◐☀ ◊◊ ƒ Z7   **Evergreen shrub**
↕ 3ft (1m) ↔ 5ft (1.5m)

FATSIA JAPONICA

The Japanese aralia is a spreading shrub grown for its large, palmately lobed, glossy green leaves. Broad, upright clusters of rounded, cream-colored flowerheads appear in autumn. An excellent architectural plant for a dry or damp, shady border, or against a wall (*see pp.216, 262, 472*). It tolerates urban pollution, thriving in urban gardens. Trim back in late spring, if necessary.

ALSO RECOMMENDED: *'Variegata' has cream-edged leaves.*

☀️◐ ◊◊ Z7b   **Evergreen shrub**
↕ 5–12ft (1.5–4m)

GAULTHERIA × WISLEYENSIS 'Pink Pixie'

This compact shrub, spreading by suckers, makes a good groundcover in a shaded border, rock garden, or wild-life area (*see pp.326, 494*). It tolerates sun if the soil remains reliably moist. Small, pink-tinged white flowers appear in late spring and early summer, followed by purple-red fruits Trim lightly after flowering to keep compact. It associates well with heathers, which also grow in neutral to acidic soil (*see p.92*).

ALSO RECOMMENDED: G. × wisleyensis *is taller; 'Wisley Pearl' is also taller, with white flowers and dark red-purple fruits.*

☀️◐ ◊◊ Z6b   **Evergreen shrub**
↕ 12in (30cm) ↔ 18in (45cm)

HYDRANGEA QUERCIFOLIA

The oakleaf hydrangea is a mound-forming shrub with large, lobed, oak-like leaves that turn rich bronze-purple in autumn. Showy, conical heads of white flowers that age to pink appear in midsummer and autumn. Excellent in a shrub border, as an architectural specimen, or in a shady container (*see p.448, 472*). Keep pruning to a minimum, in spring.

ALSO RECOMMENDED: *'Snow Flake' has arching heads of double flowers; 'Snow Queen', with large upright flowerheads, is free-flowering;* H. anomala *subsp.* petiolaris (see p.275).

☀️◐ ◊◍ Z5b   **Deciduous shrub**
‡ 6ft (2m) ↔ 8ft (2.5m)

LINDERA BENZOIN

The spicebush is named and grown for its bright green leaves that emit a spicy odor when crushed and turn golden yellow in autumn. Small, flat-headed clusters of tiny, greenish yellow flowers appear in spring, succeeded by bright red berries if male and female plants are grown together. This rounded shrub is good for acidic soils and permanently moist ground (*see pp.92, 372*), growing naturally in damp woodland. Prune after flowering, if necessary.

ALSO RECOMMENDED: *L.* obtusiloba *reaches 20ft (6m) with yellow flowers.* Z6b

☀️ ◍ *f* Z6   **Deciduous shrub**
‡↔ 10ft (3m)

PAEONIA DELAVAYI

The nodding, bowl-shaped, glossy dark red flowers of this shrubby tree peony appear in early summer amid deeply cut, dark green leaves; these are bluish green beneath and turn yellow in autumn. It is ideal as an architectural specimen (*see p.472*) grown alone, in a shrub border, or in a wildlife garden (*see p.494*). Grow in deep, fertile soil; it tolerates clay and alkaline soils (*see pp.12, 64*). Avoid regular hard pruning, but (on old specimens) occasionally cut out an old stem at the base in autumn.

ALSO RECOMMENDED: *var.* lutea *has yellow flowers; var.* ludlowii (see p.505).

☼ ☀ ◊◊ Z6   **Deciduous shrub**
‡ 6ft (2m) ↔ 4ft (1.2m)

RHODODENDRON 'Polar Bear'

One of the last to flower and among the most fragrant, this sturdy, treelike, large-leaved rhododendron bears huge clusters of waxy white flowers in late summer. It is ideal for adding color to a shaded area, being spectacular if grown in groves or avenues, and it will also grow in a large container (*see p.448*). Acidic soil is essential (*see p.92*). Little pruning is necessary.

ALSO RECOMMENDED: R. 'Nova Zembla', *an iron-clad rhododendron, has bright red flowers in late spring* Z4; Blue Diamond Group (see p.160); 'Homebush' (see p.454).

☼ ◊ *f* Z7   **Evergreen shrub**
‡ 15ft (5m) ↔ 12ft (4m)

SARCOCOCCA HOOKERIANA *VAR.* HUMILIS

A dense, suckering shrub with glossy dark green leaves that makes a good groundcover, even in dry shade (*see pp.216, 326*). Clusters of pink-tinted white flowers appear in winter and are deliciously fragrant; they are followed by small, glossy blue-black fruits. It tolerates hard pruning and makes a fine low hedge (*see p.138*); trim in late spring. Tolerant of alkaine soils and urban pollution (*see p.64*).

ALSO RECOMMENDED: S. ruscifolia *has creamy white flowers and red berries.* Z7b

☼☽ ◊◑ *f* Z6   **Evergreen shrub**
‡ 24in (60cm) ↔ 3ft (1m)

VIBURNUM *'Pragense'*

This evergreen viburnum makes a dark green, rounded bush. Its late spring flowers are pinkish then white, appearing in large, flat-headed clusters at the ends of the branches. The long and narrow leaves are deeply veined and wrinkled. Choose a site with shelter from wind. Minimal pruning is required, although it can be pruned after flowering as an informal hedge (*see p.138*).

ALSO RECOMMENDED: V. davidii *is half the size* Z7; V. rhytidophyllum (see p.134).

☼☽ ◊◑ Z7   **Evergreen shrub**
‡↔ 10ft (3m)

ACTAEA RUBRA

The red baneberry is a clump-forming plant with divided leaves. It bears spikes of fluffy white flowers in mid-spring and early summer; the glossy red berries that follow are ornamental but highly toxic. Grow in a woodland or wild garden (*see p.494*), or in a shady border. Water well in dry weather.

ALSO RECOMMENDED: *f.* neglecta *has white berries;* A. pachypoda *(syn.* A. alba) *has black-eyed white berries;* A. spicata *has black berries* Z3.

☼ ◑ Z4   **Perennial**

↕ 18in (45cm) ↔ 12in (30cm)

ANEMONELLA THALICTROIDES

Rue anemone is a spring-flowering beauty of very delicate appearance. It slowly forms a mound of blue-green, finely divided foliage and bears fragile, slender-stemmed, white or pink flowers. Use beneath shrubs or in a rock or woodland garden. It must have moist soil, but the tubers will rot in very wet soils. Protect from slugs.

ALSO RECOMMENDED: *'Oscar Shoaf' has double pink flowers.*

☼ ◑ Z5   **Perennial**

↕ 4in (10cm) ↔ 12in (30cm)

ANEMONOPSIS MACROPHYLLA

From mid- to late summer, this clump-forming perennial produces tall, dark stems of nodding, waxy textured flowers with lilac sepals and violet petals. They are held well above the mounds of divided, glossy dark green leaves. Provide shelter wind and choose a cool position in deep, fertile soil. Excellent for a shady border or woodland garden.

☀ ◐ ◊ Z5b **Perennial**
‡ 30in (75cm) ↔ 18in (45cm)

AQUILEGIA FRAGRANS

A graceful columbine that forms clumps of deeply lobed, blue-green leaves. In early summer, delicate clusters of fragrant, nodding, creamy white flowers with long, backward-pointing spurs rise above the foliage. It is ideal for naturalizing in a woodland garden or for the front of border, where its scent can be appreciated easily.

ALSO RECOMMENDED: *A. flabellata has soft blue-purple flowers* Z4; *A. 'Hensol Harebell' has soft blue flowers* Z4; *A. vulgaris 'Nivea'* (see p.511).

☀ ◐ ◊ ƒ Z4 **Perennial**
‡ 6–16in (15–40cm) ↔ 8in (20cm)

ARISAEMA CANDIDISSIMUM

This plant is cultivated for its white-striped, light pink spathe that is 3–6in (8–15cm) long and surrounds the greenish flower spike in summer. There is a sweet scent. A single leaf, palmately divided into three leaflets, emerges shortly afterward from the underground tuber. It is best in partial shade, but it tolerates some sun. Plant tubers in spring or autumn.

ALSO RECOMMENDED: *A. amurense has a dark purple, white-striped spathe* Z4; *A. flavum is hardier and has a smaller, green to yellow spathe* Z4.

☼ ☀ ◐◑ *f* Z6   **Perennial**

↕ 16in (40cm) ↔ 6in (15cm)

ARISARUM PROBOSCIDEUM

The mouse plant is named for its dark purple-brown spathes with long, curled tips that look like the tails of mice. They enclose insignificant flower spikes in spring. The long-stalked, arrow-shaped, glossy green leaves form dense mats, making a good groundcover (*see p.326*), but they often obscure the spathes. If successful, it will form a large colony in a woodland garden. Plant the rhizomes in autumn.

☼ ◐ Z7   **Perennial**

↕ 6in (15cm) ↔ 10in (25cm) or more

ATHYRIUM FILIX-FEMINA *'Frizelliae'*

Tatting fern is a diminutive form of the lady fern, with bright green fronds that resemble ribbons of hand-made lace; the frond segments are reduced to rounded lobes on either side of a midrib. Grow in a shady border or in a woodland garden, where it can be used as a groundcover (*see p.326*). It needs fertile, neutral to acidic soil (*see p.92*) and will also grow in a raised bed or shady container (*see p.448*).

ALSO RECOMMENDED: *'Minutissimum' is taller with dense, upright "shuttlecocks" of finely divided, lance-shaped fronds.*

☀️ ◐ ◊◊ Z4   **Perennial fern**
‡ 8in (20cm) ↔ 12in (30cm)

BLECHNUM TABULARE

This large, evergreen fern forms a spreading rosette of stiff, leathery fronds. It is similar to, and often confused with, *B. chilense*. In a woodland garden, shady border, or rock garden, it would make a superb architectural plant (*see p.472*). It is easy to grow in rich, acidic soils (*see p.92*).

ALSO RECOMMENDED: B. chilense *is larger with an indefinite spread (Tender);* B. penna-marina *(see p.358);* B. spicant *is smaller* Z4.

☀️ ◐ ◐ ◊ Min 40°F (5°C)   **Perennial fern**
‡ 3ft (1m) ↔ 24–48in (60–120cm)

CARDAMINE PENTAPHYLLA

An elegant addition to a shady border or woodland garden, this bittercress forms clumps of divided leaves with narrow, dark green leaflets. The loose clusters of four-petaled white, pale purple, or lilac flowers appear among the foliage in late spring and early summer. Grow in damp, leafy soil.

ALSO RECOMMENDED: C. enneaphylla *has creamy white flowers in late spring* Z6; C. pratensis *has longer heads of flowers, borne above the leaves* Z6.

☼ ☼ ◊ Z6   **Perennial**
‡ 12–20in (30–50cm) ↔ 12in (30cm)

CIMICIFUGA SIMPLEX

At the beginning of autumn, this clump-forming perennial produces wandlike, often gracefully arching spires of tiny white flowers above mounds of divided, fresh green leaves. It is at home in a damp, shaded herbaceous border or woodland garden. Grow in moist, leafy, fertile soil; it tolerates clay (*see p.12*). The flower stems may need unobtrusive support.

ALSO RECOMMENDED: *'Elstead' has purple-tinted flower buds; 'White Pearl' has greenish flower buds; 'Brunette' has maroon leaves and maroon-flushed flowers.*

☼ ◊ Z4   **Perennial**
‡ 3–4ft (1–1.2m) ↔ 24in (60cm)

DACTYLORHIZA FOLIOSA

This hardy orchid has a sheaf of narrow, green, often brown- or purple-spotted leaves. From the middle of these arise sturdy stems bearing pink to bright purple flowers. They appear between late spring and early summer. A lovely addition to a rock or woodland garden, and it may also be naturalized in fine grass.

ALSO RECOMMENDED: D. elata *bears deep purple flowers in late spring* Z6b; D. fuchsii *bears white to pale pink or mauve flowers marked deep red or purple* Z6.

☼ ◑ Z7 **Perennial**
‡ 24in (60cm) ↔ 6in (15cm)

DIGITALIS × MERTONENSIS

The spires of dusky pink flowers make this foxglove a clear favorite for shady herbaceous borders and woodland gardens. They are good for cutting (*see p.524*) and arise in late spring and early summer above a basal rosette of glossy dark green leaves. It may self-sow, coming true from seed. Tolerant of dry shade (*see p.216*).

ALSO RECOMMENDED: D. ferruginea *has golden brown flowers with red-brown veins* Z4; D. purpurea *f.* albiflora (see p.521).

☼ ◐◑ Z3 **Perennial**
‡ 36in (90cm) ↔ 12in (30cm)

ERANTHIS HYEMALIS

Winter aconite is one of the earliest spring-flowering bulbs, bearing buttercup-like, bright yellow flowers. These sit on a ruff of light green leaves, covering the ground from late winter until early spring (*see p.326*). It is ideal for naturalizing in dappled shade beneath deciduous trees and large shrubs, especially in alkaline soils (*see p.64*). Plant bulbs in autumn, and do not let the soil dry out in summer.

☀ ◊◊ Z4   **Perennial bulb**
↕ 2–3in (5–8cm) ↔ 2in (5cm)

ERYTHRONIUM CALIFORNICUM

One of the dog's-tooth violets, this clump-forming bulbous plant looks good planted in the light shade of deciduous trees and shrubs. Clusters of off-white flowers with backward-curving petals droop from the slender stems in spring, above the oval, dark green leaves. Plant bulbs in autumn.

ALSO RECOMMENDED: *'White Beauty' is vigorous;* E. dens-canis *has white, pink, or lilac flowers* Z4; E. *'Pagoda' is vigorous with yellow flowers* Z5.

☀ ◊◊ Z4   **Perennial bulb**
↕ 6–14in (15–35cm) ↔ 4in (10cm)

GENTIANA ASCLEPIADEA

The willow gentian forms clumps of lance-shaped, fresh green leaves on upright or arching stems. In late summer and autumn, these leafy stems are surrounded by whorls of trumpet-shaped, dark blue flowers, often spotted or striped with purple on the insides. It is suitable for a shady border or large rock garden, and it associates well with grasses and ferns. Grow in neutral to acidic, damp to permanently moist soils (*see pp.92, 372*).

ALSO RECOMMENDED: *var.* alba *has greenish white flowers.*

☀ ◐ ◑ Z4   **Perennial**
↕ 24–36in (60–90cm) ↔ 18in (45cm)

GLAUCIDIUM PALMATUM

This slowly spreading perennial forms a low mound of crinkly, bright green, sharply lobed leaves. From late spring to early summer it bears large, poppy-like, lilac-pink to mauve flowers, each with a small, central boss of golden stamens. Very attractive in a shady border or woodland garden. Grow in moist, leafy, fertile soil with shelter from wind.

ALSO RECOMMENDED: *var.* leucanthum *has white flowers.*

◑ ◐ ◑ ◓ Z6   **Perennial**
↕↔ 18in (45cm)

HACQUETIA EPIPACTIS

In late winter and early spring, this diminutive plant produces tiny yellow flowers, each cluster no more than 2in (5cm) tall, with a ruff of emerald-green bracts beneath. The glossy green leaves are divided into three wedge-shaped lobes and develop fully after flowering to form a low carpet. Grow in neutral to acidic soil (*see p.92*). A very pretty plant for a woodland garden, a shady niche in a rock garden, or a peat bed.

☼ ◐ Z6   **Perennial**
‡ 6in (15cm) ↔ 6–12in (15–30cm)

HELLEBORUS ORIENTALIS
SUBSP. GUTTATUS

Lenten roses are very variable and bear droopy flowers from midwinter to spring on upright stems above clumps of large and leathery, divided leaves. This one has creamy white flowers with dark red spots inside; they are good for cutting (*see p.524*). Tolerant of most sites, even dry shade (*see p.216*), but best in moist, neutral to alkaline soils (*see p.64*). Good for winter color in a shady shrub border.

ALSO RECOMMENDED: H. orientalis *is very variable with greenish white flowers, aging to pink;* H. foetidus *(see p.232);* H. niger *flowers from early winter* Z4.

☼ ◑◑ Z4   **Perennial**
↔ 18in (45cm)

HOSTA *'Wide Brim'*

This hosta is prized for its clumps of broad and crumpled leaves with wide, creamy yellow margins that pale with age. Light lavender-blue flowers appear on tall stems in summer. An architectural plant for bog gardens, pond margins, or containers (*see pp.372, 448, 472*). It tolerates clay soils and can be grown as a ground-cover (*see pp.12, 326*).

ALSO RECOMMENDED: *'Frances Williams'* (see p.381); *'Halcyon'* (see p.340); *'Shade Fanfare'* (see p.465); H. sieboldiana *var.* elegans (see p.490); H. ventricosa (see p.30). All Z4

☼ ☽ ◑◔ ◖◗ Z4   **Perennial**

‡ 18in (45cm) ↔ 3ft (1m)

JEFFERSONIA DUBIA

The delicate, two-lobed, blue-green leaves of this slender perennial are particularly beautiful as they unfold in spring; they are often tinted with purple when young. In late spring or early summer it bears cup-shaped, clear lavender-blue flowers on dark stems. A lovely addition to a shady niche in a rock garden or peat bed, needing moist, organic soil. Mulch annually with leaf mold in autumn.

ALSO RECOMMENDED: J. diphylla *is slightly taller with larger, kidney-shaped, deeply cleft, blue-gray leaves and white flowers.* Z6

☼ ◗ Z6   **Perennial**

‡ 8in (20cm) ↔ 6in (15cm)

LEUCOJUM VERNUM VAR. VAGNERI

The spring snowflake is a bulbous plant with stiffly upright, long and narrow, dark green leaves. Arising from between this thin clump of leaves a tall stem emerges; when it is fully grown, in late winter and early spring, two bell-shaped white flowers hang from its tip. Plant bulbs in autumn in a damp border or at a pond margin (*see p.372*).

ALSO RECOMMENDED: *L. vernum is slightly taller, flowering in early spring;* L. aestivum *has white spring flowers* Z4.

☀ ◐ ◊ Z5   **Perennial**
‡ 8in (20cm) ↔ 3in (8cm)

MITELLA BREWERI

This miterwort is a good groundcover perennial for the front of a damp, shady border or woodland garden (*see p.326*). It forms dense clumps of lobed leaves, and in spring and early summer it bears slender-stemmed spikes of many tiny, yellow-green flowers with fringed petals. Grow in moist and leafy, acidic soil (*see p.92*); it self-seeds freely. Protect from slugs.

ALSO RECOMMENDED: *M. stauropetala is taller and more vigorous with purple-tinted leaves and white or purple flowers.* Z5

☀ ◐ ◊ Z6   **Perennial**
‡ 6in (15cm) ↔ 8in (20cm)

OMPHALODES CAPPADOCICA

This perennial forms compact mounds of fresh green, heart-shaped leaves, making a good groundcover in a damp, shady border (*see p.326*) or in a rock or woodland garden. The loose clusters of white-eyed, azure blue flowers, reminiscent of forget-me-nots, appear in early spring. Grow in organic, moderately fertile soil. It is also good for paving crevices (*see p.348*).

ALSO RECOMMENDED: *'Cherry Ingram' is more compact with larger, deeper blue flowers; 'Starry Eyes' has larger flowers with a central white stripe on each petal.*

☀ ◐ Z6   **Perennial**
↕ 10in (25cm) ↔ 16in (40cm)

ONOCLEA SENSIBILIS

The sensitive fern forms a beautifully textured mass of arching and divided, deciduous fronds. These are tinted pinkish bronze as they unfurl, later turning matte pale green. An ideal plant for groundcover in a damp, shady border, especially at the edge of water (*see pp.326, 372*); it thrives in acidic soils and tolerates those rich in clay (*see pp.12, 92*). It must have a shady spot, because the fronds scorch in excessive sun.

☀ ◐◐ Z3b   **Perennial fern**
↕ 24in (60cm) ↔ indefinite

OSMUNDA REGALIS

The royal fern is a stately plant forming clumps of bright green, finely divided fronds. Distinctive, rust-colored fronds are produced at the center of each clump in summer. It is excellent in a damp border or at the margins of a pond or stream (*see p.372*), ideally in acidic soil (*see p.92*). It tolerates clay soils (*see p.12*).

ALSO RECOMMENDED: *'Cristata' has attractively crested fronds; the fronds of 'Purpurascens' are purplish in spring.*

☼ ◑ ◐◑ Z4   **Perennial fern**

‡6ft (2m) ↔ 12ft (4m)

PERSICARIA MILLETII

This clump-forming and upright plant is densely clothed in narrowly lance-shaped, dark green leaves and makes good, long-flowering groundcover in a damp, shady border (*see p.326*). The slender-stemmed, wandlike clusters of many tiny, crimson-red flowers appear from early summer to late autumn. Grow in any permanently damp site, including clay soils (*see p.12, 372*).

ALSO RECOMMENDED: P. affinis *'Donald Lowndes'* (see p.321); P. campanulata (see p.32); P. macrophylla *is smaller with pink or red flowers* Z6.

☼ ◑ ◐ Z6   **Perennial**

↔ 24in (60cm)

POLYSTICHUM SETIFERUM
Divisilobum Group

These soft shield ferns are tall and evergreen with finely divided, feathery dark green fronds that are soft to touch and form splayed clumps. They make fine architectural plants (*see p.472*) for shady borders or rock gardens with shelter from excessive winter moisture. They are also good as a groundcover or as pot plants (*see pp.326, 448*). Remove any dead or damaged fronds in spring. Tolerant of clay soils (*see p.12*).

ALSO RECOMMENDED: *The broad fronds of 'Herrenhausen' are more spreading;* P. munitum (see p.492).

☼ ◐ ☀ ◊◑ Z4   **Perennial fer**

↕↔ 20–28in (50–70cm)

PRIMULA VIALII

This deciduous border perennial has a basal rosette of narrow green leaves, from which emerges an upright flower stem in summer, topped by a dense spike of dark red buds. These open to violet-blue flowers. Choose a site with rich, neutral to acidic soil (*see p.92*); full sun is tolerated if the soil remains moist (*see p.372*). It can also be grown as a container plant (*see p.448*).

ALSO RECOMMENDED: P. florindae (see p.389); P. japonica *'Postford White'* (see p.389); P. polyanthus (see p.468); P. pulverulenta (see p.390); P. rosea (see p.390).

☼ ◐ ☀ ◊ Z4   **Perenni**

↕ 12–24in (30–60cm) ↔ 12in (30cm)

PRUNELLA GRANDIFLORA

Large selfheal is a vigorous plant with dark green leaves in clumps at ground level; it is good as a groundcover in a damp, shady border and may be naturalized in fine grass (*see pp.304, 326*). The two-lipped purple flowers, borne in whorls on square stems in summer, attract a host of beneficial insects (*see p.494*). It grows in any soil, including clay (*see p.12*); give it space to expand to prevent it from swamping smaller plants.

ALSO RECOMMENDED: *'Pink Loveliness' has pink flowers; those of 'White Loveliness' are pure white.*

☼ ◐ ◊◊ Z3b   **Perennial**
‡ 6in (15cm) ↔ 3ft (1m) or more

SCILLA PERUVIANA *'Alba'*

This bulbous plant bears a basal cluster of straplike leaves, to 24in (60cm) long, throughout the year; there is no dormant period, and new leaves grow in autumn as the old ones die away. Dome-shaped clusters of many white flowers rise above the leaves in early summer. Plant bulbs under deciduous trees and shrubs or in grass in autumn. It also grows in sandy and alkaline soils (*see pp.38, 64*), and coastal and hot, dry sites (*see pp.166, 190*).

ALSO RECOMMENDED: *S. peruviana has large heads of deep blue flowers.*

☼ ◐ ◊◊ Z8   **Perennial bulb**
‡ 6–12in (15–30cm) ↔ 4in (10cm)

THALICTRUM DELAVAYI *'Album'*

An upright, clump-forming perennial with finely divided, fresh green leaves and fluffy white flowers in branching heads from midsummer to autumn. This plant is an excellent textural foil for bold-leaved plants in a mixed or herbaceous border. Divide clumps every three to four years to maintain their vigor.

ALSO RECOMMENDED: *T. delavayi has purple-tinted stems and lilac or white flowers; 'Hewitt's Double' has rich mauve, double flowers and is very floriferous.*

☀ ◊◊ Z5 **Perennial**

↕ 4ft (1.2m) ↔ 24in (60cm)

TRILLIUM SESSILE

The wakerobin is an upright, clump-forming plant valued for its stemless maroon flowers of late spring; they nestle atop whorls of oval, deep green, marbled leaves. Hostas make excellent companions to this plant in a damp border. Choose leafy, neutral to acidic soil (*see p.92*), providing a mulch of leaf mold in autumn.

ALSO RECOMMENDED: *T. chloropetalum has fragrant, greenish white, yellow, or purple-brown flowers* Z6; *T. erectum (see p.117); T. luteum has sweetly scented, golden or bronze-green flowers* Z6b.

☀☀ ◊◊ Z5b **Perennial**

↕ 12in (30cm) ↔ 8in (20cm)

TROLLIUS × CULTORUM
Alabaster

This globeflower is a robust plant with pale yellow spring flowers. These are held above the clumps of midgreen leaves that are deeply cut with five rounded lobes. Good for bright color beside a pond or stream (*see p.372*) or in a damp border; the flowers can be cut for indoor decoration (*see p.524*). It grows well in heavy clay soils (*see p.12*).

ALSO RECOMMENDED: *'Earliest of All' has yellow flowers; 'Orange Princess' has golden orange flowers into summer.*

☼ ◐ ◊◖ Z3b   **Perennial**
↕ 24in (60cm) ↔ 16in (40cm)

VIOLA RIVINIANA
Purpurea Group

This group of small perennials derived from the dog violet has oval and toothed, purple-tinged leaves with long stems that emerge from ground level. Pretty purple flowers with spurs appear in late spring. These violets grow well in damp or dry shade (*see p.216*); their invasive habit makes them good as a groundcover or as a colony in a wildlife garden (*see pp.326, 494*).

ALSO RECOMMENDED: V. riviniana *is less invasive, with pale violet-blue flowers and midgreen leaves.*

☼ ◐ ◊◖ Z6   **Perennial**
↕ 4–8in (10–20cm) ↔ 8–16in (20–40cm)

PLANTS FOR NORTH- & EAST-FACING WALLS

CLIMBERS AND wall-trained shrubs establish a vertical element in a planting design, which is especially valuable in lending color and variety to small properties; no matter how extensive their vertical spread, climbers take up relatively little space at ground level. In the wild, many climbers, such as *Akebia quinata* (*see p.271*) and *Schisandra rubriflora* (*see p.278*), are to be found scrambling up and through trees, so they are well adapted to shady conditions. Walls that face east receive more light and may even be in direct sun for several hours in the morning. Plants that may be grown on east-facing walls, therefore, need not be shade-demanding plants. It is also the ideal site for plants like *Lonicera japonica* 'Halliana' (*see p.276*), which grow well in good light, but become stressed and more vulnerable to pests, such as aphids, if exposed to hot midday sun.

North- and east-facing walls can be dry places, since they often have a rain shadow at

their base, especially if overhung by the house eaves, where rainfall is unable to penetrate. To avoid this problem, plant at least 18in (45cm) away from the foot of the wall.

There is one important feature of easterly walls to be borne in mind, especially during winter and early spring. Easterly walls receive the first morning light, and its warmth can do considerable damage to the frozen leaves, buds, or flowers of otherwise hardy plants, particularly camellias (*see pp.99, 240, 264, 450*); frozen water in the plant cells causes them to rupture if thawing is rapid. The sun's warmth can also induce plants into early growth in spring, and the soft new growth is far more susceptible to cold damage. On a north wall, the temperature rises slowly, so it is much less likely to cause damage, and plants will not be tempted into early growth. Although a north wall may be relatively well lit if it is in an open site, only plants that are tolerant of shade can be expected to thrive there.

TRAINING PLANTS

Climbers use different methods to attach themselves as they climb. Some, like *Hedera colchica* 'Sulphur Heart' (*see p.275*) and *Parthenocissus tricuspidata* (*see p.277*), attach themselves by aerial roots, which cling to any surface that offers support. They usually need a little initial guidance by means of stakes, but once established, they become self-supporting. Twining or tendril climbers, like *Aconitum hemsleyanum* (*see p.271*) and *Clematis montana* (*see p.274*), must have some support that they can cling to, such as other shrubs or a framework of wires or a trellis. Wall-trained shrubs that do not climb naturally, flowering quince for example (*see p.264*), need to be trained and tied in to their support. Mount wall supports before planting, attaching them to slats 4–6in (10–15cm) thick to allow space for air circulate, which helps reduce the incidence of diseases such as mildew. There will also be more room for plant stems to expand.

CAMELLIA × WILLIAMSII *'Golden Spangles'*

This vigorous shrub is valued for its lustrous, dark green leaves with golden centers and for its elegant, single, bright red-pink flowers borne from mid- to late spring. It is ideal for a north wall, but avoid east-facing sites, since the combination of morning sun after frost is damaging. It tolerates acidic soils and damp shade (*see pp.92, 238*). Prune young plants to shape after flowering; the flowers cut well (*see p.524*).

ALSO RECOMMENDED: *'Bow Bells' has single pink flowers from winter; 'J.C. Williams' has pale pink, single flowers in spring.*

☀️ ◑ ◖◗ Z7b   **Evergreen shrub**
‡ 6–15ft (2–5m) ↔ 3–12ft (1–4m)

CHAENOMELES SPECIOSA *'Moerloosei'*

A fast-growing shrub that has tangled, spiny branches and glossy dark green leaves. It bears large, pink-flushed white flowers in early spring, followed by small, yellow-green fruits in autumn. It thrives on sunless walls; if wall-trained, shorten sideshoots to two or three leaves in late spring. It will also grow against sunnier walls as a hedge, or as a free-standing shrub (*see pp.138, 280*). Tolerant of alkaline soils (*see p.64*).

ALSO RECOMMENDED: *'Geisha Girl' has apricot-pink flowers; 'Nivalis' has pure white flowers.*

☀️◑ ◗ ◖ ◖ ◖ Z5b   **Deciduous shrub**
‡ 8ft (2.5m) ↔ 15ft (5m)

COTONEASTER HORIZONTALIS

The herringbone branches of this spreading shrub are clothed in small, glossy dark green leaves. In summer, tiny pinkish white flowers attract bees; the profusion of bright red berries that follow persist well into winter unless consumed by birds (*see p.494*). It grows in most soils, including alkaline ones, and it tolerates dry shade (*see pp.64, 216*). Keep pruning to a minimum, in winter if necessary.

ALSO RECOMMENDED: *C. integrifolius is evergreen with dark pinkish red fruits Z6b; C. simonsii is deciduous with red fruits Z7.*

☼ ◊ Z5   **Deciduous shrub**
‡ 3ft (1m) ↔ 5ft (1.5m)

CRINODENDRON HOOKERIANUM

The lantern tree is an upright shrub with elegant, narrow, leathery, dark green foliage. In late spring and early summer, it bears hanging crimson flowers that give rise to its common name. A most attractive specimen for a sheltered, north-facing or shady site (avoid east-facing positions) away from wind. Grow in organic, acidic soil (*see p.92*). Keep pruning to a minimum.

ALSO RECOMMENDED: *C. patagua bears fragrant white flowers late summer.*

☼ ◊◊ Min 35°F (2°C)   **Evergreen shrub**
‡ 20ft (6m) ↔ 15ft (5m)

DRIMYS WINTERI

Winter's bark is a superb and elegant specimen for a north wall. It forms a strongly upright shrub with elliptical, dark green leaves, and it bears large clusters of fragrant, ivory-white flowers from spring to early summer. Shelter from wind and avoid east-facing walls. Keep pruning to a minimum. It tolerates clay soils and sunnier walls (*see pp.12, 280*).

ALSO RECOMMENDED: *var.* andina *is a dwarf, to 3ft (1m) tall;* D. lanceolata *is similar with dark red stems (Tender).*

☼ ◐ ◊ Z8   **Evergreen shrub**
‡ 50ft (15m) ↔ 30ft (10m)

EUCRYPHIA MILLIGANII

This slender, upright shrub with glossy dark green leaves is valued for its cup-shaped white flowers in midsummer, which have a central boss of golden stamens. Grow in fertile, neutral to acidic soil (*see p.92*), and shelter from wind. Keep pruning to a minimum.

ALSO RECOMMENDED: E. glutinosa *is taller and deciduous with double white flowers;* E. lucida, *also taller, has white flowers in early to midsummer. Both are marginally hardy in* Z8.

☼ ◐ ◊ Z8   **Evergreen shrub**
‡ 20ft (6m) ↔ 5ft (1.5m)

FORSYTHIA SUSPENSA

An open shrub, with strongly arching branches, that is valued for its nodding, bright yellow flowers that wreathe the bare branches in early to midspring. The leaves are oval and mid-green. It is also useful as a specimen shrub, in a border, or as an informal hedge (*see p.138*). It grows in most fertile, well-drained soils, including alkaline (*see p.64*). Cut out some of the oldest stems on established plants each year after flowering. The flowers are good for cutting (*see p.524*).

ALSO RECOMMENDED: *f.* atrocaulis *and* 'Nymans' *have purplish young growth.*

☼ ◑ ○ Z5b   **Deciduous shrub**
↕↔ 10ft (3m)

GARRYA × ISSAQUAHENSIS *'Pat Ballard'*

This upright shrub, densely clothed in bright green leaves, is grown for its attractively pendent, purple-tinted, gray catkins that festoon the branches in midwinter. It is especially effective when trained against a north-facing wall. It needs minimal pruning; if necessary, shorten outward-growing shoots after flowering.

ALSO RECOMMENDED: *'Glasnevin Wine' has purplish stems and green-red catkins;* G. elliptica *(see p.219).*

☼ ◑ ○ Z8   **Evergreen shrub**
↕ 12ft (4m) ↔ 10ft (3m)

ILLICIUM ANISATUM

Chinese anise is a broadly conical shrub with glossy green leaves and clusters of fragrant, star-shaped, creamy white flowers in midspring. It does well on a north-facing wall, in a woodland garden, or in a shrub border. Grow in organic, acidic soil (*see p.92*) with shelter from wind. It needs very little pruning.

ALSO RECOMMENDED: I. floridanum *has nodding, red-purple flowers. Z7*

☼ ◐ ◊ *f* Z7   **Evergreen shrub**

‡ 25ft (8m) ↔ 20ft (6m)

JASMINUM HUMILE

Yellow jasmine is a bushy plant with bright green leaves and fragrant, rich yellow flowers from late spring to early summer. It is suitable for a north-facing wall, although it flowers more freely in sun (*see p.280*); the flowers are good for cutting (*see p.524*). After flowering, shorten flowered shoots to a strong bud; when mature, remove one in five of the oldest, flowered stems. Also good in a sunny or shady border, or as a groundcover in sun (*see p.304*). Tolerant of alkaline soils (*see p.64*).

ALSO RECOMMENDED: *'Revolutum' has larger flowers*; J. nudiflorum (see p.76).

☼ ◐ ◊ *f* Z7   **Evergreen shrub**

‡ 8ft (2.5m) ↔ 10ft (3m)

MAHONIA × MEDIA *'Charity'*

A fast-growing shrub that bears dense, upright then spreading spikes of fragrant yellow flowers from late autumn to spring, suitable for a north-facing wall. It makes a fine architectural specimen for a damp, shady border or wildlife garden (*see pp.238, 472, 494*). The glossy dark green leaves are spiny, making it useful for vandalproof barrier plantings. Prune any bare, leggy stems back hard after flowering. It tolerates alkaline soils (*see p.64*).

ALSO RECOMMENDED: *'Lionel Fortescue' and 'Winter Sun' are similar.*

☀ ◐ ◊◊ Z8　　　　**Evergreen shrub**
↕ 15ft (5m) ↔ 15ft (4m)

PYRACANTHA *'Soleil d'Or'*

This spiny, upright shrub is good for training on walls of any exposure (*see p.280*). The clustered white flowers of early summer – offset against glossy dark green leaves – attract bees, and the bright golden yellow berries that follow and persist into winter are among the last to be taken by birds (*see p.494*). It can also be grown as a hedge or in exposed sites (*see pp.118, 138*). Cut back unwanted growth in midspring. It tolerates clay soils (*see p.12*).

ALSO RECOMMENDED: *'Golden Charmer'* (see p.159); *'Mohave'* (see p.19); *'Watereri'* (see p.505).

☀ ◐ ◊ Z6b　　　　**Evergreen shrub**
↕ 10ft (3m) ↔ 8ft (2.5m)

RIBES LAURIFOLIUM

This compact shrub with scalloped, leathery, dark green leaves is valued for its hanging clusters of pale green flowers in late winter and early spring. On female plants, flowers are followed by small, egg-shaped, red then black berries if plants of both genders are grown together. It grows well on a north-facing wall. Trim after flowering, if necessary. It is also suitable for a damp, shady border (*see p.238*).

ALSO RECOMMENDED: R. alpinum (*see p.222*) *and* R. sanguineum *'Brocklebankii'* (*see p.161*) *both tolerate dry sites.*

☼☀ ◊◊ Z7   **Evergreen shrub**
↕ 3ft (1m) ↔ 5ft (1.5m)

ROSA *Danse du Feu*

The rounded, double, intense scarlet flowers of this stiff-stemmed climbing rose are borne throughout summer and autumn against very glossy dark green foliage. It does well in shade, but it flowers more profusely in sun (*see p.280*). Train the stems to cover the wall, then prune to keep it confined after flowering. It tolerates alkaline soils and can be container-grown (*see pp.64, 412, 448*). The flowers cut well (*see p.524*).

ALSO RECOMMENDED: *'Albéric Barbier' has double white flowers; 'New Dawn' has fragrant pink flowers; 'Zéphirine Drouhin' has very fragrant, deep pink flowers.* All Z6

☼☀ ◊◊ Z6   **Deciduous shrub**
↕↔ 8ft (2.5m)

Aconitum Hemsleyanum

This vigorous, twining perennial has
lobed, fresh green leaves and produces
curious, hooded, glossy violet flowers
from midsummer to early autumn.
Provide the support of a trellis if it is to
grow on a wall, or allow it to scramble
through earlier-flowering shrubs to
extend their period of interest. It is
also suitable for a shady border.

☼ ◑ ◊◑ Z6   **Climber**
↕ 6–10ft (2–3m)

Akebia Quinata

A woody-stemmed, semievergreen,
twining climber valued for its five-
parted, dark green leaves that flush
purple in winter. Fragrant, brownish
purple flowers in early spring give rise
to sausagelike purple fruits. In areas
with late frosts, avoid sites that receive
morning sun to reduce the risk of flower
damage. Grow on a wall or pergola, or
train into a tree. Trim after flowering.
It tolerates damp, shady sites
(*see p.238*).

ALSO RECOMMENDED: A. trifoliata *has
leaves that are bronzed when young,
and purple flowers and fruits.* Z6

☼ ◑ ◊◑ *f* Z5b   **Climber**
↕ 30ft (10m)

ASTERANTHERA OVATA

The bristly and rounded, bright green leaves of this evergreen climber are borne on white-hairy stems and offset by tubular, brilliant red-pink flowers in summer. It thrives in damp soils against sheltered, north-facing walls. If not tied in to a support, it becomes creeping and stem-rooting, making a good groundcover in damp shade (*see pp.238, 326*). Grow in organic, acidic soil (*see p.92*).

☀ ◊◊ Z8 **Climber**

↕ 12ft (4m) ↔ 6ft (2m)

BERBERIDOPSIS CORALLINA

The coral plant displays its hanging, spherical, dark red flowers against an evergreen backdrop of heart-shaped, dark green leaves from summer to early autumn. It is excellent on a north-facing wall if supported on wires and sheltered from wind. Grow in cool, organic, neutral to acidic soil (*see p.92*); protect the roots with a deep but loose winter mulch. Pruning is best avoided, but may be necessary in spring to keep the growth confined. It tolerates dry shade and can be grown as groundcover if allowed to trail without support (*see pp.216, 326*).

☀ ◊◊ Z8 **Climber**

↕↔ 15ft (5m)

CELASTRUS ORBICULATUS

The leaves of the Oriental bittersweet turn yellow before falling in autumn. In summer, it bears clusters of tiny green flowers that are followed by yellow fruits; these open to expose orange-red seeds. Both male and female plants must be grown in sun for reliable fruiting. Keep pruning to a minimum, removing damaged growth in early spring. It tolerates alkaline soils and will grow in dry shade (*see pp.64, 216*).

ALSO RECOMMENDED: *Plants of the Hermaphrodite Group bears both male and female flowers on the same plant.*

☼ ◑ ◊ Z4 **Climber**
↔ 46ft (14m)

CLEMATIS *'Nelly Moser'*

This deciduous clematis produces large, mauve-pink flowers in early summer and benefits from a shady root run. The flowers retain their best color in shade, as do other pale-flowered clematis; although more flowers are produced in sun, they fade quickly. Remove dead or damaged growth in early spring, and cut healthy stems back to strong buds. It tolerates alkaline soils and can be pot-grown (*see pp.64, 448*).

ALSO RECOMMENDED: *'Bee's Jubilee' has deep pink flowers; 'Bill Mackenzie' (see p.299); 'Hagley Hybrid' has pink flowers; 'Marie Boisselot' has white flowers. All Z3b*

☼ ◑ ◊ Z3b ↔ 3ft (1m) **Climber**
↕ 6–10ft (2–3m)

CLEMATIS MONTANA

This deciduous climber forms a tangled mass of stems and is almost obscured by a profusion of single white flowers in spring. It thrives on walls of any exposure (*see p.280*) as well as in containers (*see p.448*). Prune after flowering, removing dead or damaged stems; shorten others as necessary. It tolerates alkaline soils (*see p.64*).

ALSO RECOMMENDED: *f.* grandiflora *has larger flowers;* 'Tetrarose' *has pink flowers;* C. rehderiana (see p.300); C. tangutica (see p.508).

☼ ◐ ◊ Z5b   **Climber**

↕ 15–46ft (5–14m) ↔ 6–10ft (2–3m)

CODONOPSIS CLEMATIDEA

The branching stems of this twining, herbaceous climber bear narrow and pointed, gray-green leaves. In late summer, nodding, bell-shaped, pale blue-gray flowers appear; their yellow, black, and blue markings within are best seen from below. Train it against a wall or allow it to scramble through shrubs in a shady border. Provide shelter from strong winds.

ALSO RECOMMENDED: C. convolvulacea *has violet-blue flowers and needs a very sheltered site* Z4; C. tangshen *has yellow to olive-green flowers* Z4.

☼ ◐ ◊◊ Z6   **Climber**

↕ 5ft (1.5m)

HEDERA COLCHICA
'Sulphur Heart'

Persian ivy is a vigorous, self-clinging, evergreen climber that can also be grown as a groundcover or in a container (*see pp.304, 326, 412, 448*). The large, heart-shaped leaves are dark green suffused with creamy yellow. It tolerates dry shade and grows well in alkaline soils (*see pp.64, 216*). Prune at any time of year to restrict size.

ALSO RECOMMENDED: *'Dentata Variegata' has light green leaves with cream margins;* H. helix *'Erecta'* (*see p.220*); *'Glacier'* (*see p.330*); *f.* poetarum (*see p.509*); H. hibernica (*see p.331*).

☼ ◑ ◐ ◊◊ Z7   **Climber**
‡ 15ft (5m)

HYDRANGEA ANOMALA
SUBSP. PETIOLARIS

This self-clinging climber forms a woody framework that is attractive even after the heart-shaped leaves have turned yellow and fallen in autumn. Creamy white, lacecap flowerheads cover the branches for long periods in summer, illuminating a shady wall to perfection. Keep pruning to a minimum, trimming to size after flowering, if necessary. It tolerates damp, shady sites (*see p.238*) and will grow as a groundcover or in a pot (*see pp.326, 448*).

ALSO RECOMMENDED: H. seemannii *and* H. serratifolia *give similar effects but are evergreen and less hardy.* Both Z8

☼ ◑ ◐ ◊◊ Z5   **Climber**
‡↔ 50ft (15m)

LAPAGERIA ROSEA

The Chilean bellflower is a long-lived, twining climber with oval, evergreen leaves. From summer to late autumn, it produces large, narrowly bell-shaped, waxy, red to pink flowers. Where marginally hardy, it needs the protection of a sheltered, shady wall; avoid east-facing sites, and provide a deep winter mulch. Keep pruning to a minimum, removing damaged growth in spring. It tolerates sandy and acidic soils, and dry sites in shade (*see pp.38, 216*).

☀ ◊ Min 30°F (-1°C)   **Climber**
↕↔ 15ft (5m)

LONICERA JAPONICA 'Halliana'

This Japanese honeysuckle is a very vigorous, evergreen, twining climber with sweetly fragrant white flowers that age to dark yellow. They appear from spring to late summer. Cut back shoots on established plants by up to a third in spring or after flowering. It can be grown as a groundcover or in containers (*see pp.216, 448*) and tolerates alkaline soils and dry shade (*see pp.64, 216*).

ALSO RECOMMENDED: *'Hall's Prolific' is more floriferous; var.* repens *has purplish leaves and red-white flowers;* L. × americana *is deciduous with yellow flowers* Z6.

☀ ◑ ◊◊ ♦ f Z6   **Climber**
↕ 30ft (10m)

PARTHENOCISSUS TRICUSPIDATA

Boston ivy is a woody, deciduous, self-clinging climber with lobed, bright green leaves that blaze up in intense shades of scarlet, crimson, and purple in autumn. Provide young plants with some support until established. Cut out unwanted growth in autumn. It tolerates alkaline soils and can also be grown on a sunny wall (*see pp.64, 280*).

ALSO RECOMMENDED: *'Veitchii' has dark red-purple autumn foliage color;*
P. henryana (see p.77).

☼☀ ◊◊ Z5b   **Climber**
‡ 70ft (20m)

PILEOSTEGIA VIBURNOIDES

This woody, evergreen climber is slow-growing and self-clinging, and it is ideal for walls of any exposure, even deep, damp shade (*see pp.238, 280*). The glossy dark green leaves form an elegant backdrop to the clusters of small, star-shaped, creamy white flowers that appear in late summer and autumn. Keep pruning to a minimum, but trim after flowering to keep it within bounds.

 ◊ Z7   **Climber**
‡↔ 20ft (6m)

SCHISANDRA RUBRIFLORA

A twining climber with lance-shaped, dark green leaves that turn yellow before falling in autumn. In spring and summer, it bears hanging, deep crimson flowers followed (on female plants) by pendent spikes of fleshy red fruit. Male and female plants are needed to obtain fruits. Train onto a wall or up into a tree; tie in young shoots until established. It tolerates coastal sites (*see p.166*).

ALSO RECOMMENDED: S. chinensis *and* S. grandiflora *have white or pale pink flowers in late spring and early summer. Both Z7*

☼ ◐ ◊◊ Z7   **Climber**

↕ 30ft (10m)

SCHIZOPHRAGMA INTEGRIFOLIUM

This deciduous climber forms an intricate branch pattern that is attractive even when leafless in winter (*see p.472*). The dark green leaves complement the broad heads of creamy white flowers to perfection in summer. Tie to a support until it begins to cling by itself. Keep pruning to a minimum; trim to within its bounds in spring. It thrives on walls of any exposure and tolerates damp shade (*see pp.238, 280*).

ALSO RECOMMENDED: S. hydrangeoides *is similar Z5;* 'Roseum' *has flowers with pink bracts.*

☼ ◐ ◊ Z5b   **Climber**

↕↔ 40ft (12m)

TROPAEOLUM SPECIOSUM

The flame nasturtium is a slender, herbaceous climber, producing long-spurred, bright vermilion flowers throughout summer and autumn. The bright green leaves are attractively divided into several leaflets. It is very effective grown through dark-leaved hedging, such as yew (*see p.144*). If given support and cool shade at the roots it will thrive on shady walls. It will also grow as a groundcover and in containers (*see pp.304, 412, 448*).

☼ ◑ ◊◊ Z7b   **Climber**
↕↔ 10ft (3m) or more

VITIS AMURENSIS

Amur grape is a vigorous vine suitable for training against a trellis or partially shaded wall or up into a large shrub or tree. It is grown for its lobed and toothed, deep green foliage that turns to beautiful shades of red and purple before it falls in autumn. Small bunches of inedible, white-bloomed black grapes appear at the end of summer. It has woody stems and climbs using tendrils. Trim to size in midwinter. It tolerates full sun (*see p.280*).

ALSO RECOMMENDED: V. *'Brant' has copper-bronze autumn leaf color and large bunches of edible, blue-black grapes.*

☼ ◑ ◊ Z3b   **Climber**
↕↔ 40ft (12m)

PLANTS FOR SOUTH- & WEST-FACING WALLS

M ANY PLANTS give their best when allowed to bask in the heat of a warm, sunny wall, and they usually respond by producing a greater profusion of flowers. Since such walls often bound the preferred site for a patio or terrace – where the gardener may also bask during summer – they make the perfect site for wall shrubs or climbers with fragrant flowers, such as *Magnolia grandiflora* 'Goliath' (*see p.283*) or *Rosa banksiae* 'Lutea' (*see p.297*). The warm, still air of such sheltered sites quickly becomes saturated with scent, especially on warm summer evenings, creating the most pleasing ambience for outdoor dining, entertaining, or simply relaxing with a cool drink in hand.

EXTENDING THE RANGE

In cold areas, a warm wall can really make a difference to the survival of marginally hardy plants, such as *Fremontodendron* 'California Glory' (*see p.293*) or *Coronilla valentina* subsp. *glauca* (*see*

p.290). Even much hardier plants, such as *Vitis vinifera* 'Purpurea' (*see p.303*) and *Cydonia oblonga* 'Vranja' (*see p.282*), fruit better given the extra warmth. A warm wall absorbs the heat of the sun and acts like a night-storage radiator, even in winter, conferring some degree of cold protection to any plant growing against it. Wood that is well-matured by sun and warmth in summer is harder and more resistant to winter cold, and it has energy in reserve to produce better-quality flowers and fruit in greater abundance.

Since these sites do not receive the first light of morning, plants warm relatively slowly after frost, thus avoiding the damage that is often caused by the too-rapid thawing of frozen leaves and flower buds. For sun-loving plants that can't cope with scorching conditions, grow them against a southwest or west-facing wall; while these sites are still warm and sunny, they do not bear the full brunt of the midsummer sun at midday.

IMPROVING THE SITE

Unless a wall faces the direction of the prevailing wind, it is likely to be shadowed from rain at its base. This dryness is worsened when the wall faces the sun. On a south wall that receives the hottest midday sun, this is especially relevant. Plants not only need to contend with drought but also with the increased likelihood of diseases, such as powdery mildew, that proliferate in hot, dry conditions and especially when the plants are stressed. To avoid this problem, plant at least 18in (45cm) away from the foot of the wall and set supporting wires or a trellis 4–6in (10–15cm) away from the wall to permit good air circulation. Improve the moisture-retaining capacities of the soil by incorporating plenty of well-rotted organic matter before planting and by mulching well in spring. You can use an organic mulch or one of gravel or water-worn pebbles to help conserve moisture; the latter can be matched to blend with the materials used in the wall.

ACACIA PRAVISSIMA

Oven's wattle is a shrubby small tree with short branches clothed in gray-green foliage. The tiny and fluffy, bright yellow flowerheads that appear in late winter and spring are sweetly fragrant and are suitable for cutting (*see p.524*). Choose a sheltered wall in mild, almost frost-free climates; elsewhere it can be grown in a cool conservatory. Keep pruning to a minimum. It tolerates sandy soils and hot, dry sites (*see pp.38, 190*).

ALSO RECOMMENDED: *A. baileyana has feathery silver-gray leaves;* A. dealbata *has silvery blue foliage. (Both tender)*

☀ ◊ *f* Min 40°F (5°C) **Evergreen tree**
↕ 10–25ft (3–8m) ↔ 10–22ft (3–7m)

CYDONIA OBLONGA *'Vranja'*

This quince is grown for its edible, golden yellow fruits that are green before they ripen and follow the apple-blossomlike, white or pink flowers of spring. It forms a rounded crown of oval, dark green leaves and becomes increasingly picturesque with age. Ideal for fan-training on a south- or west-facing wall; in winter, cut back flowered shoots to within two to four buds of the framework; trim back inward- and outward-facing shoots.

ALSO RECOMMENDED: *Portugal (syn. 'Lusitanica') has gray-downy fruits.*

☀ ◊ Z6 **Deciduous tree**
↕↔ 15ft (5m)

MAGNOLIA GRANDIFLORA 'Goliath'

The huge and fragrant creamy flowers of this dense, conical tree nestle among glossy dark green leaves. The flowers appear sporadically from summer to late autumn, and they are displayed to perfection if the plant is grown against a south or west wall. Best in acidic soils, but it tolerates alkaline conditions (*see pp.64, 92*). Keep pruning to a minimum.

ALSO RECOMMENDED: *M. grandiflora has smaller flowers; 'Exmouth' is hardier with smaller flowers; 'Little Gem' is smaller.*

☼ ◑ ◊◊ *f* Z7　　　**Evergreen tree**
↕ 20–60ft (6–18m) ↔ 50ft (15m)

OLEA EUROPAEA

The olive tree has a Mediterranean ambience and is characterized by its beautiful habit, rough gray bark, and narrow, gray-green leaves. The summer flowers are insignificant, although they may be followed by green olives that turn black when ripe. Where winters are mild, site against a sunny, sheltered wall; otherwise, grow in a cool greenhouse or conservatory. It can be container-grown (*see p.412*). Ensure the soil is sharply drained.

☼ ◊ Z8　　　**Evergreen tree**
↕ 30ft (10m)

ABELIA SCHUMANNII

A rounded shrub with arching branches
and oval leaves that are bronze when
young. Funnel-shaped, lilac-pink
flowers appear from late summer to
autumn. It thrives against a south- or
west-facing wall, but it is also good
in a sunny border or hot, dry site (*see
p.190*). Prune back some of the oldest
growth after flowering; remove dead
or damaged growth in spring.

ALSO RECOMMENDED: A. × grandiflora *has
fragrant, pinkish white flowers* Z5b;
*A. 'Edward Goucher' is smaller, with
deeper flowers* Z5b.

☼ ◐ Z7　　　　　　**Deciduous shrub**
↕ 6ft (2m) ↔ 10ft (3m)

ABELIOPHYLLUM DISTICHUM

The white forsythia is an open,
spreading shrub with matte dark green
leaves that turn purple before falling in
autumn. The fragrant white flowers,
borne in long clusters, appear from late
winter to early spring. It flowers earlier
and most profusely when grown against
a warm, south- or west-facing wall.
Prune after flowering; if wall-trained,
cut flowered shoots back to within two
to four buds of the base, and shorten
inward- or outward-growing shoots.

☼ ◊ *f* Z5b　　　　　　**Deciduous shrub**
↕↔ 5ft (1.5m)

ABUTILON
'Souvenir de Bonn'

This treelike abutilon is suitable for a sheltered, south- or west-facing wall in mild, frost-free climates; elsewhere, grow in a conservatory. It has lobed green leaves with pale yellow margins and bears hanging, deep orange flowers from spring to autumn. Remove or shorten wayward shoots in early spring. If grown in a large pot, it can be moved under cover in winter (*see p.412*).

ALSO RECOMMENDED: *'Kentish Belle' has apricot-yellow flowers and dark green leaves; A. megapotamicum has small yellow flowers – both are a bit hardier.*

☀ ◊ Z8 **Evergreen shrub**
10ft (3m) ↔ 6–10ft (2–3m)

FEIJOA SELLOWIANA

The pineapple guava makes quite a large bush. Its silvery gray-green leaves give it the appearance of an olive tree. Instead, this plant produces showy red flowers in midsummer; they are very distinctive with long stamens and white petal backs. Edible, guavalike fruits follow in warm areas. It tolerates coastal and hot, dry conditions (*see p.166, 190*) and sandy soils (*see p.38*). Prune back excessive or damaged growth in spring.

☀ ◊ Min 35°F (2°C) **Evergreen shrub**
6ft (2m) ↔ 6ft (2.5m)

ARTEMISIA ARBORESCENS

The finely cut, silvery white, aromatic foliage of this upright shrub is at its best when grown on a south- or west-facing wall. Small yellow flowerheads appear in summer and autumn. It provides fine textural contrasts in a sunny border. Cut back hard in spring for the best foliage effects. It tolerates sandy and alkaline soils (*see pp.38, 64*), and coastal and hot, dry sites (*see pp.166, 190*).

ALSO RECOMMENDED: A. abrotanum, *lad's love or southernwood, has aromatic, gray-green leaves* Z4; A. *'Powis Castle' is more compact, with silver-gray leaves* Z5b.

☼ ◊ ƒ Z6   **Evergreen shrub**
‡ 3ft (1m) ↔ 5ft (1.5m)

BUDDLEJA CRISPA

An excellent plant for attracting bees and butterflies (*see p.494*), this arching shrub has white-woolly shoots clothed in grayish green leaves. It bears masses of fragrant, lilac to purple flowers from summer to autumn, flowering most freely on a south- or west-facing wall. Cut back all stems close to the base each year as the buds begin to swell in spring.

ALSO RECOMMENDED: B. lindleyana (*see p.69*); B. *'Lochinch' has long clusters of violet-blue flowers* Z7; B. × weyeriana *'Sungold' has dark orange-yellow flowers* Z7.

☼ ◊ ƒ Min 35°F (2°C)   **Deciduous shrub**
‡↔ 10ft (3m)

CALLISTEMON CITRINUS *'Splendens'*

The crimson bottlebrush is unmistakeable; its brilliant red, spring and summer flower spikes that appear near the tips of the arching branches radiate warmth and beauty. The narrow, leathery, gray-green leaves have a lemony eucalyptus scent when crushed. It needs neutral or acidic soils and tolerates coastal sites (*see pp.92, 166*). Pinch tips to promote bushiness; hard prune in spring, if necessary.

ALSO RECOMMENDED: C. citrinus *is similar;* C. salignus *has green or white, sometimes pink flowers.*

☼ ☼ ◊ Min 40°F (5°C) **Evergreen shrub**
‡ 6–25ft (2–8m) ↔ 5–20ft (1.5–6m)

CARPENTERIA CALIFORNICA

The tree anemone is a summer-flowering shrub bearing large, fragrant white flowers with showy yellow stamens. It has glossy dark green, narrow leaves. Where marginally hardy, it benefits from the extra warmth and shelter given by a south- or west-facing wall; protect from wind. In spring, remove branches that have become exhausted by flowering, cutting them back to their bases. Tolerant of alkaline soils, and it is good in hot, dry sites (*see pp.64, 190*).

☼ ◊ *f*Z7b **Evergreen shrub**
‡↔ 6ft (2m) or more

CEANOTHUS THYRSIFLORUS 'Skylark'

This bushy shrub has glossy green leaves and bears a profusion of deep blue flowers in late spring and early summer. Where marginally hardy, it benefits from the protection of a warm wall and flowers most freely there. Protect from wind. Tip-prune in spring when young; once established, prune only to shape after flowering.

ALSO RECOMMENDED: *C. 'Autumnal Blue'* (see p.69); *'Concha' has dark blue flowers that open from reddish buds; 'Puget Blue' is taller; 'Southmead' is more compact.*

☼ ◊ Z7b   **Evergreen shrub**
‡ 6ft (2m) ↔ 5ft (1.5m)

CESTRUM PARQUI

Willow-leaved jessamine is valued for its broad clusters of night-scented yellow flowers that are borne from summer to autumn; the berries that follow are violet-brown. Good for shrub borders against warm, south- or west-facing walls; if grown close to a window or patio area, its scent can be appreciated on summer evenings. Cut all stems back to the base in early spring. It may die back to the base in winter, but it usually recovers in spring.

ALSO RECOMMENDED: *C. 'Newellii' is evergreen with crimson flowers.*

☼ ◊ *f* Z8   **Deciduous shrub**
‡↔ 6ft (2m)

CHIMONANTHUS PRAECOX 'Grandiflorus'

Wintersweet is a vigorous shrub grown for the fragrant flowers borne on its bare branches in winter; in this cultivar, they are large, cup-shaped, and yellow, striped maroon within. It needs a sunny, sheltered site to flower well, so is ideal for a south- or west-facing wall, especially near paths and doorways, where its scent can be appreciated. Cut back flowered stems of wall-trained plants in spring.

ALSO RECOMMENDED: *C. praecox has smaller flowers;* var. luteus *has clear yellow flowers.*

☼ ◊ *f* Z7   **Deciduous shrub**
↕ 12ft (4m) ↔ 10ft (3m)

CHOISYA TERNATA

Mexican orange blossom is fast-growing, with dark green leaves, each divided into three leaflets. Fragrant white flowers appear in spring, usually with a second flush late in the season. It does well in a wide range of sites, including alkaline soils, city and coastal gardens, hot, dry sites, some dry shade, and cold walls (*see pp.64, 166, 190, 216, 262*). It needs minimal pruning and can be grown as a hedge (*see p.118*).

ALSO RECOMMENDED: *Sundance has yellow-green foliage; C. 'Aztec Pearl' has pink-tinged flowers.*

☼ ◊ *f* Z7b   **Evergreen shrub**
↔ 8ft (2.5m)

CLIANTHUS PUNICEUS *'Albus'*

Glory pea is a scrambling plant with dark green leaves, ideally suited to the warmth and shelter of south- and west-facing walls. It bears its drooping clusters of clawlike, greenish white flowers in profusion from spring to early summer. Where marginally hardy, it may be cut back by frost, but it usually recovers in spring. Pinch-prune young plants to promote bushiness; otherwise, keep pruning to a minimum. It tolerates sandy soils (*see p.38*).

ALSO RECOMMENDED: C. puniceus *has brilliant red flowers; 'Roseus' (syn. 'Flamingo') has pink flowers.*

☼ ◊ Z8   **Evergreen shrub**
↕ 12ft (4m) ↔ 10ft (3m)

CORONILLA VALENTINA *SUBSP.* GLAUCA

A compact shrub valued for its divided, blue-gray leaves and its clusters of scented, bright yellow, pealike flowers. They are borne in late winter and early spring and often again in late summer. It performs best against a south-facing wall, and it will also grow as a container plant (*see p.412*). It needs little pruning but can be cut back hard in spring to rejuvenate it.

ALSO RECOMMENDED: C. valentina *is taller with bright green leaves; 'Citrina' has pale lemon-yellow flowers.*

☼ ◊ *f* Z8   **Evergreen shrub**
↕↔ 32in (80cm)

CYTISUS BATTANDIERI

From early to midsummer, pineapple broom bears dense, upright clusters of pineapple-scented, bright yellow flowers above silky, grayish green leaves. It makes an attractive backdrop to herbaceous plantings; the loosely branched habit adapts well to training against a warm wall, where flowers are borne most freely. Good in sandy soils and hot, dry sites (*see pp.38, 190*). It needs little pruning; to rejuvenate, cut out the oldest wood after flowering.

ALSO RECOMMENDED: *'Yellow Tail' has larger flowers.*

☼ ◊ *f* Z7   **Deciduous shrub**
↕↔ 15ft (5m)

DAPHNE ODORA *'Aureomarginata'*

A dense, rounded shrub that has glossy dark green leaves irregularly margined with yellow. It is valued for its intensely fragrant, red-purple flowers that are much paler within. It benefits from the protection of a west-facing wall; provide an annual mulch of organic matter in early spring to keep the roots cool. Regular pruning is not necessary.

ALSO RECOMMENDED: *D. odora has plain green leaves;* f. alba *has cream flowers.*

☼ ☽ ◊ *f* Z6   **Evergreen shrub**
↕↔ 5ft (1.5m)

ELSHOLTZIA STAUNTONII

This open, rounded shrub is valued for its narrow and toothed, mint-scented leaves that turn red in autumn. The dense spikes of small, pink-purple flowers that appear in late summer and autumn are attractive to bees (*see p.494*). Good against a wall, but it is also good in a sheltered shrub border or mixed border. Prune in early spring as the buds swell, cutting back all shoots to a low framework.

☀ ◊ *f*Z6   **Deciduous shrub**
↔ 5ft (1.5m)

FABIANA IMBRICATA
F. VIOLACEA

A dense, mound-forming shrub with plumelike, horizontally held branches clothed in overlapping, dark green, needlelike leaves. Tubular, lavender-mauve flowers wreathe the branches in early summer. It is best with the shelter of a warm, south- or west-facing wall. It needs a neutral to acidic soil and tolerates coastal and hot, dry sites (*see pp.92, 166, 190*). Little or no pruning is required.

ALSO RECOMMENDED: *F.* imbricata *has white to pale mauve flowers; 'Prostrata' is low-growing with white flowers.*

☀ ◊ Min 35°F (2°C)   **Evergreen shrub**
↔ 8ft (2.5m)

FREMONTODENDRON
'California Glory'

This vigorous shrub has rounded, lobed, dark green leaves that are the perfect foil for the cupped, golden yellow flowers; these appear from late spring to autumn. Its upright habit makes i good for wall training, and the warmth of a south- or west-facing wall induces profuse flowering. Shelter from wind. It is best with no pruning, although wall-trained plants can be trimmed in spring. Tolerant of alkaline soils and hot, dry sites (*see pp.64, 190*).

ALSO RECOMMENDED: F. *californicum and F. 'Pacific Sunset' are similar.* Z7b

☼ ◊ Z7b   **Evergreen shrub**
↕ 20ft (6m) ↔ 12ft (4m)

ITEA ILICIFOLIA

Providing the soil is not too dry, this hollylike shrub flowers freely on a south or west wall against a mass of glossy, sharply toothed leaves. These tiny flowers are greenish white and borne in catkinlike clusters from midsummer to autumn. Shelter from wind and protect young plants with a winter mulch. It needs little pruning; trim wall-trained plants in spring. Tolerant of alkaline soils (*see p.64*).

☼ ◊ Z7b   **Evergreen shrub**
↕ 10–15ft (3–5m) ↔ 10ft (3m)

LEPTOSPERMUM SCOPARIUM *'Kiwi'*

New Zealand tea trees are compact shrubs with tiny, aromatic, dark green leaves. This dwarf form bears roselike, dark pink or red flowers that cover the plant in late spring. Suitable for a rock garden. Trim new growth in spring for bushiness, but do not cut into old wood. It tolerates coastal gardens (*see p.166*).

ALSO RECOMMENDED: *'Red Damask' has double, dark red flowers and reaches 10ft (3m) tall and wide.*

☼ ☀ ◊ *f* Min 35°F (2°C) **Evergreen shrub**
‡↔ 3ft (1m)

MYRTUS COMMUNIS *SUBSP.* TARENTINA

A compact, rounded shrub with glossy dark green leaves. Fragrant, pink-tinted, creamy white flowers appear from spring to early autumn. It thrives with the shelter of a south or west wall; where fully hardy, it makes a good informal hedge (*see p.138*). It may also be grown in a container (*see p.412*). Trim in spring; it tolerates close clipping.

ALSO RECOMMENDED: M. communis *is taller; 'Variegata' has leaves margined with creamy white.*

☼ ◊ *f* Z8 **Evergreen shrub**
‡↔ 5ft (1.5m)

OLEARIA PHLOGOPAPPA

Daisy bushes are typically dense shrubs with daisylike white and yellow flowers. This one displays its blooms in flat-headed clusters during late spring amid the wavy-margined, dark green leaves. Where marginally hardy it is best against a warm, sheltered wall; in a mild, coastal climate, try it as a hedge (*see p.138, 166*). Remove any unwanted or frost-damaged growth in late spring. It is often sold as *O. stellulata*.

ALSO RECOMMENDED: *O.* × haastii *and* O. macrodonta *are hardier and flower in summer;* O. nummariifolia *(see p.176).*

☼ ◊ Min 35°F (2°C) **Evergreen shrub**
↔ 6ft (2m)

PHYGELIUS × RECTUS *'Salmon Leap'*

This upright shrub flowers most freely in the warmth of a south or west wall. Its tubular orange-red flowers are borne in large sprays above dark green foliage throughout summer. Remove dead flowerheads regularly; cut any cold-damaged growth back in spring. It is also ideal for a mixed or herbaceous border. Tolerant of alkaline soils (*see p.64*).

ALSO RECOMMENDED: *'Devil's Tears' has red-pink flowers with yellow throats; 'Moonraker' has pale yellow flowers.*

☼ ◊◊ Z7b **Evergreen shrub**
↕ 4ft (1.2m) ↔ 5ft (1.5m)

PIPTANTHUS NEPALENSIS

This handsome shrub is valued for its yellow, pealike flowers and glossy dark green, laburnum-like leaves that are blue-white beneath. It is excellent for a site against a west-facing wall, flowering in late spring and early summer; hanging green seedpods follow. After flowering, shorten inward- or outward-growing shoots on wall-trained plants.

☀ ◐ ◊ Min 35°F (2°C)　**Evergreen shrub**
↕ 8ft (2.5m) ↔ 6ft (2m)

ROBINIA HISPIDA

The rose acacia is an upright and arching shrub with spiny shoots. Deep rose-pink, pealike flowers appear in hanging spikes during late spring and early summer; these are followed by brown seedpods. The large, fresh green leaves are divided into many oval leaflets. Provide shelter from wind to avoid damage to the brittle branches. No pruning is necessary. It is also useful for shrub borders on poor, sandy soils in hot, dry sites (*see pp. 38, 190*), but it tolerates all but waterlogged soils.

☀ ◊ Z5b　**Deciduous shrub**
↕ 8ft (2.5m) ↔ 10ft (3m)

ROSA BANKSIAE *'Lutea'*

The rambling yellow Banksian rose may need the shelter of a southwest or west wall to give its best. The long, slender stems bear light green leaves, and in late spring, clusters of double, soft yellow flowers appear. They are good for cutting (*see p.524*), have a delicate scent of violets, and are borne in abundance in a warm site. Train against a support, and prune only to remove old, unproductive wood. Tolerant of alkaline soils (*see p.64*).

ALSO RECOMMENDED: R. *'Albertine'* (see p.77); *'American Pillar'* (see p.51); *'Maigold' has semidouble, bronze-yellow flowers.* All Z6

☼ ◊ ƒ Z6b   **Deciduous shrub**
↔ 20ft (6m)

ROSA × ODORATA *'Mutabilis'*

The cupped, single flowers of this rose, borne through summer, are yellow on opening, changing to copper and deep pink as they mature; they are good for cutting (*see p.524*). If given a site on a southwest or west wall, it will climb to 10ft (3m) and flower profusely; otherwise grow in a border. Prune lightly; shorten main stems and side-shoots by no more than one-third when dormant. It will grow in a large pot and tolerates alkaline soils (*see pp.64, 412*).

ALSO RECOMMENDED: R. *Dublin Bay has double crimson flowers* Z6; *'Madame Grégoire Staechelin' has double pink flowers* Z6.

☼ ◐ ◊ Z6   **Deciduous shrub**
↕ 4–10ft (1.2–3m) ↔ 3–6ft (1–2m)

SALVIA INVOLUCRATA '*Bethellii*'

A bushy plant with upright stems that bear velvety, rich green leaves. Spikes of two-lipped, vivid crimson-purple flowers appear from late summer to autumn; they attract bees (*see p.494*). It is ideal for a border against a warm wall and is good in hot, dry sites (*see p.190*). If grown in a large container, it can be overwintered under cover (*see p.412*). Tolerant of sandy soils (*see p.38*).

ALSO RECOMMENDED: S. involucrata *has less hairy leaves;* S. officinalis '*Tricolor*' (see p.61).

☼ ◊ Min 40°F (5°C)　　**Evergreen shrub**
↕ 5ft (1.5m) ↔ 3ft (1m)

VESTIA FOETIDA

This upright shrub has glossy dark green leaves and bears hanging clusters of tubular, pale yellow flowers from spring to midsummer. Where marginally hardy, it needs the protection of a south- or west-facing wall; if grown in a pot it can be overwintered outdoors. It needs little pruning; trim to shape and remove badly placed growth in midspring.

☼ ◊ Min 35°F (2°C)　　**Evergreen shrub**
↕ 6ft (2m) ↔ 5ft (1.5m)

ACTINIDIA KOLOMIKTA

A vigorous plant valued for its deep green deciduous leaves that are purple-tinted when young, later splashed with vivid pink and white. Small, fragrant white flowers appear in early summer, and they are followed by egg-shaped, yellow-green fruits, but only if a male plant is grown nearby. Tie in new shoots as they develop; cut out badly placed shoots in summer. It tolerates alkaline soils (*see p.64*).

ALSO RECOMMENDED: A. deliciosa, *the kiwi fruit, is less hardy.* Z7

☼ ◊ *f*Z3   **Climber**
↕ 15ft (5m)

CLEMATIS *'Bill Mackenzie'*

This vigorous, deciduous clematis bears nodding yellow flowers with red anthers from midsummer to autumn; pretty, silky seedheads follow and persist into winter. It flowers freely on a warm wall but needs a cool root run; shade the roots with a stone slab or something similar. Cut all the previous year's stems back hard each year in spring. Also tolerant of cold walls and alkaline soils (*see pp.64, 262*).

ALSO RECOMMENDED: C. montana (see p.274); C. tangutica (see p.508); C. tibetana *'Orange Peel' has orange-yellow petals* Z5.

☼☼ ◊ Z4   **Climber**
↕ 22ft (7m) ↔ 6–10ft (2–3m)

CLEMATIS REHDERIANA

This rampant and unusual clematis is densely clothed with deciduous, glossy dark green leaves. Large clusters of small, bell-shaped, pale yellow flowers with a scent of cowslips cover the plant from midsummer to autumn. It is ideal for a warm wall, where it flowers profusely. Cut back hard each year in spring. Also tolerant of cold walls and alkaline soils (*see pp.64, 262*). It will grow as a groundcover (*see p.304*).

ALSO RECOMMENDED: C. *'Paul Farges' bears star-shaped white flowers* Z2; *'The President'* (see p.76); C. terniflora *bears clusters of star-shaped white flowers* Z2.

☼ ◑ ◊ **f** Z6   **Climber**

↕ 20–22ft (6–7m) ↔ 6–10ft (2–3m)

JASMINUM OFFICINALE 'Argenteovariegatum'

This variegated jasmine is a vigorous climber with cream-edged leaves made up of several pointed leaflets. Clusters of fragrant white flowers open from summer to autumn; they also do well in partial shade. If tied in initially, it will twine over a support, such as a trellis or an arch. It tolerates alkaline soils and can be pot-grown (*see pp.64, 412*). Thin out after flowering.

ALSO RECOMMENDED: J. officinale *has plain foliage; 'Aureum' has yellow-marked leaves; f. affine has pink-tinged flowers.*

☼ ◑ ◊ **f** Z7   **Climber**

↕ 40ft (12m)

LONICERA × TELLMANNIANA

A twining, woody-stemmed climber that bears clusters of deep golden orange, tubular flowers from late spring to midsummer. The deep green foliage is deciduous. Train this honeysuckle onto a fence or wall or up into a large shrub; it grows and flowers more reliably in a slightly shaded position. Trim shoots by one-third after flowering. It tolerates alkaline soils (*see p.64*) and can be grown in a container (*see p.412*).

ALSO RECOMMENDED: L. fragrantissima (*see p.526*); L. sempervirens *and* L. tragophylla *both have later flowers* Z7.

☼ ◑ ◊◊ Z5b   **Climber**
↕ 15ft (5m)

PASSIFLORA CAERULEA *'Constance Elliot'*

The blue passionflower is a vigorous, deciduous climber with lobed, rich green leaves. This white-flowered cultivar bears its intricate flowers from summer to autumn; they are followed by egg-shaped, unpalatable orange fruits. Shelter from wind. It tolerates alkaline soils (*see p.64*). Remove crowded growth in spring; shorten flowered shoots at the end of the season.

ALSO RECOMMENDED: P. caerulea *has pale blue-purple flowers.*

☼ ◊ Z7   **Climber**
↕ 30ft (10m) or more

SOLANUM CRISPUM 'Glasnevin'

The Chilean potato tree is a vigorous and shrubby climber that may benefit from the protection of a south or west wall. It bears deep purple-blue flowers from summer to autumn above narrow and deciduous, dark green leaves; small yellow berries follow. Tie in young shoots as growth proceeds; cut back weak or badly placed growth in spring. It tolerates alkaline soils (*see p.64*).

ALSO RECOMMENDED: *S. laxum has bluish white flowers and black fruits; 'Album' has white flowers and more of a climbing habit. (Tender)*

☀☀ ◊ Min 35°F (2°C)   **Climber**
‡ 20ft (6m)

TRACHELOSPERMUM JASMINOIDES

Star jasmine has oval, glossy dark green leaves, and from mid- to late summer, it produces very fragrant, creamy white flowers with twisted petal lobes. Where marginally hardy, it benefits from the protection of a sheltered, south- or west-facing wall and a winter mulch. Tie in young growth and trim in spring. It is evergreen and tolerates alkaline soils and some damp shade (*see p.64, 238*).

ALSO RECOMMENDED: *'Variegatum' has leaves splashed and margined with cream; T. asiaticum is hardier and more compact.*

☀☀ ◊ *f* Min 35°F (2°C)   **Climber**
‡ 28ft (9m)

VITIS VINIFERA *'Purpurea'*

The lobed, rounded leaves of this vine are white-downy when young, turning to plum-purple, then assuming rich purple tints before they fall. The small purple grapes in autumn are inedible. An excellent plant for a sunny wall or pergola that needs slightly alkaline soil *(see p.64)* but tolerates clay and sandy sites *(see pp.12, 38)*; autumn color is best on poor soils. Prune back to an established framework each winter.

ALSO RECOMMENDED: V. amurensis *(see p.279)*; V. *'Brant' has copper-bronze autumn foliage and large bunches of edible, blue-black grapes* Z6b.

☼ ◐ ◊ Z6   **Climber**
‡ 22ft (7m)

WISTERIA BRACHYBOTRYS *'Shiro-kapitan'*

This silky wisteria has twining stems and divided, softly hairy, deciduous leaves. In early summer, it bears short clusters of very fragrant white flowers, followed by silky green seedpods. It is a beautiful specimen for a south or west wall. Prune back new growth in summer and in late winter to control spread. Also sold as *W. sinensis* 'Shiro-capital' and *W. venusta*.

ALSO RECOMMENDED: W. floribunda *and* W. sinensis *have long clusters of lilac or white flowers*. Both Z6

☼ ◊ *f* Z7   **Climber**
‡ 28ft (9m) or more

GROUNDCOVER PLANTS FOR SUN

THE ADVENT OF low-maintenance gardening has created a great deal of interest in the use of groundcover plants to reduce weeding in the garden. At first, the term "groundcover" generally described low and dense, mat- or carpet-forming, evergreen plants. Many gardeners came to dislike the concept, however, because low, undulating mounds of planting – even when composed to form tapestries of different colors and textures – lacked the visual satisfaction of height and form.

In fact, any plant – spreading or upright – that forms a dense, light-excluding canopy will smother weeds, but it is essential that you choose plants that thrive in the growing conditions available. Unless they make dense growth quickly, they will not make effective cover, so carefully check the cultivation requirements of possible plants.

SUNNY SLOPES

The plants described in this chapter are known to perform well in full sun. Such ground-

cover is an excellent way to furnishing sunny banks, where access can be difficult and grass would prove dangerous to mow, especially where a bank slopes steeply. Many of them root where they touch the ground, so they are very useful in stabilizing the soil on sloping sites.

WEED CONTROL

Even the most vigorous ground-cover will be fully effective only if the soil is completely cleared of all perennial weeds and their roots before planting. This is especially true with thorny plants like the groundcover roses, such as Surrey (*see p.309*), because removing thistles and bindweed from among the branches is painful as well as tedious.

On small areas, thorough cultivation and hand weeding is a satisfying way to remove weeds before planting. On larger areas, treating weeds when they are in active growth with a translocated weedkiller, such as one containing glyphosate, is the most practical method. This type of weedkiller is effective because it is transferred to the roots and destroys the whole plant. Tough weeds, such as goutweed, brambles, and docks, will need more than one treatment. Organic gardeners often lay a light-excluding layer of old carpet or black plastic on the soil for a season before planting to clear the weeds.

Until plants begin to grow well, weed seedlings will still take root in the bare soil, so regular weeding is essential. Alternatively, planting through woven landscaping fabric, or matting made of jute or other fiber is ideal; unlike plastic sheeting, these materials allow plants to root into them. Jute and other fibers are bio-degradable, and the plants will have made good, dense cover by the time they decompose. Landscaping fabrics are not pretty, and they must be covered with a mulch – such as gravel or bark chips – to prevent them from degrading in sunlight. This combination suppresses weeds very effectively.

COTONEASTER CASHMIRIENSIS

This compact shrub forms a dense, wide-spreading mat of small, glossy leaves. It is studded in summer with small white flowers, followed in autumn by shiny dark red berries. These attract birds (*see p.494*). It makes excellent an groundcover for a sunny bank or at the front of a shrub border, and it tolerates clay and alkaline soils (*see pp.12, 64*). Prune only to remove wayward shoots.

ALSO RECOMMENDED: *C. dammeri has larger leaves* Z4; *those of C. procumbens are darker green* Z4.

☼ ◊ Z7   **Evergreen shrub**
↕ 12in (30cm) ↔ 6ft (2m)

ERICA CARNEA *'Springwood White'*

Early-flowering heathers are much appreciated when they bring a carpet of color to the garden from late winter. This vigorous, trailing variety gives a profusion of white flowers above bright green foliage. It tolerates acidic soils (*see p.92*) and can be pot-grown (*see p.412*). The flowers are good for cutting (*see p.524*). Trim after flowering.

ALSO RECOMMENDED: *'Foxhollow' has purplish flowers and bronze-yellow foliage; 'Myretoun Ruby' has pink to red flowers;* E. cinerea (*see p.102*) *and* E. vagans (*see p.418*) *flower from summer to autumn.*

☼ ◊ Z4   **Evergreen shrub**
↕ 8–10in (20–25cm) ↔ 22in (55cm)

GENISTA HISPANICA

Spanish gorse forms a dense mound of spiny green stems, covered by a mass of golden yellow pealike flowers in late spring and early summer. Narrow green leaves appear only on the flowering stems. Good in a rock garden or raised bed, or on a wall or sunny bank; it thrives in hot, dry sites (*see p.190*), coping with coastal conditions (*see p.166*) and flowering most freely in poor, sandy, well-drained soils (*see p.38*). Keep pruning to a minimum.

ALSO RECOMMENDED: *G. pilosa 'Vancouver Gold' is shorter, to 18in (45cm) tall. Z5*

☼ ◊ Z7b   **Deciduous shrub**
↕ 30in (75cm) ↔ 5ft (1.5m)

HEBE PINGUIFOLIA *'Pagei'*

With arching, purple stems clothed in small, leathery, blue-green leaves, this shrub makes a good groundcover for the front of a border or rock garden. Short spikes of tiny white flowers appear at the stem tips in late spring. It thrives in alkaline soils, tolerates pollution and coastal sites, and looks good in pots (*see pp.64, 166, 412*). Trim in early spring.

ALSO RECOMMENDED: *H. 'Autumn Glory' (see p.175); 'County Park' has red-margined, gray-green leaves and violet flowers; H. pimeleoides 'Quicksilver' has silver-gray leaves and lilac-blue flowers. (All tender)*

☼ ◊ Z7   **Evergreen shrub**
↕ 12in (30cm) ↔ 36in (90cm)

JUNIPERUS SABINA *'Tamariscifolia'*

The sharply pointed, bright or bluish green leaves and spreading stems of this mounded, groundcovering shrub produce an attractively tiered habit of growth. It is ideal for a shrub border, sunny bank, or gravel garden, thriving in any well-drained position, including sandy or alkaline soils (*see pp.38, 64*) and hot, dry sites (*see p.190*). Little if any pruning is necessary.

ALSO RECOMMENDED: *'Blaue Donau' (syn. Blue Danube) has blue-gray leaves; J. horizontalis 'Wiltonii' is shorter, more spreading, and has bright blue leaves* Z2.

☼ ◊ Z2   **Evergreen shrub**
‡ 3–6ft (1–2m) ↔ 6ft (2m)

MICROBIOTA DECUSSATA

A low-growing, spreading, mound-forming conifer with scalelike, bright green foliage borne in flattened sprays. In cold weather, the foliage assumes bronze tints. Its dense growth, which needs no pruning, makes an excellent, low-maintenance groundcover at the front of a shrub border or on a bank; it can also be grown in a container (*see p.412*) or in shade, where the foliage will turn less bronzy in winter.

☼ ◊ Z3   **Evergreen shrub**
‡ 3ft (1m) ↔ indefinite

RHODANTHEMUM HOSMARIENSE

A close ally of the chrysanthemum, this is a low and spreading subshrub valued for its profusion of daisylike flowers with white petals and yellow eyes. These are borne from spring to autumn, covering the silvery green, soft, hairy, finely divided leaves. Choose a very well-drained site at the base of a warm wall (*see p.280*) or in a rock garden; remove spent blooms to prolong flowering. It tolerates alkaline soils (*see p.64*). Trim after flowering.

ALSO RECOMMENDED: *R. gayanum has pink and brown summer flowers. (Tender)*

☼ ◊ Min 40°F (5°C)   **Evergreen shrub**
↕ 4–12in (10–30cm) ↔ 12in (30cm)

ROSA *Surrey*

A splendid groundcover rose with small, rich green foliage and a profusion of gentle pink blooms, borne over long periods in summer and into autumn. Excellent for confined spaces, it may also be grown in containers (*see p.412*). Prune in winter, cutting back overly long shoots to an upward- or outward-facing bud. It tolerates alkaline soils (*see p.64*).

ALSO RECOMMENDED: *'Nozomi' has pale pink flowers Z5; 'Charles Albanel' has double, bright pink blooms and is disease resistant Z2; 'Swany' has white flowers Z4b; R. pimpinellifolia (see p.131).*

☼ ◊ Z6   **Deciduous shrub**
↕ 32in (80cm) ↔ 4ft (1.2m)

THYMUS PULEGIOIDES
'Bertram Anderson'

This lemon-scented thyme is a low, wiry-stemmed subshrub with small, pleasantly aromatic leaves, often used to flavor meat. This cultivar has yellow-green foliage and heads of tiny, pale pink flowers in summer. It is an essential plant for a herb or wildlife garden with neutral to alkaline soil (*see pp.64, 494*). Also suitable for hot, dry sites and in paving (*see pp.190, 348*).

ALSO RECOMMENDED: *'Archer's Gold' has yellow-margined leaves; 'Aureus' has gold-dappled leaves;* T. serpyllum *'Annie Hall' (see p.352).*

☼ ◊ *f* Z5   **Evergreen shrub**

‡ 12in (30cm) ↔ 10in (25cm)

ACAENA SACCATICUPULA
'Blue Haze'

This vigorous, creeping evergreen forms a dense carpet of divided, gray-blue leaves that will withstand a moderate amount of traffic. It can be grown in a rock garden or raised bed, at the front of a border, or in paving crevices (*see p.348*). In summer, the spherical flowerheads are followed by decorative, dark red burrs. It is good for hot, dry sites (*see p.190*), sandy soils (*see p.38*), and sunny containers (*see p.412*).

ALSO RECOMMENDED: A. microphylla *'Kupferteppich' (syn. Copper Carpet) has bronzed leaves and bright red burrs.* Z7

☼ ◊ Z7   **Perennial**

‡ 4–6in (10–15cm) ↔ 3ft (1m)

ALCHEMILLA MOLLIS

Lady's mantle is a drought-tolerant, clump-forming border plant valued for its lobed, bright green leaves and its sprays of tiny, lime green flowers throughout summer. They are ideal for cutting and drying (*see p.524*); regular deadheading prevents nuisance self-seeding. It tolerates alkaline soils (*see p.64*) and copes with exposed and coastal sites (*see pp.118, 166*).

ALSO RECOMMENDED: A. alpina (see p.354); A. conjuncta (see p.181); A. erythropoda *is smaller with blue-green leaves* Z4; A. xanthochlora *is taller with yellowish leaves* Z4.

☼ ◐◊◊ Z4b   **Perennial**
‡ 12in (30cm) ↔ 30in (75cm)

ARTEMISIA LUDOVICIANA '*Silver Queen*'

This western mugwort is a strongly spreading plant, forming bushy clumps of narrow, silvery white, softly felted leaves; they become green with age and are sometimes jaggedly toothed. Woolly white plumes of light brown flowers appear from midsummer to autumn. It grows well in sandy soils and in hot, dry sites (*see pp.38, 190*), indispensable in a silver-themed border. Cut back in spring for the best foliage effect.

ALSO RECOMMENDED: A. ludoviciana *is similar;* '*Valerie Finnis*' *has more deeply cut leaves;* A. pontica (see p.52).

☼ ◊ Z4b   **Perennial**
‡ 30in (75cm) ↔ 24in (60cm) or more

AUBRIETA *'Joy'*

A spreading mat of midgreen foliage formed by this aubrieta is often grown in a rock garden or in cracks within walls or paving (*see p.348*). Small, double, mauve flowers appear in abundance in spring. It prefers neutral to alkaline soils (*see p.64*). Cut back after flowering to maintain a compact shape.

ALSO RECOMMENDED: *'Aureovariegata' has yellow-margined leaves and pink flowers; 'Doctor Mules' has bluish violet flowers.*

☼ ◊ Z4   **Perennial**
‡ 2in (5cm) ↔ 24in (60cm) or more

AURINIA SAXATILIS *'Dudley Nevill'*

This mound-forming evergreen bears clusters of pale orange-yellow flowers in late spring above dense clumps of oval, hairy, gray-green leaves. It is ideal for rock gardens or banks, for the front of a sunny border, or for cracks in walls and paving (*see p.348*). Trim after flowering to keep compact. It tolerates alkaline soils and hot, dry sites (*see pp.64, 190*).

ALSO RECOMMENDED: *A. saxatilis has bright yellow flowers; those of 'Citrina' are lemon yellow; 'Variegata' has leaves margined with creamy white.*

☼ ◊ Z3b   **Perennial**
‡ 8in (20cm) ↔ 12in (30cm)

CAMPANULA GLOMERATA 'Superba'

This vigorous variety of the clustered bellflower spreads to form clumps of well-foliaged, stiffly upright stems. Throughout summer, they are topped by dense clusters of purple-violet flowers. Cut back after flowering to encourage another display. It tolerates alkaline soils (*see p.64*).

ALSO RECOMMENDED: *C. 'Birch Hybrid'* (*see p.358*); *C. carpatica 'Bressingham White'* (*see p.359*); *C. cochleariifolia 'Elizabeth Oliver' is short and spreading with pale blue flowers in summer* Z3.

☼ ☀ ◊◊ Z3   **Perennial**

‡ 24in (60cm) ↔ indefinite

CENTAUREA MONTANA

This knapweed is a creeping plant and forms soft, woolly mats or clumps of broad and pointed, midgreen leaves. The thistlelike, reddish purple-blue flowers have a spidery appearance and open from late spring to midsummer; they are attractive to butterflies and bees (*see p.494*). It is tolerant of exposed sites (*see p.118*), but stakes may be needed to support the stems.

ALSO RECOMMENDED: *'Alba' has white flowers; those of 'Carnea' are pink; 'Parham' has large, dark blue flowers.*

☼ ☀ ◊◊ Z3   **Perennial**

‡ 18in (45cm) ↔ 24in (60cm)

CERASTIUM TOMENTOSUM

The dense, white-woolly foliage of snow-in-summer makes a good weed suppressant. It forms a silvery carpet that is covered by snow-white flowers in summer. It is ideal for poor, well-drained, dry and sandy soils, rock gardens, sunny banks, and crevices in dry walls and paving (*see pp.38, 348*). Its enthusiastic growth may become invasive and it self-seeds freely unless dead-headed.

ALSO RECOMMENDED: *var. columnae is slightly taller, to 6in (15cm).*

☼ ◊ Z4   **Perennial**
‡ 2–3in (5–8cm) ↔ indefinite

DIANTHUS SUBACAULIS

This low-growing evergreen forms a dense carpet of narrow, dark gray-green leaves studded with a profusion of small, deep pink flowers during summer. It makes an excellent ground-cover for a rock garden or raised bed; it may also be grown in paving crevices (*see p.348*), as border edging, or in a container (*see p.412*). Choose sharply drained, sandy, neutral to alkaline soil (*see pp.38, 64*).

ALSO RECOMMENDED: D. alpinus *has pink to crimson flowers* Z3; *the larger* D. gratianopolitanus *has fragrant flowers* Z4.

☼ ◊ Z4   **Perennial**
‡ 2in (5cm) ↔ 4in (10cm)

DIASCIA *'Salmon Supreme'*

The trailing, wiry mats of this plant are clothed by small, heart-shaped leaves that are outperformed for a long summer season by the dense clusters of pinkish apricot flowers. These have two downward-pointing spurs on the reverse, which give the plant its common name – twinspur. Grow at the front of a border or in a rock garden. Remove dead flowers, and pinch out shoot tips to encourage a bushy habit.

ALSO RECOMMENDED: *'Rupert Lambert' has pink flowers; those of* D. barbarae *'Blackthorn Apricot' and 'Ruby Field' are salmon;* D. vigilis *has pink blooms. All Z7*

☼ ◊◊ Z7   **Perennial**
‡6in (15cm) ↔ 20in (50cm)

DRYAS OCTOPETALA

An easy plant for a rock garden, dry wall, or border edge, mountain avens forms a low, evergreen mat of small, lobed leaves that resemble those of an oak tree. Aconite-like white flowers with yellow centers face the sky in late spring and early summer. It thrives in gritty soil and will grow in paving crevices (*see p.348*).

ALSO RECOMMENDED: *the foliage and flowers of 'Minor' are smaller.*

☼ ☼ ◊ Z3   **Perennial**
‡4in (10cm) ↔ 3ft (1m) or more

GERANIUM ENDRESSII

This geranium is useful for filling in between larger plants in a mixed border. It forms clumps of deeply lobed, light green leaves and has a long season of light pink summer flowers with notched petals; they darken with age, and the display continues into autumn. It is tolerant of dry shade (*see pp.216, 326*) and most but waterlogged soils. Also good for containers (*see pp.412, 448*).

ALSO RECOMMENDED: *G. 'Ann Folkard' has magenta flowers* Z4; G. clarkei *'Kashmir White' has white flowers* Z4; G. cinereum *'Ballerina'* (see p.333); G. dalmaticum (see p.363); G. renardii (see p.211).

☼ ◐ ◊◊ Z4   **Perennial**
↕ 18in (45cm) ↔ 24in (60cm)

GERANIUM × OXONIANUM

This hybrid of *G. endressii* (*above*) has similar uses in the garden, but it puts on taller, more enthusiastic growth with deeper pink, strongly veined flowers. Flowering from late spring to autumn, it is long-lived and requires minimal attention. Also suitable for containers (*see pp.412, 448*) and as a groundcover in shade (*see p.326*).

ALSO RECOMMENDED: *'A.T. Johnson' is very free flowering;* '*Claridge Druce' and 'Wargrave Pink' are very vigorous;* G. × riversleaianum *'Russell Prichard' has magenta flowers;* G. wallichianum *'Buxton's Variety' has lilac flowers.* All Z4

☼ ◐ ◊◊ Z4   **Perennial**
↕ 32in (80cm) ↔ 24in (60cm)

GYPSOPHILA REPENS
'Dorothy Teacher'

This versatile, low-spreading plant thrives in sandy or alkaline soils in hot, dry sites (*see pp.38, 64, 190*) as well as in paving and wall crevices (*see p.348*). It forms a dense mat of blue-green leaves spangled with many tiny pink flowers throughout summer, which are good for cutting (*see p.524*). It needs light, alkaline, sharply drained soil and can also be container-grown (*see p.412*).

ALSO RECOMMENDED: *G. repens has white, pink, or pink-purple flowers. 'Fratensis' has gray-green leaves and pale pink flowers.*

☼ ◊ Z4   **Perennial**

‡ 2in (5cm) ↔ 16in (40cm)

× HEUCHERELLA
TIARELLOIDES

This spreading, clump-forming plant forms a good evergreen groundcover at the front of a border. The rounded, lobed, light green leaves are often brown-marked when young. The slender-stemmed spikes of tiny pink flowers arise in midspring and early summer. Grow in light, fertile, neutral to acidic soil (*see p.92*). It is also good as a groundcover in partial shade (*see p.326*).

ALSO RECOMMENDED: × *H. alba 'Bridget Bloom' has brown-veined, midgreen leaves and white flowers.* Z5

☼☀ ◊◊ Z5   **Perennial**

↔ 18in (45cm)

HOSTA *'Birchwood Parky's Gold'*

This gold-leaved hosta has ribbed, heart-shaped leaves and bears spires of pale lavender-blue flowers in midsummer. The best foliage color is produced in sun, but it needs a little midday shade and shelter from drying winds to avoid leaf scorch. Mulch every spring and protect from slugs. A good architectural plant for groundcover and containers (*see pp.304, 326, 412, 472*), tolerating clay and permanently damp soils (*see pp.12, 238, 372*).

ALSO RECOMMENDED: *'Fragrant Gold' and 'Golden Prayers' are similar.*

☼ ☽ ◊ Z4   **Perennia**

↕ 14–16in (35–40cm) ↔ indefinite

LYCHNIS CORONARIA

Although short-lived, rose campion will form dense, ground-covering colonies by self-seeding. Its vibrant magenta flowers appear in long succession from midsummer above basal clumps of lance-shaped, silver-gray leaves. It is best in light and sandy soils (*see p.38*) but also tolerates alkaline ground (*see p.64*) and coastal and hot, dry sites (*see pp.166, 190*). Grow in a sunny, mixed or herbaceous border. It self-sows freely

ALSO RECOMMENDED: *'Alba' bears white flowers; Atrosanguinea Group has crimson flowers; Oculata Group has pink-eyed white flowers.*

☼ ◊ Z3b   **Perennia**

↕ 32in (80cm) ↔ 18in (45cm)

LYSIMACHIA PUNCTATA

This loosestrife is a robust border perennial with dense, basal clumps of dark green foliage. The plant spreads, sometimes invasively, by rhizomes. From midsummer, it bears tall spikes of bright yellow flowers. Tolerant of heavy clay and permanently moist soils (*see pp.12, 372*). Dig out excessive growth to control spread.

ALSO RECOMMENDED: L. vulgaris *is similar.* Z5

☼ ◐ ◗ Z4   **Perennial**
3ft (1m) ↔ 24in (60cm)

MENTHA SUAVEOLENS *'Variegata'*

The aromatic pineapple mint forms dense, spreading clumps of hairy and wrinkled, gray-green leaves heavily splashed with creamy white. Spikes of two-lipped, very pale pink flowers appear in summer; they attract pollinating insects (*see p.494*). It is good for creating foliage contrasts in a herbaceous border and is best in poor, damp soils, being less invasive in dry sites. It tolerates clay soils (*see p.12*).

ALSO RECOMMENDED: M. × gracilis *'Variegata' is shorter and less invasive with gold-marked, aromatic leaves.* Z5

☼ ◗ *f* Z5   **Perennial**
3ft (1m) ↔ indefinite

NEPETA × FAASSENII

Catmint is an excellent border plant, making a dense clump of arching stems clothed with aromatic, softly hairy, wrinkled, gray-green leaves. Through summer, it bears spikes of two-lipped, pale lavender-blue flowers that attract a range of pollinating insects (*see p.494*). I tolerates sandy and alkaline soils (*see pp.38, 64*) and performs well in hot, dry sites (*see p.190*). Cut back after flowering to encourage a fresh flush of foliage and flowers, and remove all old growth to the base in spring.

ALSO RECOMMENDED: *'Alba'* has white *flowers*; N. *'Six Hills Giant' is much taller.* Z4

☼ ◊ *f* Z4   **Perennial**
↕↔ 18in (45cm)

ORIGANUM VULGARE

Oregano is a spreading, bushy plant with tiny, dark green leaves that are highly aromatic and are frequently used in cooking. Short spikes of tiny, pretty pink flowers appear in summer. It is good for a well-drained bank or herb garden, growing well in sandy, alkaline soils (*see pp.38, 64*). Trim back after flowering to maintain a compact shape.

ALSO RECOMMENDED: *'Aureum'* has gold *leaves; 'Gold Tip' has yellow-tipped leaves*

☼ ◊ *f* Z3   **Perennial**
↕↔ 12–36in (30–90cm)

PERSICARIA AFFINIS
'Donald Lowndes'

This vigorous evergreen produces
dense mats of lance-shaped, dark green
leaves that take on attractive shades of
russet in autumn. From midsummer to
autumn it bears long-lasting spikes of
pale pink flowers, and these mature to
a darker, dusky pink. Position at the
front of a border, in a gravel garden, or
in a container (*see pp.412, 448*). It thrives
in any moist but well-drained soil and
tolerates partial shade (*see p.326*).

ALSO RECOMMENDED: *'Darjeeling Red'
and 'Superba' are similar.*

☼ ◐ ◊ Z3   **Perennial**
‡ 10in (25cm) ↔ 24in (60cm)

POTENTILLA MEGALANTHA

This herbaceous cinquefoil is grown
for its profusion of small and roselike,
rich yellow flowers in the second half
of summer. They are carried in upright
clusters above the dense clumps of
slightly hairy, midgreen leaves. It is
suitable for the front of a border,
where it can be used to fill patches
of bare soil between larger plants.
It will grow in sandy soils and hot,
dry sites (*see pp.38, 190*).

ALSO RECOMMENDED: *P. × tonguei is
spreading, with a long summer display of
apricot-yellow flowers with red eyes.* Z3b

☼ ◊ Z4   **Perennial**
‡ 6–12in (15–30cm) ↔ 6in (15cm)

SAPONARIA OCYMOIDES

Rock soapwort is a sprawling plant that forms a mat of bright green leaves. These are almost obscured in summer by tiny pink flowers. It is excellent for sunny banks or rock gardens; site it carefully, beacause it may swamp smaller plants. Cut back after flowering to keep it compact. Tolerant of sandy and alkaline soils (*see pp.38, 64*) and good in paving crevices and containers (*see pp.348, 412*).

ALSO RECOMMENDED: *'Alba' has white flowers and is less vigorous, 'Rubra Compacta' has dark red flowers and is more compact.*

☼ ◊ Z3   **Perennial**
‡ 3in (8cm) ↔ 18in (45cm) or more

SCUTELLARIA ORIENTALIS

A spreading, stem-rooting perennial with divided, dark green leaves that bears a profusion of tubular, two-lipped, red-marked yellow flowers in summer. It is ideal for a rock or gravel garden, or at the front of a sunny border. The flowers are attractive to bees (*see p.494*). Grow in light and gritty soil; it thrives in alkaline ground (*see p.64*).

ALSO RECOMMENDED: *S. baicalensis has pale and deep blue flowers Z6; S. indica var. parvifolia has lilac-blue flowers Z7.*

☼ ◊ Z6   **Perennial**
‡ 10in (25cm) ↔ 12in (30cm)

SEDUM KAMTSCHATICUM *'Variegatum'*

A carpeting perennial with fleshy, pink-tinted leaves margined with cream. In summer, starry yellow flowers that age to crimson nestle just above the foliage. It looks good at the front of a border, in a rock garden, or in paving crevices (*see p.348*). Grow in gritty or sandy soil (*see p.38*). It tolerates partial shade and hot, dry sites (*see pp.190, 216, 326*).

ALSO RECOMMENDED: *var.* floriferum *'Weihenstephaner Gold' is trailing with yellow flowers aging to orange*; S. acre (see p.369); S. spathulifolium *'Purpureum'* (see p.370).

☼ ◑ ◊ Z3b   **Perennial**
‡ 4in (10cm) ↔ 10in (25cm)

SEMPERVIVUM TECTORUM

Hens and chicks is a vigorous, evergreen succulent forming mats of large, open rosettes of bristle-tipped, blue-green leaves. These are often suffused wine red in summer, when clusters of starry, red-purple flowers appear on upright stems. Good for rock gardens, troughs, or paving (*see pp.348, 412*); it grows attractively on old roof tiles or among terracotta fragments. Gritty, sharply drained, sandy soil is ideal (*see p.38*). It tolerates hot, dry sites (*see p.190*).

ALSO RECOMMENDED: S. arachnoideum (see p.438); S. ciliosum (see p.370).

☼ ◊ Z4   **Perennial**
‡ 6in (15cm) ↔ 20in (50cm)

SILENE SCHAFTA

This clump-forming and spreading perennial has floppy stems bearing small, bright green leaves. From late summer to autumn it bears profuse sprays of long-tubed, rich magenta flowers. Grow in a rock or gravel garden, raised bed, in paving crevices, at the front of a border, or in a container (*see pp.348, 412*). Provide light, neutral to alkaline soil (*see p.64*). It tolerates coastal sites (*see p.166*).

ALSO RECOMMENDED: *'Shell Pink' has pink flowers*; S. uniflora *'Robin Whitebreast' (syn. 'Flore Pleno') double white flowers* Z4.

☼ ◐ ◊ Z3b   **Perennial**
‡ 10in (25cm) ↔ 12in (30cm)

STACHYS BYZANTINA *'Silver Carpet'*

This evergreen plant does not flower; it simply forms a carpet of soft-textured, furry gray leaves, hence the common name of lambs' ears. Use it to create beautiful foliage contrasts at the front of a border. Good for alkaline soils, and coastal and hot, dry sites (*see pp.64, 166, 190*), although excessive winter moisture may promote rot . It may be container-grown (*see p.412*).

ALSO RECOMMENDED: S. byzantina *has pink-purple flowers in summer; 'Big Ears' also flowers and has large leaves; 'Primrose Heron' has yellowish gray leaves.*

☼ ◊ Z3b   **Perennial**
‡ 18in (45cm) ↔ 24in (60cm)

TRIFOLIUM REPENS
'Purpurascens Quadrifolium'

This four-leaf clover spreads rapidly to form a mat of deep bronze-purple foliage; each leaflet has a narrow band of midgreen around its margin. Tiny heads of white pealike flowers appear during summer. Suitable as part of a border or in a wildflower garden, since the flowers are a source of nectar for bees (*see p.494*). Some forms of this plant are aggressive weeds.

ALSO RECOMMENDED: *T. pratense 'Susan Smith' has pink flowers, and yellow-marked leaves with three leaflets.* Z7

☼ ◊◊ Z4   **Perennial**
‡ 4in (10cm) ↔ indefinite

VERONICA PROSTRATA
'Trehane'

This form of prostrate speedwell forms dense mats of golden foliage and, in early summer, produces upright spikes of intense, deep blue flowers. It is ideal in a rock garden, at the front of a border, or in paving crevices (*see p.348*), and it performs well on alkaline soils (*see p.64*). Easily grown in any well-drained soil.

ALSO RECOMMENDED: V. prostrata *is more vigorous, with bright green leaves and pale to deep blue flowers; 'Mrs. Holt' has pink flowers.*

☼ ◊ Z4   **Perennial**
‡ 6in (15cm) ↔ 16in (40cm)

GROUNDCOVER PLANTS FOR SHADE

THERE ARE AREAS of shade in the garden beneath trees and shrubs, or at the base of walls and fences that may not receive any direct sunlight at all. Such areas are often thought of as problem sites. However, the world's woodlands and forests actually provide a wealth of plants that naturally thrive in such cool, equable, and usually damp conditions, and the choice is actually quite extensive. Most of the plants described here occur naturally on the woodland floor, where they have evolved to cope with the changing canopy of leaves and the competition of tree roots. Some plants flower early before the trees leaf out. Others, like ferns, do not flower; to them, shade is a requirement for them to produce luxuriant growth. These plants are shade-demanding rather than simply being shade-tolerant. Their lush growth is not only effective in covering the ground, but it also remains in good condition for much longer periods than it would in the face of bleaching

sunlight. Shade provides an exciting range of opportunities for creating interesting tapestries of contrasting foliage textures and shapes.

CHOOSING PLANTS

When choosing groundcovers for shady spots, it is vital to select plants that can grow in the conditions, because you need them to grow vigorously and well if they are to form the dense, light-excluding foliage canopy necessary to outcompete the weeds. It is essential that the soil be cleared thoroughly of all weeds, especially perennial ones, before planting, because they compete vigorously with your chosen ground-coverers for light, nutrients, and moisture.

Weeds can be cleared by using translocated (systemic) weed killers (see p.305), by hand (if the area is small), or covered by layers of old carpet or plastic sheeting for a season before planting. The establishment of groundcovers is also helped enormously if the soil is improved; add well-rotted organic matter to improve fertility and moisture retention before planting, and then provide a thick mulch to the soil surface after planting. Even better than this is to use a permeable sheet mulch, such as landscape fabric, in conjunction with a loose surface mulch, such as groundbark.

GROWTH RATES VARY

Even shade-tolerant plants may grow more slowly in deep shade than they would where light levels are higher in partial shade, and it will speed the completion of cover if smaller and more delicate plants, such as *Asarum europaeum* (see p.333), are planted more closely together than they would be otherwise. Rampant spreaders, like *Lamium galeobdolon* 'Hermann's Pride' (see p.341), or *Gaultheria shallon* (see p.328) need no such concessions. Quite the reverse is necessary, in fact, and it is essential to take their potential spread into account. If poorly sited, they will quickly swamp less robust plants.

GAULTHERIA SHALLON

Salal forms a spreading mound of leathery, dark green leaves, an ideal groundcover for shady banks or beneath trees. In early summer, small, pink-tinted white flowers appear, followed by purple fruits. These attract birds (*see p.494*). Grow in moist, neutral to acidic soil (*see p.92*); chop away spreading roots with a spade to restrict spread, as necessary. It tolerates urban pollution and dry shade (*see p.216*).

ALSO RECOMMENDED: *G. procumbens is low-growing with white or pale pink flowers and scarlet fruit.* Z4

☼◑ ◖ Z7   **Evergreen shrub**
↕ 4ft (1.2m) ↔ 5ft (1.5m)

HYPERICUM CALYCINUM

Aaron's beard spreads quickly by means of its creeping stems with dark green leaves, and it is an excellent groundcover plant for most soil types. Showy, bright yellow flowers are displayed from midsummer to autumn. It tolerates dry shade as well as sun, where it may flower more profusely (*see pp.216, 304*). Cut to ground level in spring. The leaves are susceptible to rust.

ALSO RECOMMENDED: *H. androsaemum is deciduous and less spreading.* Z4

☼◑ ◖◖ Z5b   **Evergreen shrub**
↕ 24in (60cm) ↔ indefinite

LEUCOTHOE *Scarletta*

This is an upright-arching bush grown for its luxuriant and very dark glossy green, pointed leaves. In this cultivar, also sold as 'Zeblid', the leaves are tinted red-purple when young and tinged with bronze in winter. Clusters of small, bell-shaped white flowers, which hang below the foliage, appear in spring. It prefers reliably damp, acidic soils (*see pp. 92, 238*). Prune after flowering, if necessary.

ALSO RECOMMENDED: L. walteri *'Rainbow' has cream- and pink-mottled leaves.* Z6

☀ ◑ ◊ Z6   **Evergreen shrub**

↕ 3–6ft (1–2m) ↔ 10ft (3m)

MAHONIA REPENS *'Rotundifolia'*

An upright, suckering shrub with leathery, dark green leaves. Clusters of fragrant yellow flowers appear in mid- to late spring, followed by spherical black berries. Best in fertile, moist but well-drained soil, but tolerant of dry, alkaline, and clay soils (*see pp. 12, 64, 216*). It can be used as an informal hedge (*see p. 138*). Prune only to remove dead wood after flowering.

ALSO RECOMMENDED: M. repens *is shorter,* M. × wagneri *'Pinnacle' has more spiny leaves, which are bronzed when young, and larger flower clusters.* Z7

☀ ◑ ◊◊ *f* Z4   **Evergreen shrub**

↕ 5ft (1.5m) ↔ 6ft (2m)

VINCA DIFFORMIS

This low and shrubby periwinkle has narrow and pointed, glossy dark green leaves all over its wide-spreading shoots. These do not flower, but in late winter and early spring, upward-growing shoots appear and bear pale blue to white flowers. It copes with relatively dry soils in shade (*see p.216*). Cut back in spring.

ALSO RECOMMENDED: *V. major* '*Variegata*' *has dark violet flowers and cream-margined leaves, tolerating deep shade, but it may be invasive* Z7; *V. minor* (*see p.237*).

☼ ◑ ◐ ◔◑ Z8   **Evergreen shrub**
‡ 12in (30cm) ↔ indefinite

HEDERA HELIX '*Glacier*'

Most ivies make excellent groundcovers in sun and shade (*see p.304*). 'Glacier' is a versatile cultivar that will also grow against a shady wall, in dry shade, in a container, or as an indoor plant (*see pp.216, 262, 412, 448*). Its climbing, self-clinging stems do not need support and are covered with small, evergreen, grayish leaves. These have triangular lobes and are variegated with gray and cream. It tolerates alkaline soils (*see p.64*).

ALSO RECOMMENDED: '*Erecta*' (see p.220); '*Ivalace*' *has dark green leaves with wavy margins; f. poetarum* (see p.509).

☼ ◑ ◔◑ Z5b   **Climber**
‡ 6ft (2m) or more

HEDERA HIBERNICA

Although Irish ivy is a climbing plant, its fast-growing, clinging stems can be allowed to spread as a groundcover in the dry shade of trees and shrubs (*see p.216*). It is valued for its broadly oval, dark green leaves with five triangular lobes. Also useful for exposed sites and shady walls (*see pp.118, 262*). It prefers alkaline soils (*see p.64*). Cut back at any time to reduce spread.

ALSO RECOMMENDED: H. colchica *'Sulphur Heart' (see p.275);* H. helix *'Spetchley' has tiny, dark green leaves* Z5b.

☼ ◑ � ◊◊ Z7   **Climber**

↕ 30ft (10m)

ADIANTUM ALEUTICUM

Tough but of delicate appearance, the Northern maidenhair fern forms a lacy mat of pale green, finely divided fronds on glossy black stalks, often pink-tinted when young. Ideal for shady borders and woodland gardens, it is easily grown in leafy soil. Remove old or damaged fronds in spring. It can be container-grown (*see p.448*), and it tolerates acidic soils and damp shade (*see pp.92, 238*).

ALSO RECOMMENDED: A. pedatum (*see p.458);* '*Japonicum' has purple-pink new fronds;* A. venustum *has fronds that are bright bronze-pink on emergence* Z6.

☼ ◐ Z3   **Perennial fern**

↕↔ 30in (75cm)

AEGOPODIUM PODAGRARIA *'Variegatum'*

Variegated goutweed is ideal for brightening a shady border or dark corner. It forms dense cover with its divided green leaves, which are broadly margined and splashed with creamy white. Although less aggressive than the green-leaved species – a pernicious weed – it may still swamp smaller, less robust species, so site it where it will not spread into other plants. Grow in any soil including poor, clay, or alkaline ones (*see pp.12, 64*). It may also be grown in a container (*see p.448*).

☼ ◐ ◊◊ Z4   **Perennial**

↕ 12–24in (30–60cm) ↔ indefinite

ANEMONE × LIPSIENSIS

The pale creamy yellow flowers of this carpet-forming anemone appear in spring above toothed, divided dark green leaves. Perfect for a woodland garden, damp and shady border (*see p.238*), or for planting beneath shrubs. It tolerates alkaline soils (*see p.64*).

ALSO RECOMMENDED: *A. nemorosa has white, often pink-flushed flowers* Z4; *A. sylvestris is taller and has nodding white flowers with gold stamens* Z3.

☼ ◊ Z6   **Perennial**

↕ 6in (15cm) ↔ 18in (45cm)

ASARUM EUROPAEUM

European wild ginger is a creeping plant that forms evergreen carpets of kidney-shaped, glossy dark green leaves. Hidden beneath them in late spring are small, narrowly bell-shaped, greenish purple to brown flowers. Excellent in a moist woodland garden or damp, shady border (*see p.238*). Grow in neutral to acidic soil (*see p.92*). Protect from slugs and snails.

ALSO RECOMMENDED: *A. hartwegii has bronze-green leaves with silver-marbled veins Z6; A. shuttleworthii has dark green, often silver-marbled leaves Z6.*

☼◑ ◊ Z4   **Perennial**

↕ 3in (8cm) ↔ 12in (30cm)

BERGENIA *'Morgenröte'*

Also sold as Morning Red, this early-flowering, evergreen perennial forms clumps of rich green, fleshy and leathery, paddle-shaped leaves. Clusters of deep pink flowers on upright stems emerge in spring. Good underplanting for shrubs, which give necessary winter shelter, or grow in a pot (*see p.448*). Provide a mulch in autumn. It tolerates alkaline soils and reasonably dry or damp shade (*see pp.64, 216, 238*).

ALSO RECOMMENDED: *'Abendglut' (syn. 'Evening Glow') has magenta-crimson flowers; 'Baby Doll' has pink flowers; 'Sunningdale' (see p.226); B. ciliata (see p.79).*

☼◑ ◊◊ Z3b   **Perennial**

↕ 12in (30cm) ↔ 20in (50cm)

CARDAMINE TRIFOLIA

Trifoliate bittercress is a creeping plant with divided, dark green leaves that are tinted red beneath. In late spring, it bears dense clusters of four-petaled, white (occasionally pink) flowers. It is ideal for a permanently damp, shady border (*see pp.238, 372*) or for naturalizing in a woodland garden. Grow in moist, organic soil.

ALSO RECOMMENDED: C. pratensis *'Flore Pleno' has double, lilac-pink flowers* Z5; C. raphanifolia *has lilac, red-violet, or white flowers* Z4.

☀◐● ◊ Z6　　　　**Perennial**
‡ 6in (15cm) ↔ 12in (30cm)

CHELIDONIUM MAJUS
'Flore Pleno'

This double-flowered form of the greater celandine is perfect for naturalizing in a woodland garden. Above a clump of lobed, deeply divided leaves it bears a mass of deep yellow flowers in summer. It tolerates most soils and almost any situation, including dry shade (*see p.216*).

ALSO RECOMMENDED: C. majus *has single, bowl-shaped, poppylike yellow flowers and self-seeds freely; var.* laciniatum *has deeply cut leaves and petals.*

☀◐ ◊◊ Z4　　　　**Perennial**
‡ 24in (60cm) ↔ 8in (20cm)

CHRYSOGONUM VIRGINIANUM

Goldenstar produces a long succession of star-shaped yellow flowers from early spring to late summer. The heart-shaped leaves with toothed or scalloped margins are borne on red-green stalks; they form dense clumps and, in mild winters, often remain evergreen. Ideal groundcover for a shady border or woodland garden, and it may also be grown in sun where soils remain moist (*see p.304*).

☼ ◐ ◊ Z3   **Perennial**
↕ 10in (25cm) ↔ 24in (60cm)

CYCLAMEN HEDERIFOLIUM

The Neapolitan cyclamen produces pale to deep pink flowers with backswept petals in autumn. These appear in advance of the ivylike leaves that are patterned with silvery gray. Excellent in dry shade beneath trees or shrubs (*see p.216*), or in containers (*see p.448*). Mulch each year as the leaves wither. It self-seeds freely, forming substantial colonies if protected from summer rainfall. Plant tubers in autumn. It tolerates alkaline soils (*see p.64*).

ALSO RECOMMENDED: *f.* albiflorum *has white flowers;* C. purpurascens *bears red flowers with its leaves in late summer* Z6.

☼ ◊ Z7   **Perennial**
↕ 4–5in (10–13cm) ↔ 6in (15cm)

DICENTRA *'Bacchanal'*

The clusters of dusky crimson spring flowers of this spreading perennial appear to glow among the ferny, deeply cut, grayish green leaves. It forms a very attractive groundcover for a woodland garden or damp, shady border (*see p.238*). It will grow in slightly alkaline soils (*see p.64*).

ALSO RECOMMENDED: *'Adrian Bloom' is similar; 'Langtrees' has silvery foliage and pinkish white flowers*; D. cucullaria (see p.229); D. spectabilis (see p.82).

☀ ◐ ◊◊ Z3   **Perennial**
‡ 14in (35cm) ↔ 18in (45cm)

DISPOROPSIS PERNYI

This rhizomatous perennial produces arching, mottled, deep green stems clothed in lance-shaped, dark green leaves. In early summer, lemon-scented flowers hang from the stems like waxy white bells. A very elegant plant for a woodland garden or damp, shady border (*see p.238*). It associates beautifully with ferns. Grow in leafy, moist but well-drained soil.

☀ ◐ ◊ *f* Z7   **Perennial**
‡ 16in (40cm) ↔ 12–16in (30–40cm)

DUCHESNEA INDICA

The Indian strawberry produces clumps of deeply veined, palmately divided, bright green leaves that are more or less evergreen; it spreads freely by means of rooting runners. Five-petaled yellow flowers appear in early and late summer followed by bright red, strawberry-like, unpalatable fruits. It is excellent as edging in a shady border and will also grow in a container (*see p.448*). Tolerant of most soils and sites.

☼ ◐ ◊◊ Z4   **Perennial**
‡ 4in (10cm) ↔ 4ft (1.2m) or more

EPIMEDIUM × WARLEYENSE

This evergreen, clump-forming plant has fresh green leaves that are tinted red in spring and autumn. It spreads freely by rhizomes. In mid- to late spring, slender stems carry nodding, cup-shaped yellow flowers with orange-red sepals. It is perfect for a mixed or herbaceous border or for a woodland site. Cut off old leaves in late winter or early spring. It tolerates dry shade (*see p.216*).

ALSO RECOMMENDED: *E. × perralchicum has bright yellow flowers* Z4; *E. × versicolor has pink and yellow flowers with reddish spurs* Z5.

☼ ◊◊ Z5   **Perennial**
‡ 16in (40cm) ↔ 30in (75cm)

EUPHORBIA SIKKIMENSIS

A spreading plant with upright shoots that are bright pink when young; they are clothed in narrow green leaves that become paler with red veins and margins as they age. Heads of yellow flowers appear from midsummer. It is ideal for a shady borders. Remove dead flowerheads after flowering but wear gloves, since the milky sap can irritate skin. Tolerant of alkaline soils (*see p.64*).

ALSO RECOMMENDED: E. amaygdaloides *var.* robbiae (see p.230); E. dulcis (see p.230); E. griffithii *'Dixter' has coppery leaves and orange flowers* Z4; E. schillingii *has bluish leaves and green-yellow flowers* Z7b.

☀ ◑ ◊ Z7   **Perennial**
↕ 4ft (1.2m) ↔ 18in (45cm)

GALAX URCEOLATA

The rounded and leathery, dark green leaves of this evergreen plant turn red-bronze in autumn. It is a robust and long-lived plant suitable for the front of a shady border, woodland garden, or large rock garden; it forms an excellent groundcover beneath shrubs in both dry and damp shade (*see pp.216, 238*). Slender-stemmed spikes of many tiny white flowers appear late spring and early summer. Grow in acidic soil (*see p.92*) and apply a mulch of pine needles or leaf mold annually in spring.

☀ ◊ Z6   **Perennial**
↕ 12in (30cm) ↔ 3ft (1m)

GALIUM ODORATUM

Tolerant of almost any soil and site, sweet woodruff makes a good groundcover, especially since its dense clusters of pure white, star-shaped summer flowers are very effective at brightening shady spots. It spreads rapidly, so site it away from less robust plants. The whorls of brilliant green leaves develop a strong scent of newly mown hay when dried. It is best with shade from the hottest sun. Excessive growth can be pulled out easily by hand to limit its spread.

☼☀ ◊◑ *f* Z4   **Perennial**
‡18in (45cm) ↔ indefinite

GERANIUM MACRORRHIZUM

This geranium spreads to form a cover of light green, finely cut, sticky and strongly aromatic foliage, coloring well in autumn. Clusters of pink, purplish, or white flowers appear above the carpet of leaves in early summer. Tolerant of clay soils and dry shade (*see pp.12, 216*); it will also grow in a container (*see p.448*).

ALSO RECOMMENDED: *'Album' has white flowers; 'Czakor' has magenta flowers; 'Ingwersen's Variety' has pink flowers; G. endressii (see p.316); G. nodosum (see p.231); G. × oxonianum (see p.316); G. phaeum (see p.232).*

☼☀ ◊◑ *f* Z4   **Perennial**
‡12in (30cm) ↔ 24in (60cm)

HEUCHERA *'Green Ivory'*

This coral bells forms clumps of bright green, lobed and rounded foliage that makes an effective evergreen groundcover or edging if grouped together. Sprays of small, pale green flowers are borne on upright stems in early summer; they are good for cutting and attract bees (see pp.494, 524). It tolerates full shade where the soil is reliably damp (see p.238). Also suitable for containers (see p.448).

ALSO RECOMMENDED: *'Chocolate Ruffles'* has brown, ruffled leaves; *'Rachel'* has pink flowers; H. micrantha *'Palace Purple'* (see p.464).

☼☀ ◊◊ Z4   **Perennial**
↕↔ 30in (75cm)

HOSTA *'Halcyon'*

The bright grayish blue foliage of this perennial make it a striking groundcover or architectural plant (see p.472). The leaves are heart-shaped, about 8in (20cm) long, forming clumps from which emerge clusters of lavender flowers on upright stems in summer. Good for clay and damp or permanently moist soils (see pp.12, 238, 372) as well as containers (see p.448).

ALSO RECOMMENDED: *'Birchwood Parky's Gold'* (see p.318); *'Frances Williams'* (see p.381); *'Shade Fanfare'* (see p.465); *'Wide Brim'* (see p.254); H. sieboldiana (see p.490); H. ventricosa (see p.30).

☼☀ ◊ Z4   **Perennial**
↕ 14–16in (35–40cm) ↔ 28in (70cm)

LAMIUM GALEOBDOLON
'Hermann's Pride'

This form of yellow archangel makes a dense carpet of silver-burnished green leaves, and it bears whorled spikes of yellow flowers in summer. It spreads vigorously, so site it well away from smaller plants. Growth is best on moist but well-drained soil; drier soils help reduce vigor. Tolerates both dry and damp shade (*see pp.216, 238*), and clay and alkaline soils (*see pp.12, 64*).

ALSO RECOMMENDED: *L. galeobdolon is more vigorous; 'Silver Angel' is more trailing, with silvery leaves.*

☀☀ ◐ ◊◊ Z3   **Perennial**

↕ 24in (60cm) ↔ indefinite

LUZULA SYLVATICA *'Aurea'*

This bright-foliaged cultivar of the greater woodrush is a grasslike woodland plant that makes a useful, dense groundcover for dry or damp, shady places (*see pp.216, 238*); it copes with full sun if the soil is reliably moist. The clumps of evergreen, strap-shaped leaves are yellow-green, fading to yellow in winter. Airy clusters of light brown flowers appear from spring to early summer.

ALSO RECOMMENDED: *'Hohe Tatra' is shorter; 'Marginata' has cream-margined, rich green leaves.*

☀ ◐ ◊◊ Z5   **Perennial**

↕ 28–32in (70–80cm) ↔ 18in (45cm)

MAIANTHEMUM BIFOLIUM

The false lily-of-the-valley is a vigorous, spreading plant with paired, broadly heart-shaped, dark green leaves. The slender-stemmed clusters of fluffy, star-shaped white flowers appear in early summer and are followed by red berries. An excellent groundcover for a wild or woodland garden or on a cool, damp, and shady bank (*see p.238*). It tolerates acidic soils (*see p.92*) and can be invasive.

ALSO RECOMMENDED: M. canadense *is similar with narrower leaves.* Z4

:☼: ☼: ◐ Z6   **Perennial**
‡ 6in (15cm) ↔ indefinite

PACHYPHRAGMA MACROPHYLLUM

The rounded and scalloped, dark green leaves of this spreading perennial are semievergreen, persisting partially in basal clusters over winter. In early spring, dense heads of four-petaled, malodorous white flowers appear; the stems later elongate, so the heart-shaped fruits that follow are held well above the foliage. Good as a groundcover beneath trees or shrubs, or at the front of a shady border. It tolerates dry shade (*see p.216*).

:☼: ◐◐ Z6   **Perennial**
‡ 16in (40cm) ↔ 36in (90cm)

PHUOPSIS STYLOSA

The Caucasian crosswort is a creeping, mat-forming plant with whorls of narrow, pale green leaves. It is ideal for a bank, rock garden, or the front of a border. It bears rounded heads of many tiny pink flowers over long periods in summer. The plant forms good cover in both shade and sun (*see p.304*). Trim after flowering to keep it compact.

☀ ◐ ◊◊ Z6   **Perennial**

‡ 6in (15cm) ↔ 20in (50cm) or more

POLYPODIUM VULGARE

The common polypody is a robust fern with deeply divided, lance-shaped and leathery, dark green fronds. It makes good cover on shady banks or borders and can be established on fallen tree trunks. Tolerant of alkaline and dry soils (*see pp.64, 216*). It grows well in organin, gritty or stony, well-drained soils and can be container-grown (*see p.448*).

ALSO RECOMMENDED: *'Bifidomultifidum' has lacy, very finely divided fronds; 'Cornubiense Grandiceps' has finely divided fronds that are crested at the tips.*

☀ ◐ ◊ Z4   **Perennial fern**

‡ 12in (30cm) ↔ indefinite

PULMONARIA SACCHARATA *'Frühlingshimmel'*

This plant forms an evergreen mat of silver-spotted leaves. From late winter to late spring, pink buds open to sky blue flowers with darker eyes. Also good for a damp, shady border, wildlife garden, or container (*see pp.238, 448, 494*). Remove old leaves after flowering to induce new growth and reduce risk of powdery mildew. It tolerates clay soils and exposed sites (*see pp.12, 118*).

ALSO RECOMMENDED: *Argentea Group has very silvery leaves and red flowers that age to deep violet; 'Mrs. Moon' has pink buds that open to bluish lilac flowers.*

☼ ◐ ◖ Z4 **Perennial**
‡ 10in (25cm) ↔ 24in (60cm)

RANUNCULUS ACONITIFOLIUS *'Flore Pleno'*

White bachelor's buttons is a double-flowered form of a buttercup. Its late spring, pure white flowers are almost spherical in shape and are borne above the clumps of large and luxuriant, deeply lobed and toothed, dark green leaves. It tolerates clay soils (*see p.12*) and makes a good groundcover for a woodland or shady garden.

ALSO RECOMMENDED: *R. aconitifolius is similar, with single flowers.*

☼ ◐ ◖◖ Z5 **Perennial**
‡ 24in (60cm) ↔ 18in (45cm)

SANGUINARIA CANADENSIS

Bloodroot forms a low mat of kidney-shaped, blue-gray leaves and makes excellent cover in a wild or woodland garden or in a shady niche in a rock garden. The lovely, crystalline-textured, white or pink-tinged flowers emerge from between vertically folded leaves as they unfurl in spring. It will also grow in containers (*see p.448*) and tolerates clay soils and damp sites in shade (*see pp.12, 238*).

ALSO RECOMMENDED: *'Plena' has longer-lasting, double white flowers.*

☀ ◐ ◊ Z4   **Perennial**
‡ 6in (15cm) ↔ 12in (30cm)

SAXIFRAGA *'Tricolor'*

A woodland saxifrage grown for its colorful rosettes of rounded to deeply cut, red, white, and green leaves. Airy clusters of tiny white flowers with uneven petals rise above the foliage in summer on slender stems. It also tolerates alkaline soils and dry shade (*see pp.64, 216*). Grow in a border, rock garden, or container (*see p.448*).

ALSO RECOMMENDED: S. fortunei *is similar;* S. cuneifolia *and* S. × urbium *both form spreading mats.*

☀ ◐ ◊◊ Z7   **Perennial**
‡↔ 12in (30cm)

SYMPHYTUM *'Goldsmith'*

This plant, less rampant than variants with plain green leaves, spreads vigorously to form a dense cover of wrinkled, gold- and cream-variegated, dark green leaves. From midspring, a mass of tubular, pale blue, pink, or cream flowers rise just above the foliage. Grow in a woodland garden or in a dry or damp, shady border (*see pp.216, 238*).

ALSO RECOMMENDED: *'Hidcote Blue' has plain, dark green leaves and pale blue flowers; 'Hidcote Pink' has pale pink and white flowers; S. tuberosum (see p.235).*

☼ ◐ ◔ ◊ Z6　　　　**Perennial**
↕↔ 12in (30cm)

TIARELLA CORDIFOLIA

Foam flower is named for its clouds of starry, creamy white flowers that appear in summer. It makes a weed-smothering, evergreen mat of lobed, pale green leaves that flush bronze-red in autumn. Excellent in a woodland garden or at the front of a damp, shady border (*see p.238*). It copes with a wide range of soils.

ALSO RECOMMENDED: *T. wherryi is less vigorous, with maroon-tinted foliage and white or pink flowers Z3b; 'Bronze Beauty' has red-bronze foliage.*

◑ ◐ ◔ ◊ Z4　　　　**Perennial**
↕ 4–12in (10–30cm) ↔ 12in (30cm)

TRADESCANTIA *Andersoniana Group 'Osprey'*

This perennial is admired for its bright white, summer to autumn flowers that are illuminated by the arching, deep purplish green leaves. The blooms have three triangular petals and appear at the tips of the stems. A long-flowering plant for filling gaps in a border or for a container (*see p.448*).

ALSO RECOMMENDED: *'Isis' makes a fine, dark-blue-flowered companion; 'Purple Dome' has rich purple flowers.*

☼ ☽ ◊ Z3b   **Perennial**
‡ 24in (60cm) ↔ 18in (45cm)

VANCOUVERIA HEXANDRA

Tough but of delicate appearance, this spreading perennial is ideal for a large, shady rock garden or under trees or shrubs. The lobed leaves are smooth-textured and bright green, and loose clusters of small, nodding white flowers appear on wiry stems in late spring and summer. It is best with shelter from wind, and it tolerates damp shade (*see p.238*).

ALSO RECOMMENDED: V. chrysantha *is wider spreading with leathery, evergreen leaves and yellow flowers.* Z6b

☼ ◊ Z6   **Perennial**
↕ ↔ 16in (40cm)

PLANTS FOR WALLS & PAVING

First and foremost, walls, paths, and patios are practical features. Paths allow people to use the garden without getting their feet dirty; patios provide an area for dining and outdoor entertaining; and walls serve to divide the garden into separate areas. Although these surfaces may seem to be mundane, there is no reason why they cannot form yet another planting niche for the gardener to exploit.

Walls and paving can appear hard, monotonous, and bland without plants to soften their severe lines. When paths are studded with aromatic herbs, such as *Mentha requienii* (*see p.365*) or thyme (*see pp.310, 352, 507*), that release their fragance when gently walked on by passing feet, and walls are softened by flowers and handsome foliage, these areas become features of real beauty.

Many plants that do well in wall and paving crevices do best with hot, dry conditions at their heads (*see p.190*), good drainage at their necks, and cool, damp conditions at their

roots (which they find beneath the slabs or stones).

The stonework also insulates the roots, keeping temperatures more even in summer and protecting them from frost heave in the winter months.

IDEAL PLANTS FOR PAVING

In paving, plants need to be small enough not to impede progress and low-growing so that they do not cause the unwary to trip. Larger mound-formers, like lavenders (*see pp.155, 200*), *Euryops acraeus* (*see p.350*), or *Artemisia schmidtiana* 'Nana' (*see p.357*), have a role to play in softening the hard lines at the margins; place them carefully away from lines of pedestrian access across the paving. Bear in mind that few plants will withstand constant foot traffic or having garden furniture placed on top of them.

CULTIVATION TIPS

Instead of mortaring all wall and paving crevices, fill them or some of them with a gritty or sandy soil mix to provide a good, well-drained growing medium. Plants can be introduced either by sowing seed directly into the crevices or by planting them when still small – before the root system becomes too large to introduce without damaging it. You will need to weed around young plants and seedlings and keep them well watered until they are established. Once they get going, they will help prevent further invasion by weeds. Some plants, such as *Alchemilla alpina* (*see p.354*) or *Geranium dalmaticum* (*see p.363*), will find their own way into crevices by self-seeding; the only aid they need is to thin the seedlings to give them sufficient space to grow.

If you are building a new patio or wall, consider omitting some slabs or bricks to form planting pockets to accommodate a few taller or larger species – you could even create a checkerboard effect in paving by leaving out alternate slabs. Top-dress the soil surface with gravel, which will serve as a weed-suppressing mulch.

CYTISUS ARDOINOI

This ground-hugging broom forms a hummock of arching stems and small, deep green leaves that are palmately divided into three narrow leaflets. Bright yellow pea flowers are borne in the axils of these leaves from late spring to summer. It grows well on poor, sandy or acidic soils (*see pp.38, 92*), where it likes to remain undisturbed. Minimal pruning is necessary. Also suitable for rock gardens.

☼ ◊ Z7   **Deciduous shrub**
↕↔ 8–24in (20–60cm)

EURYOPS ACRAEUS

This silver-gray-leaved shrub forms a tight dome of foliage that is studded in late spring and early summer by a mass of bright yellow, daisylike flowerheads. Both foliage and flowers are offset beautifully by mellow stone or brick pavers. Excellent in hot, dry sites and in containers (*see pp.190, 412*), but it is also suitable for a rock garden, raised bed, or at the front of a sunny border. Trim lightly after flowering to keep compact.

☼ ◊ Min 40°F (5°C)   **Evergreen shrub**
↕↔ 12in (30cm)

HELIANTHEMUM LUNULATUM

The spreading stems of this low shrub
are clothed in gray-green leaves. In late
spring and early summer, a profusion
of small, saucer-shaped yellow flowers
cover the plant. It thrives on sandy
and alkaline soils, and in hot, dry sites
(*see pp.38, 64, 190*), and it also makes a
good groundcover (*see p.304*). Trim
after flowering to keep compact. It is
suitable for a sunny container (*see
p.412*).

ALSO RECOMMENDED: *H. 'Ben Hope' has
pale gray-green leaves and carmine red
flowers; H. oelandicum subsp. alpestre has
gray-green leaves and yellow flowers Z7.*

☼ ◊ Z6   **Evergreen shrub**
6in (15cm) ↔ 10in (25cm)

LINUM ARBOREUM

The tree flax is actually a dwarf shrub
with spatula-shaped, thick, dark blue-
green leaves crowded along its shoots.
It is grown for its lengthy season of
bright yellow, funnel-shaped flowers
that appear for many weeks from late
spring to summer. Also suitable for a
rock garden and alkaline soils (*see
p.64*), but shelter it from excessive
winter moisture.

ALSO RECOMMENDED: *L. 'Gemmel's
Hybrid' is smaller. Z6*

☼ ◊ Z7   **Evergreen shrub**
↔ 12in (30cm)

TEUCRIUM POLIUM

This rounded shrub has aromatic, wrinkled, white-woolly, gray-green leaves and dense heads of purple or yellow, two-lipped flowers that appear in summer; they are attractive to bees (*see p.494*). Also good for rock gardens and raised beds. In paving, grow it in pockets of gritty, well-drained, neutral to alkaline soil (*see p.64*). Trim in early spring to keep it compact. It may also be clipped as a low hedge (*see p.138*).

ALSO RECOMMENDED: *T. aroanium is compact with silver-hairy leaves and purple flowers Z7; T. subspinosum is spiny with gray-green leaves and pink flowers Z8.*

☼ ◊ *f* Z8   **Deciduous shrub**
‡↔ 12in (30cm)

THYMUS SERPYLLUM *'Annie Hall'*

A creeping, mound-forming plant with tiny, aromatic green leaves and tight heads of two-lipped purple-pink flowers in summer; they attract bees (*see p.494*). In paving, the foliage releases a lovely fragrance when stepped on. Thyme thrives in alkaline soils and hot, dry sites (*see pp.64, 190*) and makes a good groundcover (*see p.304*). Trim after flowering to keep the growth compact.

ALSO RECOMMENDED: *'Coccineus' has crimson-pink flowers; 'Pink Chintz' has gray-green leaves and flesh pink flowers; 'Snowdrift' has white flowers.*

☼ ◊ *f* Z5   **Evergreen shrub**
‡ 10in (25cm) ↔ 18in (45cm)

ACANTHOLIMON GLUMACEUM

This compact evergreen forms a mat of stiff and needlelike, dark green leaves. In summer, it is covered by dense, short-stemmed spikes of rose-pink flowers. Grow in pockets of sharply drained, gritty soil. It tolerates alkaline soils and hot, dry sites (*see pp.64, 190*), and it is good for raised or scree beds. Susceptible to rot in areas with wet winters, but planting in wall crevices helps protect the vulnerable plant neck. Leave undisturbed once established.

☼ ◊ Z5   **Perennial**
‡ 2–3in (5–8cm) ↔ 12in (30cm)

AETHIONEMA GRANDIFLORUM

This pretty stonecress is a woody-based, evergreen perennial. It bears masses of pale to deep pink, cross-shaped flowers in late spring and early summer above its neat and narrow, blue-green leaves. It is best in light, sandy or alkaline soils (*see pp.38, 64*), but it tolerates acidic conditions (*see p.92*). Good for coastal and hot, dry sites (*see pp.166, 190*). It is often short-lived.

ALSO RECOMMENDED: *A. armenum is more compact with pale pink flowers* Z5; *A. 'Warley Rose' has blue-gray leaves and rich pink flowers* Z5b.

☼ ◊ Z5   **Perennial**
‡↔ 8–12in (20–30cm)

AJUGA REPTANS
'Catlin's Giant'

An excellent evergreen perennial for both paving and groundcover (*see pp.304, 326*). It bears whorls of dark blue flowers along the upright stems in early summer. The glossy, deep bronze-purple leaves can be up to 6in (15cm) long. Also useful as border edging, coping with both dry and damp shade (*see pp.216, 238*). It is tolerant of clay soils (*see p.12*).

ALSO RECOMMENDED: *'Multicolor'* (see p.225); *'Variegata'* is denser, with cream-splashed leaves.

☼☀ ◊◊ Z3   **Perennial**
‡ 8in (20cm) ↔ 3ft (1m)

ALCHEMILLA ALPINA

Alpine lady's mantle has a creeping rootstock and forms low mats of lobed, dark green leaves that are densely silver-hairy beneath. Loose clusters of yellow-green flowers appear throughout summer. It is ideal for paving crevices, where it may spread by self-seeding, and it is also good for a rock garden or as a groundcover (*see p.304*). It tolerates coastal conditions (*see p.166*).

ALSO RECOMMENDED: A. conjuncta (see p.181); A. ellenbeckii *has pale green leaves on wiry red stems* Z6b.

☼ ◊ Z4   **Perennial**
‡ 3–5in (8–12cm) ↔ 20in (50cm)

ANAGALLIS TENELLA
'Studland'

This mat-forming plant has bright green leaves that are almost obscured in late spring and early summer by a profusion of small, fragrant pink flowers. Also good as a groundcover at the front of a sunny border (*see p.304*) or in a rock garden. It may be short-lived.

ALSO RECOMMENDED: A. monellii *is taller and has blue flowers.* Z6

☼ ◐ ƒ Z6   **Perennial**
‡ 2–4in (5–10cm) ↔ 16in (40cm)

ANDROSACE CARNEA
SUBSP. LAGGERI

This evergreen, cushion-forming plant has rosettes of narrow, fleshy leaves and produces yellow-eyed, deep pink flowers in late spring. Grow in pockets of gritty, moist, but sharply drained soil, and top-dress with gravel to keep the crown and leaves dry. Also good for a rock garden, trough, or raised bed. It tolerates alkaline soils (*see p.304*).

ALSO RECOMMENDED: A. lanuginosa *has grayish leaves and pink flowers* Z4; A. semper-vivoides *has fragrant pink flowers* Z4.

☼ ◊ Z4   **Perennial**
‡ 2in (5cm) ↔ 3–6in (8–15cm)

ARABIS BLEPHAROPHYLLA 'Frühlingszauber'

A mat-forming evergreen with dark green leaves that bears compact clusters of fragrant, deep pink flowers in late spring and early summer. As well as for paving, it is suitable for rock gardens and raised beds, and tolerates hot, dry sites (*see p.190*). It may be short-lived. Protect from excessive winter moisture. Also sold as 'Spring Charm'.

ALSO RECOMMENDED: *A. alpina 'Flore Pleno' has double white flowers* Z3; *A.* × *arendsii 'Rosabella' has rose-pink flowers* Z4.

☼ ◊ *f* Z4   **Perennial**

‡ 4in (10cm) ↔ 8in (20cm)

ARENARIA PURPURASCENS

This sandwort is a low-growing and spreading perennial, freely bearing an abundance of starry pink flowers in midsummer. They are highlighted by the background of small and narrow, sharply pointed, grayish green leaves on wiry, mat-forming stems. It is easily grown in both wall and paving crevices, or in a rock garden. It tolerates sandy soils (*see p.38*).

ALSO RECOMMENDED: *A. montana has white flowers in early summer.* Z4

☼ ◊ Z4   **Perennial**

‡ ¾–2in (2–5cm) ↔ 8in (20cm)

ARTEMISIA SCHMIDTIANA 'Nana'

A compact, evergreen plant with very
finely divided, silvery gray foliage and
heads of tiny yellow flowers in summer.
The pale foliage is beautifully offset
by stone or brick pavers. Plant it in
pockets of gritty soil. It is also good
for a rock garden or raised bed.
Tolerant of sandy and alkaline soils (*see
pp.38, 64*), and hot, dry sites (*see p.190*).

ALSO RECOMMENDED: *A. stelleriana
'Boughton Silver' has deeply toothed
or lobed, silver-white leaves.* Z4b

☀ ◊ Z4   **Perennial**
‡ 3in (8cm) ↔ 12in (30cm)

ASARINA PROCUMBENS

The trailing stems of this evergreen
plant are for good for paving in partial
shade. They display pretty pale yellow,
snapdragon-like flowers through
summer among pairs of heart-shaped,
hairy green leaves. It prefers sandy soils
(*see p.38*) and copes with dry shade
(*see p.216*). The stems can also be
allowed to cascade over the sides
of walls, rocks, raised beds, or dry
banks. It can be grown as a groundcover (*see p.326*).

☀ ◊ Z5   **Perennial**
‡ 2in (5cm) ↔ 24in (60cm)

BLECHNUM PENNA-MARINA

The attractive, dark green, narrow fishbone foliage of this evergreen fern is useful in any damp and shady site (*see p.238*). As well as wall and paving crevices, it also grows well as a ground-cover in rock gardens, herbaceous borders, or woodland, where it forms sizeable mats. The leaves may be reddish when young. It thrives in acidic soils (*see p.92*).

ALSO RECOMMENDED: B. spicant *is taller and less spreading.* Z3

☼ ☼ ◖ Min 40°F (5°C)　　**Perennial fern**
‡ 4–8in (10–20cm) ↔ indefinite

CAMPANULA *'Birch Hybrid'*

An attractive, ground-hugging bellflower with small, evergreen, heart-shaped, bright green leaves. Plentiful clusters of deep mauve-blue flowers appear in summer. It can also be used as ground cover (*see p.304*), or in a rock garden or container (*see p.412*). Alkaline soils are tolerated (*see p.64*).

ALSO RECOMMENDED: C. cochleariifolia *has white to blue flowers* Z3; C. latiloba *'Hidcote Amethyst'* (see p.26); C. portenschlagiana *and* C. poscharskyana *are similar, both* Z3.

☼ ☼ ◊◖ Z4　　**Perennial**
‡ 4in (10cm) ↔ 20in (50cm) or more

CAMPANULA CARPATICA
'Bressingham White'

Forming low clumps of heart-shaped leaves, this plant bears its pure white, upward-facing bellflowers over a long summer season. It grows well on dry stone walls, in paving crevices or rock gardens, in containers, or as a ground-cover (*see pp.304, 412*). It tolerates alkaline soils (*see p.64*).

ALSO RECOMMENDED: *'Blaue Clips' (syn. 'Blue Clips') has blue flowers; 'Weisse Clips' (syn. 'White Clips') is white-flowered.*

☀ ◊◊ Z4 **Perennial**

‡ 6in (15cm) ↔ 12–24in (30–60cm)

CHIASTOPHYLLUM
OPPOSITIFOLIUM

This is fleshy plant that is naturally found in shady rock crevices, so it is ideal for a drystone wall or rock garden. Its spreading, evergreen growth forms dense mats of rounded, fleshy, pale green leaves. Long, arching stems of yellow flowers decorate the plant in early summer. Prone to slug and snail damage.

ALSO RECOMMENDED: *'Jim's Pride' is low and spreading, with cream-margined leaves.*

☀ ◊◊ Z5 **Perennial**

‡ 6–8in (15–20cm) ↔ 6in (15cm)

COLCHICUM AGRIPPINUM

This perennial bears its narrow, funnel-shaped, purplish pink flowers, marked with darker veins, in autumn. The leaves appear in spring and die down in early summer. It is also good at the foot of a sunny bank, in a rock garden, or at the front of a border. To grow in paving crevices, plant corms in early summer in pockets of fertile, moist but well-drained soil. It tolerates alkaline soils and hot, dry sites (*see pp.64, 190*).

ALSO RECOMMENDED: C. autumnale (*see p.80*); C. speciosum *has pale to deep pinkish purple flowers* Z4.

☼ ◊ Z5b   **Perennial corm**
‡ 3–4in (8–10cm) ↔ 3in (8cm)

CRASSULA SARCOCAULIS

This compact and bushy succulent has fleshy stems that carry narrow green leaves. These are tinted red and are relatively small, as are the unpleasantly scented, star-shaped, pinkish white summer flowers. Choose a hot, dry site (*see p.190*) with sharply drained, sandy soil (*see p.38*), where it may grow with other succulents.

☼ ◊ Min 40°F (5°C)   **Perennial**
‡↔ 12in (30cm)

CROCUS CORSICUS

This dwarf perennial brings vase-shaped violet flowers to the garden in spring. They emerge from the corm at about the same time as the narrow, dark green leaves. It tolerates sandy and alkaline soils (*see pp.38, 64*) as well as coastal and hot, dry sites (*see pp.166, 190*). Also effective in drifts at the front of a border or rock garden, or in a raised bed or container (*see p.412*). Plant corms in autumn; keep it completely dry over summer.

ALSO RECOMMENDED: C. angustifolius *has orange-yellow flowers.* Z3

☼ ◊ *f* Z6b   **Perennial corm**
‡3–4in (8–10cm) ↔ 1½in (4cm)

DIANTHUS *'La Bourboule'*

This evergreen pink bears a mass of clove-scented, clear pink flowers with fringed petals. They are borne in summer above a neat mound of narrow, gray-green leaves. It is also good for a rock garden, raised bed, trough, or container (*see p.412*). In paving, grow in sharply drained, gritty soil. It thrives in shallow, alkaline soil (*see p.64*) and in sandy soils (*see p.38*).

ALSO RECOMMENDED: D. *'Annabelle' has double, cherry pink flowers* Z5; *D.* deltoides *'Leuchtfunk' has dark green leaves and cherry flowers* Z4 ; D. subacaulis (*see p.314*).

☼ ◊ *f* Z4   **Perennial**
‡3–4in (8–10cm) ↔ 8in (20cm)

EDRAIANTHUS PUMILIO

This diminutive plant produces dense tufts of grasslike foliage and upturned, bell-shaped flowers of pale to deep violet in early summer. It thrives in light, sharply drained, alkaline soils (*see p.64*), but it tends to be short-lived. Good in a dry wall or rock garden.

ALSO RECOMMENDED: *E. graminifolius is taller with spherical heads of bell-shaped, deep purple flowers* Z4; *E. serpyllifolius is mat-forming with deep violet flowers* Z4.

☼ ◊ Z4   **Perennial**

↕ 1in (2.5cm) ↔ 6in (15cm)

ERIGERON KARVINSKIANUS

This evergreen perennial, sometimes sold as *E. mucronatus* or 'Profusion', forms a carpet of gray-green foliage that is covered by yellow-centered, daisylike flowerheads in summer. The outer petals are white, aging to pink or purple. It can also be grown as a trailing container plant (*see p.412*). Tolerant of coastal conditions (*see p.166*). Grow as an annual where it is not fully hardy.

☼ ◊ Z6   **Perennial**

↕ 6–12in (15–30cm) ↔ 3ft (1m) or more

GERANIUM DALMATICUM

This low-growing, usually evergreen plant forms mounds of glossy light green leaves and bears profuse clusters of pale to bright pink flowers in summer. An undemanding plant that is also good for groundcover (*see p.304*), containers (*see p.412*), rock gardens, and the fronts of sunny borders. It tolerates a range of soils and sites.

ALSO RECOMMENDED: G. cinereum *subsp.* subcaulescens *has black-eyed, brilliant magenta flowers* Z4; G. 'Kate' *has bronzed leaves and pale pink flowers* Z4.

☼ ◊ Z4   **Perennial**

↕ 6in (15cm) ↔ 20in (50cm)

HELICHRYSUM *'Schwefellicht'*

Fluffy heads of sulfur yellow flowers appear on this clump-forming plant in late summer above a mound of woolly, silver-gray leaves. It works well at the front of a sunny, mixed or herbaceous border and tolerates hot, dry sites (*see p.190*). Also sold as 'Sulfur Light'.

ALSO RECOMMENDED: H. sibthorpii *is more compact, with white-woolly leaves and gold flowerheads*; H. thianschanicum *'Goldkind'* has papery, golden yellow flowerheads. Both are tender but good for containers.

☼ ◊ Min 40°F (5°C)   **Perennial**

↕ 16in (40cm) ↔ 12in (30cm)

LEONTOPODIUM ALPINUM

With its mounds of gray-green leaves and densely white-woolly, yellowish white flowerheads that appear in spring or early summer, edelweiss is a charming addition to a planting pocket in paving. It also thrives on top of dry stone walls and in rock gardens. Grow in sharply drained, neutral to alkaline soil (*see p.64*). It may be short-lived.

ALSO RECOMMENDED: *'Mignon' is compact, with white flowerheads; subsp. nivale has densely white woolly leaves and pure white flowerheads;*

☼ ◊ Z4   **Perennial**
‡ 8in (20cm) ↔ 4in (10cm)

LEWISIA *'George Henley'*

This evergreen plant has rosettes of fleshy, dark green leaves and bears open sprays of funnel-shaped flowers from late spring to late summer; they are purplish pink with magenta veining. Excellent planted on its side in a dry-stone wall. In planting pockets, provide sharply drained, neutral to acidic soil (*see p.92*). Always choose a site where plants will be protected from excessive winter moisture.

ALSO RECOMMENDED: *L. cotyledon hybrids have bright pink, magenta, orange, or yellow flowers Z3b; L. tweedyi has white to peach-pink flowers Z3b.*

◑ ◊ Z4   **Perennial**
‡↔ 4in (10cm)

MENTHA REQUIENII

Corsican mint is a mat-forming plant with creeping, rooting stems. The glossy bright green leaves are tiny but have a strong peppermint scent; this is released if brushed by passing feet, although it will not withstand heavy traffic. Short spikes of tiny, tubular lilac flowers appear in summer; they attract bees (*see p.494*).

ALSO RECOMMENDED: M. pulegium *has sharply scented leaves.* Z5

☼ ◑ *f* Z5b   **Perennial**

‡ ½in (1cm) ↔ indefinite

MYOSOTIS SYLVATICA *'Music'*

Although most often used as short-lived bedding plants, compact cultivars of the forget-me-not are ideal for crevices in damp, lightly shaded areas of paving. This cultivar has very large, bright blue flowers from spring to early summer. It will self-seed, but its offspring may not retain the same characteristics. Tolerant of clay soils (*see p.12*).

ALSO RECOMMENDED: *'Blue Ball' is more compact, with azure flowers; 'Pompadour' has deep rose-pink flowers; 'Ultramarine' has indigo blue flowers.*

☼ ◑ ◊◑ Z3   **Perennial**

‡ 10in (25cm) ↔ 6in (15cm)

OXALIS ENNEAPHYLLA *'Rosea'*

This spreading, rhizomatous plant produces umbrella-like tufts of pleated, blue-gray leaves and bears widely funnel-shaped, pale purple-pink flowers in early summer. Excellent for paving, it may also be used as a groundcover in sun (*see p.304*). It tolerates coastal and hot, dry sites (*see pp.166, 190*).

ALSO RECOMMENDED: *O. enneaphylla has fragrant, white to deep pink flowers; 'Minutifolia' is more compact, with white flowers; O. 'Ione Hecker' has blue-violet flowers with darker veins* Z8.

☼ ◊ Z7   **Perennial**
‡ 3in (8cm) ↔ 6in (15cm)

PRATIA PEDUNCULATA

Paving crevices make an ideal home for this creeping, ground-hugging plant that forms a carpet of rounded leaves. Above these, a scattering of starry, pale blue flowers appear over long periods in summer. Also good as a groundcover in damp, shady spots (*see pp.238, 326*). It can be invasive, but not rampant, even in dry shade (*see p.216*).

ALSO RECOMMENDED: *'County Park' is similar; P. angulata 'Treadwellii' is larger and more invasive, with white flowers* Z6.

◐☼ ◊◊ Z6   **Perennial**
‡ ½in (1.5cm) ↔ indefinite

PUSCHKINIA SCILLOIDES

This small bulb, with grasslike foliage, produces densely packed spikes of bell-shaped, pale blue spring flowers, each petal with a darker blue stripe. It looks charming in paving crevices and is equally suitable for a rock garden. It can also be grown in containers (*see p.412*) or beneath shrubs. Plant bulbs in early autumn in any well-drained soil.

ALSO RECOMMENDED: *var.* libanotica *has smaller, white flowers.*

☼ ☼ ◊ Z4   **Perennial bulb**
↕ 8in (20cm) ↔ 2in (5cm)

RHODOHYPOXIS
'Margaret Rose'

This alpine plant forms a compact clump of grasslike, grayish green, hairy foliage. Clear pink flowers bloom all over the plant through summer, bringing life to the foliage. As well as in paving and wall crevices, it can be grown in a trough, rock garden, or alpine house. It must have well-drained soil and shelter from excessive winter moisture.

ALSO RECOMMENDED: R. baurii *has pale to deep reddish pink flowers.* Z8

☼ ◊ Z8   **Perennial**
↕↔ 4in (10cm)

SAPONARIA × OLIVANA

Ideal for sunny areas of paving, this cushion-forming plant forms a tight mound of narrow leaves that are almost obscured by pale pink flowers in summer. It may also be grown in a rock garden or scree bed, or in a container (*see p.412*). Provide gritty, sharply drained, preferably alkaline soil (*see p.64*) and top-dress with gravel.

ALSO RECOMMENDED: S. 'Bressingham' *is mat-forming, with deep pink flowers* Z6; *S. caespitosa has pink to purple flowers* Z4.

☼ ◊ Z4   **Perennial**
↕ 2in (5cm) ↔ 6in (15cm)

SAXIFRAGA 'Gregor Mendel'

The tiny rosettes of this saxifrage are densely packed to form a deep green mat of foliage that sprouts flower stems in early spring; these form a sheet of pale yellow flowers above the leaves. Good for a rock garden as well as wall and paving crevices. Grow in neutral to alkaline soil (*see p.64*), in a site protected from hot sun to prevent leaf scorch. It can be pot-grown (*see p.412*). Sometimes sold as *S. × apiculata*.

ALSO RECOMMENDED: 'Cranbourne' *has deep pink flowers; 'Faldonside' grows vigorously, with bright yellow flowers.*

☼◑ ◊ Z6   **Perennial**
↕ 4in (10cm) ↔ 12in (30cm)

SAXIFRAGA *'Cloth of Gold'*

This moss-textured saxifrage forms a golden cushion of tightly packed leaf rosettes. Flat-topped clusters of small and starry, creamy yellow flowers rise above this mat of foliage from late spring to early autumn. It is best in partial shade to keep the sharply drained soil reliably moist. It prefers neutral to alkaline soils and can be container-grown (*see pp.64, 448*).

ALSO RECOMMENDED: *'Jenkinsiae' has pale pink flowers with dark centers in spring; 'Southside Seedling' has red-spotted white flowers in early summer.*

☼ ◊ Z6   **Perennial**
↕ 4in (10cm) ↔ 12in (30cm)

SEDUM ACRE

Common stonecrop forms an evergreen mat of small and rounded, fleshy, pale green leaves. This is topped by starry, yellow-green flowers over long periods in summer. Any small piece will root easily if pushed carefully into a paving crevice. It grows well in hot, dry sites and in shallow containers, and it can be grown as a groundcover (*see pp.190, 304, 412*). Tolerant of sandy and alkaline soils (*see pp.38, 64*). It can become a bad lawn weed.

ALSO RECOMMENDED: *'Aureum' has bright yellow leaves; S. lydium has tight rosettes of red-tipped leaves and white flowers Z4.*

☼ ◊ Z4   **Perennial**
↕ 2in (5cm) ↔ 24in (60cm) or more

SEDUM SPATHULIFOLIUM *'Purpureum'*

This fast-growing, summer-flowering succulent forms tight, evergreen mats of fleshy purple leaves; young foliage is covered with a silvery bloom. Flat clusters of small, star-shaped, bright yellow flowers appear through summer. Also good for rock gardens and the fronts of well-drained borders, and it will grow as a groundcover in sun (*see p.304*). Tolerant of sandy soils and hot, dry sites (*see pp.38, 190*). Contain to prevent encroachment on other plants.

ALSO RECOMMENDED: *'Cape Blanco'* has silvery green leaves.

☼ ◐ ◊ Z6   **Perennial**
↕4in (10cm) ↔ 24in (60cm)

SEMPERVIVUM CILIOSUM

This evergreen succulent makes dense and hairy rosettes of gray-green leaves that will form a spreading mat. Heads of star-shaped, yellow-green flowers rise above the foliage through summer; the rosettes that flower die afterward, but they are rapidly replaced. Grow in gritty, sharply drained soil; it survives drought but not high humidity or winter moisture. Tolerant of sandy soils and hot, dry sites (*see pp.38, 190*); will grow as a groundcover in sun (*see p.304*).

ALSO RECOMMENDED: S. arachnoideum (see p.438); S. tectorum (see p.323).

☼ ◊ Z7b   **Perennial**
↕3in (8cm) ↔ 12in (30cm)

SOLEIROLIA SOLEIROLII

This mat-forming perennial forms a very fine-textured carpet of tiny, rounded, emerald green leaves. It is evergreen in frost-free areas but is deciduous in slightly colder areas; it recovers quickly in spring. Any soil is suitable, in sun or shade. Although it is invasive and difficult to eradicate, it is useful as a groundcover in difficult sites (*see pp.304, 326*). An ideal solution to containment is to plant it in paving crevices, where it spreads to form an exceptionally pretty, neat green outline to pavers.

☼ ☀ ◊◊Min 40°F (5°C) **Perennial**
↕2in (5cm) ↔ indefinite

TANACETUM ARGENTEUM

Valued for its filigree carpet of silver-gray leaves, this mat-forming, usually evergreen perennial bears white, daisy-like flowerheads in summer. It tolerates most soils, as long as they are neither heavy nor wet; it grows best on sandy, well-drained soil (*see p.38*). In addition to paving crevices, it is suitable in a rock garden or as a groundcover at the front of a sunny border (*see p.304*).

ALSO RECOMMENDED: T. densum *subsp.* amani *and* T. haradjanii *are similar, with yellow flowerheads.* Both Z7

☼ ◊ Z6 **Perennial**
↕8in (20cm) ↔ 12in (30cm)

PLANTS FOR RELIABLY MOIST SOILS

An AREA OF permanently moist soil in the garden, perhaps in a low-lying hollow, can be a cause for rejoicing rather than a perennial problem if you select the right plants – and there are many to choose from. Nearly all of the plants that thrive in such conditions occur naturally in damp meadows, bogs, and by watersides, whether a stream, river, or lake. There is also a great number of other plants that are normally grown in shade but will thrive in full sun where the soil stays constantly moist (*see p.238*). Collectively, these plants are known as moisture-lovers, but they are sometimes offered for sale as bog plants. This can be misleading, since many moisture-loving plants will not tolerate totally water-logged soils. Boggy soil saturated with water is usually better for shallow-water, or marginal aquatic plants (*see p.394*).

PLANTING PLACES

An area of permanently moist soil is the perfect opportunity to create a luxuriant moisture

garden, populated by beautiful, ground-covering foliage plants and stately heads of flowers. These plants can also be used to surround ponds or pools to bridge the gap between water and land. Here, they will mask the water's edge in a most attractive way, and if the water is still and clear, plants like *Salix alba* 'Britzensis' (*see p.375*) or *Lysichiton camtschatcensis* (*see p.385*) give more than double the value when their form is reflected in its mirrorlike surface. Moisture-lovers thrive in the muddy margins of ponds or streams, where their roots are kept just above water level. These plants provide cover for the wildlife that lives in or around water, or for those that visit to drink and bathe.

MAINTAINING MOISTURE

When constructing a new pond, it is always worth the effort to provide planting pockets or shallow ledges of moist soil to accommodate moisture-loving plants. Barring accidents, the soil will never dry out in these situations.

In other sites, you may need to take a few steps to ensure that the soil does remain moist. Few plants, particularly moisture-lovers, can withstand being almost inundated with water at one moment and then left high and dry the next. This is often the case with damp hollows that lie over impermeable clay, which are wet as long as the moisture is replenished by rain, but they are often baked as hard as brick come summer. It may be sufficient to improve drainage by breaking up the soil, adding coarse sand and generous amounts of organic matter before planting, with an annual autumn or spring mulch. Alternatively, you may wish to go whole hog and create a proper permanently moist garden by excavating the top 10in (25cm) or so of soil then lining the hollow with plastic liner. Before backfilling with the excavated soil (improved with copious quantities of organic matter), stab the plastic with a garden fork to allow water to drain slowly and prevent waterlogging.

ALNUS CORDATA

The Italian alder is a large and fast-growing, conical tree with shiny, dark green leaves. The bark is smooth and gray, and yellow-brown catkins emerge on the bare branches in late winter. Small brown cones follow, persisting into the next season. It grows well in most soils, including dry ones, but it is at its best next to water. Useful as a windbreak or hedge (*see pp.118, 138*). Prune in winter, if necessary.

ALSO RECOMMENDED: A. glutinosa *'Imperialis'* (see p.121); A. incana (see p.140); A. rubra *is similar* Z7.

☼ ◊◊ Z6   **Deciduous tree**

‡ 80ft (25m) ↔ 20ft (6m)

METASEQUOIA GLYPTOSTROBOIDES

This elegant conifer with a neat, narrowly conical outline has soft, fern-like leaves that are emerald green on emergence; they contrast beautifully with the shaggy, cinnamon brown bark. In autumn, the leaves assume warm, russet-gold tones before falling. An ideal architectural waterside specimen (*see p.472*). It tolerates clay and alkaline soils (*see pp.12, 64*) and atmospheric pollution. Pruning is seldom required.

☼☀ ◊ Z5b   **Deciduous tree**

‡ 70–130ft (20–40m) ↔ 15ft (5m)

SALIX ALBA *'Britzensis'*

The white willow has narrow green leaves and bears yellow catkins as the leaves emerge in spring. This form is valued for its orange-red winter stems and makes a large tree if left unpruned. For the best stem effects, cut all shoots to the base or to a short trunk each or every other year in late winter. It is excellent for waterside plantings and can be grown as a hedge (*see p.138*). It tolerates coastal sites (*see p.166*).

ALSO RECOMMENDED: *subsp.* vitellina *has rich yellow to orange stems;* S. exigua (*see p.50*); S. purpurea (*see p.162*).

☀ ◊ Z2   **Deciduous tree**
↕ 80ft (25m) ↔ 30ft (10m)

ARONIA ARBUTIFOLIA

Red chokeberry is an ideal specimen or border shrub of manageable size. It is grown for its yellow or orange-red autumn leaves, its flat-headed clusters of white flowers in late spring, and for the profusion of bright red berries that follow, which are favored by birds (*see p.494*). It tolerates clay soils (*see p.12*).

ALSO RECOMMENDED: A. melanocarpa, *black chokeberry, has black berries.* Z4

☀◐ ◊ Z4   **Deciduous shrub**
↕ 10ft (3m) ↔ 5ft (1.5m)

CORNUS ALBA
'Elegantissima'

This variegated form of the red-barked dogwood has grayish green, white-margined leaves as well as bright red young stems. For the best stem and foliage display, cut all shoots on established plants back hard and fertilize each spring. Particularly effective in a prominent site close to water. It tolerates clay soils and exposed sites (*see pp.12, 118*).

ALSO RECOMMENDED: *'Kesselringii'* (see p.128); *'Spaethii' has yellow-margined leaves.*

☼ ◊◊ Z2   **Deciduous shrub**
↕↔ 10ft (3m)

VACCINIUM CORYMBOSUM

The highbush blueberry is a dense, arching shrub with oval leaves that turn yellow or red in autumn. In late spring and early summer, it bears hanging clusters of small, white or pink flowers, followed by edible, blue-black berries. Grow in a shrub border or woodland garden, in acidic, organic soil (*see p.92*) Prune in winter to remove dead, badly placed, or old, unproductive wood.

ALSO RECOMMENDED: *'Bluecrop' has brilliant red autumn color;* V. floribundum *is evergreen, with pink flowers and red fruits (Tender).*

☼◐ ◊◊ Z4   **Deciduous shrub**
↕↔ 5ft (1.5m)

ASTILBE × CRISPA *'Perkeo'*

This clump-forming plant is shorter
than many other astilbes and produces
upright plumes of tiny, star-shaped,
rich pink flowers in summer that
are useful for indoor arrangements
(*see p.524*). It makes a dense mound
of finely cut, crinkled dark green leaves
and is good as a groundcover in damp,
shady spots (*see pp.238, 326*). Tolerant
of clay soils (*see p.12*).

ALSO RECOMMENDED: *A. 'Bronce Elegans'
has dark green leaves and pink-red
flowers; 'Deutschland'* (*see p.25*); *'Willie
Buchanan'* (*see p.530*).

☀ ◊ Z3b   **Perennial**
↕ 6–8in (15–20cm) ↔ 6in (15cm)

ASTILBOIDES TABULARIS

This clump-forming perennial forms
a dense mound of enormous, rounded
and lobed, pale green leaves, up to
36in (90cm) long. Tall plumes of many
small, creamy white flowers rise well
above the foliage in early summer.
It forms an architectural specimen
(*see p.472*) ideal for woodland and
streamside plantings. It is also excellent
as a groundcover in shade (*see p.326*),
and it tolerates clay soils (*see p.12*).
Protect from slugs, which may eat
resting winter buds. It is sometimes
sold as *Rodgersia tabularis*.

☀ ◊ Z4   **Perennial**
↕ 5ft (1.5m) ↔ 4ft (1.2m)

CAREX ELATA *'Aurea'*

Bowles' golden sedge is a colorful and tussock-forming, deciduous perennial for a moist border, bog garden, or the margins of a pond or stream. The bright leaves are narrow and golden yellow. In spring and early summer, small spikes of relatively inconspicuous, dark brown flowers are carried above the leaves. Often sold as 'Bowles' Golden'.

ALSO RECOMMENDED: *C. grayi has rich green foliage and spiky flowerheads Z6; C. siderosticha 'Variegata' is shorter, with white-striped leaves Z5.*

☼ ◐ ◖◗ Z5   **Perennial**
↕ 28in (70cm) ↔ 18in (45cm)

CAREX PENDULA

Weeping sedge is named for its catkin-like, dark brown flower spikes in late spring and early summer that are upright at first then droop with age. They are carried on tall, arching flower stems above the evergreen clumps of shiny green leaf blades. It self-seeds where conditions are favorable. Also suitable for a wildlife garden (*see p.494*).

ALSO RECOMMENDED: *C. muskingumensis is half the size with bright green leaves and upright flower spikes. Z4*

☼ ◐ ◖◗ Z4   **Perennial**
↕ 4½ft (1.4m) ↔ 5ft (1.5m)

CIMICIFUGA RACEMOSA

Black snakeroot is a clump-forming plant that produces long spikes of unpleasantly scented, tiny white flowers in midsummer, above a mound of divided, dark green leaves. It is suitable for a damp, shady border or woodland garden (*see p.238*), preferably away from paths or seating areas.

ALSO RECOMMENDED: *C. simplex 'Brunette'
has maroon leaves and maroon-flushed
flowers; 'White Pearl' has white flowers.* Z4

☼ ◐ Z3   **Perennial**

↕ 4–7ft (1.2–2.2m) ↔ 24in (60cm)

DARMERA PELTATA

The sturdy stems of this spreading plant arise from the bare soil in late spring, terminating in a broad, flat cluster of many tiny, white to bright pink, star-shaped flowers. The enormous, rounded, and deeply lobed leaves that follow form a handsome and imposing, umbrella-like clump (*see p.472*). It makes an excellent groundcover in shady or sunny, damp sites (*see pp.238, 304, 326*). Tolerant of clay soils (*see p.12*).

☼ ◐ ◑ Z6   **Perennial**

↕ 6ft (2m) ↔ 3ft (1m)

EUPHORBIA PALUSTRIS

For bright color in a damp border or alongside water in sun, this clump-forming perennial is ideal. Its sturdy, pale green stems bear narrow, bright green leaves that turn orange and yellow in autumn. Large yellow flowerheads appear in spring. It will grow in any reliably moist soil.

☼ ◊ Z6 **Perennial**
↕↔ 36in (90cm)

FILIPENDULA RUBRA 'Venusta'

A vigorous, upright perennial that bears feathery plumes of tiny, fragrant, deep rose-pink flowers on tall branching stems in midsummer. The dark green leaves that underpin the flower display are large and jagged. This plant is excellent for waterside plantings and damp sites in shade (see p.238).

ALSO RECOMMENDED: *F. camtschatica is taller, with fragrant, white or pale pink flowers* Z4; *F. purpurea(see p.28)*; *F. rubra has deep peach-pink flowers on red stems* Z4.

☼ ◊◊ ƒZ3 **Perennial**
↕ 6–8ft (2–2.5m) ↔ 4ft (1.2m)

GUNNERA MANICATA

A massive, clump-forming perennial
that produces the leaves to 6ft (2m)
long. These are rounded, lobed, sharply
toothed, and dull green, with thick,
prickly stalks. Large conelike clusters of
tiny, greenish red flowers appear in
summer. An imposing, architectural
plant by water or in a bog garden (*see
p.472*). Fold the dead leaves over
the dormant crown before winter.
It tolerates clay soils (*see p.12*).

ALSO RECOMMENDED: *G. tinctoria (syn.
G. chilensis) is shorter and denser.* Z4

☼ ◑ ♦♦ Z6   **Perennial**
‡ 8ft (2.5m) ↔ 10–12ft (3–4m) or more

HOSTA *'Frances Williams'*

This blue-green plantain lily forms a
clump of heart-shaped, very crinkled
leaves with paler margins; white
flowers emerge in early summer. A fine
architectural plant for a damp, shady
border (*see pp.238, 472*) that can be
grown as a groundcover or confined
to a container (*see pp.326, 448*).
It tolerates clay soils (*see p.12*).

ALSO RECOMMENDED: *'Birchwood Parky's
Gold'* (see p.318); *'Halcyon'* (see p.340);
'Shade Fanfare' (see p.465); *'Wide Brim'*
(see p.254); H. sieboldiana *var.* elegans
(see p.490); H. ventricosa (see p.30).

☼ ◑ ♦ Z4   **Perennial**
‡ 24in (60cm) ↔ 3ft (1m)

IRIS FORRESTII

The scented, pale yellow blooms of this early summer-flowering iris possess a subtle elegance that looks good by water or in a border. The clumps of narrow leaves, which are green above and gray-green beneath, are also attractive. Grow in reliably moist but well-drained soil with plenty of space to allow it to spread. The flowers can be cut for use indoors (*see p.524*).

ALSO RECOMMENDED: I. chrysographes (see p.536); I. laevigata '*Variegata*' (see p.401).

☼ ☀ ◐◑ *f* Z6   **Perennial**
‡ 14–16in (35–40cm) ↔ indefinite

IRIS VERSICOLOR '*Kermesina*'

This red-purple-flowered form of the blue flag (*I. versicolor*) is a pretty water iris with upright, long and narrow leaves. It flowers in the first half of summer, each stem bearing up to five flower buds. The downward-pointing fall petals are marked with white. Particularly effective at the margin of a pond or stream in acidic soils (*see p.92*).

ALSO RECOMMENDED: I. ensata (see p.400); I. pseudacorus (see p.401).

☼ ☀ ◐◑ Z3   **Perennial**
‡ 24in (60cm) ↔ 3ft (1m)

LIGULARIA *'Gregynog Gold'*

This large and vigorous perennial forms clumps of luxuriant, toothed leaves. From late summer to early autumn, tall stems rise above the foliage, bearing pyramidal spikes of daisylike golden flowers. This is an excellent plant with a strong architectural form (*see p.472*) for reliably moist soil close to water, where it may naturalize freely. Shelter from strong winds. It tolerates clay soils (*see p.12*).

ALSO RECOMMENDED: L. *'The Rocket' has yellow flowers on very dark green stems from early summer.* Z4

☼ ◐ ◊ Z5b   **Perennial**
6ft (2m) ↔ 3ft (1m)

LIGULARIA PRZEWALSKII

An imposing waterside plant with a similar habit to L. *'Gregynog Gold' (above)* and valued for its tall pillars of sunny yellow flowers on purplish stems in the later half of summer. The irregularly lobed and toothed, deeply cut leaves heighten its architectural stature (*see p.472*). It tolerates clay soils (*see p.12*).

ALSO RECOMMENDED: L. dentata *'Desdemona' and 'Othello' are shorter and have orange flowers in flattened, rather than spirelike, flowerheads.* Z4

☼ ◊ Z4   **Perennial**
6ft (2m) ↔ 3ft (1m)

LOBELIA CARDINALIS

The cardinal flower forms clumps of bronze-tinged green leaves. In late summer and early autumn it produces spires of two-lipped, luminous scarlet flowers. It is very effective at the edge of water or in a border. It is often short-lived; divide the clumps in spring.

ALSO RECOMMENDED: *L. 'Bees' Flame' has red-purple leaves and crimson flowers; 'Queen Victoria' has vivid red flowers and deep purple-red leaves.*

☼ ◐ Z3   **Perennial**
‡ 36in (90cm) ↔ 12in (30cm)

LOBELIA SIPHILITICA

The blue cardinal flower bears spires of two-lipped, rich bright blue flowers on leafy stems from late summer to midautumn. Its basal clumps of softly hairy, lance-shaped leaves are light green. An excellent plant for a damp mixed or herbaceous border, or beside a pool or stream.

ALSO RECOMMENDED: *'Alba' has white flowers; L. × gerardii 'Vedrariensis' (syn. L. vedrariensis) bears spires of deep violet-purple flowers throughout summer Z4.*

☼ ◐ Z4   **Perennial**
‡ 24–48in (60–120cm) ↔ 12in (30cm)

LYSICHITON AMERICANUS

The yellow skunk cabbage is a
strikingly architectural plant (*see p.472*).
In early spring, the bright yellow
spathes, which enclose a spike of tiny
green flowers, look fabulous if reflected
in still water; they appear before the
foliage has expanded fully. Grow at the
water's edge, or in shallow water up to
3in (8cm) deep (*see p.394*), allowing
plenty of room for the huge leaves to
develop. It tolerates clay soils and
provides shelter for aquatic animals
(*see pp.12, 494*). The entire plant has a
musky scent.

☼☀ ◐◖ Z6   **Perennial**
‡ 3ft (1m) ↔ 4ft (1.2m)

LYSICHITON CAMTSCHATCENSIS

With similar ornamental virtues to the
yellow-flowered species (*above*), the
white skunk cabbage has an elegant
combination of creamy white spathes
and green flower spikes. As with
the yellow skunk cabbage, it is an
architectural plant, good in clay soils
and for sheltering aquatic animals
(*see pp.12, 472, 494*). It grows well in
shallow water to 3in (8cm) deep
(*see p.394*).

☼☀ ◐◖ Z6   **Perennial**
‡ 3ft (1m) ↔ 4ft (1.2m)

Lysimachia clethroides

This vigorously spreading, clump-forming plant is grown for its tapering spires of tiny, star-shaped white flowers. The spires droop sinuously when in bud, straightening as the flowers open in the later half of summer. The narrow, bright green leaves turn red in autumn. An excellent plant for a woodland or bog garden. Protect from slugs and snails.

ALSO RECOMMENDED: L. barystachys *is shorter* Z4; L. ephemerum *is slightly less hardy* Z6; L. nummularia *'Aurea'* (see p.136); L. punctata (see p.319).

☼ ◑ ◊ Z4　　　　　　**Perennial**

↕ 3ft (1m) ↔ 24in (60cm)

Lythrum salicaria 'Feuerkerze'

Purple loosestrife is a clump-forming plant with narrow, midgreen leaves. Its upright shape is defined by the tall, slender flower spikes, which are an intense deep pink in this cultivar and rise above the foliage from midsummer to early autumn. 'Firecandle' is a common alternative name. It tolerates clay soils (see p.12). Note: do not plant purple loosestrifes where they might escape into wetlands.

ALSO RECOMMENDED: L. salicaria *is taller, with purple-pink flowers;* 'Blush' *is similar.*

☼ ◊ Z4　　　　　　**Perennial**

↕ 3ft (1m) ↔ 18in (45cm)

MATTEUCCIA STRUTHIOPTERIS

The ostrich fern forms architectural clumps of upright or gently arching, pale green fronds (*see p.472*). From the centre of each clump in summer, smaller, dark brown fronds appear and persist through winter, long after the green fronds have withered away. It is excellent for a damp, shady border or container (*see pp.238, 448*), in a woodland garden, or beside water. It tolerates clay and acidic soils (*see pp.12, 92*).

☀ ◐◗ Z3   **Perennial fern**
↕ 3–5ft (1–1.5m) ↔ 30in (75cm)

OENANTHE JAVANICA '*Flamingo*'

This spreading, moisture-loving plant has celery-like leaves variegated with pink, cream, and white; they are divided into many toothed leaflets. Flat-headed clusters of tiny, star-shaped white flowers appear in late summer. A fine foliage perennial for a bog garden. Protect from slugs and snails. Overwinter indoors.

☀◑ ◐◗ Min 35°F (2°C)   **Perennial**
↕ 24in (60cm) ↔ 3ft (1m)

PARNASSIA PALUSTRIS

This grass of Parnassus is a low-growing, rosette-forming plant with heart-shaped, pale green leaves and star-shaped, green-veined white flowers that appear in late spring and early summer. It makes a very pretty addition to a bog garden and may be naturalized in marshy grass. Grow in organic, slightly alkaline soil (*see p.64*).

☼ ◐◆ Z5 **Perennial**
↕ 8in (20cm) ↔ 4in (10cm)

PONTEDERIA CORDATA

Pickerel weed is an elegant, architectural plant (*see p.472*) with smooth, fresh green, lance-shaped leaves and dense spikes of tubular blue flowers that appear in late summer. As well as beside a pond or stream, or in a reliably damp border, it can also be grown in up to 5in (12cm) of water (*see p.394*). It may even be accommodated in large, water-filled containers on a sunny, sheltered patio. Tolerant of clay soils (*see p.12*).

☼ ◆ Z4 **Perennial**
↕ 4ft (1.2m) ↔ 24–30in (60–75cm)

PRIMULA FLORINDAE

The giant cowslip produces tall stems topped by clusters of scented, nodding, funnel-shaped, sulfur yellow flowers in early summer. The fresh green leaves are deciduous. It is ideal for bog garden and waterside plantings, and it makes an excellent groundcover in damp, shady places (*see pp.238, 326*). It tolerates clay and acidic soils (*see pp.12, 92*), self-seeding if conditions are favorable.

ALSO RECOMMENDED: P. prolifera *is evergreen with candelabra-like tiers of pale to golden yellow flowers* Z7; P. sikkimensis *has yellow or cream flowers* Z3.

☼ ◐ ◑ *f* Z3   **Perennial**
↕ 4ft (1.2m) ↔ 36in (90cm)

PRIMULA JAPONICA *'Postford White'*

The Japanese primrose is a vigorous, deciduous perennial for damp, shady places (*see p.238*). At ground level, it forms a rosette of spoon-shaped and scalloped, pale green leaves, from which emerges a tall and sturdy flower stem in late spring. In this cultivar, it is topped with white, red-eyed flowers. It tolerates clay soils (*see p.12*).

ALSO RECOMMENDED: P. japonica *has red-purple flowers;* 'Miller's Crimson' *has crimson flowers;* P. viallii (see p.258).

◐ ◑ Z3   **Perennial**
↕↔ 18in (45cm)

PRIMULA PULVERULENTA

This deciduous candelabra primrose has rosettes of lance-shaped leaves and produces tiered spires of tubular, dark red or red-purple flowers in late spring and early summer. It is lovely when grown *en masse* in a bog garden or waterside planting or in a damp, shady border (*see p.238*). It tolerates acidic soils (*see p.92*).

ALSO RECOMMENDED: *'Bartley Pink' has red-eyed, shell pink flowers;* P. beesiana *has yellow-eyed, rich red-pink flowers.* Z3

☼ ◐ ◊ Z4   **Perennial**
‡ 3ft (1m) ↔ 24in (60cm)

PRIMULA ROSEA

This deciduous primrose has rounded clusters of glowing pink, long-throated flowers on sturdy, upright stems in spring. The oval, toothed, midgreen leaves, which are tinted red-bronze when young, emerge fully after flowering. It is good for a bog garden or waterside planting or in a damp, shady border (*see p.238*). It tolerates acidic soils and full sun if the soil remains moist (*see pp.92*).

ALSO RECOMMENDED: *'Grandiflora' is more vigorous, with larger flowers;* P. sieboldii *is taller, with rose-violet to lilac-purple, or deep crimson flowers* Z4.

☼ ◊ Z3   **Perennial**
‡↔ 8in (20cm)

RHEUM PALMATUM
'Atrosanguineum'

Chinese rhubarb is a big, architectural perennial (*see p.472*) with palmately lobed and toothed, dark green leaves to 36in (90cm) long. In this cultivar, the foliage has a purplish tint when young, and tall and feathery, cherry pink flowerheads rise above it in early summer. It will grow as a groundcover (*see p.304*); provide a mulch in spring. It tolerates clay soils (*see p.12*).

ALSO RECOMMENDED: R. *'Ace of Hearts' is half the size, with white flowers;* R. palmatum *and var.* tanguticum *have cream to red flowers.*

☼ ◐ ◊◊ Z4   **Perennial**
‡ 8ft (2.5m) ↔ 6ft (2m)

RODGERSIA PINNATA
'Superba'

A clump-forming, architectural plant (*see p.472*) that bears upright clusters of starry, bright pink flowers above bold, heavily veined, deep green leaves; these are purplish bronze when young. It is ideal for a bog garden or waterside planting and can be grown as a groundcover in damp shade (*see pp.238, 326*). Shelter from wind.

ALSO RECOMMENDED: R. aesculifolia (see p.34); R. pinnata *has white, pink, or red flowers.*

☼ ◐ ◊ Z4   **Perennial**
‡ 4ft (1.2m) ↔ 30in (75cm)

RODGERSIA PODOPHYLLA

A robust, architectural perennial that forms mounds of deeply lobed, glossy dark green leaves suitable for a damp border or waterside planting. The leaves are bronzed when young and bronze-red in autumn. In mid- to late summer it bears sprays of creamy green flowers. Shelter from wind. It tolerates clay soils and can be grown as a groundcover in partial shade (*see pp.12, 326*).

ALSO RECOMMENDED: R. sambucifolia *has white or pink flowers from early summer.* Z4

☼ ☀ ◐ ◗ Z4   **Perennial**
↕ 5ft (1.5m) ↔ 6ft (1.8m)

SAGITTARIA LATIFOLIA

The duck potato is named for its walnut-sized tubers that attract ducks and other water birds (*see p.494*). As well as moist ground, it also grows in water no deeper than 12in (30cm), so it is ideal for a pond margin (*see p.394*). White flowers appear on tall flower stems in summer above the arrow-shaped leaves; these are large and distinctive. Trim back spreading growth in late summer.

☼ ◐ ◗ Z4   **Perennial**
↕ 18–36in (45–90cm) ↔ 36in (90cm)

VERATRUM ALBUM

White hellebore is an imposing plant that forms an elegant mound of deeply pleated, bright green foliage. In early to midsummer, sturdy stems rise to bear many starry white flowers. It is invaluable as a feature plant in a mixed or herbaceous border or in a woodland setting (*see p.472*). It also makes a good groundcover in sun or shade (*see pp.304, 326*).

ALSO RECOMMENDED: *V. nigrum has dusky red-brown to almost black flowers* Z5b; V. viride *has green flowers and tolerates the wettest soils* Z3b.

☼◑ ◊◊ Z6　　　　　　**Perennial**
‡ 6ft (2m) ↔ 24in (60cm)

ZANTEDESCHIA AETHIOPICA

The calla lily is well known for its large, pure white spathes that enclose fingerlike flower spikes in the first half of summer; they are proudly held up above the arrowlike leaves. It is a strong, architectural plant (*see p.472*) that can be grown in shallow water or in a container in sun(*see pp.394, 412*). It tolerates coastal sites (*see p.166*). The flowers cut well (*see p.524*).

ALSO RECOMMENDED: *'Crowborough' has smaller spathes; 'Green Goddess' has green spathes with white centers.*

☼◑ ◊◊ Z8　　　　　　**Perennial**
‡ 36in (90cm) ↔ 24in (60cm)

PLANTS FOR WATER GARDENS

PONDS AND POOLS not only make superb focal points in the garden, but they are also the most effective way of bringing wildlife into the garden, even if they are not designed for that purpose. Water gardens provide a web of interdependent mini-habitats, with niches that are good for a variety of plants as well as for a range of aquatic and amphibious creatures and visiting birds and mammals.

A healthy pond requires plantings at several levels. Within the water itself, there should be floating or bottom-rooting plants, such as curled pondweed (*see p.408*), hornwort (*see p.398*), and curly water thyme (*see p.402*). These plants perform the vital function of oxygenating the water; without dissolved oxygen in the water, fish and amphibians would not be able to survive. Submerged plants also help remove excess nutrients from the water, which would otherwise fuel the rapid growth of algae and turn the water green. Introduce these

plants to the pond simply by casting them in as weighted bundles of stems.

ORNAMENTAL PLANTS

Floating water plants, such as water fringe (*see p.407*), that root at the bottom of the pond, cover the surface of the water with their floating leaves. As well as being pretty, the leaves offer shade and shelter to fish and reduce algal growth by excluding light. To grow them, they can either be allowed to root in the muddy bottom of the pond, but more usually they are grown in aquatic planting baskets lined with burlap and filled with a heavy soil-based mix. The soil surface is then topped with a layer of gravel to prevent the soil from muddying the water. Planting baskets are ideal in smaller ponds, because they help contain the spread of vigorous plants.

For the poolside, select marginal plants. These will root in the mud or moist soil that surrounds the pond, and they tolerate shallow to relatively deep water, depending on the species. They can also be very vigorous, although their spread will be limited by their depth tolerance. Popular marginal plants include the bog bean (*see p.403*), which spreads its leathery leaves over the surface of the water, and more upright plants such as the variegated club rush (*see p.402*). Marginal plants look good around the edge of a pool, softening the transition from water to land, and more upright species with reedy or grasslike stems, such as the flowering rush (*see p.397*), form a perfect egg-laying perch for creatures such as dragon-flies and damselflies. Marginals can also be planted in aquatic baskets, as for floating-leaved plants, but it is easier to create naturalistic clumps if they are allowed to root directly into wet soil confined in special planting bays. They are planted exactly as for dryland plants but should not be given fertilizer, since this will leach into the water, causing the proliferation of algae. Fertilizers are also directly detrimental to fish and other pond life.

APONOGETON DISTACHYOS

Water hawthorn is valued for its handsomely shaped, bright green, floating foliage that is accompanied from spring until autumn by V-shaped white flowerheads. These are held above the water's surface, then they fold over and fade to green. It is easy to grow in water 12–36in (30–90cm) deep, preferably in full sun, but do not let the water freeze over. It tends to smother waterlilies (*see pp.405–406*), so keep these plants apart. Also suitable for a water-filled container.

☼☀ Z4   **Perennial**
↔ 4ft (1.2m)

AZOLLA FILICULOIDES

Fairy moss lives and grows on the surface of water, and its fractal-like, floating leaves make an attractive, fast-growing cover with a soft appearance. This will help keep the pond water clear by suppressing the growth of algae; thin out invasive growth as necessary. Where not hardy, scatter small bunches of overwintered or new stock on the pool surface after the danger of frost has passed. It will grow in a water-filled container. Sometimes sold as *A. caroliniana*.

☼☀ Z7   **Perennial**
↔ indefinite

BUTOMUS UMBELLATUS

The flowering rush is a robust marginal plant of delicate appearance. In spring, bronzed shoots develop into long and twisted, rushlike leaves, bronze-purple at first then dark olive-green. Tall cylindrical stems emerge in late summer, bearing open sprays of fragrant, cup-shaped pink flowers. Grow in fertile mud at the water's edge in water 2–16in (5–40cm) deep. It will also grow in planting baskets, but they must be lifted and divided frequently to maintain flowering. Tolerant of clay soils (*see p.12*).

☼ *f*Z4   **Perennial**
↕ 30in (75cm) ↔ 18in (45cm)

CALLA PALUSTRIS

The bog arum has heart-shaped, glossy dark green leaves that form an attractive feature in themselves at the margin of a pool or slow-moving stream. It also bears shapely, cowl-like white bracts in midsummer; these surround a spike of insignificant flowers, later giving rise to dull red berries in autumn. Grow in mud or in planting baskets in water no deeper than 10in (25cm). Bog arum must have acidic conditions

☼ Z4   **Perennial**
↕ 5ft (1.5m) ↔ 4ft (1.2m)

CALTHA PALUSTRIS

The marsh marigold is a clump-forming plant with kidney-shaped, glossy dark green leaves. In spring, it bears wax-textured, buttercup-like, glossy bright yellow flowers. It does well in water no more than 9in (23cm) deep as well as in fertile, permanently moist sites (*see p.372*). Tolerant of clay soils (*see p.12*).

ALSO RECOMMENDED: *var.* alba *has white flowers;* 'Flore Pleno' *has double yellow flowers.*

☼ ♦ Z3   **Perennial**
‡ 4–16in (10–40cm) ↔ 18in (45cm)

CERATOPHYLLUM DEMERSUM

Hornwort is a deciduous perennial with slender stems and forked leaves. It grows underwater and is valued for its ability to oxygenate pond water; since it tolerates shade, it grows in deeper water than most other oxygenators. Young plantlets break away from the main plant, and they may sink to the pond bottom and overwinter as dormant buds. Grow in water up to 24in (60cm) deep.

☼◑ Z4   **Perennial**
↔ indefinite

FONTINALIS ANTIPYRETICA

This evergreen perennial moss with submerged stems has olive green, scale-like leaves. It is grown for its ability to oxygenate water and is best in cold streams, since it is much less vigorous in still water. Plant in water up to 18in (45cm) deep by weighing the plant down between boulders, on which the roots will cling and spread. Thin the growth if it begins to dominate.

☀ ◑ Z4   **Perennial**

‡ 3in (8cm) ↔ indefinite

HOTTONIA PALUSTRIS

The water violet is a deciduous, underwater perennial with masses of spreading, light green and deeply divided foliage both on and under the surface of the water. Pale lilac flower spikes emerge above the water on upright stems in spring. It is a useful plant to keep a pond clear and well oxygenated. Thin periodically.

☀ Z6   **Perennial**

‡ 12–36in (30–90cm) ↔ indefinite

HYDROCHARIS MORSUS-RANAE

Frogbit is a free-floating water plant with rosettes of kidney-shaped, shiny green leaves. They are accompanied throughout summer by white flowers with yellow centers. It provides useful shelter for pond creatures, but it is vulnerable to snail damage. New plantlets form on the runners. Grow in water up to 12in (30cm) deep; it prefers still and shallow conditions.

☼ Z4   **Perennial**
↔ indefinite

IRIS ENSATA

This Japanese iris will grow either in a pond or in permanently moist ground (*see p.372*). In a pond, grow it in a planting basket, since it needs to be removed from saturated soil in winter. Dense tufts of bold, sword-shaped leaves rise up from ground level, and large purple flowers open in midsummer; they are good for cutting (*see p.524*). It needs acidic soil (*see p.92*).

ALSO RECOMMENDED: *'Moonlight Waves'
bears white flowers with lime green centers;
'Rose Queen' has pink flowers; 'Variegata'
has variegated leaves.*

☼ ◐◖ Z5   **Perennial**
‡ 24–36in (60–90cm) ↔ indefinite

IRIS LAEVIGATA *'Variegata'*

This deciduous iris forms clumps of sword-shaped, white- and green-striped leaves. Its sparsely branched flower stems produce up to four purple-blue, broad-petaled flowers in early summer. It thrives in pond margins and other reliably moist places (*see p.372*), and tolerates clay soils (*see p.12*). The flowers can be cut for indoors (*see p.524*).

ALSO RECOMMENDED: I. laevigata *has plain green leaves;* 'Alba' *has white flowers.*

☼ ◊◢ Z4　　　　　　**Perennial**

‡32in (80cm) ↔ indefinite

IRIS PSEUDACORUS

The yellow flag is a very vigorous, rhizomatous iris that will spread widely at the edge of water. It has ribbed, sword-shaped, gray-green leaves and, from early to late summer, bears golden yellow flowers marked with brown or violet on the lower petals; they can be cut for indoor decoration (*see p.524*). Plant in water up to 12in (30cm) deep or in permanently moist soil (*see p.372*). It tolerates alkaline soils (*see p.12*).

ALSO RECOMMENDED: I. pseudacorus *var.* bastardii *has sulfur yellow flowers;* 'Variegata' *has cream-variegated leaves.*

☼☼ ◢ Z4　　　　　　**Perennial**

‡3–5ft (1–1.5m) ↔ indefinite

LAGAROSIPHON MAJOR

Also sold as *Elodea crispa*, curly water thyme is an underwater plant that is used to keep pond water oxygenated. It forms a dense mass of dark green, snaking, fragile stems that are covered by incurved, scalelike leaves. Insignificant, tiny pink flowers appear in summer. Grow in a submerged planting basket in water up to 3ft (1m) deep, and thin growth in summer as necessary, cutting back in autumn; remove dead stems to prevent them from decomposing in the water.

☼ Z8   **Perennial**
↔ indefinite

MARSILEA QUADRIFOLIA

Water clover is actually a fern and is grown for its shamrocklike leaves that are downy when young and form a floating canopy on the water's surface. In muddy shallows, the leaves may rise above the water. Grow at the margins of a pond, either in open soil or in lattice baskets at a depth of up to 24in (60cm).

☼ Min 45°F (7°C)   **Perennial**
↕ 15cm (6in) ↔ indefinite

MENYANTHES TRIFOLIATA

The dark stems of the bog bean rise above the water, keeping the leathery green leaves clear of the surface. In summer, it produces upright clusters of star-shaped white flowers with attractively fringed and bearded petals. Grow in shallow, still or slow-moving water, planting in the muddy margins of a pool or in water no deeper than 9in (23cm). It is excellent for disguising hard edges in formal water features. Confine its spread by planting in a basket.

☼ Z3   **Perennial**
↕ 8–12in (20–30cm) ↔ indefinite

MIMULUS LUTEUS

Yellow musk is a spreading plant, bearing a profusion of yellow, snapdragon-like flowers, often with dark red spots, from midsummer to autumn. It self-seeds freely and is well suited to shallow, still or fairly fast-moving water at streamsides or pool margins and in permanently moist ground (*see p.372*).

ALSO RECOMMENDED: M. guttatus *has yellow flowers with red-spotted throats* Z7; M. ringens *is taller, with violet, violet-blue, white, or pink flowers* Z4.

☼ ◐◗ Z7   **Perennial**
↕ 12in (30cm) ↔ 24in (60cm)

MYRIOPHYLLUM AQUATICUM

Parrot feather is a submerged oxygenating plant with spreading stems covered by whorls of delicate, bright green leaves. It is ideal for shallow water, where the stems may extend above the surface, but it will grow to a depth of 3ft (1m) or more. Inconspicuous flowers appear in summer. Where not hardy, overwinter plants under cover or start with new plants in spring. Young shoots may be eaten by fish. The leaves provide a valuable refuge for fish fry.

ALSO RECOMMENDED: M. verticillatum *is much hardier.* Z3

☀ Min 40°F (5°C)　　　　**Perennial**
↔ indefinite

NUPHAR LUTEA

The yellow pond lily is a deciduous perennial with large, heart-shaped, floating leaves. While the plant is valued for its round yellow flowers that are held just above the water's surface in summer, its deep green foliage provides valuable shelter for pond creatures and shades out the growth of algae. It grows in still or slowly moving water to a depth of 12in (30cm), preferably in acidic water and with a free root run. It is suitable for a wildlife pond.

☼ ☀ Z5　　　　　　　**Perennial**

↔ 6ft (2m)

NYMPHAEA *'Froebelii'*

A good waterlily for barrels or small ponds, since it grows in shallow water up to 12in (30cm) deep. Its bronzed young leaves mature to small, round or heart-shaped, pale green lily pads, useful for reducing algae growth. Deep red flowers, 4–5in (10–13cm) across, force their heads up between the foliage in summer; they are cup-shaped at first, then star-shaped. Grow in still water.

ALSO RECOMMENDED: *'Aurora' has mottled leaves and yellow flowers that age to orange with red flecks.*

☼ Z3　　　　　　　**Perennial**
↔ 3ft (1m)

NYMPHAEA *'Gonnère'*

This magnificent, white-flowered water-lily is ideal for any size pond. Its slightly bronzed young leaves mature to round, pea green lily pads up to 9in (22cm) across; they help keep the pond cool and shade out algal growth. The fully double, globe-shaped, fragrant white flowers stay open until late in the afternoon, closing at night. Grow in still water at a depth of 12–18in (30–45cm).

ALSO RECOMMENDED: *N. alba, the white waterlily, is more spreading, with larger leaves and fragrant white flowers.*

☼ *f* Z3　　　　　　**Perennial**
↔ 3–4ft (1–1.2m)

NYMPHAEA *'Lucida'*

This free-flowering waterlily is good for any size pond with still water 12–18in (30–45cm) deep. Its large, dark green lily pads keep the pond cool and shaded, and they are heavily marked with dark purple. Star-shaped flowers, 5–6in (12–15cm) wide, emerge from below in summer; they have red inner petals and outer petals of pale pink with deeper pink veins.

ALSO RECOMMENDED: *'James Brydon' has vivid rose-red flowers.*

☼ Z3   **Perennial**
↔ 4–5ft (1.2–1.5m)

NYMPHAEA *'Marliacea Chromatella'*

Also sold as 'Tuberosa Flavescens', this is one of the most reliable yellow waterlilies, bearing its large, primrose-colored, semidouble summer flowers in abundance. It will grow in any size pond at a depth of 12–18in (30–45cm) in calm water. Its coppery, purple-streaked young leaves mature to an attractive purple-mottled green.

ALSO RECOMMENDED: *'Marliacea Albida' has white flowers with yellow stamens; 'Marliacea Carnea' has light pink flowers with yellow stamens.*

☼ Z3   **Perennial**
↔ 4–5ft (1.2–1.5m)

NYMPHOIDES PELTATA

The water fringe has floating, glossy green, heart-shaped leaves that look rather like those of a miniature water-lily. The small, funnel-shaped flowers are bright yellow with fringed petals; they appear just above the water's surface through summer. Grow in water to a depth of 18in (45cm) deep; in small pools, confine the spreading rhizomes by planting in a basket.

☼ Z4   **Perennial**
↔ indefinite

ORONTIUM AQUATICUM

Golden club is a deciduous perennial that grows in water up to 18in (45cm) deep. The blue-green leaves with silvery undersides float on the surface of the water, and from late spring to summer, pokerlike, yellow-tipped flowerheads rise well above the foliage. Remove them when they fade. It is ideal at the margin of a pool among water irises.

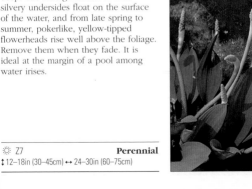

☼ Z7   **Perennial**
‡ 12–18in (30–45cm) ↔ 24–30in (60–75cm)

PERSICARIA AMPHIBIA

The amphibious bistort roots itself
in soil up to 18in (45cm) underwater,
sending out floating, narrow, willowlike leaves on long stalks. In midsummer, light pink flowers in dense
heads are held above the water on
upright stems. It will also grow in
boggy pond margins. Thin out
growth as necessary

☀ Z4 **Perennial**
↔ indefinite

POTAMOGETON CRISPUS

Curled pondweed is a seaweedlike
aquatic with submerged, translucent
green leaves. Insignificant crimson and
creamy white flowers are carried just
above the water in summer. It spreads
rapidly in mud-bottomed pools and
tolerates cloudy or shady water better
than any other oxygenating plant. Grow
in water up to 3ft (1m) deep, thinning it
frequently to keep it in check.

☀◑ Z7 **Perennial**
↔ indefinite

RANUNCULUS AQUATILIS

Water crowfoot is a submerged, evergreen perennial that holds its yellow-centered white buttercup flowers and some of its rounded leaves just above water. It flowers in midsummer and is best in large wildlife ponds or streams at a depth of 6–24in (15–60cm), where it will spread and root in muddy bottoms.

ALSO RECOMMENDED: *R. lingua has bright yellow flowers and prefers still or slow-moving water at pond margins.* Z4

☀ Z5   **Perennial**
↔ indefinite

SCHOENOPLECTUS LACUSTRIS *'Zebrinus'*

This variegated club rush has almost leafless, gray-green stems banded with creamy white. In early to late summer, it bears branched clusters of brown flower spikelets. Grow in water up to 12in (30cm) deep or in permanently moist soil at the water's edge (*see p.372*). In small pools, restrict growth by cutting back rhizomes annually. Trim nonvariegated stems back to the base, as necessary. May be sold as *Scirpus lacustris.*

ALSO RECOMMENDED: *'Albescens' has white stems with vertical green stripes.*

☀ ◗ Z5   **Perennial**
↕ 3ft (1m) ↔ 24in (60cm) or more

STRATIOTES ALOIDES

Water soldier is a free-floating, semi-evergreen perennial that grows as an attractive foliage plant in still or slow-moving water up to 3ft (1m) deep. "Pineapple-top" rosettes of deep green, spiky leaves rise above the surface of the water in midsummer, when the plant bears cup-shaped, white or pink-tinged flowers. It must be thinned regularly to control its spread.

☼ Z6   **Perennial**
↕ 16in (40cm) ↔ indefinite

TYPHA LATIFOLIA

The cattail is a deciduous perennial forming a dense stand in shallow water, to 10in (25cm) deep; it is suitable only for the margin of a large wildlife pool, where deep water limits its spread. The characteristic, dark brown, cylindrical flower spikes, useful for dried flower arrangements (*see p.524*), are carried on top of tall, grasslike stems in summer. Flexible pond liners may be punctured by the thick, spreading rhizomes.

ALSO RECOMMENDED: *'Variegata' is much less vigorous, with cream-striped leaves;* T. minima *is suitable for a small pond, reaching 30in (75cm) tall* Z4.

☼☀ Z3   **Perennial**
↕ 6ft (2m) or more ↔ indefinite

URTICULARIA VULGARIS

Great bladderwort is a deciduous, submerged perennial with pouched, bright yellow, crimson-streaked flowers held well above the water in summer. An amazing feature of this oxygenating plant is its feathery, bronze-green leaves that bear bladder-like structures. These trap insects. The plant thrives in still or stagnant water that attracts insect larvae. Grow in acidic water to 3ft (1m) deep.

☼ Z4   **Perennial**
→ 24–36in (60–90cm)

VERONICA BECCABUNGA

Brooklime is an excellent scrambling plant for a pond's edge, either in water up to 5in (12cm) deep or in permanently moist soil (*see p.372*). Its succulent, creeping stems are covered by fleshy, semievergreen leaves, and from late spring until the end of summer, clusters of light blue flowers appear in the leaf axils. Replace plants when the growth becomes straggly.

☼ ◊ Z5   **Perennial**
‡ 4in (10cm) ↔ indefinite

PLANTS FOR CONTAINERS IN SUN

GROWING PLANTS in containers is an extremely versatile way of decorating sunny patios. They can also be used to mark an entrance or to create a focal point, and windowboxes and hanging baskets are a great way of introducing living color to even the smallest of spaces. Container and bedding plants are also very useful for creating quick displays in new gardens.

You can use containers, too, for permanent plantings of frost-tender plants, such as lemon verbena (*see p.415*) or lemon trees (*see p.414*), which will lend a Mediterranean air to a sunny patio. They can be moved to a cool greenhouse or brought indoors for winter, before the first frosts. Another idea is to plant containers with seasonal bulbs to observe the changes through winter, spring, summer, and autumn.

CHOOSING CONTAINERS
Provided a container has drainage holes in the bottom, almost any receptacle can be used. Materials should be cold-

resistant if they are to be left outdoors in winter, and choose containers that are in balance with the plants to ensure that plants are not top-heavy in the face of the wind.

TIPS ON CULTIVATION

Container-grown plants rely heavily on the gardener for nutrients and water, so site them within easy reach of a water source. They dry out more rapidly than in the open border and, in sunny sites, are likely to need watering at least daily in hot, dry weather. A soil mix containing water-retaining granules helps. Soil-based mixes are ideal for containers, because they are heavy and lend stability; they also contain fertilizers and retain moisture well. Soil-free mixes are excellent for hanging baskets or windowboxes, where weight is a disadvantage, but they are more prone to drying out and can be difficult to rewet. You could add a layer of stones or broken pots at the bottom of the pot for ballast (but don't block the drainage hole), and leave about 3/4–1in (2–2.5cm)

between the soil surface and the rim of the pot to allow for watering.

A top-dressing of gravel helps retain water and keep the roots cool. Give container plants a balanced liquid fertilizer every two weeks, or use a slow-release granular fertilizer. Deadhead regularly to ensure continuous and abundant flowering.

Plants in containers seldom achieve the height and spread that they would in open ground, so for mixed displays of summer bedding, pack plants closely in pots and hanging baskets. For permanent plants, remove the top 2–3in (5–8cm) of soil mix and replace with fresh mix each spring. When the roots fill the pot, repot into a slightly larger container in spring, or prune the roots and refresh the soil mix. Even in mild regions plants in pots are vulnerable to damage by cold. Some kind of protection is often needed if they are to remain outside during winter, such as insulating with a layer or two of bubble-wrap or a pad of straw under a piece of burlap (*see p.449*).

CITRUS LIMON

This small tree is an ideal specimen for a large pot on a sunny patio. Its glossy dark green leaves form the perfect backdrop for its fragrant, waxy white flowers that appear from spring to summer. The lemons that follow take a year to ripen. Water freely when in growth; apply a balanced fertilizer every 2–3 weeks when in growth. Keep just moist in winter. Prune to shape in early spring.

ALSO RECOMMENDED: *C. × meyeri 'Meyer' is more compact, with fragrant flowers and small, almost spherical fruits.*

☼ ◊ *f* Min 40°F (5°C)   **Evergreen tree**
‡ 6–22ft (2–7m) ↔ 5–10ft (1.5–3m)

CORDYLINE AUSTRALIS 'Variegata'

The New Zealand cabbage palm is a palmlike, architectural tree with spiky leaves (*see p.472*). 'Variegata' has matte green leaves with cream stripes. Where not hardy, it must be brought under cover during winter. Remove dead leaves and faded flower stems as necessary. It tolerates coastal sites (*see p.166*).

ALSO RECOMMENDED: *C. australis has plain light green leaves; 'Torbay Dazzler' has boldly cream-striped leaves.*

☼☀ ◊ Min 50°F (10°C)   **Evergreen tree**
‡ 10ft (3m) ↔ 3ft (1m)

SALIX CAPREA *'Kilmarnock'*

The Kilmarnock willow is a small and weeping tree, ideal for a pot. It forms a dense, umbrella-like crown of yellow-brown shoots studded with silvery catkins in spring, before the arrival of the new foliage. These broad, toothed leaves are dark green on top and gray-green beneath. Prune annually in late winter to prevent the crown from becoming congested, and remove shoots that arise on the clear trunk. Plant in soil-based mix.

☼ ◊◊ Z5   **Deciduous tree**
‡5–6ft (1.5–2m) ↔ 6ft (2m)

ALOYSIA TRIPHYLLA

Lemon verbena is grown mainly for its strongly lemon-scented, bright green foliage, used in both cooking and pot-pourri. Slender spikes of pale lilac or white flowers appear in late summer. It is ideal in a container; where not hardy, move it outside for the summer and overwinter under cover. Water freely when in growth and apply a balanced liquid fertilizer monthly; keep the soil just moist in winter. Trim to shape in spring. It could be grown against a warm, sheltered wall (*see* p.280). It is also sold as *A. citriodora*.

☼ ◊ *f* Z8   **Deciduous shrub**
↔ 6ft (2m)

ARGYRANTHEMUM
'Vancouver'

This compact, summer-flowering subshrub is valued for its double, daisy-like pink flowerheads with rose-pink centers and fernlike, gray-green leaves. Where not hardy, grow as summer bedding or in a container that can be sheltered in frost-free conditions over winter. It tolerates coastal conditions (*see p.166*). Pinch out growing tips to encourage bushiness. .

ALSO RECOMMENDED: *'Jamaica Primrose' has light yellow flowerheads.*

☼ ◊ Min 35°F (2°C)   **Evergreen shrub**
‡ 36in (90cm) ↔ 32in (80cm)

BRUGMANSIA × CANDIDA
'Grand Marnier'

Festooned with hanging, trumpet-shaped flowers, this frost-tender shrub is an impressive plant. The apricot-colored, night-scented flowers appear from summer to autumn. Water freely and apply a balanced liquid fertilizer monthly in growth; keep just moist in winter. Prune to a woody framework in spring, and move under cover for winter. Also known as datura.

ALSO RECOMMENDED: B. × candida has white, or soft yellow flowers; *'Knightii' has double flowers. (Tender)*

☼ ◊ *f* Min 45°F (7°C)   **Evergreen shrub**
‡ 10–15ft (3–5m) ↔ 8ft (2.5m)

CESTRUM AURANTIACUM

A vigorous shrub with arching branches that bear matte mid-green leaves and clusters of tubular orange flowers in spring and early summer. It is ideal for decorating a sunny patio in summer; move under cover for the winter where not hardy. Water freely and apply a balanced liquid fertilizer monthly; keep just moist in winter. Trim to shape in spring.

ALSO RECOMMENDED: *C. elegans has crimson to purple-red or pink flowers from late summer to autumn; crimson-flowered C. 'Newellii' withstands light frosts. (Tender)*

☼ ◊ Min 41°F (5°C)   **Evergreen shrub**
↔ 10ft (3m)

× CITROFORTUNELLA MICROCARPA

The Panama orange is a large shrub with leathery, bright glossy green leaves, occasionally with a few spines on the stems. White flowers appear from spring to summer, followed by small, orangelike, inedible fruits. Move under cover where not hardy, or grow as a greenhouse or indoor plant all year round. Prune to size and shape in late winter. It is also sold as × C. mitis.

ALSO RECOMMENDED: *Tiger' (syn. 'Variegata') has leaves streaked and margined with white.*

☼ ◊ Min 40°F (5°C)   **Evergreen shrub**
↕ 10–20ft (3–6cm) ↔ 6–10ft (2–3m)

ERICA VAGANS *'Birch Glow'*

This summer-flowering heather is a low and spreading shrub, looking good on its own in a pot of bark-based acidic soil mix . Its deep pink flowers continue well into autumn. Trim in early spring. In the garden, grow in acidic soil, although it tolerates alkaline soil (*see pp.64, 92*). It can be grown as a groundcover (*see p.304*) and is suitable for coastal gardens (*see p.166*).

ALSO RECOMMENDED: *'Lyonesse' has white flowers; 'Mrs. D.F. Maxwell' has deep pink flowers; 'Valerie Proudley' has yellow foliage and white flowers.*

☼ ◊ Z5   **Evergreen shrub**
↕ 12in (30cm) ↔ 20in (50cm)

FELICIA AMELLOIDES *'Read's White'*

This white-flowered form of the blue daisy has narrow, deep green foliage and flowers from late spring to autumn. It is excellent in hanging baskets and mixed container displays. Treat it as an annual where not hardy, pinching out the tips to promote bushiness and deadheading to prolong flowering. Take cuttings in autumn for plants next year. It tolerates coastal sites (*see p.166*).

ALSO RECOMMENDED: *'Read's Blue' is compact, with blue flowerheads; 'Santa Anita' bears large, rich blue flowerheads.*

☼ ◊ Min 45°F (7°C)   **Evergreen shrub**
↕↔ 12–24in (30–60cm)

FUCHSIA *'Thalia'*

This small and vigorous bush performs well in sun. It makes a superb patio or bedding plant. Masses of long-tubed, rich orange-scarlet flowers appear continuously from summer to autumn among and above the dark green leaves. Pinch-prune when young to encourage bushiness or train as a standard to lend height to displays.

ALSO RECOMMENDED: *'Billy Green' has salmon pink flowers; those of 'Coralle' are orange-red; 'Mary' has brilliant crimson flowers.*

☼ ◑ ◊◊ Min 35°F (2°C) **Evergreen shrub**
↔ 18–36in (45–90cm)

HELICHRYSUM PETIOLARE

Licroice plant is a silvery, mound-forming, shrubby evergreen with trailing stems that cascade beautifully over the sides of hanging baskets and other containers. Its small leaves are densely felted and silver-gray and combine well with flowering plants in mixed displays. Often grown as an annual in frost-prone areas. Pinch-prune young stems to encourage bushiness.

ALSO RECOMMENDED: *'Variegatum' has cream-variegated foliage.*

☼ ◊ Min 35°F (2°C) **Evergreen shrub**
↕ 20in (50cm) ↔ 6ft (2m) or more

IBERIS SEMPERVIRENS

This subshrubby candytuft bears dense, rounded heads of tiny white flowers in late spring and early summer, sometimes in such profusion as to obscure the dark green foliage. It is often grown in a rock garden, but it is also suitable for troughs and other containers. Trim lightly after flowering to keep the growth compact. It tolerates coastal conditions (*see pp.166, 304*).

ALSO RECOMMENDED: *'Schneeflocke'* ('Snowflake') *is mound-forming, with snow-white flowers; 'Weisser Zwerg' is more compact.*

☼ ◊ Z3   **Evergreen shrub**
↕ 12in (30cm) ↔ 16in (40cm)

LANTANA *'Radiation'*

This prickly stemmed shrub with wrinkled, dark green leaves is usually grown as annual bedding in cold areas, but it is ideal for containers in warm, sunny sites. Its vibrant heads of brilliantly colored, fiery red and orange flowers from late spring to late autumn are extremely eye-catching. Water freely and apply a balanced liquid fertilizer once a month in summer.

ALSO RECOMMENDED: *L. camara has flowers in shades of white, yellow, pink, or red.*

☼ ◊ Min 40°F (5°C)   **Evergreen shrub**
↕ 18–24in (45–60cm) ↔ 10in (25cm)

LOTUS BERTHELOTII

Known as parrot's beak for its hooked flowers, this trailing subshrub is used in hanging baskets and containers for its narrowly cut, silvery leaves on long, trailing stems. The striking orange-red to scarlet flowers may appear in summer. Cut out some older stems after flowering to encourage new growth.

ALSO RECOMMENDED: *L. maculatus is similar, with red-tipped yellow flowers. (Tender)*

☼ ◊ Min 40°F (5°C)   **Evergreen shrub**
‡ 8in (20cm) ↔ indefinite

MELIANTHUS MAJOR

The honey bush is an excellent architectural foliage shrub (*see p.472*) with gray-green to bright blue-green divided leaves. Spikes of blood red flowers may appear in summer, but it is grown in pots for its outstanding foliage. Where hardy, it can be grown in the open or against a warm wall (*see p.280*); where not hardy, it must be overwintered under cover. It tolerates coastal sites (*see p.166*), needing protection from wind and winter moisture.

☼ ◊ Z7b   **Evergreen shrub**
‡ 6–10ft (2–3m) ↔ 3–10ft (1–3m)

NERIUM OLEANDER

Oleander is an upright shrub with narrow, dark gray-green leaves. The flowers, usually pink, red, or white, appear throughout summer. It looks good on a patio in summer, where it tolerates coastal and hot, dry conditions (*see pp.166, 190*). Where not hardy, move it into a greenhouse or conservatory for winter. Cut back in late winter. All parts of this plant are toxic.

☀ ◊ Min 45°F (7°C)   **Evergreen shrub**
↕ 6ft (2m) ↔ 10ft (3m)

OSTEOSPERMUM *'Whirligig'*

Like other osteospermum hybrids, 'Whirligig' is grown for its bright and cheerful daisylike flowers, borne from spring to autumn. It is ideal for a sunny summer border or container; treat as an annual where not hardy, or take autumn cuttings to overwinter. Plants can also be overwintered under cover. Tolerant of coastal and hot, dry sites (*see pp.166, 190*). Good in mixed displays with other tender perennials. Also sold as 'Tauranga'.

ALSO RECOMMENDED: *'Buttermilk'*
has primrose yellow flowerheads;
O. jucundum (see p.188).

☀ ◊ Min 40°F (5°C)   **Perennial**
↕↔ 24in (60cm)

PARAHEBE CATARRACTAE

A small shrub bearing loose clusters of red-eyed, purple-veined white flowers throughout summer. It is very effective when tumbling over the edges of large containers or hanging baskets. Where not hardy, overwintered it in a cool greenhouse or conservatory. It tolerates coastal conditions (*see p.166*). In the garden, shelter from cold, drying winds.

ALSO RECOMMENDED: *'Delight' has blue flowers; 'Miss Willmott' has rose-lilac flowers with mauve veins.*

☼ ◊ Z7b   **Evergreen shrub**
‡ 24–30in (60–75cm) ↔ 18in (45cm)

PICEA MARIANA *'Nana'*

This diminutive variant of the black spruce forms a short, dense mound of soft, blue-gray needles and is ideal in containers – a pair flanking a path or entrance can be very effective. Keep it well watered in hot weather, and shelter it from wind. Every spring replace the top 2in (5cm) with fresh soil mix. In the garden, it is useful as an architectural plant in a rock garden. It tolerates acidic soils (*see p.166*).

ALSO RECOMMENDED: P. abies *'Ohlendorffii'* (see p.106); P. glauca *'Conica' is taller, slow-growing, and pyramidal with short, blue-green needles* Z2.

☼☀ ◊ Z2b   **Evergreen shrub**
‡↔ 20in (50cm)

PROSTANTHERA ROTUNDIFOLIA

The round-leaved mint bush is a spreading shrub with very aromatic, small and rounded, deep green leaves. Short clusters of bell-shaped, purple to lilac flowers appear in late spring and early summer. Where not hardy, overwinter container plants under cover. Trim after flowering. It tolerates partial shade (*see p.448*).

ALSO RECOMMENDED: *'Rosea' (syn. 'Chelsea Girl') has grayish leaves and rich pink flowers.*

☼ ◐ ◊◒ ƒ Min 35°F (2°C) **Evergreen shrub**
↕ 6–12ft (2–4m) ↔ 3–10ft (1–3m)

RICINUS COMMUNIS *'Impala'*

The castor bean is an upright shrub, usually grown as an annual for its shapely, palmately lobed foliage, which is reddish purple in this variety. Less significant are the yellowish green male flowers and red female flowers in summer. In the garden, it makes a good feature plant in a sunny border, where it may need to be staked. Usually grown as an annual in Canada.

ALSO RECOMMENDED: *'Zanzibarensis' is taller, with large, white-veined, midgreen leaves.*

☼ ◊ Min 35°F (2°C) **Evergreen shrub**
↕ 4ft (1.2m) ↔ 3ft (1m)

ROSA *'The Fairy'*

This dwarf rose forms a dense cushion of glossy green leaves, topped from early summer to autumn by a mass of small, double, soft pink flowers. Fertilize regularly throughout summer. Prune in late winter as for other roses. In the garden, it tolerates alkaline soils (*see p.12*) and is effective planted among pinks or violas.

ALSO RECOMMENDED: *Angela Rippon has rose- to salmon-pink flowers; Queen Mother has pink flowers; Surrey has double pink flowers; 'White Pet' has white flowers. All Z6*

☼ ◊ Z5   **Deciduous shrub**
‡↔ 24–36in (60–90cm)

SENECIO CINERARIA *'Silver Dust'*

This mound-forming shrub is usually grown as an annual for its attractive, lacy leaves that are velvety, deeply cut, and almost white. Plants kept into the second year bear loose heads of mustard yellow flowers in midsummer; most gardeners prefer to remove them. It is ideal for massed foliage effects in bedding designs and for mixed plantings in containers. In the garden, it tolerates sandy soils, and coastal, and hot, dry sites (*see pp.38, 166, 190*).

ALSO RECOMMENDED: *'White Diamond' has oaklike, gray-white leaves*

☼ ◊ Z7b   **Evergreen shrub**
‡↔ 12in (30cm)

BOUGAINVILLEA 'San Diego Red'

This vigorous climber needs the protection of a frost-free greenhouse or conservatory if it is to grow in a cold climate, but it is worthwhile for its incredibly vibrant, bright scarlet flower bracts from summer to autumn. The oval, midgreen leaves may fall in winter. Also sold as 'Scarlett O'Hara' or 'Hawaiian Scarlet'. Bring outside during summer onto sheltered sunny patios. Fertilize regularly in summer. Keep on the dry side in winter.

☼ ◊ Min 50°F (10°C)   **Climber**
↕ 25–40ft (8–12m)

PASSIFLORA 'Amethyst'

This is a strong-growing passionflower with slender, climbing stems and three-fingered leaves. It is valued for its large, purple-blue flowers, to 4 1/2in (11cm) across, in late summer and autumn. Orange fruits follow. Grow in a large pot in a greenhouse or conservatory. Water freely in summer, and sparingly in winter. Provide shade from strong sun. Prune back after flowering to keep within bounds.

ALSO RECOMMENDED: *P. antioquiensis, the red banana passionflower, has bright rose-red, pendulous flowers.*

☼ ☼ ◊◊ Min 50°F (10°C)   **Climber**
↕ 12ft (4m) or more

PLUMBAGO AURICULATA

Cape leadwort is a scrambling, semi-evergreen plant that can be tied to a support and trained as a climber. It bears dense clusters of long-throated, sky blue flowers from summer to late autumn amid the oval leaves. In cold climates, plants overwintered under glass can be moved outside in summer. Pinch out the tips of young plants to promote bushiness, and cut back to a permanent framework in early spring. Also sold as *P. capensis*.

ALSO RECOMMENDED: *var.* alba *has white flowers.*

☼ ☼ ◊ Min 45°F (7°C)   **Climber**
‡ 10–20ft (3–6m) ↔ 3–10ft (1–3m)

RHODOCHITON ATROSANGUINEUS

This slender, evergreen climber has heart-shaped, rich green leaves and pendulous flowers from summer to autumn. These have a dark purple-black tube beneath a flaring, dusty red-purple "skirt." It is very effective grown in a container with a pyramidal trellis support or allowed to spill from a hanging basket, especially in association with plants with deep blue flowers. It can be grown as an annual in cold climates. It is best with the roots in shade.

☼ ◊◊ Min 37°F (3°C)   **Climber**
‡ 10ft (3m)

THUNBERGIA ALATA

Black-eyed Susan vine is an evergreen climber named for its brilliant, orange-yellow, flat-faced flowers with distinctive black centers. The twining stems need support unless the plant is grown to cascade from a hanging basket. To keep over winter, take into a warm greenhouse or conservatory. Otherwise, grow as an annual.

ALSO RECOMMENDED: T. grandiflora, *the blue trumpet vine, has light violet-blue flowers. (Tender)*

☼ ◊◊ Min 45°F (7°C)   **Climber**
↕ 5–8ft (1.5–2.5m)

AEONIUM *'Zwartkop'*

This upright and shrubby, succulent perennial is sparsely branched, but it bears neat rosettes of leathery, deep black-purple leaves at the tip of each stem. In a container, grow in a freely draining soil mix, and water regularly. Overwinter in a conservatory or greenhouse. Keep plants almost dry in winter. Shade from the midday sun in summer.

ALSO RECOMMENDED: A. arboreum *'Atropurpureum' is similar. (Tender)*

☼ ☼ ◊ Min 50°F (10°C)   **Perennial**
↕↔ 6ft (2m)

AGAPANTHUS PRAECOX
SUBSP. ORIENTALIS

Useful in a large container as a late-flowering perennial, this African blue lily bears its large and showy, spherical clusters of rich blue, trumpetlike flowers in late summer and early autumn. Below are the evergreen clumps of straplike, dark green leaves. Tolerant of coastal conditions (*see p.280*). At edge of hardiness, protect crowns with gravel in fall.

ALSO RECOMMENDED: *var.* albiflorus *has white flowers;* A. *'Blue Giant' (see p.181) and 'Bressingham Blue' are hardier.*

☼ ◊ Z7   **Perennial**
↕ 24–36in (60–90cm) ↔ 24in (60cm)

AGAVE AMERICANA
'Variegata'

This barbed succulent is grown for its spiny-margined and spine-tipped, fleshy leaves with bold yellow stripes. They eventually form a large, evergreen rosette that makes an excellent architectural feature plant for a large container (*see p.472*). Grow in a freely draining soil mix.

ALSO RECOMMENDED: A. americana *has plain green leaves.*

☼ ◊ Min 50°F (10°C)   **Perennial**
↕↔ 5ft (1.5m)

BIDENS FERULIFOLIA

This clump-forming plant, often grown as an annual, is a spreading, short-lived perennial with finely divided, fresh green leaves. During summer it bears a profusion of yellow, daisy-like flowerheads. It is excellent for hanging baskets or other containers, where its sprawling flowering stems will spill over the sides.

☼ ◊ Z7b   **Perennial**
↕ 12in (30cm) ↔ indefinite

CAMPANULA ISOPHYLLA

The Italian bellflower is also known as falling stars for its plentiful, pale blue, bell-shaped flowers on trailing stems in midsummer. It is ideal for cascading over the side of a large container or hanging basket. The small, heart-shaped leaves are light green. Usually grown as an annual.

ALSO RECOMMENDED: *'Alba'* has white flowers; C. *'Birch Hybrid'* (see p.358); C. carpatica *'Bressingham White'* (see p.359).

☼◑ ◊◊ Min 35°F (2°C)   **Perennial**
↕ 6–8in (15–20cm) ↔ 12in (30cm)

CANNA *'Assaut'*

Cannas are popular summer bedding plants grown as much for their upright stature (*see p.472*) and handsome foliage as for their bright, gladiolus-like flower spikes. 'Assaut' bears broad, rounded, purple-brown leaves and orange-red flowers from midsummer to autumn. Overwinter dormant plants in a cool basement but protect from freezing. Many colorful varieties exist.

ALSO RECOMMENDED: *'Black Knight' has dark red flowers; 'King Midas' (see p.486); 'Striata' has orange flowers and variegated leaves.*

☼ ◊ Min 35°F (2°C)　　　**Perennial**
↕ 6ft (2m) ↔ 20in (50cm)

CHRYSANTHEMUM *'Mary Stoker'*

This bushy chrysanthemum bears sprays of apricot flowerheads in late summer and early autumn. The green centers turn to yellow as the flowers open. It is excellent on a sunny patio and is also suitable for cutting (*see p.524*). Use a soil-based potting mix. Water freely when in growth, and apply a balanced liquid fertilizer weekly from midsummer until the end of the season.

ALSO RECOMMENDED: *'Bronze Elegance' has pomponlike bronze flowerheads; 'Emperor of China' has silvery pink flowerheads with quilled petals.*

☼ ◊ Z4　　　**Perennial**
↕ 4ft (1.2m) ↔ 30in (75cm)

CONVOLVULUS SABATIUS

A compact, trailing perennial bearing trumpet-shaped, vibrant blue-purple flowers from summer into early autumn. The slender stems are clothed with small, oval leaves. It is ideal for trailing over the sides of a container. Sometimes sold as *C. mauritanicus*. It prefers very well-drained or sandy soil.

ALSO RECOMMENDED: C. cneorum (see p.44).

☼ ◊ Z8   **Perennial**
‡ 6in (15cm) ↔ 20in (50cm)

GAZANIA *Mini-star Series*

These useful, vigorous and spreading summer bedding plants are often grown as annuals. They are valued for their long summer display of large and fiery, daisylike flowers, similar to sunflowers, although they close in cool or dull weather. Colors range from orange to golden yellow, beige, bronze, or bright pink, some zoned with contrasting colors. The leaves are dark green. They grow well in containers and are tolerant of coastal conditions (*see p.166*).

ALSO RECOMMENDED: *Daybreak Series also has flowers in a spectrum of colors.*

☼ ◊ Z8   **Perennial**
‡ 8in (20cm) ↔ 10in (25cm)

HYACINTHUS ORIENTALIS 'Ostara'

This violet-flowered hyacinth is a bulbous perennial grown as spring bedding for its dense, upright spikes of bell-shaped, fragrant blooms. Bright green leaves emerge from the base of the plant. Prepared bulbs can be started indoors in autumn for winter flowers. Outdoors, plant bulbs in autumn and shelter from excessive winter moisture. Tolerant of coastal conditions (see p.166).

ALSO RECOMMENDED: *'Anna Marie' has pale pink flowers; 'Delft Blue' has soft blue flowers; those of 'Gipsy Queen' are salmon-orange.*

☀ ☼ ◊ *f* Z4   **Perennial bulb**

↕ 8–12in (20–30cm) ↔ 3in (8cm)

LILIUM REGALE

Regal lilies bear fragrant, trumpet-shaped white flowers in midsummer; each stem carries up to 25 blooms that can be cut for indoor display (see p.524). It makes an elegant, architectural plant for containers (see p.472), but it needs staking. Ideal for patios, where the scent can be appreciated easily. Plant bulbs in autumn or early spring. It tolerates most soils, and sunny sites (see pp.38, 64, 190).

ALSO RECOMMENDED: *'Fire King', orange Z3; 'Journey's End' (see p.538); L. longiflorum, white, scented Z7; 'Star Gazer', crimson red Z5.*

☀ ◊ *f* Z4   **Perennial bulb**

↕ 2–6ft (0.6–2m)

MATTHIOLA INCANA
Cinderella Series

Stocks are short-lived perennials, usually grown as annuals, valued for their dense spikes of sweetly scented, double flowers. This selection comes in a range of colors from white through pink to dark blue and purple. Single colors are also available. They make an attractive addition to a summer border; the flowers are good for cutting (*see p.524*). Sow seeds in spring. Plant out in a sheltered site after the danger of frost has passed. Tolerant of coastal conditions (*see p.166*).

☼ ◊ *f* Z7   **Perennial**
↕ 8–10in (20–25cm) ↔ 10in (25cm)

MIMULUS *'Andean Nymph'*

This spreading monkey flower can be allowed to sprawl over the sides of containers and hanging baskets, showing its patchy pale pink, trumpet-shaped flowers for a long summer season among the pale green leaves. Keep the soil moist at all times. Also suitable for containers in shade.

ALSO RECOMMENDED: *Seed selections* *Magic Series and Mystic Series. (Tender)*

☼◐ ◊ Min 35°F (2°C)   **Perennial**
↕ 8in (20cm) ↔ 12in (30cm)

MUSCARI ARMENIACUM

A strong-growing, bulbous plant that bears dense spikes of tubular, rich blue flowers in early spring. The midgreen leaves are straplike and begin to emerge in autumn. Plant bulbs in autumn, either in containers, massed together in borders, or in grass, where they may naturalize, although they can be invasive. Tolerant of sandy soils and hot, dry sites (*see pp.38, 190*).

ALSO RECOMMENDED: M. azureum *is half as tall and suitable for a rock garden.* Z4

☀ ◊ Z3   **Perennial bulb**

‡8in (20cm) ↔ 2in (5cm)

NARCISSUS *'Tête à Tête'*

This miniature daffodil is famous for its twin- or triple-headed, golden yellow spring flowers above strap-shaped leaves. Good for both indoor and outdoor displays and very effective when planted *en masse*. Plant bulbs in late summer. Fertilize with a high-potassium fertilizer at flowering time and after flowering. Tolerant of alkaline soils and coastal conditions (*see pp.64, 166*).

ALSO RECOMMENDED: *'February Gold' taller with solitary flowers; 'Hawera' has up to five flowers per stem; 'Jack Snipe' has white and yellow flowers.*

☀ ◊ Z4   **Perennial bulb**

‡6in (15cm) ↔ 2–3in (5–8cm)

PELARGONIUM
'Happy Thought'

Geraniums are mostly bushy, evergreen perennials grown as annuals, with bold flowers from spring to summer, making them popular bedding plants. In containers, they can be grown indoors or outside in summer. 'Happy Thought' bears clusters of bright red flowers above leaves with greenish yellow centers. Keep rather dry during winter.

ALSO RECOMMENDED: *Trailing ivy-leaved 'Barbe Bleu' with dark purple flowers is good for hanging baskets; 'The Boar' has pink flowers and also trails.*

☼☀ ◊ Min 35°F (2°C)   **Perennial**
‡ 16–18in (40–45cm) ↔ 8–10in (20–25cm)

PELARGONIUM
'Lady Plymouth'

This geranium is grown specifically for its prettily lobed and silver-margined, eucalyptus-scented foliage. The bluish pink flowers are less showy and more delicate than those bred purely for their flowers. It will perfume a greenhouse or conservatory and can be used as summer edging along a path or in pots on a patio, the leaves releasing their scent when brushed against.

ALSO RECOMMENDED: *'Attar of Roses', 'Chocolate Peppermint', and 'Prince of Orange' also have scented leaves.*

☼ ◊ *f* Min 35°F (2°C)   **Perennial**
‡ 12–16in (30–40cm) ↔ 6–12in (15–30cm)

PETUNIA *'Purple Wave'*

Petunias are grown as annuals. This one is ideal for hanging baskets, containers, or summer bedding, where it may cover an area up to 3ft (1m) across. The trumpet-shaped flowers open over a long period from late spring to autumn. Plant out in spring only when danger of frost has passed, preferably in a sheltered site. It grows well in poor soils. The Wave Series comes in a range of colors

ALSO RECOMMENDED: *Surfinia Series is very vigorous and trailing, with abundant flowers; Ultra Series has a profusion of large flowers. Both stand up to bad weather.*

☼ ◊ Min 30°F (-1°C) **Perennial**
‡18in (45cm) ↔ 12–36in (30–90cm)

PTEROCEPHALUS PERENNIS

This low-growing, scabiosa-like perennial forms an evergreen mat of fiddle-shaped, gray-green leaves. It bears flat, clustered heads of pale pinkish purple flowers in summer; papery seedheads follow. Grow in any well-drained soil. It is effective both in a container or at the front of a sunny border.

☼ ◊ Z6 **Perennial**
‡3in (8cm) ↔ 8in (20cm)

SALVIA SPLENDENS 'Scarlet King'

The scarlet sage is a compact and bushy perennial, commonly grown as an annual in cold climates, with dense spikes of tubular flowers that are an invaluable, long-lasting addition to any bedding or container display. 'Scarlet King' is one of several cultivars that have brilliant scarlet flowers from summer to autumn above dark green, toothed leaves.

☀ ◊ Min 35°F (2°C) **Perennial**
‡ 10in (25cm) ↔ 9–14in (23–35cm)

SEMPERVIVUM ARACHNOIDEUM

The cobweb hens and chicks is a mat-forming, evergreen succulent with rosettes of reddish green leaves webbed with silvery white hair. Flat clusters of star-shaped, red-pink flowers appear on leafy stems in summer. Grow in sharply drained soil; it is good for scree beds, troughs, or in drystone wall crevices (*see p.348*). Tolerant of sandy soils and coastal and hot, dry sites (*see pp.38, 166, 190*).

ALSO RECOMMENDED: S. tectorum (see p.323).

☀ ◊ Z4 **Perennial**
‡ 3in (8cm) ↔ 12in (30cm)

TULIPA *'Keizerskroon'*

Whether massed in spring bedding, in groups in a border, or filling a container on the patio, this tulip brings welcome color to the spring garden. Plant bulbs in autumn. After flowering, the bulbs can be lifted, heeled in until the foliage dies down, then stored in a cool greenhouse or shed. It tolerates alkaline soils and coastal and hot, dry sites (*see pp.64, 166, 190*). The flowers can be cut for indoor use (*see p.524*).

ALSO RECOMMENDED: *'Apricot Beauty'* has soft salmon-pink flowers; *'Red Riding Hood'*.

☼ ◊ Z4   **Perennial bulb**
‡12in (30cm) ↔ 3–5in (8–13cm)

VERBENA *'Sissinghurst'*

This pretty, sprawling verbena has deeply cut, dark green leaves and bears heads of magenta-pink flowers from late spring to autumn. It is best used in mixed plantings in containers, including hanging baskets. Take cuttings in late summer or pot up and overwinter in a cool greenhouse.

ALSO RECOMMENDED: *'Peaches and Cream'* (*see p.215*); *Tapien Series, trailing and comes in a range of colors*.

☼ ◊ Z8   **Perennial**
‡8in (20cm) ↔ 3ft (1m)

AGERATUM HOUSTONIANUM *'Adriatic'*

Floss flowers are popular little plants for edging in summer beds and containers. Their compact flowerheads form a frothy or fluffy mass of color just above the deep green leaves from summer until the first frosts. 'Adriatic' is one of several blue-flowered ageratums. Water freely and deadhead to encourage an extended display. Also suitable for the cracks between paving and alkaline soils (*see pp.64, 348*).

ALSO RECOMMENDED: *'Summer Snow' has white flowerheads; 'Swing Pink' has pink flowerheads.*

☼ ◐◖   **Annual**
↕ 6–8in (15–20cm) ↔ 6–12in (15–30cm)

BASSIA SCOPARIA *F.* TRICHOPHYLLA

The burning bush is named for its bushy, cone-shaped habit and the feathery, close-set, light green leaves that, in autumn, turn to bright red and purple. The flowers are inconspicuous. Sow in late spring in the growing position, or raise in cell packs and plant into pots. In the garden, plant in small groups in a bedding design or in a line to make a temporary low screen. It tolerates coastal conditions (*see p.166*). May be listed as *Kochia*.

☼ ◖   **Annual**
↕ 12–60in (30–150cm) ↔ 12–18in (30–45cm)

BRACHYSCOME IBERIDIFOLIA

The Swan River daisy is a dependable
bedding plant grown for its profusion
of daisylike flowerheads. These are
borne in summer and early autumn and
are normally mauve-blue in color,
although they are sometimes white,
purple, or pink. The weak-stemmed,
trailing growth makes it useful for
containers and hanging baskets.

ALSO RECOMMENDED: *Splendour Series
has black-eyed, white, lilac-pink, or purple
flowerheads.*

☼ ◊ **Annual**

↕ 18in (45cm) ↔ 14in (35cm)

BRACTEANTHA BRACTEATA
'Dargan Hill Monarch'

This strawflower is an upright annual
with papery, daisylike, rich yellow
flowerheads from late spring to autumn.
The leaves are gray-green. Sow in pots
and use to fill gaps in a border; the
flowers are long-lasting and cut and
dry well (*see p.524*). It tolerates sandy
soils (*see p.38*). Also listed under
Helichrysum.

ALSO RECOMMENDED: *Bright Bikinis
Series is low-growing, suitable for border
edging or a windowbox; 'Skynet' has pink-
cream flowerheads.*

☼ ◊ **Annual**

↕ 3–5ft (1–1.5m) ↔ 12in (30cm)

DAHLIA *'Yellow Hammer'*

Dwarf bedding dahlias are raised from seed and treated as annuals. Sow in spring with heat. Pinch out growing tip when young to encourage bushiness. Deadhead regularly. Useful for containers or to fill gaps in a border display. 'Yellow Hammer' has showy yellow flowers above bronze-tinged, divided leaves. The flowers are ideal for cutting (*see p.524*) and perform from midsummer to autumn, when many other plants are past their best.

ALSO RECOMMENDED: *Double 'Diablo' is a mix of colors with dark red foliage. 'Harlequin' is a single mix.*

☼ ◯ ◌　　　　　　　　　**Annual**

‡ 24in (60cm) ↔ 18in (45cm)

ESCHSCHOLZIA CAESPITOSA

California poppies are known for their colorful, poppylike flowers that close in dull weather. This short, upright species is ideal for containers and has finely divided, bluish leaves and many bright yellow, scented flowers in summer. Sow where it is to grow in spring or early autumn. It prefers sandy soils (*see p.38*) and tolerates coastal and hot, dry sites (*see pp.166, 190*).

ALSO RECOMMENDED: *'Mission Bells' has a mix of semi-double flower colors.*

☼ ◌　　　　　　　　　　**Annual**

‡↔ 6in (15cm)

LIMNANTHES DOUGLASII

The poached-egg plant forms a carpet of glossy, bright yellow-green leaves and produces a profusion of shining yellow, white-edged, buttercup-like flowers from summer to autumn. It is excellent for troughs, path edging, and paving crevices (*see p.348*). Sow where it is to grow; it self-seeds freely and can become an almost permanent fixture once introduced. The flowers attract hoverflies, which help control aphids. In containers, it makes a cheerful addition to a patio. It tolerates sandy soils and coastal sites (*see pp.38, 166*).

☼ ◊ **Annual**

↔ 6in (15cm) or more

NEMESIA STRUMOSA '*KLM*'

A fast-growing and colorful annual with a bushy habit that is useful in containers or bedding displays, where it produces blue and white, lipped flowers with yellow throats during the second half of summer. Sow seed indoors in spring, and plant out seedlings only after the danger of frost has passed. Pinch out growing tip for bushy plants.

ALSO RECOMMENDED: '*Blue Gem*' has bright blue flowers; '*Danish Flag*' has red and white flowers; those of '*Prince of Orange*' are orange.

☼ ◊◊ **Annual**

↕ 7–12in (18–30cm) ↔ 4–6in (10–15cm)

NEMOPHILA MACULATA

Five-spot is a fleshy-stemmed annual
with divided, bright green leaves. It
bears saucer-shaped white flowers,
each petal with a small, blue-violet spot
at its tip. Often grown as border edging,
it is also suitable for containers and
hanging baskets. Keep it well watered
in hot weather to ensure a succession
of flowers throughout summer.

ALSO RECOMMENDED: *N. menziesii has
bright blue flowers, paler at the center and
with darker spots; 'Oculata' has pale blue,
purple-centered flowers.*

:☼::☀: ◊   **Annual**
↕↔ 6–9in (15–30cm)

PAPAVER RHOEAS
Shirley Mixed

A colorful selection derived from the
field poppy (*P. rhoeas*); like it, they are
upright annuals with solitary, nodding
flower buds borne on slender stalks in
summer. These open to bowl-shaped,
crepe-paperlike flowers that are single,
semidouble, or double in yellow, pink,
orange, and sometimes red. They
tolerate sandy soils (*see p.38*). Sow
seeds where they are to grow.

ALSO RECOMMENDED: *P. rhoeas has
bright red flowers with black marks on the
petal bases.*

:☼: ◊   **Annual**
↕ 24in (60cm) ↔ 12in (30cm)

SALPIGLOSSIS SINUATA
Casino Series

These upright and compact, weather-resistant annuals, ideal for summer bedding, freely produce a contrasting display of funnel-shaped flowers through summer and autumn. Colors range from blue and purple to red, yellow, or orange, heavily veined in deeper tints. The lance-shaped, mid-green leaves have wavy margins. Plant out after the risk of frost has passed; staking is usually necessary. Remove dead flowers regularly.

ALSO RECOMMENDED: *Bolero Hybrids are similar; 'Kew Blue' has deep blue flowers.*

☼ ◊   **Annual**

‡24in (60cm) ↔ 12in (30cm)

SANVITALIA PROCUMBENS

Creeping zinnia forms a low mat of midgreen foliage that is covered throughout summer and into autumn by single, bright yellow daisylike flowers with black centers. It is ideal for border edging and containers, including troughs, pots, and hanging baskets. Sow seed where it is to grow in spring.

ALSO RECOMMENDED: *'Gold Braid' has golden flowerheads; 'Mandarin Orange' has semidouble, rich orange flowerheads – both are more compact, to 4in (10cm) tall.*

☼ ◊   **Annual**

‡8in (20cm) ↔ 18in (45cm)

SCHIZANTHUS *'Hit Parade'*

The poor man's orchid is known for its dense clusters of very pretty, orchid-like, lipped flowers that come in shades of white, yellow, pink, purple, or red. 'Hit Parade' has deep pink flowers with yellow throats, almost covering the light green, fernlike leaves for a long season from spring to autumn. Pinch back young growth to encourage bushiness. It tolerates sandy soils (*see p.38*).

☼ ◐◑   **Annual**
‡ 8–20in (20–50cm) ↔ 9–12in (23–30cm)

TAGETES *Boy Series*

Marigolds are compact plants with extremely colorful, bright yellow, orange, or red-brown, velvety, pompon-like flowers from late spring to frost. They are suitable for containers or as edging in mixed summer borders and tolerate sandy or alkaline soils (*see pp.38, 64*) and coastal sites (*see p.166*). The finely divided, rich green foliage gives a feathery or fernlike effect.

☼ ◊   **Annual**
‡ 6in (15cm) ↔ 12in (30cm)

THYMOPHYLLA TENUILOBA

Dahlberg daisy has pungently scented, feathery leaves and produces an abundance of daisylike, bright yellow flowers from spring to summer. It is excellent for hanging baskets and other containers, as well as for summer bedding. Sow seed under glass in mid-spring and set out when danger of frost has passed or sow seed where it is to grow in late spring.

☼ ◊ *f*   **Annual**

↔ 12in (30cm)

TROPAEOLUM MAJUS *'Alaska'*

A fast-growing, scrambling annual that has very bright and eye-catching spurred flowers in shades of yellow, orange, mahogany, or cream in summer and autumn. It is ideal for a hanging basket or as a groundcover (*see p.304*) in a summer border. The light green, rounded leaves are attractively speckled white. It tolerates coastal sites (*see p.166*) and flowers best in poor soils.

ALSO RECOMMENDED: *'Hermine Grashoff' has double red flowers;* T. peregrinum, *the canary creeper, is an annual climber with small yellow flowers and prettily lobed leaves.*

☼ ◊◊   **Annual**

↕ 12in (30cm) ↔ 18in (45cm)

PLANTS FOR CONTAINERS IN SHADE

MANY GARDENS have shady areas, such as beds over-shadowed by trees and shrubs or a patio bordered by a wall. In paved or concreted areas, containers provide the obvious solution to brightening the gloom. The plants themselves often benefit from the protection of walls and fences, making permanent plantings of shrubs or herbaceous perennials particularly suitable. Since they are under less stress than when sited in full sun, plants grow well. Shade narrows the choice of bedding plants, but those that do enjoy shade, such as lobelia (*see p.466*), go on flowering for longer than when growing in sun.

An enormous range of shade-loving plants are amenable to container cultivation. Even relatively large shrubs can be grown, such as the architectural × *Fatshedera lizei* (*see p.450*), which often respond to "captivity" by growing more slowly and becoming more compact. Many shade-loving plants, like the Japanese painted

fern (*see p.459*), are grown mainly for their graceful foliage and can be used in containers. Introduce vibrant color with jewel-bright Polyanthus primroses in spring (*see p.468*), or impatiens, coleus, and begonias in summer (*see pp.466, 459, 460*), and add fragrance with flowering tobacco (*see p.471*).

TIPS ON CULTIVATION

Container plants in shade are planted and fertilized as for those in sun (*see p.412*) but do not need such meticulous attention to watering, since they usually dry out less rapidly than those in hot, sunny sites. Avoid standing containers in spots where walls or fences may have created a wind tunnel, since plants are unlikely to thrive.

Because surfaces in shady spots are often damp, the drainage from the bottom of the pot can become critical, especially during the cooler months. Pots in direct contact with damp surfaces may not drain freely, and soil mix can easily become waterlogged. Then, not only does the root system suffer, but the pots themselves become more susceptible to cracking and flaking when subjected to the freeze-thaw cycle in winter. Choose cold-resistant pots for permanent plants and use special pot feet, or old bricks, to assist drainage by creating a gap between the floor and pot.

If containers are to be left outdoors during the colder winter weather, group pots together and take steps to insulate them and the plant roots by wrapping a layer of bubble wrap or straw around the outside of the pot. Make sure that the wrapping does not interfere with drainage.

While many insects pests, such as aphids, proliferate more freely in sunny sites, a few, notably slugs and snails, thrive in damp shade, so be vigilant. Check beneath pot rims in the evening, which are a favorite lurking place for slugs. Either remove slugs and snails by hand or place pellets in the containers, perhaps under a small, upturned pot, so that they are not accessible to children, pets, or other animals.

CAMELLIA JAPONICA
'Adolphe Audusson'

This compact camellia is fine both in the open garden and in a container. Choose a site sheltered from early morning sun, wind, and late-season frosts, and it will repay with healthy, glossy, dark green leaves and large, semidouble red flowers in spring. Trim young plants to shape and size, and maintain a mulch. Grow in acidic soil mix. In the garden, it tolerates damp shade and north-facing walls (*see pp. 238, 262*).

ALSO RECOMMENDED: *'Hagoromo', pink semidouble; 'Lady Vansittart' (see p.99).*

☀ ◐ ◊ Z7   **Evergreen shrub**
‡ 6ft (2m) ↔ 5ft (1.5m)

× FATSHEDERA LIZEI

The tree ivy is a spreading shrub with very glossy, ivylike leaves. Pinch out young shoots to promote bushiness. In autumn, it produces clusters of greenish white flowers. An elegant container plant for a shady terrace or courtyard. In the garden, it will grow against a shady wall (*see p.262*).

ALSO RECOMMENDED: *'Annamieke' (syn. 'Lemon and Lime', 'Maculata') has yellow-variegated leaves; 'Variegata' has green leaves narrowly cream-margined.*

☀ ◊ Z7   **Evergreen shrub**
‡ 4–6ft (1.2–2m) ↔ 10ft (3m)

FUCHSIA *'Annabel'*

An especially floriferous and versatile
fuchsia that is suitable for both pots
and hanging baskets. It can also be
trained with a clear stem as a treelike
standard. 'Annabel' has pendulous,
pinkish white flowers through summer
and into autumn. Shelter from wind and
move to a frost-free environment
for winter. Pinch out growing tips to
promote bushiness.

ALSO RECOMMENDED: *'Checkerboard'
has red and white flowers. 'Alice Hoffman',
with pink and white flowers, and
'Display', with red and pink flowers, are
suitable for training as standards.*

☼◐ ◊◊ Min 35°F (2°C) **Evergreen shrub**
↕↔ 12–24in (30–60cm)

FUCHSIA *'Lady Thumb'*

'Lady Thumb' is a small fuchsia in
all respects, which makes it a superb
choice for a windowbox. Its
low growth is made up of small midgreen
leaves and little, red and white, hanging
flowers. Shelter from wind, and keep it
above freezing in winter. Pinch out
growing tips of young plants to
promote bushiness.

ALSO RECOMMENDED: *'Dark Eyes' has
red and violet flowers; 'Son of Thumb'
and 'Tom Thumb' are both compact.*

☼◐ ◊◊ Min 35°F (2°C) **Evergreen shrub**
↕ 6–12in (15–30cm) ↔ 12–18in (30–45cm)

FUCHSIA PROCUMBENS

A fascinatingly unusual fuchsia with small, upward-looking flowers that are like miniature golden goblets with green sepals and blue pollen – colors very rarely found in fuchsias. Plumlike fruits follow. The long, creeping stems with rounded leaves make this plant good for a hanging basket. It is easy to grow.

ALSO RECOMMENDED: *More traditional trailing fuchsias include: 'Autumnale', with reddish young leaves and scarlet flowers; 'Jack Shahan', with pink flowers; 'La Campanella', with white and purple flowers; 'Marinka', with dark red flowers.*

☼ ◐ ◊◊ Min 35°F (2°C) **Evergreen shrub**
‡ 4–6in (10–15cm) ↔ 3–4ft (1–1.2m)

ILEX CRENATA *'Convexa'*

This form of Japanese holly has a dense, broadly rounded habit and bears very glossy leaves on dark purple stems. The small white flowers of spring and early summer give rise to a profusion of shiny black berries, which are a food source for birds (*see p.494*). It makes an elegant specimen for a shady courtyard, especially in formal designs. Clip to shape in summer.

ALSO RECOMMENDED: *'Convexa' makes a dense bush with small leaves; 'Golden Gem' is compact, with golden leaves; 'Mariesii' has tiny leaves and grows slowly.*

☼ ◐ ◊ Z7 **Evergreen shrub**
‡ 8ft (2.5m) ↔ 6ft (2m)

NANDINA DOMESTICA

Heavenly bamboo is not actually a bamboo, but an upright shrub with fine spring and autumn color. The divided leaves are red when young, maturing to green, then flushing red again in late autumn. Conical clusters of small white flowers with yellow centers appear in midsummer, followed by long-lasting, bright red fruits. Move to a sheltered site wherre marginally hardy, and prune in spring to keep the plant shapely.

ALSO RECOMMENDED: *'Firepower' is dwarf and compact, to 18in (45cm) tall.*

☀ ◐ ◊ Z7　　　　　**Evergreen shrub**
↕ 6ft (2m) ↔ 5ft (1.5m)

PIERIS JAPONICA
'Little Heath'

A dwarf form of *P. japonica* suitable for container cultivation. It has a rounded shape and bears small, pink-flushed white flowers in late winter and early spring. These are carried in drooping clusters among glossy dark green leaves with silver margins; the young foliage is bronze-tinted. A good early-flowering shrub, although it needs acidic soil mix. In the garden, it succeeds in damp, shady places (*see p.238*).

ALSO RECOMMENDED: *P. formosa 'Wakehurst' (see p.107) is larger.*

☀ ◐ ◊◊ Z5b　　　　　**Evergreen shrub**
↕ 12ft (4m) ↔ 10ft (3m)

PITTOSPORUM EUGENIOIDES *'Variegatum'*

This pretty foliage shrub tolerates clipping. It has glossy leaves with wavy, creamy yellow-splashed margins. The leaves release a lemon scent when crushed, giving the plant its common name – lemonwood. Clusters of tiny flowers appear in spring and summer. It must be given a sheltered site and moved under cover where not hardy. If necessary, prune in winter to keep an open balanced shape.

ALSO RECOMMENDED: *'Garnettii' is similar but with smaller leaves.*

☼ ◑ ◊◑ ƒ Min 40°F (5°C) **Evergreen shrub**
↕ 15–40ft (5–12m) ↔ 6–15ft (2–5m)

RHODODENDRON *'Homebush'*

A compact rhododendron with a bushy habit that is suitable for a large pot. Its dense clusters of neat, bright pink, trumpet-shaped flowers make a fine, late-spring display. It needs an acidic soil mix. In the garden, it is happy in damp, shady sites (*see p.238*). Deadhead carefully; otherwise, little pruning is needed.

ALSO RECOMMENDED: *'Gibralta' has orange flowers Z6; 'Rosy Lights' has mid-pink flowers Z3; 'Strawberry Ice' has very pale pink blooms Z5.*

☼ ◑ ◊◑ Z6 **Deciduous shrub**
↕↔ 5ft (1.5m)

SASA VEITCHII

What appears to be a variegated bamboo is actually a plain-leaved species with glossy dark green leaves that wither attractively at the edges from late autumn. It has slender, branching, usually purple canes. Plant in a large container to contain its spreading habit; pots can be sunk into the ground over winter.

ALSO RECOMMENDED: S. palmata *and f.* nebulosa *are similar, with paler leaves.* Z6b

☼ ◐ ◊◊ Z6   **Evergreen bamboo**
‡ 3–4ft (1–1.2m) ↔ indefinite

SKIMMIA × CONFUSA 'Kew Green'

This compact, dome-shaped, male shrub bears conical spikes of creamy white flowers in spring. It is an excellent pollinator for berry-bearing female skimmias. In a container, it is ideal for a courtyard. Little or no pruning is required. In the garden, it is ideal for a dry, shady bed or border (*see p.216*). It tolerates clay and acidic soils (*see pp.12, 92*).

ALSO RECOMMENDED: S. japonica (see p.223); 'Rubella' (see p.108); 'Veitchii' is female, with red berries.

☼ ◐ �685 ◐ Z7   **Evergreen shrub**
‡ 1½–10ft (0.5–3m) ↔ 5ft (1.5m)

VACCINIUM GLAUCOALBUM

This blueberry forms a mound of dense, dark green, oval leaves with bright whitish blue undersides. Hanging clusters of small, pinkish white flowers appear from the leaf axils in early summer, and these are followed by the edible, blue-black berries. Plant in acidic soil mix; where not hardy, it needs to be brought under cover. Good for a woodland garden, but it must have an acidic soil (*see p.92*).

ALSO RECOMMENDED: V. corymbosum *is the highbush blueberry, grown specifically for its edible fruits* Z4; V. floribundum *has red fruits (Tender).*

☼ ☀ ◊◊ Min 40°F (5°C) **Evergreen shrub**
↕ 20–48in (50–120cm) ↔ 3ft (1m)

VIBURNUM TINUS *'Variegatum'*

A compact bush that has dense, dark green foliage with creamy yellow margins. Flattened heads of pink buds open to tiny star-shaped white flowers from late winter to spring; small, dark blue-black fruits follow. Trim to shape after flowering. In the garden, it can be grown as an informal hedge (*see p.138*). Tolerant of alkaline soils, coastal sites, and dry shade or sun (*see pp.64, 166, 216, 412*).

ALSO RECOMMENDED: *'Eve Price' has pink flower buds; 'Gwenllian' has pink-flushed flowers and red buds.*

☼ ☀ ◊◊ Z7b   **Evergreen shrub**
↕↔ 10ft (3m)

CISSUS ANTARCTICA

The kangaroo vine is usually grown as a house or conservatory plant in cold areas, but it may be moved outdoors for the summer months. Train up a support or allow to trail. Ideal for hanging baskets, it is valued for its glossy, dark green leaves; the flowers are small and insignificant. Apply a balanced fertilizer monthly when in growth. Keep just moist in winter.

ALSO RECOMMENDED: C. rhombifolia *has diamond-shaped leaves with rusty-hairy undersides; 'Ellen Danica' is bushier, with lobed leaves.*

☼ ◐ ◊ Min 41°F (5°C)   **Climber**
↕ 15ft (5m)

FICUS PUMILA

The creeping fig is an evergreen perennial, clinging by means of aerial roots. On climbing stems, the leathery, dark green leaves are asymmetrically oval, and on nonclimbing ones, the leaves are narrower and very glossy. It is ideal as a house or conservatory plant; provide support or grow in a hanging basket. When in growth, water moderately and apply a high-nitrogen fertilizer once a month; keep the soil just moist in winter.

☼ ◐ ◊ Min 35°F (2°C)   **Climber**
↕ 10–15ft (3–5m)

ADIANTUM PEDATUM

This maidenhair fern bears long, mid-green fronds up to 14in (35cm) tall that die down in winter. These have glossy dark brown or black stalks that emerge from creeping rhizomes. Remove dead fronds in spring. In the garden, it is also suitable for light woodland or a damp, shady border (*see p.238*), where it can be planted as a groundcover (*see p.326*).

ALSO RECOMMENDED: A. aleuticum (*see p.331*); A. venustum *is short, to 6in (15cm) tall* Z6.

☼ ◑ ◊ Z4   **Perennial fern**
↔ 12–16in (30–40cm)

ASPIDISTRA ELATIOR *'Variegata'*

Although commonly grown indoors, the cast-iron plant is a useful, very shade-tolerant foliage perennial for pots. Small cream flowers appear in early summer. It will overwinter outside in the garden in mild climates, where it can be planted as a groundcover in shade (*see p.326*). This variegated variety has large, dark green, cream-striped leaves to 28in (70cm) long. Grow in a sheltered site.

ALSO RECOMMENDED: A. elatior *has shorter, plain dark green leaves.*

☼ ◑ ◊◊ Min 35°F (2°C)   **Perennial**
↔ 24in (60cm)

ATHYRIUM NIPONICUM

The Japanese painted fern has finely divided, gray-green, deciduous fronds with purplish midribs and makes an elegant container plant for a shady courtyard or a cool conservatory. Use acidic or bark-based soil mix containing some coarse sand and leaf mold. In the garden, it is excellent as a groundcover in damp, partially shaded sites (*see pp.238, 326*); it spreads by red-brown rhizomes.

ALSO RECOMMENDED: *var.* pictum *has silvery fronds;* A. filix-femina *'Frizelliae'* (see p.248).

☀️ ☼ ◊ Z5   **Perennial fern**

↕ 8–12in (20–30cm) ↔ indefinite

BEGONIA *Non Stop Series*

Often grown outdoors as bedding, these tuberous begonias have bold, double blooms throughout summer in white, red, orange, apricot, pink, or yellow. They are excellent in containers and hanging baskets. Apply a balanced fertilizer at alternate waterings when in full growth. In cold climates, lift tubers before first frosts in autumn and store dry at 41–45°F (5–7°C).

ALSO RECOMMENDED: *'Can-can' has yellow flowers with red edges; Illumination Series begonias are pendulous, with pink or orange flowers, ideal for hanging baskets.*

☼ ◊ Min 50°F (10°C)   **Perennial**

↕ 12in (30cm)

BEGONIA SUTHERLANDII

Pendulous or trailing begonias like this orange-flowered species are ideal for hanging baskets and other containers. It has long and slender stems clothed with large, oval, bright green leaves with red veins. The relatively small flowers are freely borne in hanging clusters during summer. Fertilize regularly when in growth, and move under cover for winter. Allow to go dormant, then start into growth again in spring.

ALSO RECOMMENDED: *B. grandis subsp. evansiana is upright and has pink or white flowers. Z7*

☀ ◑ ○ Min 40°F (5°C)　　**Perennial**
‡ 30in (75cm) ↔ 18in (45cm)

BROWALLIA SPECIOSA *'White Troll'*

The sapphire flower is grown as an annual in cold-winter climates and is ideal for summer bedding and containers. This cultivar bears a profusion of white flowers through summer above a mound of sticky, matte green leaves. Water freely and apply a balanced liquid fertilizer monthly when in full growth. Pinch out growing tips to promote bushiness.

ALSO RECOMMENDED: *'Blue Bells' is compact, with violet-blue flowers; 'Silver Bells' has white flowers.*

☀ ◑ ○ Min 55°F (13°C)　　**Perennial**
‡ 24in (60cm) ↔ 10in (25cm)

CHLOROPHYTUM COMOSUM *'Vitiatum'*

Spider plants are famous for their clumps of ribbonlike, fresh green leaves, which have an off-white central stripe in this cultivar. Long, slender flower stems freely arch over the foliage, tipped by small, starry white flowers and miniature plantlets; in a hanging basket, the plantlets can cascade over the edge. Ideal for year-round display in a conservatory, they can be moved outside in summer.

ALSO RECOMMENDED: *'Variegatum'*
is similar, with white-margined leaves.

☀◐ ◌ ◊◊ Min 45°F (7°C) **Perennial**
↕6–8in (15–20cm) ↔ 6–12in (15–30cm)

CYCLAMEN PERSICUM

A tender cyclamen available in white and many shades of pink and purple. It is ideal for a cool greenhouse or conservatory in light shade, or on a windowsill, and bears its flowers from early winter to early spring above deep green, often silver-marbled leaves. Avoid drafts and hot, dry air, and water moderately when in leaf; cease watering when the foliage begins to wither after flowering. Lovely in winter windowboxes where hardy.

☀◐ ◌ ◊ Min 50°F (10°C) **Perennial**
↕6in (15cm) or more

CYRTOMIUM FALCATUM

The Japanese holly fern has evergreen, glossy dark green fronds with hollylike leaflets; these make a strong contrast among other ferns with more delicate, lacy foliage. Where not hardy, move the plant indoors in winter, where it will make a handsome foliage plant. Pot up in equal parts bark-based soil mix, coarse sand, and leaf mold. In the garden, its spreading habit is also good for dry areas in quite deep shade (*see p.216*). Choose a sheltered site.

ALSO RECOMMENDED: C. fortunei *is less hardy and less spreading.* Z7b

☼ ◑ ● ◊◊ ● Z7   **Perennial fern**

‡ 24in (60cm) ↔ 3½ft (1.1m)

DRYOPTERIS WALLICHIANA

Wallich's wood fern is a handsome plant for a large container. The long, upright fronds form an elegant, dark green shuttlecock. They are golden green when young, and the midribs are clothed in shaggy dark brown scales. The fronds die down in winter. Choose a site sheltered from wind. Pot up into equal parts bark-based soil mix and leaf mold.

ALSO RECOMMENDED: D. cycadina *is compact, with bright green fronds* Z7; D. erythrosora *has dark green fronds that are copper-red when young* Z7.

☼ ◑ ● ◊ ● Z7   **Perennial fern**

‡ 36in (90cm) ↔ 30in (75cm)

EPIMEDIUM GRANDIFLORUM 'Lilafee'

Also sold as 'Lilac Fairy', this small, deciduous plant produces spikes of delicate, violet-purple flowers above the light green foliage in mid- and late spring. The leaves are tinged bronze when young. Evergreen, but cut back the old leaves in late winter for the best display. In the garden, this is useful in the dry shade of trees and shrub (*see p.216*).

ALSO RECOMMENDED: *'Rose Queen' has rose-pink flowers;* E. × perralchicum *has bright yellow flowers* Z4; E. × rubrum *has crimson and pale yellow flowers* Z3.

☀ ◌◑ Z4   **Perennial**
‡ 8–12in (20–30cm) ↔ 12in (30cm)

FRAGARIA VESCA 'Multiplex'

Ornamental strawberries make pretty pot plants with trailing stems. Typical characteristics include leaves split into three, toothed leaflets; roselike flowers; and fleshy, edible red fruits. This cultivar has bright green foliage and relatively large white flowers in spring and summer, followed by small strawberries. In the garden it grows well in alkaline soils and can be used as a groundcover (*see pp.64, 326*).

ALSO RECOMMENDED: F. *'Pink Panda' has rich pink flowers but rarely bears fruits. Fruiting strawberries are also suitable for growing in containers.*

☀☀ ◌◑ Z5   **Perennial**
‡ ↔ 12in (30cm)

HAKONECHLOA MACRA *'Aureola'*

This colorful, deciduous grass forms a clump of narrow, arching, bright yellow leaves with cream and green stripes. They flush red in autumn and persist well into winter. Reddish brown flower spikes appear in late summer. It tolerates full sun, but the leaf color is best in partial shade. It is a versatile plant that can also be used in a border or rock garden.

ALSO RECOMMENDED: *'Alboaurea' has gold-striped leaves.*

☼ ◐ ◊◑ Z5   **Perennial**
‡ 14in (35cm) ↔ 16in (40cm)

HEUCHERA MICRANTHA *'Palace Purple'*

A clump-forming perennial valued for its dark purple-red, almost metallic foliage. It is topped by airy sprays of white flowers in summer. The leaves have five pointed lobes. It tolerates deep shade if the soil mix is kept moist. In the garden, plant in groups as groundcover for a damp, shady site (*see pp.238, 326*), but it can be slow to spread.

ALSO RECOMMENDED: H. *'Green Ivory'* (see p.340) *is less upright; 'Pewter Moon' has large, pale pink flowers.*

☼ ◐ ◊◑ Z4   **Perennial**
‡↔ 18–24in (45–60cm)

HOSTA *'Shade Fanfare'*

A variegated-leaved hosta that is also suitable as a groundcover in damp, shady places (*see pp.238, 326*). It forms clumps of bright green, boldly cream-margined leaves; their broad, heart shape gives an architectural quality (*see p.472*). Lavender-blue flowers appear in summer. Growing in pots reduces slug damage.

ALSO RECOMMENDED: *'Frances Williams'* (see p.381); *'Halcyon'* (see p.340); H. sieboldiana *var.* elegans (see p.490); H. ventricosa (see p.30); *'Wide Brim'* (see p.254).

☼◐ ◊ Z4   **Perennial**

↕ 18in (45cm) ↔ 24in (60cm)

IPHEION UNIFLORUM *'Wisley Blue'*

The vigorous bulb produces clumps of narrow, strap-shaped, bluish green leaves in autumn and bears scented, star-shaped, lilac-blue flowers in spring. Ideal for a container in a lightly or partially shaded courtyard; it tolerates sun. Plant bulbs in autumn. In the garden, it enjoys sandy soils (*see p.38*) and sun.

ALSO RECOMMENDED: *'Album' has pure white flowers; 'Froyle Mill' has dusky violet flowers.*

☼◐ ◊ *f* Z5   **Perennial bulb**

↕↔ 6–8in (15–20cm)

LOBELIA ERINUS
'Lilac Fountain'

This trailing perennial, usually grown as an annual bedding plant, is ideal for mixed container plantings, including hanging baskets. It bears a profusion of two-lipped, lilac-pink flowers throughout summer into autumn. The tiny leaves are dark green and bronzed. Plant out after the risk of frost has passed in spring. Many colorful trailing and nontrailing varieties are available.

ALSO RECOMMENDED: *Cascade Series has red, violet-blue, blue, pink, or white flowers.*

☀◐ ◊ Min 40°F (5°C)   **Perennial**

‡6in (15cm) ↔ 4–6in (10–15cm)

NEPHROLEPIS CORDIFOLIA

The sword fern has long and arching, fishbonelike, bright green fronds that hang over the side of a pot or hanging basket. It makes an easy indoor, greenhouse, or conservatory plant, and it can be grown outdoors in summer. The fronds are evergreen. Water sparingly in the colder months. It needs an open soil mix, bark based or with added coarse sand and leaf mold.

ALSO RECOMMENDED: N. exaltata *is very similar. (Tender)*

☀ ◊◊ Min 50°F (10°C)   **Perennial fern**

‡32in (80cm) ↔ 5ft (1.5m) or less

OPHIOPOGON JABURAN *'Vittatus'*

White lilyturf is a grasslike plant with clumps of arching foliage. This variety has cream and yellow-striped leaves. Spikes of small white flowers appear in late summer and are followed by round, blue-black fruits. Grow in an acidic or bark-based soil mix. In the garden, it can be used to edge a summer border. Grow in acidic soil; it tolerates dry shade (*see pp.92, 261*).

ALSO RECOMMENDED: *O. planiscapus 'Nigrescens' is smaller and hardier, with nearly black foliage.* Z6

☼◑ ◊◊ Z7b   **Perennial**
‡ 24in (60cm) ↔ 12in (30cm)

PAROCHETUS AFRICANUS

The shamrock pea is an ideal winter-flowering trailing plant for a hanging basket in a frost-free greenhouse or conservatory. It is named for its pretty, trifoliate, cloverlike leaves. The flowers are small and bright blue, borne from late autumn until late spring. Use a coarse soil mix.

☼ ◊◊ Min 40°F (5°C)   **Perennial**
‡ 4in (10cm) ↔ 24–39in (60–100cm)

PRIMULA *Polyanthus Group*

Polyanthus primroses are rosette-forming evergreens with colorful clusters of flat-faced flowers from late winter to early spring; they are available in an array of pastel and primary colors. These plants are splendid for containers, as well as in mixed plantings or on their own. Plant out in autumn. In the garden, they tolerate damp sites in shade (*see p.238*).

ALSO RECOMMENDED: *Cowichan Series has bronzed leaves and red, yellow, blue, or purple flowers; Crescendo Series has large flowers.*

☼ ◑ ◊◊ Z5   **Perennial**
↕ 6in (15cm) ↔ 12in (30cm)

STRELITZIA REGINAE

The bird of Paradise is a clump-forming evergreen with long, paddle-shaped leaves. The exotic orange and purple flowers appear from winter to spring. Grow in a greenhouse or conservatory in sun or light shade (*see p.412*); in hot weather, provide plenty of ventilation and extra shade. Water freely and fertilize every month when in growth, and water sparingly in winter. Use a soil-based potting mix.

ALSO RECOMMENDED: *'Humilis' is a dwarf form, reaching 32in (80cm) tall.*

☼ ◑ ◊ Min 50°F (10°C)   **Perennial**
↕ 6ft (2m) ↔ 3ft (1m)

VIOLA × WITTROCKIANA

Pansies are bushy, short-lived perennials with bold and colorful flowers. They make reliable, free-flowering container or windowbox plants if deadheaded regularly. Many different selections exist in a wide range of flower colors. They also include pansies that have been bred to flower in winter and early spring; these are popular plants for winter color. In the garden, they are tolerant of clay soils (*see p.12*).

☼◐ ◊◊ Z4   **Perennial**

‡ 6–9in (15–23cm) ↔ 9–12in (23–30cm)

WOODWARDIA RADICANS

The European chain fern is a tall, architectural plant (*see p.472*) with large and arching, dark green, feathery fronds. It is evergreen. Best potted in a bark-based soil mix with coarse sand and leaf mold. An impressive plant for a large container. In the garden, site in a damp, shady place near water. Tolerant of clay soils (*see p.12*).

◐ ◊ Z8   **Perennial fern**

‡ 6ft (2m) ↔ 10ft (3m)

CALCEOLARIA *'Bright Bikinis'*

Grown in containers, these pouch flowers offer summer-long color with their dense heads of slipperlike flowers in hot shades of yellow, orange, and red. Provide shelter from wind, water freely, and apply a balanced fertilizer every month when in full growth. Raise from seeds sown late in late summer or early spring. These plants can be used in mixed displays. Plant out once fear of frost has passed. Usually grown as an annual.

ALSO RECOMMENDED: *Anytime Series is early- and free-flowering and compact.*

☀◐ ◊ Min 40°F (5°C)　　**Biennial**
↕↔ 8in (20cm)

LUNARIA ANNUA

Honesty bears spires of red-purple flowers in late spring and summer that later give rise to flat, oval, silvery seedheads. Raise plants from seeds sown early in summer, and pot up in autumn. It is also good in mixed borders and cottage gardens; the self-seeding habit makes it ideal for naturalizing. The seedheads are popular for indoor arrangements, either fresh or dried (*see p.524*). It tolerates alkaline soils (*see p.64*).

ALSO RECOMMENDED: *var. albiflora has white flowers; 'Variegata' has red-purple or purple flowers and white-variegated leaves.*

☀◐ ◊ Z3　　**Biennial**
↕ 36in (90cm) ↔ 12in (30cm)

IMPATIENS WALLERIANA
Swirl Series

These impatiens are excellent annual
bedding or container plants that bear
long-lasting summer flowers of pink
and orange edged rose-red. The oval
leaves are light green. Many other types
of impatiens exist in a wide range of
pastel colors from white to orange,
red, pink, and violet; there are also
bicolored forms. Plant out after the
last frost, and give shelter from wind.
They tolerate coastal sites (*see p.166*).
Use alone or in mixed displays.
Suitable for hanging baskets.

☀ ◐ ⬥   **Annual**

↕ 6–8in (15–20cm) ↔ 24in (60cm)

NICOTIANA × SANDARAE
Domino Series

The abundant, flat-faced, fragrant
flowers of these flowering tobaccos
come in many shades, including white,
yellow, lime green, pink, red, and purple.
They are borne throughout summer and
are excellent for containers or bedding
in either sun or shade (*see p.412*). Plant
out in spring only after the danger of
frost has passed.

ALSO RECOMMENDED: *Havana Series
is compact in pink and lime green shades;
Starship Series has pink, white, lime green,
or lilac flowers.*

☀ ◐ ◑ ⬥ *f*   **Annual**

↕ 12–18in (30–45cm) ↔ 12in (30cm)

PLANTS FOR SHAPE & STRUCTURE

BY VIRTUE OF THEIR SIZE, and distinctive bold outlines, "architectural" plants are ranked among the star performers of the garden. In many cases, their sculptural beauty is not necessarily reliant on flowers, so they can often be guaranteed to provide an exceptionally long season of interest.

The elegant, tiered branching habit of *Cornus alternifolia* 'Argentea' (*see p.476*), for example, is exquisite when in full leaf, but it is almost equally beautiful when forming a leafless tracery of branches against a winter sky. *Rhus tybina* (*see p.482*) also forms a starkly elegant outline in winter, when it holds its staghorn branches like an organic candelabra. The South American bamboo, *Chusquea couleou* (*see p.481*), forms an arching, fountainlike clump of glossy canes fringed with whiskery tufts of narrow leaves, which are as good to look at in the depths of winter as at the height of summer. Some architectural plants have other

virtues, too: the cardoon (*see p.487*) has huge, jagged, arching, silver-gray leaves and towering heads of thistlelike flowers, and *Eupatorium purpureum* (*see p.488*) has massive, flattened heads of tiny dark pink flowers – both deserve a place in a wildlife garden. Their nectar-rich flowerheads are an invaluable, late-summer food source for butterflies and bees (*see p.494*).

DESIGN IDEAS

Many architectural plants really do deserve a spot in center stage, and they are best used as stand-alone specimens. Examples include *Liriodendron tulipifera* 'Aureomarginata' (*see p.477*) on a clear sweep of grass, or *Magnolia campbellii* (*see p.478*) in an open glade in a woodland garden, distantly framed by other lower, less spectacular plants. Most cacti and other succulents are very architectural in the open garden and in containers.

Spiky plants such as cordyline (*see p.414*) and yucca (*see pp.215, 483*) can look fabulous set in a container on a sea of gravel; a flat surface of muted color sets off a sharp outline to perfection. You can use such plants as a living exclamation point to draw the gaze from several viewpoints. Yet others, such as the billowing *Macleaya microcarpa* 'Kelway's Coral Plume' (*see p.491*) or tall hollyhocks, including *Alcea rosea* 'Nigra' (*see p.493*), can be used as focal points in beds and borders. Their height and strong vertical outline stand out from lower, more horizontally spreading plants and draw the eye into and along the design.

CARE AND CULTIVATION

If architectural plants are to give their best, they do need to be grown well. Before choosing, check each plant's individual cultivation requirements and then adhere to them closely. These plants will probably perform poorly in less-than-ideal sites. All they require is a little imagination in seeking a site that will display their ornamental virtues to their full potential.

ARAUCARIA ARAUCANA

The monkey puzzle is an unmistakeable, umbrella-shaped tree that forms a perfectly dome-shaped shrub when young. As it grows, it gradually loses its lower branches, which are in whorls around the dark gray-brown trunk. The sharply pointed leaves are very tough and scalelike, bright at first, then deepening to dark green; they persist for up to ten years. It is slow to reach maturity. No pruning is necessary.

☼ ◊◑ Z7   **Evergreen tree**
‡ 50–70ft (15–20m) ↔ 22–30ft (7–10m)

BETULA PENDULA *'Tristis'*

This European white birch is an elegant tree for a reasonably small garden. It has a narrow shape with drooping branchlets and attractive white bark. Yellow-brown male catkins appear in early spring before the triangular green leaves that turn golden yellow in autumn. It tolerates sandy, alkaline, and acidic soils (*see pp.38, 64, 92*). Prune in late winter, if necessary.

ALSO RECOMMENDED: *The trunk base of* B. pendula *becomes fissured with age;* 'Laciniata' *has deeply cut leaves and strongly pendent branchlets;* 'Youngii' *is much shorter, dome-shaped, and weeping.*

☼ ◊ Z2   **Deciduous tree**
‡ 80ft (25m) ↔ 30ft (10m)

CATALPA BIGNONIOIDES

The Southern catalpa forms an irregular, spreading canopy of large and handsome, heart-shaped, midgreen leaves. Upright clusters of white flowers appear in summer, followed by long and slender, beanlike pods that persist through winter. It tolerates clay and alkaline soils (*see pp.12, 64*). Branches can be pruned back heavily when dormant to create a compact shape.

ALSO RECOMMENDED: *'Aurea' has bright yellow foliage and is less vigorous.*

☼ ◊◊ Z5   **Deciduous tree**
↔ 50ft (15m)

CEDRUS DEODARA *'Aurea'*

This slow-growing, dwarf form of the deodar cedar is a conical conifer with spreading branches covered in golden yellow needles that become greener with age. The drooping shoot tips give the tree a shaggy appearance. The bark is very dark brown, and upright cones appear on the branches. Tolerant of exposure and hot, dry sites (*see pp.118, 190*). Little pruning is necessary.

ALSO RECOMMENDED: C. deodara *and* C. libani, *the cedar of Lebanon* (Z6), *are for larger properties only.*

☼ ◊ Z7   **Evergreen tree**
↔ 15ft (5m)

CORNUS ALTERNIFOLIA
Argentea

With spreading, tiered branches clothed in elliptical, white-margined green leaves, this dogwood makes an irresistibly elegant specimen in woodland or other sheltered sites. The leaves turn red and purple in autumn. Its light canopy allows for an underplanting of spring-flowering bulbs. Keep pruning to a minimum.

ALSO RECOMMENDED: *C. alternifolia has plain dark green leaves; C.* controversa *'Variegata' has white-margined leaves* Z5.

☀️◐ ◊ Z4   **Deciduous tree**
↕↔ 20ft (6m)

CORYLUS AVELLANA
Contorta

The corkscrew hazel has strongly twisted shoots that are striking in winter. Later in this season, the display is enhanced with the appearance of pale yellow catkins. The midgreen leaves are almost circular and jaggedly toothed. Thin out congested branches in late winter; these can be displayed indoors (*see p.524*). The autumn nuts attract wildlife (*see p.494*).

ALSO RECOMMENDED: *'Aurea' has straight shoots and bright yellow then yellow-green foliage; C.* maxima *'Purpurea' (see p.141).*

☀️◐ ◊ Z5   **Deciduous tree**
↕↔ 15ft (5m)

LARIX DECIDUA

Unlike most conifers, the European
larch sheds its soft, pale green needles
in autumn, fading to straw yellow
beforehand. It has a conical shape with
a spreading crown and smooth, scaly
gray bark. Small, rounded cones appear
in spring, and they usually persist on
the branches. A useful, easily grown
specimen tree that tolerates a wide
range of conditions.

ALSO RECOMMENDED: *L. kaempferi,
the Japanese larch, is very similar.* Z2b

☼ ◊ Z3 **Deciduous tree**
↕ 100ft (30m) ↔ 12–20ft (4–6m)

LIRIODENDRON TULIPIFERA
'Aureomarginata'

This tulip tree makes a stately and
elegant specimen. The columnar crown
of distinctive, saddle-shaped leaves with
broad, golden yellow margins turns
yellow in autumn. Cupped, orange-
banded, pale green flowers may appear
in midsummer. Plant young saplings
and allow them to grow undisturbed.
Keep pruning to a minimum.

ALSO RECOMMENDED: *L. tulipifera is
taller, with plain green leaves; 'Fastigiatum'
is narrowly conical, with upright branches.*

☼☀ ◊◊ Z5b **Deciduous tree**
↕ 70ft (20m) ↔ 30ft (10m)

MAGNOLIA CAMPBELLII

This vigorous tree magnolia becomes increasingly picturesque as it spreads with age. It has long, narrow leaves, and after 25 years or so bears its waxy, cup-and-saucer-shaped white, rose-pink, or crimson flowers on its bare branches in late winter and early spring. Mulch with leaf mold in spring, and shelter the early flowers from frost and wind. Keep pruning to a minimum.

ALSO RECOMMENDED: *For specimens that flower on younger plants, grow* M. × loebner 'Leonard Messel', *a small tree with pink flowers* Z5, *or* M. × soulangeana (*see p.15*).

☼ ◐ ◊◑ Z7   **Deciduous tree**
‡ 50ft (15m) ↔ 30ft (10m)

PAULOWNIA TOMENTOSA

The empress tree bears fragrant, trumpet-shaped, pinkish lilac flowers that appear in late spring; upright clusters of light brown seed capsules follow. The large, heart-shaped, bright green leaves make this an excellent shade tree. It is fast-growing, and if pruned back hard each winter, it will give especially big leaves on smaller, shrubby, nonflowering plants. It tolerates urban pollution and alkaline soils (*see p.64*), but choose a site sheltered from wind.

☼ ◊ *f* Z6b   **Deciduous tree**
‡ 40ft (12m) ↔ 30ft (10m)

PICEA OMORIKA

The Serbian spruce is a narrow, spire-like tree, popular as a landscape tree on larger properties. Its branches hang downward, curving back up at the tips, and are clothed with dense, dark blue-green needles and the occasional hanging, red-brown cone. It copes with a range of soils, from alkaline to acidic (*see pp.64, 92*).

ALSO RECOMMENDED: *P. abies 'Ohlendorffii' (see p.106); P. glauca 'Conica' is a compact, conical shrub Z3; P. mariana 'Nana' (see p.423); P. pungens 'Koster' is a silvery blue tree with horizontal branches Z2.*

☼ ◊ Z3b   **Evergreen tree**
↕ 70ft (20m) ↔ 6–10ft (2–3m)

PRUNUS
'Kiku-shidare-zakura'

Also sold as 'Cheal's Weeping', this small cherry tree is grown for its weeping branches and clear pink blossoms in spring. They appear with or just before the midgreen leaves, which are flushed bronze when young. Prune after flowering, if necessary, and remove any shoots growing from the bare trunk as they appear. It tolerates alkaline soils (*see p.64*).

ALSO RECOMMENDED: *'Spire' is taller, to 30ft (10m), and cone- to vase-shaped; P. serrula has glossy, mahogany-red bark and white spring blossoms Z7.*

☼ ◊◊ Z6   **Deciduous tree**
↔ 10ft (3m)

TRACHYCARPUS FORTUNEI

The Chusan palm is one of the hardiest palm trees. It has a single, upright stem with a head of fan-shaped, dark green leaves with many pointed lobes. Small yellow flowers may appear in large, hanging clusters in early summer, followed by small, round black berries on female plants. It will grow in a large container (*see p.412*).

☼ ◊ Z7b   **Evergreen palm**
↕ 70ft (20m) ↔ 8ft (2.5m)

ZELKOVA SERRATA

The Japanese zelkova is an imposing, elmlike tree for larger properties only. It has a spreading habit with smooth gray, peeling bark. The narrow, toothed, dark green foliage gives good autumn color when it turns to yellow, orange, or red.

ALSO RECOMMENDED: *'Goblin' is a dwarf, bushy shrub to 3ft (1m) tall and wide.*

☼◑ ◊◊ Z5b   **Deciduous tree**
↕ 100ft (30m) ↔ 80ft (25m)

CHUSQUEA CULEOU

This is among the most graceful of bamboos, forming an elegant, fountain-like clump of whiskered, glossy olive green canes with papery white leaf sheaths. The narrow leaves are subtly checkered and midgreen. It is a perfect specimen for a woodland garden, but provide ample space for its graceful habit to develop fully. Alternatively, confine the roots with slabs or metal plates sunk into the soil. Provide shelter from wind.

☼ ◐ ◊ Z8 　　**Evergreen bamboo**
↕ 20ft (6m) ↔ 8ft (2.5m) or more

ERIOBOTRYA JAPONICA

The loquat is a vigorous, easily grown shrub with thick shoots and large and leathery, downward-curving leaves. They are glossy dark green and deeply veined. Open clusters of fragrant white flowers appear from autumn to winter, followed by rounded, orange-yellow, ornamental fruits in spring. Keep it compact by pruning once the fruiting display is over.

☼ ◊ ƒ Min 50°F (10°C)　**Evergreen shrub**
↔ 25ft (8m)

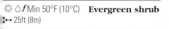

EUPHORBIA CHARACIAS

A dramatic, blue-green bush that bears large, rounded heads of dark-eyed, pale yellow-green flowers at the tips of the upright stems in spring and early summer. It is ideal for long-lasting color in a spacious, Mediterranean-style garden. Shelter from wind. Cut back to the base in autumn; wear gloves, because the milky sap can irritate skin. It is good for sandy soils (*see p.38*) and coastal and hot, dry sites (*see pp.166, 190*).

ALSO RECOMMENDED: *subsp.* wulfenii *and its cultivars 'John Tomlinson' and 'Lambrook Gold' are similar.*

☼ ◊ Z7b   **Evergreen shrub**
↕↔ 4ft (1.2m)

RHUS GLABRA

The smooth sumac is a suckering shrub with large, divided, shining blue-green leaves that blaze rich red in autumn; color is best in full sun. In summer, it produces large clusters of yellow-green flowers; these give rise to flame-shaped, winter-persistent clusters of red fruits on female plants only. It is an ideal specimen for a shrub or mixed border. Keep pruning to a minimum.

ALSO RECOMMENDED: R. typhina *is reliable and even more elegant, with orange-red autumn color; 'Dissecta' has finely cut leaves.* Z3

☼ ◊ Z2b   **Deciduous shrub**
↕↔ 8ft (2.5m)

TROCHODENDRON ARALIOIDES

This large, bushy plant is sometimes known as the wheel tree for its spirally arranged, handsome foliage. Clusters of unusual, vivid green flowers appear in late spring and early summer at the shoot tips. The dark green leaves have a leathery texture, and the bark is aromatic. It is suitable for a woodland garden or among other shrubs and trees, in a site sheltered from wind. It tolerates acidic soils (*see p.92*). Remove badly placed growth in spring.

☼ ☀ ◊◊ Z7   **Evergreen shrub**
↕ 30ft (10m) ↔ 25ft (8m)

YUCCA FILAMENTOSA *'Bright Edge'*

An almost stemless plant with basal rosettes of rigid, lance-shaped, dark green leaves, to 30in (75cm) long, with broad yellow margins. Nodding, bell-shaped white flowers, on spires to 6ft (2m) or more tall, are borne in the second half of summer; remove old flower stems at the end of the season. It is good in a border or courtyard, and is good in coastal and hot, dry sites (*see pp.166, 190*), and sandy soils (*see p.38*).

ALSO RECOMMENDED: *'Variegata' has white margins;* Y. whipplei (*see p.215*).

☼ ◊ Z4   **Evergreen shrub**
↕ 30in (75cm) ↔ 5ft (1.5m)

ACANTHUS MOLLIS

Bear's breeches is a striking border plant that makes mounds of arching, deeply lobed, glossy dark green leaves. In summer, spires of two-lipped white flowers with purple-shaded bracts rise well above the foliage, persisting as equally attractive seedheads. It is good as a groundcover in sun or dry, partial shade (*see pp.216, 304, 326*).

ALSO RECOMMENDED: *Latifolius Group has broader, conspicuously veined leaves;* A. spinosus *has spiny, deeply cut leaves* Z6.

☼ ◐ ◊ Z6b **Perennial**
↕ 5ft (1.5m) ↔ 36in (90cm)

ACIPHYLLA AUREA

This clump-forming plant bears its majestic spikes of tiny, golden brown flowers with spiny bracts from early to late summer, but it must have a mild, sunny climate to do so. The narrow, grayish leaves with bold yellow edges and midribs have sharp, terminal spines, so site with care. A superb specimen for a gravel garden. It resents root disturbance, so set out plants when they are young and small.

ALSO RECOMMENDED: A. pinnatifida *has bronzed, dark green leaves.* Z8

☼ ◊ Z7b **Perennial**
↕↔ 3ft (1m)

ANGELICA ARCHANGELICA

This short-lived perennial forms clumps of large and divided, glossy green, very aromatic leaves. In its second summer it produces huge, rounded heads of greenish yellow flowers on sturdy, ridged stems. Grow in a mixed or herbaceous border. It will self-seed if conditions are favorable; thin out seedlings as necessary, or transplant when small.

ALSO RECOMMENDED: *A. gigas has dark purple flowers on dark red stems* Z4; *A. sylvestris has white or pale pink flowers and is suitable for a wild garden* Z5.

☼ ☀ ◗ ƒ Z4   **Perennial**

‡ 6ft (2m) ↔ 4ft (1.2m)

BESCHORNERIA YUCCOIDES

This fleshy plant forms an impressive rosette of strap-shaped, gray-green leaves at ground level. A tall red, yellow, or orange flower spike emerges from the center of the rosette in summer. It is a good plant for a Mediterranean-style or gravel garden or against a sunny, sheltered wall. In frost-prone climates, grow it in a large container (*see p.412*) and move it into a cool conservatory or greenhouse for winter. It must have sharply drained soil.

☼ ◊ Min 45°F (7°C)   **Perennial**

‡ 5ft (1.5m) ↔ 3ft (1m) or more

CANNA 'King Midas'

This canna is an upright perennial with a single, canelike stem clothed with large, oval, dark green leaves. It is topped by golden yellow flowers from midsummer to early autumn. Its color and stature make it popular in summer bedding (*see p.412*). Where not hardy, lift plants in late autumn and store over winter in a cool, frost-free place in barely moist soil mix. Replant in late spring. Many colorful varieties exist.

ALSO RECOMMENDED: *'Assaut'* (see p.431); *'Endeavour' has red flowers; C. indica has bright red or soft orange flowers.*

☀ ◑ Min 35°F (2°C)   **Perennial**
↕ 5ft (1.5m) ↔ 20in (50cm)

CIRSIUM RIVULARE 'Atropurpureum'

The thistlelike, deep crimson flowerheads of this clump-forming plant arise on pale, branched stems in the first half of summer. They are held well above the prickly, divided, dark green foliage. It is excellent in a mixed or herbaceous border or in a meadow garden. Remove dead flowerheads to prevent nuisance self-seeding; the flowers can be cut for indoor arrangements (*see p.524*).

ALSO RECOMMENDED: *C. japonicum 'Rose Beauty' has carmine-red flowerheads; those of 'Pink Beauty' are rose-pink. Z6*

☀ ◊ Z5   **Perennial**
↕ 4ft (1.2m) ↔ 24in (60cm)

CORTADERIA SELLOANA *'Sunningdale Silver'*

This evergreen pampas grass forms huge, weather-resistant clumps of arching, sharp-edged leaf blades; silvery flower plumes appear in late summer. Cut out any dead foliage with the previous year's flower plumes in late winter – wear gloves to protect your hands. It tolerates sandy and alkaline soils (*see pp.38, 64*), and exposed, coastal, and hot, dry sites (*see pp.118, 166, 190*).

ALSO RECOMMENDED: *'Aureolineata' (syn. 'Gold Band') is shorter, with yellow-margined leaves; 'Pumila' is shorter still, with silvery yellow plumes.*

☼ ◊ Z7   **Perennial**

‡ 10ft (3m) or more ↔ 8ft (2.5m)

CYNARA CARDUNCULUS

The cardoon forms a sculptural mound of arching, deeply divided, silvery gray leaves. It is topped in mid- to late summer by thick, gray, woolly-stemmed, thistlelike purple flowerheads; these attract bees and butterflies and are useful in dried flower arrangements (*see pp.494, 524*). It makes a fine focal point in a mixed or herbaceous border with shelter from wind. The leaf stalks are edible when blanched. Prepare them like asparagus.

ALSO RECOMMENDED: *The flowerheads of Scolymus Group, the globe artichoke, are edible in bud.*

☼ ◊ Z7b   **Perennial**

‡ 5ft (1.5m) ↔ 4ft (1.2m)

DICKSONIA ANTARCTICA

This tree fern has a very fibrous, upright trunk topped by an umbrella of very large, feathery, bright green fronds. Each one can measure up to 10ft (3m) long; as they age, they turn to dark green. A fine specimen for a sheltered, damp and shady spot (*see p.238*), but it will survive winters in mild climates only; elsewhere, grow it in a large container in a cool, north-facing greenhouse or conservatory (*see p.448*). Grow in acidic soil (*see p.92*) and hose the trunk down in hot weather. It is very slow-growing.

☼◐◑ ◗ Min 40°F (5°C)   **Perennial fern**
↕ 10ft (3m) ↔ 12ft (4m)

EUPATORIUM PURPUREUM

Joe Pye weed is a versatile plant, at home in clay, alkaline, or permanently moist soils (*see pp.12, 64, 372*), in a border or woodland garden. Stiff, upright stems clothed in purple-tinged leaves are topped with domed, fluffy heads of tiny pink, purple, or white flowers in summer and autumn; they are very attractive to bees and butterflies (*see p.494*).

ALSO RECOMMENDED: E. cannabinum *has flat-topped heads of pink, purple, or white flowers.* Z4

☼◐ ◗◖ Z3   **Perennial**
↕ 7ft (2.2m) ↔ 3ft (1m)

FERULA COMMUNIS

The giant fennel is an excelent foliage
plant. It grows strongly to produce a
mass of finely divided, light green
foliage. After several years, the plant
may finally flower in the first half of
summer, when many globular clusters
of tiny yellow flowers are borne on a
tall, thick stem. The plant sometimes
dies after producing seeds. Grow it at
the back of a border or as a specimen
plant; provide a dry mulch during
winter. This is not the culinary fennel
(*Foeniculum*).

☼ ◊ *f* Z7   **Perennial**
↕ 6–10ft (2–3m) ↔ 24in (60cm)

GLADIOLUS COMMUNIS
SUSBP. BYZANTINUS

In late spring, this elegant, upright plant
gives a blaze of magenta flowers. These
are arranged in spikes above fans of
narrow leaves. It is ideal for a border,
and the flowers are good for cutting
(*see p.524*). Plant corms in spring on a
bed of coarse sand to improve
drainage. It tolerates clay and alkaline
soils (*see pp.12, 64*), and hot, dry sites
(*see p.190*). Mulch well in fall at the
limits of its hardiness.

ALSO RECOMMENDED: G. papilio
is less hardy, with yellowish flowers. Z8

☼ ◊ Z5b   **Perennial corm**
↕ 3ft (1m) ↔ 3in (8cm)

HOSTA SIEBOLDIANA
VAR. ELEGANS

Also sold as 'Elegans' or 'Robusta', this hosta forms gray-blue clumps of broad, heart-shaped, puckered foliage, giving an architectural quality. It is suitable as a groundcover in damp, shady places (*see pp.238, 326*) and tolerates clay and moist soils (*see pp.12, 372*). Pale lilac-gray flowers appear in early summer. It will also grow in a container (*see p.448*).

ALSO RECOMMENDED: *'Birchwood Parky's Gold'* (see p.318); *'Frances Williams'* (see p.381); *'Halcyon'* (see p.340); *'Shade Fanfare'* (see p.465); *'Wide Brim'* (see p.254); H. ventricosa (see p.30).

☼◐ ◊ Z4   **Perennial**
‡3ft (1m) ↔ 4ft (1.2m)

LILIUM CANDIDUM

The Madonna lily has upright stems, each bearing up to 20 highly fragrant, trumpet-shaped, pure white flowers in midsummer. They are good for cutting (*see p.524*). The leaves are lance-shaped and glossy. Grow in neutral to alkaline soils (*see p.64*) in full sun with the base in shade. It is also suitable for hot, dry sites (*see p.190*). Plant bulbs just below the soil surface in winter, unlike other lilies, which are planted deeper.

ALSO RECOMMENDED: L. martagon *has rich pink, turkscap flowers* Z4; L. regale (see p.433); L. superbum (see p.113).

☼ ◊ *f* Z5   **Perennial bulb**
‡3–6ft (1–2m)

MACLEAYA MICROCARPA
'Kelway's Coral Plume'

This clump-forming perennial is grown
for its foliage and graceful plumes of
tiny, coral pink to buff flowers. These
open from pink buds in early and
midsummer, above large, olive green
leaves. Grow in a mixed or herbaceous
border with shelter from wind. Confine
to bounds by chopping away excess
roots from the margins, as necessary.
It tolerates clay soils (*see p.12*).

ALSO RECOMMENDED: *M. cordata
has buff-white flowers; 'Flamingo' has
pink buds and buff-pink flowers.* Z3

☀️ ◐ ◊◊ Z4　　　　　　**Perennial**

‡ 7ft (2.2m) ↔ 3ft (1m) or more

MUSA BASJOO

The Japanese banana is hardier than
most and produces several slender,
arching green leaves over 6ft (2m) long.
A large brown flower spike may appear
in summer from the center of the plant.
Greenish bananas may develop, which
are small and inedible. This exotic plant
must have a sheltered site, because
strong winds will shred the leaves.
Grow as a specimen or as part of a
summer border; in autumn, provide a
thick mulch in mild areas or pot it up
and overwinter under cover.

☀️ ◊◊ Min 40°F (5°C)　　　　**Perennial**

‡ 15ft (5m) ↔ 12ft (4m)

PLEIOBLASTUS AURICOMUS

This upright bamboo forms an evergreen screen of brilliant green, yellow-striped foliage. The bristly edged, lance-shaped leaves are carried on purple-green canes. Plant in an open glade in a woodland garden, or against a backdrop of trees or tall shrubs. Provide shelter from wind, and thin overcrowded clumps in late spring. To confine its invasive spread, bury a barrier around the roots.

ALSO RECOMMENDED: *P. variegatus is shorter, to 30in (75cm) tall, with cream- and green-striped leaves.* Z7b

☼ ◊◑ Z7b   **Perennial bamboo**
↕↔ 5ft (1.5m)

POLYSTICHUM MUNITUM

The sword fern, with its evergreen shuttlecocks of leathery, dark green fronds, is an attractive specimen plant for a damp or dry, shady border (*see pp.216, 238*). The spiny-toothed leaf segments add to its spiky, hard-edged appearance. Remove old fronds as new ones unfurl in spring. It can be pot-grown (*see p.412*).

ALSO RECOMMENDED: *P. aculeatum is similar, with prickly, dark green fronds* Z3b; *P. setiferum Divisilobum Group* (see p.258).

◑◐ ◑ Z4   **Perennial fern**
↕ 36in (90cm) ↔ 4ft (1.2m)

ALCEA ROSEA *'Nigra'*

This is the darkest-flowered of all the hollyhocks, bearing impressive spires of funnel-shaped, chocolate-maroon flowers in early and midsummer. These rise above a mound of crinkled, lobed, light green leaves. Indispensable in a cottage garden, it looks good at the back of a herbaceous border. Hollyhocks can be raised from seed and come in white, pink, purple, yellow, and red shades, with double or single flowers. Those with single flowers are most attractive to bees and butterflies (*see p.494*).

☀ ◊ Z3   **Biennial**

↕ 5–8ft (1.5–2.5m) ↔ 24in (60cm)

AMARANTHUS TRICOLOR *'Illumination'*

This amaranth is a fast-growing, upright and bushy plant grown for its brightly colored foliage. The upper leaves are brilliant rose-red topped with gold, and the lower leaves are copper-brown. The flowers are insignificant. Choose a sheltered site. It can also be container-grown (*see p.412*).

ALSO RECOMMENDED: *'Flaming Fountains' has narrow, red and bronze leaves; 'Joseph's Coat' has red, green, yellow, and brown lower leaves.*

☀ ◊   **Annual**

↕ 18in (45cm) ↔ 12–18in (30–45cm)

PLANTS FOR WILDLIFE GARDENS

PLANTING FOR WILDLIFE conjures a picture of chaotic, jungle-like plantings that only the most committed of enthusiasts could tolerate. Wild creatures, however, don't pass judgement on style – their primary concerns are food, water, and shelter – so even those who garden in a more formal, neater manner can provide a valuable haven for birds, mammals, and insects.

To attract wildlife into your garden, grow a diversity of native species; these include several so-called weeds, but remember that many of these are essential food for emerging caterpillars of butterflies and moths. You will be able to observe wild creatures at close quarters, and enjoy the feel-good factor that derives from playing a small part in their conservation. A healthy wildlife population also helps with pest control; birds pick off aphids, while other birds pick out soil pests from upturned earth. Toads and frogs consume large quantities of slugs, while lacewings, ladybugs, and

hoverflies have young that eat aphids and other sap-sucking pests. Wildlife gardeners seldom use chemical pest controls because of the risks it carries to wild creatures, but once a wildlife garden is established, chemical controls are seldom needed. Infestations of pests hardly ever reach damaging levels when controlled by predatory insects and birds.

ATTRACTING WILDLIFE

Bring beneficial insects into the garden by planting plenty of colorful, nectar-rich flowers, such as *Melissa officinalis* 'Aurea' (*see p.516*) or *Buddleja davidii* 'Empire Blue' (*see p.500*). Other inviting flowers include nearly all daisylike blooms and those with two-lipped flowers, such as *Hyssopus officinalis* (*see p.504*). Aim to provide a nectar supply from early spring onward; bees particularly need access to a source of nectar and pollen when they emerge from hibernation. To help, plant spring flowers such as snowdrops (*see p.231*) and

pulmonarias (*see pp.34, 344*). A shrub border provides good shelter for nesting and can lend cover for birds that come to the bird feeder. Choose autumn-fruiting shrubs to feed birds then and into winter. Red fruits, like those of *Sorbus commixta* (*see p.499*) and *Rosa rugosa* (*see p.178*), are almost always the birds' first choice, so choose some of other colors, too. Birds take yellow, white, or purple berries sooner or later, especially in hard winters, but you will at least get some pleasure from them before they are consumed. Grow thistlelike plants and grasses, such as *Stipa tenuissima* (*see p.521*), for seed-eating birds; they also like the seedheads of perennials, so delay cleaning up the border until early spring.

A garden pond is the single most important feature for attracting wildlife (*see p.394*). Make the sides slope gently so that animals can get down easily to drink and bathe, and can escape if they fall in. Also provide log piles in out-of-the-way places as a home for hibernating butterflies, toads and snakes.

ABIES KOREANA

The Korean fir is a dense, conical tree with shiny, dark green leaves that are silver beneath. It bears very ornamental, violet-blue cones, even on very young trees. A superb architectural specimen tree (*see p.472*) that lends good cover for birds; owls often use the uppermost branches as a viewpoint when hunting, and finches may extract seeds from the cones. Grow in neutral to slightly acidic soil; it tolerates clay (*see pp.12, 92*). Shelter from wind. Normally, little pruning is necessary.

ALSO RECOMMENDED: *'Silberlocke' has twisted leaves with pale silvery undersides.*

☀ ◊ Z4   **Evergreen tree**
‡ 30ft (10m) ↔ 20ft (6m)

ACER CAMPESTRE

The field maple is a small tree with lobed leaves that are red when young then dark green, turning yellow and red in autumn. The green flowers give rise to winged fruits, and these are a food source for small animals. It makes excellent hedging (*see p.138*), providing a good nesting site for birds; trim hedges in winter. Tolerant of alkaline soils (*see p.64*).

ALSO RECOMMENDED: *'Postelense' has red-stalked, golden yellow leaves.*

☀ ◊ Z5   **Deciduous tree**
‡ 25ft (8m) ↔ 12ft (4m)

ILEX × ALTACLERENSIS
'Golden King'

A shrubby holly that has glossy dark
green leaves edged with gold; their
margins may be smooth or toothed.
Red berries develop in autumn if a male
plant is nearby; these are a food source
for birds. It tolerates urban pollution and
coastal sites, making a good windbreak
or impenetrable hedge (*see pp.118, 138,
166*). Trim or prune in spring,
as necessary.

ALSO RECOMMENDED: *'Camelliifolia' has
plain, dark green leaves; 'Lawsoniana' has
gold-splashed leaves; I. aquifolium 'Golden
van Tol' (see p.154).*

☼◑ ◊ Z6   **Evergreen tree**

↕ 20ft (6m) ↔ 12ft (4m)

MALUS *'Professor Sprenger'*

This round-headed tree is very attractive
to wildlife. In spring, its pink buds hum
with bees as they open to fragrant white
flowers, and the amber crabapples
that follow will be consumed by birds,
especially in hard winters. The leaves
turn gold in late autumn. It will grow
in any but waterlogged soil, including
clay and alkaline (*see pp.12, 64*).
Remove crossing branches in winter
when young to form an open crown;
older trees need little pruning.

ALSO RECOMMENDED: *'Evereste' has red-
orange fruits; 'John Downie' (see p.16);
'Red Sentinel' has glossy, dark red fruits.*

☼◑ ◊◊ Z4   **Deciduous tree**

↕↔ 22ft (7m)

PHOTINIA DAVIDIANA

This upright tree has lance-shaped, dark green leaves; the old ones turn red before they fall – at any time of year – especially in autumn. In midsummer, it bears clusters of small, rather ill-scented white flowers, which attract beneficial insects. Matte bright red fruits follow. Grow in a shrub border or on its own as a specimen.

ALSO RECOMMENDED: *P. 'Redstart' is smaller, with bronze-red young leaves and orange-red fruits; P. serratifolia has red young leaves and scarlet fruits. Z7*

☼ ◑ ◊◊ Z7   **Evergreen tree**
‡ 25ft (8m) ↔ 20ft (6m)

PRUNUS PADUS

The European bird cherry is a spreading, often multistemmed tree with dark green leaves that turn red or yellow in autumn. In late spring, it bears hanging clusters of small, fragrant white flowers, attractive to pollinating insects. The small, pea-sized black cherries that follow are readily consumed by birds. Keep pruning to a minimum, in midsummer if necessary.

ALSO RECOMMENDED: *'Albertii' is free-flowering; 'Colorata' has red-purple young foliage and pink flowers; P. laurocerasus is a dense, evergreen shrub Z7.*

☼ ◑ ◊ Z2   **Deciduous tree**
‡ 50ft (15m) ↔ 30ft (10m)

SORBUS ARIA *'Lutescens'*

This compact whitebeam forms a beautiful specimen tree that tolerates a range of conditions, including clay and alkaline soils (*see pp.12, 64*). The broad and toothed leaves are silvery gray and turn russet and gold in autumn. Clusters of white spring flowers are followed by dark red berries that are a food source for birds. It is also good for exposed, city, or coastal gardens (*see pp.118, 166*). Remove any dead wood in summer.

ALSO RECOMMENDED: *'Magnifica' has larger, glossier leaves; 'Majestica' is taller, with larger leaves.*

☼ ◐ ◊◊ Z4   **Deciduous tree**

‡ 30ft (10m) ↔ 25ft (8m)

SORBUS COMMIXTA

This mountain ash is a small, conical tree with finely divided, dark green leaves that flush yellow, red, and purple in autumn. In late spring, it produces broad clusters of white flowers, followed by an abundance of orange-red or red berries. These are eagerly eaten by birds. Keep pruning to a minimum. It tolerates exposed sites (*see p.118*).

ALSO RECOMMENDED: S. aucuparia (see p.126); S. sargentiana *bears bright red berries in profusion* Z6.

☼ ◐ ◊◊ Z7   **Deciduous tree**

‡ 30ft (10m) ↔ 22ft (7m)

BERBERIS DICTYOPHYLLA

This upright shrub has white-bloomed shoots clothed in spiny leaves that turn red in autumn. The pale yellow flowers of late spring form a valuable nectar source for bees; they later give rise to red fruits favored by birds.

It tolerates alkaline and clay soils and coastal and urban sites (*see pp.12, 64, 166*). Thin out dense growth in winter.

ALSO RECOMMENDED: *B. julianae* (see p.146); *B. × stenophylla 'Corallina Compacta'* (see p.127); *B. thunbergii 'Dart's Red Lady'* (see p.147).

☼ ◐◊Z7   **Deciduous shrub**
↕ 6ft (2m) ↔ 5ft (1.5m)

BUDDLEJA DAVIDII
'Empire Blue'

The arching flower spikes of all *B. davidii* cultivars attract a profusion of butterflies and other pollinating insects in summer and autumn. This one has violet-blue flowers. All are fast-growing, arching shrubs with grayish green leaves. Prune back hard to a woody framework in spring for the best foliage and flowers. It tolerates alkaline soils and exposed sites (*see pp.64, 118*).

ALSO RECOMMENDED: *'Black Knight' has dark purple-blue flowers; 'Royal Red' has red-purple flowers; 'White Profusion' has white flowers.*

☼ ◊*f*Z5b   **Deciduous shrub**
↕ 10ft (3m) ↔ 15ft (5m)

CARYOPTERIS × CLANDONENSIS *'Kew Blue'*

This upright shrub has dark gray-green leaves and, in late summer and early autumn, dense clusters of dark blue flowers. As well as lending late color to the border, they provide a useful nectar source for pollinating insects. Cut all stems back to low buds in late spring. It tolerates alkaline soils and hot, dry sites (*see pp.64, 190*).

ALSO RECOMMENDED: *'Heavenly Blue' is similar; 'Worcester Gold' has yellow leaves and lavender-blue flowers.*

☼ ◊ Z6   **Deciduous shrub**
‡ 15ft (1m) ↔ 5ft (1.5m)

CLERODENDRUM TRICHOTOMUM

This upright shrub with dark green leaves is valued for its large, sweetly fragrant clusters of white flowers that appear in the leaf axils from late summer to autumn. Each flower is surrounded by a ring of pinkish red sepals. Like the shiny blue berries that follow, the flowers make quite a display. Good in a border where it will attract beneficial insects. Prune in early spring, if necessary.

ALSO RECOMMENDED: *var.* fargesii *has bronze young leaves and flowers with green sepals.*

☼ ◊◑ ƒ Z6   **Deciduous shrub**
‡↔ 15–20ft (5–6m)

DAPHNE MEZEREUM

Mezereon has pale to soft gray-green leaves, and in late winter and early spring, its upright stems are wreathed to the tips in very fragrant, deep purple-pink flowers. The fleshy red fruits that follow, though highly poisonous to humans, are enjoyed by birds. Pruning should be avoided.

ALSO RECOMMENDED: *f.* alba *has creamy white flowers and yellow fruits;* 'Bowles' Variety' *is vigorous, with pure white flowers and yellow fruits.*

☼ ☀ ◊ *f* Z5   **Deciduous shrub**
‡ 4ft (1.2m) ↔ 3ft (1m)

DECAISNEA FARGESII

This distinctive, upright shrub with long, divided, dark green leaves bears hanging clusters of bell-shaped, yellow-green flowers in early summer. They are followed, in autumn, by fat, sausage-shaped, deep blue pods that contain energy-rich seeds and jelly enjoyed by birds. A good architectural plant for a shrub border (*see p.472*); shelter from wind. It normally needs very little pruning.

☼ ☀ ◊ Z6   **Deciduous shrub**
‡↔ 3ft (6m)

HEBE *'Great Orme'*

A rounded shrub that from midsummer
to autumn carries slender spikes of
small, deep pink flowers that fade to
white and attract beneficial insects. The
leaves are lance-shaped and glossy dark
green. It is ideal for a mixed or shrub
border; shelter from wind at the base
of a warm wall where marginally hardy
(*see p.280*). Pruning is unnecessary, but
leggy plants can be cut back in spring.
It can be pot-grown, and it tolerates
alkaline soils (*see pp.64, 412*).

ALSO RECOMMENDED: *H. × franciscana
'Variegata' has cream-margined leaves
and purple flowers. (Tender)*

☼◑ ◊◊ Min 40°F (5°C) **Evergreen shrub**
↨ 4ft (1.2m)

HELIOTROPIUM ARBORESCENS

Heliotrope is a compact shrub, normally
grown as an annual for summer
bedding or as a conservatory plant.
(*see p.412*). It is prized for its sweetly
fragrant heads of deep violet-blue
summer flowers that attract butterflies
and appear above the wrinkled leaves.

ALSO RECOMMENDED: *'Chatsworth'
has strongly scented, deep purple flowers.*

☼ ◊◊ƒ Min 45°F (7°C) **Evergreen shrub**
‡ 18–48in (45–120cm) ↔ 12–18in (30–45cm)

HYSSOPUS OFFICINALIS

Hyssop is an upright, aromatic shrub with narrow, dark green leaves. The dense spikes of nectar-rich, two-lipped, deep blue flowers that appear from midsummer to early autumn are attractive to bees and butterflies. Grow at the front of a mixed border or in a herb garden, where it is effective as low edging (*see p.138*). It thrives on alkaline soils and in hot, dry sites (*see pp.64, 190*).

ALSO RECOMMENDED: *f. albus has white flowers; 'Roseus' has pink flowers.*

☼ ◊ *f* Z7   **Evergreen shrub**
↕ 24in (60cm) ↔ 3ft (1m)

LEYCESTERIA FORMOSA

Himalayan honeysuckle is an attractive flowering shrub with bamboolike, dark green young stems. Chains of white flowers with wine red bracts dangle from the branches in summer and early autumn; these are followed by maroon to purple-black fruits that are a food source for birds. Trim or cut back hard in spring. It is suitable as an informal hedge (*see p.138*).

ALSO RECOMMENDED: *L. crocothyrsos has arching shoots, golden yellow flowers from late spring, and small green berries. (Tender)*

☼ ◑ ◊ Min 40°F (5°C)   **Deciduous shrub**
↕ 20ft (6m)

PAEONIA DELAVAYI
VAR. LUDLOWII

This vigorous tree peony has an open, upright form that is displayed to best effect standing on its own as an architectural shrub (*see p.472*) or in a shrub border. In late spring, the nodding, glossy, bright yellow flowers open among deeply cut, bright green leaves. The flowers are attractive to bees. Cut back old, leggy stems to the base occasionally in autumn. It tolerates clay and alkaline soils, and damp, shady sites (*see pp.12, 64, 238*).

ALSO RECOMMENDED: P. delavayi (see p.243).

☼ ☀ ◊◊ Z6   **Deciduous shrub**
↔ 8ft (2.5m)

PYRACANTHA *'Watereri'*

A vigorous, upright, spiny shrub that forms a dense screen of dark green foliage, ornamented by an abundance of white spring flowers and bright red berries in autumn. It makes an attractive nesting place for birds and has many uses in the garden: as a barrier hedge, border plant, or as a wall-trained shrub (*see pp.138, 262, 280*). It tolerates clay soils and exposed sites (*see pp.12, 118*). Cut back unwanted growth in mid-spring, if necessary.

ALSO RECOMMENDED: *'Golden Charmer'* (see p.159); *'Mohave'* (see p.19); *'Soleil d'Or'* (see p.269).

☼ ☀ ◊ Z6   **Evergreen shrub**
↔ 8ft (2.5m)

RIBES ODORATUM

The clove currant is valued for its fragrant yellow flowers in spring; these are followed by small black berries – a food source for birds. It has an upright habit with broad, three-lobed, bright green leaves that turn red and purple before they fall. Selectively remove wayward shoots after flowering.

☀ ◊ *f* Z2   **Deciduous shrub**
↕↔ 6ft (2m)

ROSA *'Geranium'*

This shrub rose forms a clump of thorny, arching stems clothed in dark green leaves. In summer, it is covered in single, sealing-wax-red flowers and a humming mass of pollinating bees. The large, brilliant red hips of autumn are eaten by birds and small mammals. Cut out old, spent stems at the base after flowering. Grow in a border, as an informal hedge, or as a pot plant (*see pp.138, 412*); it tolerates alkaline soils (*see p.64*).

ALSO RECOMMENDED: *'Jens Munk' is repeat-flowering, with bright pink flowers and thorns* Z2; *R. pimpinellifolia (see p.131).*

☀ ◊ Z6   **Deciduous shrub**
↕ 8ft (2.5m) ↔ 5ft (1.5m)

RUBUS SPECTABILIS
'Olympic Double'

Salmonberry is a suckering shrub that forms thickets of raspberry-like canes; the leaves are lobed and bright green. In late spring and early summer it bears double, bright magenta flowers that are attractive to bees; there are no fruits. Cut spent stems back to the base after flowering. Good as part of a barrier planting.

ALSO RECOMMENDED: R. odoratus *has purple-pink flowers and red fruits* Z3; R. spectabilis *has single flowers and bears red or yellow fruits.*

☼ ◐ ◊ Z5   **Deciduous shrub**
↕↔ 6ft (2m)

THYMUS VULGARIS
'Silver Posie'

This thyme forms a rounded, wiry-stemmed subshrub clothed with tiny, white-margined, grayish leaves. Masses of bright purple flowerheads are borne in summer. Good in a herb garden – the aromatic foliage is useful in cooking – and as a groundcover or in paving crevices (*see pp.304, 348*). It tolerates alkaline soils and hot, dry sites (*see pp.64, 190*). Attractive to beneficial insects.

ALSO RECOMMENDED: T. pulegioides *'Bertram Anderson'* (see p.310); T. serpyllum *'Annie Hall'* (see p.352); T. vulgaris *has plain leaves.*

☼ ◊ ƒ Z4   **Evergreen shrub**
↕ 6–12in (15–30cm) ↔ 16in (40cm)

VIBURNUM OPULUS *'Compactum'*

This slow-growing, compact and very dense form of the guelder rose bears maplelike leaves that turn red in autumn. Flat heads of showy white flowers are borne in early summer, followed by large bunches of bright red berries – a food source for birds. Prune after flowering, if necessary. It tolerates clay, permanently moist soils, and exposed sites (*see pp.12, 118, 372*).

ALSO RECOMMENDED: *'Roseum' (syn. 'Sterile') has pinkish flowers and purple autumn leaves; 'Xanthocarpum' has yellow berries – both plants grow to 12ft (4m) tall.*

☼ ◐ ◊ ♦ ƒ Z2b   **Deciduous shrub**
↔ 5ft (1.5m)

CLEMATIS TANGUTICA

This vigorous, deciduous, late-flowering clematis bears its hanging, bell-shaped flowers from midsummer to autumn, followed by silky-hairy seedheads that last well into winter. As with many yellow flowers, they attract beneficial insects. Grow against a wall or support with the roots in shade and the top-growth in sun or partial shade (*see pp.262, 280*). Cut back hard before growth begins in early spring. It grows well in alkaline soils (*see p.64*).

ALSO RECOMMENDED: *C. 'Aureolin' is similar, with lemon yellow bells.*

☼ ◐ ◊ Z3   **Climber**
↕ 15–20ft (5–6m) ↔ 6–10ft (2–3m)

HEDERA HELIX F. POETARUM

This and the English ivy, *H. helix*, are
both wonderful wildlife plants, giving
cover and food to birds, insects, and
small mammals. This form is known as
poet's ivy. The round heads of yellowish
flowers in autumn are a valuable source
of nectar, and the small, orange-yellow
fruits that follow are winter sustenance
for wildlife. A versatile, evergreen plant,
tolerant of alkaline soils and dry shade
(*see pp.64, 216*), and will grow on most
walls, as a groundcover, or in a pot (*see
pp.262, 280, 304, 326, 412, 448*).

ALSO RECOMMENDED: *H. helix, English
ivy, has smaller leaves and black fruits.*

☀️◐ ◊◊ Z6   **Climber**
‡ 10ft (3m)

LONICERA PERICLYMENUM 'Serotina'

The late Dutch honeysuckle is a fast-
growing, twining climber for training
onto a support or up into a large shrub
(*see p.280*). It has deciduous, oval
leaves and very fragrant, rich red-
purple, tubular flowers from midsummer; red berries may follow.
Prune by up to one-third after flowering
to keep it in bounds. Keep the base
in shade. It tolerates alkaline soils
(*see p.64*).

ALSO RECOMMENDED: *'Graham Thomas'
has white to yellow flowers; L. tatarica (see
p.129); L. japonica 'Halliana' (see p.276).*

☀️◐ ◊◊ *f* Z4b   **Climber**
‡ 22ft (7m)

ACHILLEA MILLEFOLIUM *'Cerise Queen'*

This yarrow is fast-growing, forming a mat of finely divided, dark green foliage. In summer, long-lasting flat heads of many tiny, deep pink flowers hover above the foliage on upright stems. They attract pollinating insects and the flowerheads dry well (*see p.524*). Grow at the front of a sunny border. It tolerates sandy soils (*see p.38*).

ALSO RECOMMENDED: A. filipendulina *'Gold Plate'* (see p.52); A. ptarmica, *sneezewort, has off-white flowers* Z4; A. *'Summerwine'* (see p.527).

☼ ◊ Z3   **Perennial**
↕↔ 24in (60cm)

ALLIUM SCHOENOPRASUM

Chives are grown mainly for their grass-like, edible leaves and round heads of pale purple flowers. This is a very versatile herb and may be grown as edging in the herb or vegetable garden, or at the front of a herbaceous border. The flowers attract pollinating insects. It tolerates sandy and alkaline soils and hot, dry sites (*see pp.38, 64, 190*). Clip off the flowers once faded for a fresh flush of foliage.

ALSO RECOMMENDED: *'Forescate' is tall and vigorous, with deep purple-pink flowers;* A. cernuum (see p.203).

☼ ◊ Z3   **Perennial bulb**
↕ 12–24in (30–60cm) ↔ 2in (5cm)

AQUILEGIA VULGARIS *'Nivea'*

An upright, vigorous, clump-forming plant, sometimes sold as 'Munstead White', bearing leafy clusters of nodding, short-spurred, pure white flowers in late spring and early summer. Each grayish green leaf is deeply lobed. An attractive, luminous perennial for light woodland or herbaceous borders. It tolerates clay soils (*see p.12*).

ALSO RECOMMENDED: *A. vulgaris, granny's bonnet, has purple, pink, blue, or white flowers with short spurs; Vervaeneana Group has variegated leaves with white, pink, and purple flowers.*

☀ ◐ ◊ Z3　　　　　**Perennial**
↕ 2in (90cm) ↔ 18in (45cm)

ASTER × FRIKARTII *'Wunder von Stäfa'*

This upright, bushy plant bears a long succession of daisylike, orange-centered blue flowerheads from late summer to autumn. As well as lending useful late color to the herbaceous border, it provides a rich source of nectar for bees and butterflies. Tolerant of clay and alkaline soils (*see pp.12, 64*). Mulch annually after cutting back in late autumn. The flowers are good for indoor display (*see p.524*). Also sold as 'Wonder of Stafa'.

ALSO RECOMMENDED: *'Flora's Delight' has lilac flowers; 'Mönch' has lavender flowers.*

☀ ◊ Z4　　　　　**Perennial**
↕ 28in (70cm) ↔ 14–16in (35–40cm)

CAREX FLAGELLIFERA

This sedge is a densely tufted evergreen, forming an arching mound of tough, narrow, grasslike, red-brown leaves. The flowering stems, which appear in mid- to late summer, bear brown inflorescences, followed by red-brown seeds that attract birds. Grow in any soil that is not dry or waterlogged. It is suitable for mixed and wildflower borders, and it will grow in a container (*see p.412*).

ALSO RECOMMENDED: C. pendula (see p.378); C. testacea *is taller, with pale olive-green to orange-brown leaves (Tender).*

☼ ◑ ◊ ◊ Z7   **Perennial**
↕ 3½ft (1.1m) ↔ 36in (90cm)

CENTAUREA DEALBATA '*Steenbergii*'

All knapweeds attract bees and butter-flies with their thistlelike flowerheads and are ideal for herbaceous borders. This is a clump-forming plant with light green leaves, bearing pink flowerheads over long periods in summer. It is easily grown and does well on alkaline soil (*see p.64*). Remove dead flowerheads to encourage a second flush of flowers.

ALSO RECOMMENDED: C. dealbata *has white-centered flowerheads; those of* C. hypoleuca *'John Coutts' are deep pink* Z5; C. macrocephala (see p.27); C. montana (see p.313).

☼ ◊ Z4   **Perennial**
↕↔ 24in (60cm)

CENTRANTHUS RUBER

Red valerian is a clumping perennial with slightly fleshy, cloudy green stems and oval leaves. It has a long flowering season (from late spring to early summer), when it bears very colorful, rounded flowerheads of small, rose-pink flowers. It self-seeds freely. Grow in alkaline soil; it also tolerates sandy sites (*see pp.38, 64*). Good for coastal gardens and for naturalizing in drystone walls (*see pp.166, 348*).

ALSO RECOMMENDED: *'Albus' is a white-flowered cultivar.*

☼ ◊ Z4   **Perennial**
↔ 3ft (1m)

CEPHALARIA GIGANTEA

The giant scabious is an imposing plant for the back of a wildflower or herbaceous border. It forms a mound of rather coarse, divided, dark gray-green leaves and bears pincushion flowers of soft primrose yellow on tall, branched stems in summer. They are attractive to bees, butterflies, and other pollinating insects. Tolerant of alkaline soils (*see p.64*).

ALSO RECOMMENDED: *C. alpina is slightly shorter; C. flava is about 3ft (90cm) tall, so it is more suited to smaller borders. Both Z4*

☼ ◊ Z3   **Perennial**
↕ 3ft (2.5m) ↔ 24in (60cm)

ECHINACEA PURPUREA *'Robert Bloom'*

This upright coneflower is grown for its large, daisylike flowerheads, up to 5in (12cm) across, from midsummer to autumn. They have cone-shaped, dark orange-brown centers and mauve-crimson, slightly downward-facing petals. The oval leaves are rough and hairy. Cut back as the flowers fade to encourage another display; they are useful for indoor arrangements (*see p.524*). Good for coastal gardens (*see p.166*).

ALSO RECOMMENDED: *'Magnus' has orange and purple flowerheads; 'White Swan' has orange and white flowerheads.*

☼ ◑ ◊ Z3b   **Perennial**
↕ 5ft (1.5m) ↔ 18in (45cm)

ECHIUM VULGARE

Viper's bugloss is a bushy, short-lived perennial with bristly hairy leaves, stems, and flowers. It is grown for its early summer flowers that are borne in short spikes among the narrow leaves. The flowers are purple in bud, opening to broadly bell-shaped, violet-blue, sometimes pink or white flowers. Suitable for coastal gardens (*see p.166*).

☼ ◊ Z5   **Perennial**
↕ 24–36in (60–90cm) ↔ 12in (30cm)

EPILOBIUM ANGUSTIFOLIUM *VAR.* ALBUM

This form of fireweed, less invasive than the pink-flowered species, attracts a range of beneficial insects into the garden. It is a tall, clump-forming perennial, bearing spires of saucer-shaped white flowers from midsummer to early autumn. Grow in a wild garden or herbaceous border; it self-seeds freely unless the dead flowerheads are removed.

ALSO RECOMMENDED: E. dodonaei *is shorter, with deep pink-purple flowers* Z6; E. glabellum *is even shorter* (see p.185).

☼ ◐ ◊ Z4   **Perennial**

↕ 5ft (1.5m) ↔ 3ft (1m) or more

INULA HOOKERI

This daisylike, clump-forming perennial is ideal for late color in a wild garden. It has golden yellow flowerheads with fine, narrow petals from late summer to midautumn; they attract pollinating insects. The hairy green leaves are borne on willowy stems. It tolerates clay soils (*see p.12*).

ALSO RECOMMENDED: I. magnifica *is taller, to 6ft (2m), with flowers from midsummer;* I. racemosa *is even taller, to 8ft (2.5m) – both may need support. Both Z4.*

☼ ◊ ◊ Z5   **Perennial**

↕ 24–30in (60–75cm) ↔ 24in (60cm) or more

IRIS *'Shelford Giant'*

This vigorous spuria iris forms upright clumps of sword-shaped leaves. In early summer it produces large, very pale lemon yellow flowers with a yellow patch on each of the drooping fall petals. A beautiful plant for a mixed or herbaceous border. The marks on the lower petals act as guides for insect pollinators. It tolerates alkaline soils and the flower can be cut for indoor arrangements (*see pp.64, 524*).

ALSO RECOMMENDED: *'Imperial Bronze' has brown-veined, deep yellow flowers.*

☼ ◊ Z4   **Perennial**
↕ 6ft (1.8m) or more

MELISSA OFFICINALIS *'Aurea'*

Lemon balm is a bushy perennial named for its spikes of small white summer flowers that attract bees and other insects. This cultivar has dark green leaves heavily splashed gold at the margins; they smell strongly of lemons when bruised and may be used in potpourri or herbal tea. A decorative, drought-tolerant plant useful for sandy soils (*see p.38*). Cut back in early summer and protect from excessive winter moisture.

ALSO RECOMMENDED: M. officinalis *has plain green leaves;* 'All Gold' *has golden yellow leaves and lilac-tinted white flowers.*

☼ ◊ ƒ Z3   **Perennial**
↕ 24–48in (60–120cm) ↔ 12–18in (30–45cm)

MELITTIS MELISSOPHYLLUM

This clump-forming perennial is very attractive to bees. It has oval, honey-scented leaves, and its whorls of lipped flowers are rich in nectar; they are white, pink, purple, or creamy white with pink and purple lips and spots – these markings direct the bees to the nectar-secreting glands. The flowers appear in late spring and early summer. It is good in a shady, mixed or herbaceous border.

☼ ◑ *f* Z7   **Perennial**

↕ 8–28in (20–70cm) ↔ 20in (50cm)

MONARDA *'Croftway Pink'*

This beebalm bears shaggy heads of tubular pink flowers above small and aromatic, light green leaves from midsummer to early autumn. It is good for mixed or herbaceous borders, and the flowers are attractive to bees. Choose a site sheltered from excessive winter moisture. It tolerates clay soils (*see p.12*).

ALSO RECOMMENDED: *'Mahogany'* (see p.32); M. didyma *has red or pink flowers* Z4; M. fistulosa *is taller, with pinkish purple flowers* Z4.

☼ ☼ ◑ Z3b   **Perennial**

↕ 3ft (1m) ↔ 18in (45cm)

NEPETA SIBIRICA

This catmint is an upright, leafy perennial with branching stems clothed by aromatic, dark green foliage. Its long, whorled clusters of lavender-blue flowers appear in the second half of summer; they attract bees. Good in sandy soils and hot, dry sites (*see pp.38, 190*).

ALSO RECOMMENDED: N. × faassenii (*see p.320*); N. *'Six Hills Giant' forms large clumps* Z4.

☼ ◊ *f* Z4   **Perennial**
↕ 36in (90cm) ↔ 18in (45cm)

PENSTEMON *'Sour Grapes'*

Penstemons are elegant perennials valued for their spires of tubular, foxglovelike flowers, which are rich pink-purple in this cultivar. They appear from midsummer to autumn and attract beneficial insects. Suitable for a border or container (*see p.412*). It may be short-lived.

ALSO RECOMMENDED: *'Andenken an Friedrich Hahn' (syn. 'Garnet') has deep red flowers; 'Schoenholzeri' (syn. 'Firebird') has scarlet flowers. Both are hardier.*

☼ ☼ ◊ Z7   **Perennial**
↕ 24in (60cm) ↔ 18in (45cm)

PRUNELLA VULGARIS

Selfheal is a low, vigorously creeping plant with pointed, oval leaves. Its spikes of lipped violet flowers, which are occasionally white or pink, appear from early summer to autumn. They are much visited by bees and other nectar-feeding insects. It is suitable for a wildflower border and makes a good groundcover in either sun or shade (*see pp.304, 326*). It grows in all but waterlogged soil.

ALSO RECOMMENDED: P. grandiflora (see p.259).

☼ ◑ ◊◊Z4　　　　**Perennial**

↕ 6in (15cm) ↔ 3ft (1m) or more

SAPONARIA OFFICINALIS

Soapwort spreads rapidly by runners and forms a ground-covering carpet of tough, oval leaves in sunny spots (*see p.304*). From summer to autumn it produces profuse clusters of pink, white, or red flowers that attract a range of nectar-feeding, beneficial insects. It is good in a wildflower border but can be invasive. Tolerant of clay soils (*see p.12*).

ALSO RECOMMENDED: 'Dazzler' is less vigorous, with variegated foliage.

☼ ◊Z3　　　　**Perennial**

↕ 24in (60cm) ↔ 20in (50cm)

SCABIOSA CAUCASICA

The beautiful pincushion flower is named for its solitary, pale to lavender-blue flowerheads that are ideally suited to a cottage garden. They are borne above the clumps of gray-green leaves during the later half of summer and are good for indoor arrangements (*see p.524*). Remove dead flowerheads to prolong flowering. It tolerates alkaline soils (*see p.64*).

ALSO RECOMMENDED: *The annual S. atropurpurea is taller and has scented lilac flowers.*

☼ ◊ Z4   **Perennial**
↕↔ 24in (60cm)

SEDUM 'Herbstfreude'

Often sold as 'Autumn Joy', this fleshy perennial forms a clump of unbranched stems clothed in succulent, dark gray-green leaves. In late summer, flat heads of many tiny, star-shaped, deep pink flowers appear and age to pink-bronze and copper-red. Bees and butterflies find them irresistible. Grow in a mixed or herbaceous border; it tolerates sandy soils and hot, dry sites (*see pp.38, 190*).

ALSO RECOMMENDED: *'Ruby Glow' is shorter with red flowers;* S. spectabile *has gray-green leaves and pink flowers* Z4.

☼ ◊ Z3   **Perennial**
↕↔ 24in (60cm)

STIPA TENUISSIMA

This fluffy grass forms a dense tuft of midgreen leaves. Throughout summer a profusion of greenish white, feathery flowerheads top the display. The whole plant billows in the slightest breeze. The seedheads provide a winter food source for finches and other seed-eating birds. It tolerates exposed sites (*see p.118*).

ALSO RECOMMENDED: *S. arundinacea is taller, with purplish green flower spikes Z7; S. calamagrostis has blue-green leaves and silvery, purple to buff spikelets Z7.*

☀ ◊ Z7　　　　　**Perennial**
↕ 24in (60cm) ↔ 12in (30cm)

DIGITALIS PURPUREA
F. ALBIFLORA

This ghostly foxglove bears tall, stately spires of tubular, pure white flowers during summer. They attract bees and open above a rosette of coarse, bright green leaves. A fine addition to a woodland garden or mixed border, tolerating damp or dry sites in sun or partial shade (*see pp.216, 238*). Sow the seed where it is to grow; the emergent plants will not flower until their second year. Sometimes sold as 'Alba'.

ALSO RECOMMENDED: *D. purpurea has pink-purple flowers and self-seeds freely; D. obscura (see p.229).*

☀ ◑ ◊ ◊ Z4　　　　　**Biennial**
↕ 3–6ft (1–2m) ↔ 24in (60cm)

SILYBUM MARIANUM

Mary's thistle is an excellent plant for attracting bees and butterflies. It bears purple-pink flowerheads from summer to autumn the year after sowing; they are followed by fluffy seedheads. The clump of basal leaves are glossy dark green with white veins and marbling. Grow as an architectural plant in free-draining, sandy soil (*see pp.38, 472*), or in a hot, dry site mulched with gravel (*see p.190*). Sow the seed where it is to flower in late spring or early summer. It tolerates alkaline soils (*see p.64*).

☼ ◊ Z5   **Biennial**
↕ 5ft (1.5m) ↔ 24–36in (60–90cm)

CONVOLVULUS TRICOLOR *'Royal Ensign'*

The beautiful royal blue, funnel-shaped, white- and yellow-eyed flowers of this bushy bindweed attract a number of beneficial and pollinating insects, such as as hoverflies. It is attractive in a sunny hanging basket (*see p.412*). Individual flowers last just one day, but they are soon replaced by new ones throughout summer. May be a short-lived perennial in Zones 9–10.

ALSO RECOMMENDED: *C.* tricolor *(syn. C. minor) has slightly smaller flowers.*

☼ ◊   **Annual**
↕ 12–16in (30–40cm) ↔ 9–12in (23–30cm)

HELIANTHUS ANNUUS

The sunflower is a well-known summer-flowering plant grown for its large, golden yellow flowerheads on top of tall, thick stems. Allow them to stand over winter so the birds can pick the seeds. The large, heart-shaped leaves are coarsely textured and mid-green. A good architectural plant for a sheltered, sunny border (*see p.472*). Tolerant of clay soils (*see p.12*). It may need support.

ALSO RECOMMENDED: *'Autumn Beauty' has flowerheads with zones of red, brown, and gold; 'Music Box' is a much shorter form with pale yellow to dark red flowerheads.*

☀ ◊　　　　　　　　　**Annual**

↕ 6ft (2m) or more ↔ 24in (60cm)

NIGELLA DAMASCENA
'Persian Jewels'

These love-in-a-mist cultivars are tall and slender annuals bearing pretty summer flowers in a range of colors from sky blue to violet, deep pink, and white; each flower is surrounded by a feathery ruff of bright green foliage. Attractive, inflated seedpods follow. The flowers last well when cut, and the seedpods can be dried for indoor flower arrangements (*see p.524*). It self-seeds freely.

ALSO RECOMMENDED: *Miss Jekyll' has sky blue flowers; 'Mulberry Rose' has pale pink flowers, deepening with age.*

☀ ◊　　　　　　　　　**Annual**

↕ 16in (40cm) ↔ 9in (23cm)

PLANTS FOR CUTTING & DRYING

THE PERFECT SITUATION for many gardeners would be to have enough space to devote a border entirely to cut flowers and foliage. The dilemma of whether or not to leave plants looking beautiful in the garden – or to cut them in their prime for the house – would therefore be solved. Since most modern properties have too little room for a cutting border, however, a compromise is necessary. Perhaps the best approach is to show restraint when pillaging the border, with the aim of getting as good value as possible from the flowers that are cut.

The best time for cutting is in the cool of early morning, when plants are firm and full of water, and before the blooms are fully open. If flowers are cut when they are in bud, make sure that the buds show good color, otherwise; they may not open indoors. Choose healthy material with sound stems and foliage, avoiding any diseased or old material, because it rots rapidly and fouls the water.

CUTTING FLOWERS

For maximum vase life, speed is of the essence, especially for hollow-stemmed flowers, such as delphiniums (*see pp.81, 534*); if plants wilt, they may recover, but seldom last very long. Carry a bucket of warm to almost hot water with you on your cutting forays, then plunge stems into it immediately after they are cut. Failing that, place stems as soon as possible after cutting in warm, deep water up to their necks for a few hours. Cut the stems again, at an angle across their base – while they are still under water – before arranging. It's a good idea to use a commercial cut-flower preservative in the water and to refresh water frequently, since this also helps prolong the vase life.

PROFESSIONAL IDEAS

Before arranging, professional florists often scald the stems of sappy plants such as poppies to lengthen their life in an arrangement. Plunge the bottom inch or so of the stems into boiling water, then transfer them immediately to deep, cold water up to the neck. This helps expel air bubbles from the stem so that water can be drawn up the stem unimpeded. This may also be effective with heavy-headed plants, such as roses (*see pp.270, 297, 506, 527*), chrysanthemums (*see p.533*), dahlias (*see pp.442, 547*), and tulips (*see pp.439, 544*); if they are plunged into the cold water through wire mesh so that their heads are held in position, they remain upright when they are arranged, instead of flopping as they usually do. Use a scrunch of wire, wire mesh, or florists' foam to help keep the stems upright or at the desired angle.

DRYING FLOWERS

In some plants, such as statice (*see p.538*), and many grasses, such as *Panicum virgatum* 'Heavy Metal' (*see p.541*), the flowerheads are excellent for dried indoor arrangements. Cut them before they are fully open and hang them upside down in small bundles in a cool, dry, and airy place out of direct sunlight, which will bleach the colors.

LONICERA FRAGRANTISSIMA

This bushy honeysuckle has dark green leaves with blue-green undersides and very fragrant, creamy white flowers in winter and early spring. Together, the flowers and foliage make pretty, if short-lived, winter posies. After flowering, prune flowered shoots back to strong buds; on mature plants, prune out one in five of the oldest shoots. It tolerates alkaline soils (*see p.64*).

ALSO RECOMMENDED: L. × purpusii *'Winter Beauty' has white flowers with yellow anthers* Z7; L. standishii *has intensely fragrant, creamy white flowers* Z6.

☼ ◑ ◊ *f* Z6   **Deciduous shrub**
↕ 6ft (2m) ↔ 10ft (3m)

PITTOSPORUM TENUIFOLIUM *'Tom Thumb'*

A compact and rounded shrub grown for its bronze-purple foliage, useful in flower arrangements. It is good in a sheltered border designed for year-round interest. It can also be pot-grown (*see p.412*). Tiny, honey–scented purple flowers are borne in early summer. Trim to shape in spring, if necessary. It tolerates coastal sites (*see p.166*).

ALSO RECOMMENDED: P. tenuifolium (*see p.157*); *'Warnham Gold' has golden leaves. Both are larger, to 30ft (10m) tall.*

☼ ◑ ◊◊ *f* Z8   **Evergreen shrub**
↕ 3ft (1m) ↔ 24in (60cm)

ROSA *'Remember Me'*

This hybrid tea rose has lovely, deep copper-orange, double flowers borne singly or in small clusters from early summer; repeat displays continue until autumn. The abundant foliage is glossy dark green on a vigorous, spreading plant, good for a summer border. It tolerates alkaline soils (*see p.64*).

ALSO RECOMMENDED: *Blessings has pink flowers; Just Joey has apricot flowers; those of 'Madame Isaac Pereire' are purple-pink; Royal William has red flowers; Tequila Sunrise has yellow flowers with red-rimmed petals.*

☼ ◊◊ Z6   **Deciduous shrub**
‡ 3ft (1m) ↔ 24in (60cm)

ACHILLEA *'Summerwine'*

This upright, evergreen yarrow is grown for its flat, dark red flowerheads and feathery, deep green foliage. The mid- to late summer flowers can be used when fresh or allowed to dry; take care when handling, since the leaves may aggravate skin allergies. Suitable for a mixed or herbaceous border or in a rock or wildlife garden (*see p.494*). It tolerates sandy soils (*see p.38*).

ALSO RECOMMENDED: *'Taygetea' has creamy yellow flowers Z3b; A. filipendulina 'Gold Plate' (see p.52); A. millefolium 'Cerise Queen' (see p.510).*

☼ ◊◊ Z5   **Perennial**
‡ 24in (60cm) ↔ 18in (45cm)

ALSTROEMERIA LIGTU
Hybrids

These summer-flowering, tuberous perennials bear heads of widely flared flowers that are considerably varied in color, from white to shades of pink, yellow, and orange – often spotted or streaked with contrasting colors. They are ideal for sunny borders in moist but well-drained soil. Mulch thickly for winter where marginally hardy. Leave undisturbed to form clumps.

ALSO RECOMMENDED: *A. aurea (syn. A. aurantiaca) has bright orange or yellow flowers Z6; A. psittacina (syn. A. pulchella) has green flowers marked with red Z8.*

☼ ◑ ◊◗ Z7b   **Perennial**
‡ 20in (50cm) ↔ 30in (75cm)

ANEMONE HUPEHENSIS
'Bressingham Glow'

This lovely Japanese anemone bears its wiry-stemmed, silky-hairy, deep pink flowers over long periods from mid- to late summer, and they are excellent for cutting. The lobed, dark green leaves are less significant, held below the upright flower stems. Grow in a mixed or herbaceous border; it tolerates clay and alkaline soils (*see pp.12, 64*), and damp sites in shade (*see p.238*).

ALSO RECOMMENDED: *'Prinz Heinrich' (syn. Prince Henry) is similar but more vigorous; A. × hybrida 'September Charm' has pale pink flowers Z4.*

☼ ◑ ◊◗ Z3   **Perennial**
‡ 24–48in (60–120cm) ↔ indefinite

AQUILEGIA *McKana Group*

These vigorous, often short-lived columbines are indispensable in a cottage garden and excellent for a mixed or herbaceous border. The spurred flowers, which last well in water, come in single and bicolored shades of blue, yellow, and red. They rise well above the clumps of divided, midgreen leaves from late spring to midsummer.

ALSO RECOMMENDED: *A. vulgaris 'Nivea' (see p.511);'Nora Barlow' has double pink, white, and green flowers Z3.*

☼ ◊ Z3   **Perennial**
‡ 30in (75cm) ↔ 24in (60cm)

ASTER PRINGLEI *'Monte Cassino'*

This dainty aster has slender stems with dark green leaves. From late summer to late autumn it bears open sprays of small, daisylike flowers with white petals and golden centers. It makes a beautiful border perennial, and its cut flowers are especially useful for providing an airy backdrop to flowers of more substantial weight.

ALSO RECOMMENDED: *A. ericoides 'Blue Star' has sprays of small blue flowerheads; 'Esther' has sprays of pink flowerheads Z5; A. × frikartii 'Wunder von Stäfa' (see p.511).*

☼ ◑ ◊◖ Z4   **Perennial**
‡ 3ft (1m) ↔ 12in (30cm)

ASTILBE *'Willie Buchanan'*

A leafy, clump-forming dwarf perennial good for damp, shady borders and waterside plantings (*see pp.238, 372*). It bears feathery, tapering plumes of tiny, star-shaped, creamy pink flowers in summer that arch elegantly over a mass of broad, red-tinted leaves composed of many narrow leaflets. It tolerates clay and alkaline soils (*see pp.12, 64*).

ALSO RECOMMENDED: *'Deutschland'* (see p.25); *'Sprite' is larger with shell pink plumes;* A. × crispa *'Perkeo'* (see p.377).

☼ ◐ ○ Z3b   **Perennial**
‡ 9–12in (23–30cm) ↔ 8in (20cm)

BAPTISIA AUSTRALIS

Blue false indigo is a spreading perennial with a long season of interest. It has bright blue-green leaves on gray stems and bears spires of lupinelike, soft indigo blue flowers in early summer. They last well in water. The dark gray seedpods that follow can also be cut and dried for winter arrangements. Grow in a mixed or herbaceous border; it tolerates sandy soils and hot, dry sites (*see pp.38, 190*).

ALSO RECOMMENDED: B. lactea *(syn.* B. leucantha*) has creamy white flowers with purple marks.* Z5

☼ ○ Z3b   **Perennial**
‡ 5ft (1.5m) ↔ 24in (60cm)

CALAMAGROSTIS × ACUTIFLORA *'Overdam'*

This feather reed grass forms a clump of flat, narrow green leaves that are striped and margined with pale yellow. In mid- to late summer, airy, stiff-stemmed, glistening, purple-tinted inflorescences appear and age to grayish pink; they can be used in fresh or dried arrangements. For drying, cut before the flower spikes open fully.

ALSO RECOMMENDED: *'Karl Foerster' has pink-bronze flowerheads that age to buff.*

☼◐ ◗ Z4   **Perennial**
↕ 4ft (1.2m) ↔ 24in (60cm)

CAMASSIA LEICHTLINII *SUBSP.* SUKSDORFII

This bulbous border perennial with long, linear leaves is grown for its spires of relatively large, creamy white flowers in late spring. As each flower ages, its segments twist together. Plant bulbs in autumn. It tolerates damp shade (*see p.372*), but do not allow the soil to become waterlogged.

ALSO RECOMMENDED: *'Semiplena' has semidouble flowers;* C. quamash *has bright blue flowers* Z4b.

☼◐ ◊◊ Z4   **Perennial bulb**
↕ 24–52in (60–130cm) ↔ 4in (10cm)

CAMPANULA LACTIFLORA *'Prichard's Variety'*

An upright plant that produces sprays of large and nodding, bell-shaped, deep purple flowers from midsummer above midgreen leaves. It is an excellent border perennial, but it may need staking in an exposed site. Trim after flowering to encourage a second, although less profuse flush of flowers. It tolerates clay and alkaline soils (*see pp.12, 64*).

ALSO RECOMMENDED: *'Alba' has white flowers; 'Loddon Anna' has lilac-pink flowers.*

☼ ◐ ◊◊ Z3   **Perennial**

↕ 30in (75cm) ↔ 24in (60cm)

CHIONOCHLOA CONSPICUA

The plumed tussock grass is grown for its strong, elegant shape and attractive flowerheads that are ideal for dried flower arrangements if cut before they are fully mature. It forms tussocks of stiff and arching, red-brown-tinted leaves, and from midsummer, strong, tall stems emerge bearing droopy, feathery, creamy brown flower clusters. Choose a sheltered site protected from excessive winter moisture, and cut out old, flowered stems at the base in early winter. Grow as a feature plant in a border or as a specimen on its own.

☼ ◊◊ Z7b   **Perennial**

↕ 6ft (2m) ↔ 3ft (1m)

CHRYSANTHEMUM
'Mary Stoker'

Above a bushy clump of dark green leaves, this chrysanthemum bears single, rose-tinted, apricot-yellow, daisy-like flowerheads from late summer to autumn. The centers of the flowers turn from green to yellow as they open fully. It is a reliable border plant, and the flowers last well when cut. It can be container-grown (*see p.412*).

ALSO RECOMMENDED: *'Clara Curtis' has clear pink flowers; those of 'Duchess of Edinburgh' are rich coppery red .*

☼ ◊ Z4   **Perennial**

‡ 30in (75cm) ↔ 24in (60cm)

CROCOSMIA ×
CROCOSMIIFLORA
'Star of the East'

An orange-flowered crocosmia that is valuable as a border plant for its late summer to early autumn display of bright flowers. They are borne on arching spikes over the fans of mid-green leaves. It is suitable for coastal gardens (*see p.166*). Plant corms in spring, and cover with a dry mulch in winter. Tolerant of clay soils (*see p.12*).

ALSO RECOMMENDED: *'Jackanapes' (syn. 'Fire King') has orange-red and yellow flowers; C. 'Lucifer' (see p.184); C. masoniorum has orange-red flowers* Z6b.

☼ ☀ ◊◗ Z6   **Perennial corm**

‡ 30in (70cm) ↔ 3in (8cm)

DELPHINIUM GRANDIFLORUM 'Blue Butterfly'

This delphinium makes an excellent border plant, with bright blue flowers that are lovely for cutting. Unlike the tall hybrid delphiniums, this one has open spires of elf-cap-shaped flowers in early summer. They appear among the five-lobed, divided foliage. It tolerates clay and alkaline soils (*see p.12, 64*) and seldom needs staking. Cutting and removal of dead flowerheads will induce further flowering.

ALSO RECOMMENDED: *D. grandiflorum (syn. D. chinense) has blue, violet, or white flowers* Z4; *D. tatsiense (see p.81).*

☼ ◊◊ Z4   **Perennial**
↕ 8–20in (20–50cm) ↔ 9–12in (23–30cm)

DORONICUM PARDALIANCHES

A vigorous colonizer for a woodland garden or wildflower border (*see p.494*), the great leopard's bane bears wiry-stemmed, daisylike, light yellow flowerheads from late spring to early summer. They appear above narrowly oval, softly hairy leaves and last well as cut flowers. It grows in most moist, organic soils, including alkaline ones (*see p.64*).

ALSO RECOMMENDED: *D. 'Miss Mason' (see p.83); 'Frühlingspracht' (syn. 'Spring Beauty') has double yellow flowerheads* Z4.

☼ ◐ ◊ Z4   **Perennial**
↕ 36in (90cm) ↔ 24–36in (60–90cm)

ERYNGIUM GIGANTEUM

Miss Willmott's ghost is a steely blue-green perennial with spiny leaves along its stems. In summer, clusters of flowers rise above the foliage; each flowerhead is ringed by a spiky ruff of silver bracts. Shelter from excessive winter moisture. It is short-lived, but it may self-seed. Suitable for coastal and hot, dry sites (*see pp.166, 190*), and tolerant of sandy and alkaline soils (*see pp.38, 64*). It can be used for fresh or dry arrangements.

ALSO RECOMMENDED: *'Silver Ghost' has very silvery bracts;* E. bourgatii *(see p.208);* E. × oliverianum *(see p.186);* E. × tripartitum *(see p.56).*

☼ ◐ ◊ Z4   **Perennial**
↕ 5ft (1.5m) ↔ 24–36in (60–90cm)

GEUM *'Red Wings'*

This sturdy plant forms a clump of hairy, fresh green, divided leaves. In early and midsummer, it produces bowl-shaped, semidouble, bright scarlet flowers that last well when cut. It also looks good in a mixed or herbaceous border, especially one with a hot-colored theme.

ALSO RECOMMENDED: *'Lady Stratheden' has semidouble, rich yellow flowers; 'Mrs. J. Bradshaw' has semidouble scarlet flowers.*

☼ ◊◊ Z5   **Perennial**
↕ 24in (60cm) ↔ 16in (40cm)

IRIS CHRYSOGRAPHES

This iris has a sheaf of narrow, grayish leaves and bears fragrant, deep red-violet flowers with gold-streaked fall petals in early summer. It is an elegant border perennial, making an exquisite cut flower. If flowers cannot be removed from the garden, grow several plants in a cutting border; the clumps can be increased by division in late summer. It tolerates alkaline soils (*see p.64*).

ALSO RECOMMENDED: I. bucharica (see p.86); I. ensata (see p.400); I. foetidissima *var.* citrina (see p.233); I. forrestii (see p.382); I. innominata (see p.112); I. pseudacorus (see p.401); I. 'Shelford Giant' (see p.516).

☼ ◊ Z6   **Perennial**
‡ 16–20in (40–50cm) ↔ 12in (30cm)

KNIPHOFIA *'Royal Standard'*

A classic red-hot poker that bears tall, conical flowerheads from midsummer. Its bright yellow, tubular flowers open from red buds, from the base up. The clumps of arching, grasslike leaves die back in winter. Provide a thick mulch in autumn. An architectural plant for coastal and hot, dry sites (*see pp.166, 190*); it tolerates sandy and alkaline soils (*see pp.38, 64*).

ALSO RECOMMENDED: *'Jenny Bloom' has pink flowers; 'Percy's Pride' (see p.187); 'Shining Sceptre' has yellow flowers;* K. caulescens *has red flowers that turn yellow with age Z7.*

☼ ◊◊ Z6   **Perennial**
‡ 3ft (1m) ↔ 24in (60cm)

LEUCANTHEMUM × SUPERBUM *'Phyllis Smith'*

This Shasta daisy is a robust, clump-forming plant with glossy, dark green basal leaves. In early summer, its tall, strong stems bear single, daisylike flowerheads with golden centers and narrow, twisted white petals. They are ideal for cutting. It tolerates exposed sites (*see p.118*).

ALSO RECOMMENDED: *'Aglaia' has fringed, semidouble flowerheads; 'Wirral Supreme' has double flowers.*

☼ ◑ ◊◊ Z5　　　　　**Perennial**
‡ 36in (90cm) ↔ 30in (75cm)

LIATRIS SPICATA

Gayfeather is an upright perennial with leafy stems that bear fluffy spikes of bright mauve-pink or white flowers in late summer and autumn. They open from the top of the spike downward and are long-lasting when cut. This plant is ideal for late color in a mixed or herbaceous border.

ALSO RECOMMENDED: *'Alba' has white flowerheads; 'Kobold' (syn. Goblin) has deep bright purple flowerheads.*

☼ ◊◊ Z4　　　　　**Perennial**
‡ 5ft (1.5m) ↔ 18in (45cm)

LILIUM *'Journey's End'*

A robust Oriental lily that produces a number of large, broad, very showy flowers in late summer; the spreading petals, which curve back on themselves slightly, are deep pink with maroon spots and white margins. Choose a site in full sun, preferably with the base of the plant in shade. Plant bulbs in autumn; it can be container-grown (*see p.412*).

ALSO RECOMMENDED: *'Lilac Ice' has large, star-shaped pink flowers;* L. candidum (see p.490); L. regale (see p.433); L. superbum (see p.113).

☼ ◊ Z5   **Perennial bulb**
↕ 3–6ft (1–2m)

LIMONIUM SINUATUM *'Iceberg'*

This stiff, papery plant bears tightly packed heads of white flowers from summer to early autumn; they are very long-lasting in a vase, keeping their color well as a dried flower. It has upright stems with narrow wings and dark green leaves and is good for a sunny border or gravel garden. Like other statice, it is usually grown as an annual. Grow in sandy soil; it tolerates dry, stony, and alkaline sites (*see pp.38, 64*).

ALSO RECOMMENDED: *Forever Series has a mixture of blue, pink, and yellow flowers;* L. platyphyllum (see p.56).

☼ ◊ Z8   **Perennial**
↕ 24in (60cm) ↔ 12in (30cm)

MALVA SYLVESTRIS
'Primley Blue'

A spreading, almost ground-hugging perennial producing upright spires of funnel-shaped, pale blue-violet flowers with darker veins. They appear from late spring to midautumn, which gives many opportunities for interesting associations with cut flowers from different times in the season. It is useful in a mixed or herbaceous border; it tolerates alkaline soils (*see p.64*).

ALSO RECOMMENDED: *'Brave Heart' is upright, to 36in (90cm) tall, with large, dark-veined purple flowers.*

☼ ◐◊ Z4 **Perennial**

‡ 8in (20cm) ↔ 12–24in (30–60cm)

MISCANTHUS SINENSIS
'Silberfeder'

This tall grass forms substantial clumps of arching, bright green leaves that look good in a mixed or herbaceous border, or as a screen. In early and midautumn, it bears straight-stemmed, silvery to pale pink-brown flowerheads. They can be dried for indoor display if cut before the spikelets are fully open. It is also sold as 'Silver Feather'.

ALSO RECOMMENDED: *'Rotsilber' has red-tinted, silvery plumes; 'Zebrinus' has maroon-tinted spikelets and creamy yellow-banded leaves.*

☼☀ ◊◊ Z5 **Perennial**

‡ 8ft (2.5m) ↔ 4ft (1.2m)

MORINA LONGIFOLIA

This prickly whorlflower forms evergreen rosettes of aromatic, glossy bright green leaves. Whorls of tubular, two-lipped, waxy white flowers arise on sturdy stems in midsummer, turning pink after fertilization. They are ideal for cutting, and the seedheads are useful for drying. Grow in a herbaceous border in poor to moderately fertile, gritty, well-drained soil.

☀ ◊ *f* Z7   **Perennial**
↕ 36in (90cm) ↔ 12in (30cm)

NARCISSUS *'Bridal Crown'*

A highly scented daffodil that bears heads of several, double white flowers, each with clustered, orange-yellow petals at the center. It makes a beautiful cut flower and can be grown in a spring border or container (*see p.412*). It tolerates alkaline soils and coastal sites (*see pp.64, 166*). Plant bulbs in early autumn.

ALSO RECOMMENDED: *'Cheerfulness' has double white flowers with creamy centers; 'Tahiti' has double yellow flowers with bright red-orange centers.*

☀ ◊ *f* Z4   **Perennial bulb**
↕ 16in (40cm) ↔ 15cm (6in)

PAEONIA LACTIFLORA
'Sarah Bernhardt'

With its large, fragrant, fully double flowers in early summer, this peony is indispensable in a herbaceous border. Its flowers are light pink with ruffled, silver-margined inner petals. Mulch with well-rotted organic matter in autumn. It tolerates alkaline soils (*see p.64*).

ALSO RECOMMENDED: *'Bowl of Beauty' has carmine flowers with creamy centers; 'Karl Rosenfield' has double, deep red flowers.*

☼ ◑ ◊◊ ♦ *f* Z2   **Perennial**
↕↔ 3ft (1m)

PANICUM VIRGATUM
'Heavy Metal'

This metallic-looking form of switch grass is valued for its light and airy, weeping, bronze to purple-green inflorescences that can be cut and dried for indoor flower displays. These appear in early autumn above stiff clumps of blue-green leaves; the foliage fades to yellow in autumn. It is good for a mixed or herbaceous border.

ALSO RECOMMENDED: *'Hänse Herms' has red-purple autumn foliage and a fountain-like habit; 'Rubrum' has red-tinted leaves, red in autumn, and brown inflorescences.*

☼ ◊ Z4   **Perennial**
↕ 3ft (1m) ↔ 30in (75cm)

PENNISETUM SETACEUM

This fountain grass forms deciduous mounds of rough-textured green leaf blades to 12in (30cm) long. It flowers from midsummer to early autumn to produce fluffy, tail-like, pink or purplish spikes; they can be used in both fresh and dried flower arrangements. It is often grown as an annual border plant; it tolerates hot, dry sites (*see p.190*). Cut back dead top-growth by early spring. Also known as *P. rueppellii*.

ALSO RECOMMENDED: P. alopecuroides *has yellow-green to purple inflorescences* Z5; P. orientale *has pink inflorescences* Z7.

☼ ◊ Min 35°F (2°C)   **Perennial**
‡ 3ft (1m) ↔ 18in (45cm)

PHLOX PANICULATA *'Eventide'*

Perennial phloxes are upright plants, excellent for herbaceous borders. They are grown for their clusters of bright, flat-faced, lightly fragrant flowers in summer and autumn above midgreen foliage. 'Eventide' has lavender-blue flowers, and it may need staking for support. Larger flowers can be encouraged by removing the weakest shoots in spring. Cut back after flowering.

ALSO RECOMMENDED: *'Bright Eyes' has pink, red-eyed flowers; 'Starfire' has crimson flowers; 'White Admiral' has white flowers.*

☼◑ ◊ ƒ Z3   **Perennial**
‡ 36in (90cm) ↔ 18in (45cm)

RUDBECKIA *'Goldquelle'*

A tall but compact perennial that bears large, fully double, bright lemon yellow flowers from midsummer to autumn. These are carried above loose clumps of deeply divided, midgreen leaves. The long-stalked flowers are ideal for cutting. It tolerates alkaline soils and exposed sites (*see pp.64, 118*).

ALSO RECOMMENDED: *'Herbstonne'* (see p.90); *R. fulgida 'Goldsturm' has large, golden yellow, daisylike flowerheads with dark centers Z3b.*

☼◐ ◊◊ Z3   **Perennial**

↕ 36in (90cm) ↔ 18in (45cm)

SCHIZOSTYLIS COCCINEA *'Sunrise'*

A strong-growing, clump-forming plant with a stiff and upright habit that bears gladiolus-like spikes of salmon-pink flowers. They appear in late summer and autumn above the narrow, almost floppy, midgreen leaves and last well in water when cut. In the garden, it is good near the front of a sheltered border; it tolerates permanently moist soils (*see p.372*). Divide crowded clumps every few years.

ALSO RECOMMENDED: *f.* alba *has white flowers;* 'Jennifer' *has pink flowers;* 'Major' *has large red flowers.*

☼ ◊ Z7b   **Perennial**

↕ 24in (60cm) ↔ 12in (30cm)

× SOLIDASTER LUTEUS

This upright, branching perennial with relatively large leaves is grown for its attractive clusters of small, daisylike flowerheads that appear in profusion from midsummer to early autumn; they have pale yellow petals and golden centers. It is good for late color in a mixed or herbaceous border. The flower clusters attract beneficial insects (*see p.494*) and last well as cut flowers. It is also known as *S. × hybridus*.

ALSO RECOMMENDED: *'Lemore'* *has light lemon yellow petals.*

☼ ◊ Z5   **Perennial**
‡ 36in (90cm) ↔ 12in (30cm)

TULIPA *'Purissima'*

Also sold as 'White Emperor', this tulip has pure white flowers in midspring, and they make for a bold indoor display. In the garden, group them together with other tulips in a spring border, or grow in a large container (*see p.412*). Plant bulbs in autumn. Lift the bulbs after the foliage has died down and store them in a cool greenhouse. It tolerates sandy and alkaline soils (*see pp.38, 64*) and coastal and hot, dry sites (*see pp.166, 190*).

ALSO RECOMMENDED: *'Keizerskroon'* (see p.439); T. hageri *'Splendens'* (see p.63); T. praestans *'Unicum'* (see p.214).

☼ ◊ Z4   **Perennial bulb**
‡ 14in (35cm)

DIPSACUS FULLONUM

The teasel is an architectural plant (*see p.472*), but with its prolific self-seeding, it is best confined to a wild garden, where goldfinches will enjoy the seedheads in winter (*see p.494*). It has a basal rosette of prickly dark green leaves; the branching stems above bear thistlelike, pink-purple or white flowerheads from midsummer. Harvest the dried heads in autumn for dried arrangements. Sow seeds in autumn or spring where it is to grow, and it will flower the year after. It tolerates clay soils (*see p.12*). Also known as *D. sylvestris*.

☼ ☽ ◊◊ Z4   **Biennial**
↕ 5–6ft (1.5–2m) ↔ 32in (80cm)

ONOPORDUM ACANTHIUM

This architectural biennial (*see p.472*) forms a basal rosette of large, densely white-hairy, spiny leaves in its first year. The massive, candelabra-like, white-woolly stems of thistlelike, pale purple or white flowerheads arise in the summer of the second year. They are good for cutting and drying. Grow in a sunny border or in a gravel garden. It self-seeds freely; transplant seedlings to the flowering site when small.

ALSO RECOMMENDED: O. nervosum (*syn. O. arabicum*) *has bright purple-red to purple-pink flowerheads.* Z6

☼ ◊ Z5   **Biennial**
↕ 10ft (3m) ↔ 3ft (1m)

AMARANTHUS CAUDATUS

Love-lies-bleeding is a bushy, upright annual with red, purple, or green stems clothed with broad, light green leaves. It is valued for its drooping, tassel-like clusters of crimson-purple flowers that appear freely in summer and are good for fresh or dried cut-flower displays. It tolerates poor soils, but it needs plenty of water. Sow seed where it is to grow in late spring, after the last frosts. Use to add height to a summer border.

ALSO RECOMMENDED: *'Viridis' has bright green tassels that age to cream; cultivars of A. hypochondriacus have plumelike flower clusters in several colors.*

☼ ◑   **Annual**
↕ 3–5ft (1–1.5m) ↔ 18–30in (45–75cm)

BRIZA MAXIMA

Greater quaking grass is an upright annual that bears green, red- or brown-tinged flowerheads from late spring until the end of summer. They hang from hair-fine stalks and ripen to a beautiful straw color. The green leaves fade to the same color. It is suitable for a mixed or herbaceous border or in a rock garden. The flowerheads are popular in dried flower arrangements. Sow seed where it is to grow in spring or autumn.

ALSO RECOMMENDED: *B. media is a perennial Z5; B. minor is shorter Z5.*

☼ ◊   **Annual**
↕ 18–24in (45–60cm) ↔ 10in (25cm)

CALLISTEPHUS CHINENSIS
Ostrich Plume Series

These sturdy, variably colored, fast-growing annuals are ideal for summer bedding and sunny pots (*see p.412*). They have feathery, rounded flowerheads from late summer to late autumn in shades of pink and crimson; their long stems make them ideal for cutting. Choose a sheltered, moist site and remove dead flowerheads to extend flowering. They tolerate alkaline soils (*see p.64*). Sow seed in spring.

ALSO RECOMMENDED: *Compliment Series has pink, light blue, and white flowerheads with quilled petals.*

☼ ◊◊   **Annual**

‡ 24in (60cm) ↔ 12in (30cm)

DAHLIA *'Fascination'*

This dwarf dahlia has large and showy, daisylike, purplish pink flowerheads above dark bronze, divided leaves. The flowering period lasts from midsummer to autumn; flowers removed for cutting will soon be replaced. It is useful for filling gaps in a border display or in a sunny container (*see p.412*). Dwarf bedding dahlias are usually raised each year from seed and discarded at the end of the season.

ALSO RECOMMENDED: *'Border Princess' freely bears strong-stemmed, golden bronze, spiky, rounded flowerheads; 'Yellow Hammer' (see p.442).*

☼ ◊   **Annual**

‡ 24in (60cm) ↔ 18in (45cm)

LAGURUS OVATUS

Hare's tail is an annual grass that bears fluffy, oval flowerheads in summer. These are pale green, often purple-tinged, and fade to a pale creamy buff. The flat, narrow leaf blades are light green. It is effective in a border. The flowerheads can be cut for either fresh or dried arrangements; for drying, pick the heads before they are fully mature. Sow seed where it is to grow in late spring.

ALSO RECOMMENDED: *'Nanus' is much more compact, to 5in (12cm) tall.*

☼ ◊   **Annual**

↕ 20in (50cm) ↔ 12in (30cm)

LATHYRUS ODORATUS
Bijou Group

Sweet peas are annual climbers. Cut them regularly for a long display of beautiful flowers, which are available in most colors. This selection has pink, blue, red, or white flowers; its bushy growth is more or less self-supporting. The widely grown Spencer sweet peas are tall-growing and the best for cutting with their long stems and sweet scent. Most types will need to be trained on a pyramid of stakes or a trellis or allowed to scramble among larger plants. Sow seed in spring.

☼☀ ◊◊ ♦ *f*   **Annual climber**

↕↔ 18in (45cm)

LAVATERA TRIMESTRIS
'Pink Beauty'

Annual lavateras are excellent bushy plants for grouping in a summer border, flowering continuously from midsummer to autumn, which makes them an excellent source of cut flowers. 'Pink Beauty' has purple-veined, very light pink flowers, complemented by the soft green leaves. Water young plants well until established, and check for aphids. It tolerates alkaline soils and coastal sites (*see pp.64, 166*). Sow seed in late spring.

ALSO RECOMMENDED: *'Silver Cup' has bright rose-pink flowers; 'White Beauty' and 'White Cherub' have white flowers.*

☼ ◊   **Annual**
‡ 24in (60cm) ↔ 18in (45cm)

MALOPE TRIFIDA *'Vulcan'*

The annual mallow is a bushy plant with hairy stems and round-lobed, mid-green leaves. It flowers from summer to autumn, bearing magnificent magenta-pink, trumpet-shaped flowers; flowering is further stimulated by regular picking. It is best in full sun and thrives in coastal gardens (*see p.166*). Grow in the middle of a summer border. The flowers last well when cut. Sow seed where it is to grow in midspring.

ALSO RECOMMENDED: *'Rosea' has rose-red flowers; 'White Queen' has white flowers.*

☼ ◊◊   **Annual**
‡ 36in (90cm) ↔ 9in (23cm)

MOLUCCELLA LAEVIS

Bells of Ireland is named for its unusual flower spikes that grow up to 12in (30cm) tall and appear in summer; each small, fragrant, white to pale pink, two-lipped flower is enclosed by an expanded, pale green calyx that has the shape of a shell ot cap and becomes papery with age. The pale green leaves are deeply scalloped. Grow in a mixed or summer border. The flower spikes are useful for dried arrangements. Sow seed where it is to grow in late spring.

☼ ◊ *f*   **Annual**

‡ 24–36in (60–90cm) ↔ 9in (23cm)

PAPAVER SOMNIFERUM *'Peony Flowered'*

The opium poppy (*P. somniferum*) has attractive blue-green seedpods thta are good for dried flower arrangements. This double-flowered form has frilly flowers in red, purple, pink, salmon-pink, maroon, or white. It is a spectacular, upright annual for a summer border. All parts of the plant are toxic. Sow seed where it is to grow in spring.

ALSO RECOMMENDED: *'Hen and Chickens'* has a very large central seedpod with clusters of baby pods around it.

☼ ◊   **Annual**

‡ 4ft (1.2m) ↔ 12in (30cm)

SALVIA VIRIDIS *'Claryssa'*

Annual clary is an upright and bushy plant for summer bedding, with hairy green foliage. It bears upright spikes of insignificant flowers in summer, but these are enclosed by very colorful bracts. 'Claryssa' has bracts in shades of pink, blue, purple, or white, available in mixtures or single colors. These are long-lasting as cut flowers, and they also dry well. It tolerates alkaline soils (*see p.64*), and it can be container-grown (*see p.412*).

☼ ◐ ◊◊ **Annual**

‡ 16in (40cm) ↔ 9in (23cm)

XERANTHEMUM ANNUUM

The immortelle is named for its everlasting flowers that keep their color indefinitely when dried. It is an upright plant with silvery green leaves, bearing its pink-purple flowerheads on long, wiry stems in summer and autumn. It is suitable for an annual border. The cut flowers can be used fresh; for drying, cut them before they have fully opened, then hang them upside down in a cool, dark, well-ventilated area until dry. It tolerates alkaline soils (*see p.64*).

ALSO RECOMMENDED: *'Snow Lady' has single white flowerheads.*

☼ ◊ **Annual**

‡ 10–30in (25–75cm) ↔ 18in (45cm)

INDEX

Page numbers in *italics* refer to illustrations.

ACKNOWLEDGMENTS

Picture Research: Marie Osborn
Picture Library: Romaine Werblow, Richard Dabb, Neale Chamberlain, Denise O'Brien
Index: Dorothy Frame

The publisher would like the thank the following for their kind permission to reproduce their images:
(key: t=top, b=bottom, c=center)

Heather Angel: 399t, 408b. **A-Z Botanical Collection:** 400t; Michael Jones 398b. **John Fielding:** 64c, 64-65, 216c, 216-217. **Garden Picture Library:** 387t; Howard Rice 399b; Ron Evans 470t. **Andrew Lawson:** 38c, 38-39, 394c,

394-395. **N.H.P.A.:** 411t. Clive Nichols: 211b. **Photos Horticultural:** 75b, 83t, 118c, 118-119, 123t, 141b, 160t, 165b, 209t, 272t, 279b, 314b, 403t, 443t, 551t. **Howard Rice:** Beth Chatto 190c, 190-191.**Harry Smith Collection:**148b, 162b, 282b, 414t, 440b, 502b, 536t, 545t, 545t.

Dorling Kindersley would also like to thank the following for editorial assistance: Candida Frith-Macdonald, Louise Abbott, Pam Brown; at the Royal Horticultural Society, Vincent Square; Barbara Haynes, Susanne Mitchell, and Karen Wilson.

Based on the Plant Hardiness Zones of Canada 2000 map developed by Natural Resources Canada and Agriculture and Agri-Food Canada, this map indicates the different zones in Canada where various types of trees, shrubs, and flowers will most likely survive. Ranging from 0 (the harshest) to 8 (the mildest), there are 9 major zones split into 17 subzones.

Reproduced with the permission of the Minister of Public Works and Government Services Canada, 2003.

CONTENTS

Writers **Lin Hawthorne, Simon Maughan**
Project Editor **Simon Maughan**
Art Editor **Ann Thompson**
Managing Editor **Anna Kruger**
Managing Art Editor **Lee Griffiths**
DTP Design **Louise Waller**
Production **Liz Cherry, Mandy Inness**
US Editor **Ray Rogers**
Editor, Canada **Julia Roles**

First Canadian Edition, 2004
Copyright © 2001, 2002, 2004 Dorling Kindersley Limited

Dorling Kindersley is represented in Canada by
Tourmaline Editions Inc., 662 King Street West, Suite 304,
Toronto, Ontario M5V 1M7

National Library of Canada Cataloguing in Publication
What Grows Where in Canadian Gardens/Trevor Cole, editor –
Canadian edition.

Includes index.
ISBN 1-55363-026-2

1. Gardening -- Canada. I. Cole, Trevor J.
SB453.3.C2 W47 2004   635'.0971   C2003-901924-1
Printed and bound by Graphicom (Italy)
04 05 06 6 5 4 3 2 1

Discover more at
www.dk.com

WHAT GROWS WHERE

IN
CANADIAN GARDENS

EDITOR-IN-CHIEF
TREVOR COLE